# REBELLIOUS YOUNGER BROTHER

# REBELLIOUS
## YOUNGER BROTHER

ONEIDA LEADERSHIP AND

DIPLOMACY, 1750–1800

DAVID J. NORTON

Northern

Illinois

University

Press

*DeKalb*

Library of Congress Cataloging-in-Publication Data

Norton, David J. (Jeffrey), 1945–

Rebellious younger brother : Oneida leadership and diplomacy, 1750–1800 / David J. Norton.

   p.   cm.

Includes bibliographical references and index.

ISBN 978-0-87580-399-9 (clothbound : alk. paper)

1. Oneida Indians—Wars. 2. Oneida Indians—Politics and government. 3. Oneida Indians—Government relations. 4. Indians of North America—History—Revolution, 1775–1783. 5. United States—History--Revolution, 1775–1783. I. Title.

E99.O45N67 2009

973.3—dc22

2009002431

*Dedicated to*
*Harry, Peggy, and Jay*

# CONTENTS

ACKNOWLEDGMENTS    ix

INTRODUCTION—The Oneida as a Nation Apart, prior to 1750    3

1—The Oneida during War, in the 1750s    17

2—The Oneida at Peace, 1760–1765    35

3—The Oneida as Diplomats, 1765–1770    54

4—The Oneida as Neutrals, 1770–1776    72

5—The Oneida as Rebels, 1777–1783    90

6—The Oneida as Survivors, 1784–1800    111

CONCLUSION—Oneida Leadership Maintained, 1750–1800    132

APPENDIX 1—Names of Oneida and Tuscarora Participants at
Fort Stanwix Conference    149

APPENDIX 2—Oneida Members Involved at the Treaty of Fort Stanwix    150

APPENDIX 3—Petitioners to the State of New York to Lease Land
to Peter Smith    151

APPENDIX 4—Oneida Signatories to an Act Relative to the Lands
Appropriated by the State of New York    152

APPENDIX 5—Oneida Signers of Letter to Timothy Pickering Complaining
about Samuel Kirkland    153

APPENDIX 6—Oneida Overseers of East and West Ends of Kanowalohale    154

BIOGRAPHICAL INFORMATION OF ONEIDA LEADERS    155

NOTES    193

SELECTED BIBLIOGRAPHY    221

INDEX    233

# ACKNOWLEDGMENTS

It is fascinating to look back and reflect on how a relatively minor undergraduate assignment can grow into a complex venture. A brief paper I presented at a history class at the University of Western Ontario—based on the cultural complexities experienced by an itinerant Presbyterian preacher of the Mohegan First Nation—has morphed through various renditions into this present volume. During the process, my relationship with Dr. Ian Steele has also developed and matured. He was first my professor when I was in his history class during the late 1960s, then later an academic director while I was under his guidance for my master of arts degree, then recently my doctoral supervisor. More important, he has become a friend, as we chatted in his library or solarium or wandered through his garden and he challenged me to attain a deeper understanding of the topic at hand. His scholastic wealth, unstinting encouragement, and personal friendship have been unequalled.

Many others have accompanied and guided me since I first started my research. I am greatly indebted to those working at numerous libraries who have assisted me with that extra amount of tolerance needed for one such as myself who gets easily befuddled at a computer. I thank two key people in the D. B. Weldon Library at the University of Western Ontario: David Murphy in interlibrary loans for his extraordinary patience as I struggled to complete what seemed incomprehensible and innumerable forms needed to procure distant manuscripts, and Walter Zimmerman in the research department for his tireless enthusiasm, which energized me when the road ahead began to seem impossibly convoluted. My visits to the Burke Library at Hamilton College in Clinton, New York, were made especially pleasant and productive by the warm welcome and considerable expertise of the head archivist, Frank Lorenz. His assistant, Katherine Collett, took extra time to scan and mail to my home numerous documents in the Kirkland Collection, which would not have been at my disposal without her help. Three research assistants worked on the Gideon Hawley Papers at the Congressional Library in Boston, but special thanks are extended to Michael Feldhusen who donated extra time to organize and collate the very disparate collection. The staff at the Wisconsin Historical Society were extremely helpful in guiding me through the intricacies of the Draper Collection.

I greatly appreciate the financial assistance I have received throughout the production of this volume. The University of Western Ontario granted me Special University Scholarships in addition to teaching assistantships within the

Department of History. Additional funding resulted from my being awarded an Ontario Graduate Scholarship, and financial assistance was granted by the Anglican Foundation, under the auspices of the Anglican Church of Canada.

Words cannot express my gratitude for the personal support afforded me by both Archbishop Percy O'Driscoll and Bishop Bruce Howe of the Anglican Diocese of Huron, who extended tremendous encouragement as well as considerable freedom from diocesan functions to allow me time to travel and conduct research. The congregation of the Anglican Parish of St. Mark in London, Ontario, have been extremely understanding when I have frequently avoided undertaking new initiatives as their parish priest, bowing to the pressures of meeting deadlines in the production of this book. Unique opportunities have arisen to discuss aspects of my research through my involvement with the Leni-Lennape Algonkian Iroquois Council of the Anglican Diocese of Huron (LAIC), and I have consistently benefited from the expertise of this erudite group of First Nation leaders from the various reserve communities of southwestern Ontario.

Since my teenage years in the 1960s when members of the Oneida of the Thames First Nation, located southwest of London, Ontario, welcomed me into their community, their friendship and ongoing guidance have molded my fascination with First Nation history and spirituality, in general, and those of the Oneida in particular. The political and cultural knowledge of former Grand Chief of the Association of Iroquois and Allied Indians, Harry Doxtator, and elder and Anglican lay pastor Garfield Nicholas have constantly sustained me. I could not have made the connection between Oneida and English renditions of leaders' names found in the manuscripts without the help of Olive Elm and the late Mercy Doxtator, both Oneida elders and linguists within the Christian tradition, and brothers and community activists Perry, Alex, and John Elijah of the Oneida Longhouse traditional movement.

It seems a very long time ago that Melody Herr, former acquisitions editor for Northern Illinois University Press, contacted me expressing an interest in my doctoral thesis on the Oneida, which she had unearthed. Her patient and professional recommendations, in numerous e-mails and phone calls, provided the necessary incentive for me to keep on track; they are largely responsible for the reading that lies ahead. Thanks also go to Sara Hoerdeman, who took up the reins as Melody's successor and ensured that this volume came to completion. Two anonymous reviewers requested the necessary revisions hidden within these pages. And without the skills of Patricia Connor, a cartographer in London, this book would not be complete.

Special thanks go to my family. I could not have traveled to New York State as frequently as I did without the help of my sister, Joan, and her husband, Sid, in maintaining the homestead during my absence. My brother, Bill, endured my constant departing to the tranquility of my room to work on the manuscript when I retreated to his and June's home in Stafford, England. And to my son, Jay, no words can adequately convey my thanks for his constant refusal to let me abandon what I had started.

REBELLIOUS YOUNGER BROTHER

# THE ONEIDA AS A NATION APART,

# PRIOR TO 1750

A log, hewn and placed ceremoniously across the main trail following the south bank of the Mohawk River, for the Oneida held considerable significance, but significance that to a stranger might have seemed inflated. The trail connected the colonial settlement at Albany with the Iroquois villages to the west. In the early eighteenth century, for the numerous travelers on foot or on horseback, a fallen tree limb traversing any of the many narrow paths through the vast forest covering the northeastern section of continental America would usually not have caused a moment's hesitation. To the residents of the Oneida village of Kanowalohale, located a short distance to the south of the main trail, however, the log was of strategic importance. The log served as an obligatory stopping point for all passersby. The connecting path to this leading village was marked by a fallen timber that was maintained and replaced when necessary by the Oneida community, as mandated by their ancestral traditions. As a member nation of the Six Nations (also known since the seventeenth century as the Iroquois Confederacy), the Oneida were known as the people of the Standing Stone. Within the more ancient cultural framework of the Great Law that established the earlier Iroquois League, however, the Oneida were associated with the fallen timber, the people of the "Big Tree."[1]

This time-honored distinction, being called the people of the Standing Stone, was only one factor providing Oneida leadership with the justification they needed to pursue the independent course of action they adopted during the revolution in the latter part of the eighteenth century. The nation's status within the Confederacy was based on additional well-established considerations. The teachings of the Great Law and the Oneida creation epic gave added support to the nation's perceived singularity, the pivotal geographic position of its people's homelands and main villages was complemented by the existing land and water trade routes, and the diplomatic expertise of their political leaders was recognized by the Confederacy. The Confederacy granted them supervisory capacity in their southern lands, and in their assigned role as adoptive parents to refugee nations. The challenges presented by the arrival of European traders and missionaries prior to 1750 would prove minor in comparison to the stresses besetting the Oneida in the tumultuous years between 1750 and 1800, when their ability to maintain their political and diplomatic leadership would be greatly tested. These features of Oneida's history as a nation with a unique role within the Six Nations Confederacy augment the existing rationale for their independent action during the American Revolution—that it was for utilitarian reasons that the Oneida separated themselves as rebellious younger brothers from their fellow Iroquois and sided with the American rebel Patriots. The weakening effects of the internal conflict between traditional hereditary and more modern warrior-based leadership has been misunderstood.[2] Recognition of the dominance of their ancestrally sanctioned diplomatic role—as perceived by their political and spiritual leaders, and as presented in this study—contributes to a better understanding of the Oneida's actions during the latter part of the eighteenth century.

The Iroquois, so named by French traders and explorers who encountered them in the Great Lakes area in the early 1600s, for many generations maintained established villages and associated hunting grounds in the territory immediately south of Lake Ontario. Five tribal configurations, unified by linguistic and historical similarities, formed a loose political alliance in the seventeenth century. The Mohawk lived at the eastern extremity of their homelands, close to the Hudson River; to the west of them were the Oneida. The Onondaga were located geographically at the center of the Iroquoian territory and below the eastern end of Lake Ontario; to their west were the Cayuga; and the Seneca maintained control of a vast area south of the lake stretching as far as the Niagara region.

At this early stage of cooperation between the Five Nations, the traditions of the Iroquois League—connected with the formation of the Great Law, an ancient charter whose origin is practically impossible to trace—unified each of the original nations. John Norton, a youth of Scottish Cherokee parentage, in his journal accentuated aspects of the formation of the Iroquois League that he found particularly significant. He recounts with considerable detail the legends depicting efforts of the Peacemaker (Deganawida) to establish the Great Law of Peace from which the Iroquois would later formulate their Confederacy. Following the acceptance of the Peacemaker's teachings by the Mohawk (the most eastern nation of the five), Hiawatha joined Deganawida in his attempt to create a similar affiliation among the Onondaga. So fierce was the antagonism of an Onondaga demon-possessed

Area of north-eastern United States influenced by the Iroquois Confederacy, 1750–1800.

Oneida homelands and neighbouring territory, 1750–1800.

cannibal that, once Hiawatha was able to subdue him, the depth of the tribe's appreciation to Hiawatha and their acceptance of the Peacemaker's message earned the Onondaga the distinction of being named the keeper of the council fires of the future Confederacy. Eventually the Seneca, living at the western extremity of Iroquoia, accepted Hiawatha and Deganawida's message, and as the original nations amenable to the teachings of the Great Law, they with the Mohawk and Onondaga were known as the Elder Brothers. The Cayuga and Oneida were termed the Younger Brothers, the Cayuga because they accepted the Great Law indirectly by sending a delegation to the Onondaga, and the Oneida because of their intervention in the process of establishing the Great Law.[3]

Oneida's importance as receivers and conveyors of information, and as key players when decisions were to be made, was symbolized in the Great Law by reference to the log situated near Kanowalohale. It was the Oneida who blocked the passage of Hiawatha and Deganawida on their way from the Mohawk to the Onondaga. Being situated between these two nations, the Oneida promised to "throw a tree in the path" so that Hiawatha and Deganawida would have no option but to spend time at the Oneida community and inform them of their progress among the Onondaga. This meeting took place some time later, as the spokesmen returned and indeed found the path "blocked" by the tree. Deganawida related the difficulties they had encountered in persuading the Onondaga wild man, stating that he understood they would be required to stop among the Oneida again on their subsequent visit to the Onondaga. Deganawida then established the name of the Oneida as "Big Tree."[4]

It was largely in response to subsequent colonial incursions into the economic and political life of the Five Nations that they crafted the concept of a political Iroquois Confederacy, expanding on precepts of the Iroquois League incorporated in the Great Law. Pressures introduced by French traders and political authorities operating in the lands north of Iroquois territory were augmented by similar developments on the part of the Dutch, who ventured up the Hudson River to the east and into Iroquoia during the mid-1600s. To increase the sense of a unified political and cultural response, capable of withstanding ever-increasing numbers of European strangers, each nation now had responsibilities assigned by rules established within the Confederacy in order to ensure its continued existence. Using the symbolism of the longhouse, the Mohawk and Seneca (as keepers of the eastern and western doors, respectively) were responsible for matters of trade, security, and diplomacy with neighboring Indians that concerned the Confederacy as a whole. The centrally located Onondaga ensured the continuation of the council fire and the associated ceremonial. As Younger Brothers, the Cayuga and Oneida provided the reflection and reaction required to make informed decisions. While this system theoretically ensured stability based on League principles, dissent was permitted but resolution was expected when the Grand Council of the Confederacy representatives met to discuss matters relating to the Iroquois as a whole. The nine Grand Council chiefs of the Oneida, possessing hereditary titles handed down through matrilineage, like all Confederacy chiefs were constantly aware of their interests and responsibilities as representatives of the Confederacy, but this was tempered by their loyalty to the concerns and expectations of their own nation and the particular clan who bestowed their names.[5]

Of great significance is the fact that the checks and balances built into the Grand Council system forming the center of the Iroquois League—as observed at the council fire of each nation and as reflected in the consensual form of Confederacy government—provided a sustainable national identity within each community. Contrary to the opinion of some, Iroquois villages did not become tribal melting pots with an amorphous character in which no distinct national allegiance was identifiable. Oneida communities retained their Oneida identity. Discussion at the village council meeting involved preservation of tribal lands and boundaries, relocation of village sites, monitoring and protection of hunting grounds, concerns brought from the Grand Council, and diplomatic relations with other nations both within and outside the Confederacy. Many forms of council leadership functioned at the village level. Resident League chiefs would convey information between their nation and the Confederacy. Hereditary sachems, referred to as peace chiefs and endorsed by the village clan mothers, would discuss issues affecting the nation and the village. Warriors, often young men who had risen to prominence in times of war, were allowed to belong to the council, if approved by the chiefs and clan mothers. Their position was not hereditary, and permission to remain on council depended on their continuing military value to the community. Individuals known as Pine Tree chiefs, appointed for their skill in oratory and negotiation rather than for their family connection or their performance in war, could also attend council. Recognized by the council for their eloquence and their excellent memory, the Pine Tree chiefs regularly spoke at meetings and conferences as representatives of the sachems whose opinions they conveyed. As with the warriors, there was no requirement to replace Pine Tree chiefs after their death. Although they were appointed for life, in the event of failing health or diminished memory, or of a political revolution that rendered them unable to speak for community leaders, their pronouncements were ignored rather than superseded.[6] This system augmented rather than diminished tribal identity and allegiance within Indian communities, despite the ramifications inherent on the occasion of an influx of refugees or colonists.

The ability of the Iroquois' political leadership to contend with increasing confrontation with colonial authorities in the latter eighteenth century (and to adapt to forces of change they could have little anticipated in the preceding decades) is worthy of study. The challenges faced and modifications made by the Oneida should be appreciated: the system for choosing and advising speakers in order to obtain favorable results at conferences; the possibility that League chiefs, peace sachems, Pine Tree chiefs, or warriors could all serve as speakers, or hold more than one position simultaneously; the likelihood that the status, qualifications, and expectations made of the leaders could change over time and in varying situations; and the ramifications that ensued when colonial secretaries at conferences erroneously mistook speakers to be chiefs. Indians from differing tribal affiliations, migrating in search of safe communities to live in, would bring additional need for adjustment on the part of a village's political leaders attempting to maintain its national identity.

Shickellamy's function as an Oneida representative of Iroquois authority in territory outside Six Nations' control exemplifies the adaptability and the extent of the geographic and diplomatic roles of the Oneida. Living in the Susquehanna valley during the 1730s and 1740s, when British and French competition for Indian allegiance was intensifying, Shickellamy's leadership defied standard definitions yet served the Confederacy well. Much about him is unknown: his actual name, tribal background, youth, and training for leadership are all a matter of conjecture. Although possibly a Frenchman, a Cayuga, or a member of the Iroquoian-speaking Susquehannock nation indigenous to the area, Shickellamy had been adopted by the Oneida. He could thus not be a hereditary chief, and there is no record he was recognized as a warrior, but his influence was such that members of the Pennsylvanian Provincial Council, meeting in Philadelphia in 1728, accepted his account that he had been appointed by the Confederacy as their representative, to reside among and negotiate with the Shawnee, a nation of Algonquian background who had inhabited the Ohio region since the late 1600s and frequently resisted Iroquoian interference. Having been formally installed with traditional Iroquoian ceremonies at his home in Shickellamy's Town, when in 1737 he moved to Shamokin in central Pennsylvania approximately two hundred miles northeast of Philadelphia, Shickellamy frequented meetings both at Philadelphia's council chambers and at Onondaga's Grand Council fires. Perhaps he was seen as a Pine Tree chief, valued for his eloquence and viewed as an Oneida ambassador for the Confederacy. It is possible, given his background, that he would never have risen to this prominence had he lived within the Oneida heartlands, for at Shamokin he yielded to temptation that might have cost him his position were his actions under closer Oneida scrutiny. He repeatedly but unsuccessfully tried to manipulate the citizens of Shamokin and some newly arrived Moravian missionaries into building a fence around his property (the ultimate symbol of colonial prestige). As a Pine Tree chief, he was unable to grant hereditary rights to his successor. After his death in 1748, his eldest son, John Tachnechdorus, tried to fill his father's role as mediator—but, lacking both eloquence and tact, Tachnechdorus gradually dropped from view in the turmoil stirring between the Ohio and Iroquois Indians that his father had worked so hard to prevent.[7]

Basic to Oneida identity was their spiritual foundation, as embodied within their creation epic, a myth whose origins extended as far back as those of the Great Law. Iroquoian belief regarding the formation of Turtle Island (the name given to North America) was centered on a common mythology involving the descent of Skywoman from the Skyworld to the watery abyss below. Here numerous aquatic animals assisted the turtle in creating an island on its back, where Skywoman would give birth to a daughter who would herself bear offspring.

Each Iroquoian nation developed particular elements within the basic epic, contributing to the nation's sense of self-identity. James Dean was a non-native youth who grew up among the Oneida at their southern community of Oquaga in the 1760s, became fluent in their language, was actively involved in their political affairs in the revolutionary period, and had a keen interest in Oneida traditions. Dean's writings have preserved features of the basic epic that are unique to the Oneida. For example, strawberry and tobacco plants were brought to Turtle Island by Skywoman (not created by her granddaughter as in other renditions), reminding the Oneida of their direct link with the spirit realm. The first clump of earth brought to the turtle's back reproduced spontaneously, not being dependent on contributions from other animals, which gives the Oneida a special sense of their territory's creative and nurturing properties. In preparing Turtle Island for human habitation, the Oneida benefited from the daughter's placement of rivers, allowing them access to the Atlantic Ocean, both the bays of Chesapeake and Delaware, and Lake Ontario.[8]

The responsibility for nurturing and protecting those placed under their care, as portrayed in the Oneida's creation legends, further bolstered their unique status within the Confederacy. Under the Great Law, their position as Younger Brother, in company with the Cayuga, charged them with the responsibility of discussing and offering solutions to the issues raised by the three Elder Brothers at Grand Council meetings. However, the extent of their territory, combined with their creative and regenerative powers as described in their creation legend, bestowed on them a distinctive female contribution to the Confederacy when compared with the contribution of the Cayuga. Geographical equilibrium had been established when the Confederacy was formed: the eastern nations embodied a harmony between male (Mohawk) and female (Oneida) as did the western male (Seneca) and female (Cayuga), with their synthesis maintained by the central male (Onondaga). Stability within the Iroquois, both corporately and individually, required the cooperation of the female responsibility (for production and distribution of food, rearing of future generations, selection of clan chiefs, and settling of disputes) and the male duty (to conduct the hunt, confer with outside nations, protect the community, and when necessary, go to war).[9] The trust that the Confederacy placed in the Oneida to maintain a viable "motherly" presence in the southern territory was of significance for the Oneida beyond that of merely being a buffer against colonial encroachment.

Although the adoption of non-Iroquois nations into the Confederacy was a means of bolstering the Iroquoian population base depleted by war and disease, tradition augmented location in tipping the balance in the Oneida's direction when concerns for shouldering the responsibility of taking refugee nations into Iroquoian jurisdiction were discussed at Grand Council meetings. The addition of the Tuscarora as the sixth nation of the Confederacy provides a good illustration. In the late seventeenth century, English colonists encroaching on their land in Carolina continually harassed the Tuscarora, who after staging a series of attacks against the intruders sought help from the Iroquois Confederacy, which in July 1712 agreed to assist. The following year the Iroquois, meeting at Grand Council in Onondaga, regretted their failure to mediate the dispute, and the Tuscarora sought asylum in Pennsylvania. A subsequent provincial council was called by the Pennsylvanian authorities at which some Seneca chiefs were present. "Moved . . . with their pitiful messages . . . to take steps to shield and protect the Tuscarora," the Seneca supported their reception into the Five Nations, and with the proclamation of the Onondaga that they were a "new string fixed to the cradle" and "living among [them] as their children," the Tuscarora were placed under the protection of the Oneida.[10] The sequence of events conformed to Iroquois protocol; supported by the Seneca, the keepers of the western door, and with a decision approved by the Onondaga at the Grand Council, the Tuscarora progressed from the status of children to that of younger brother with their guardians, the Oneida. Settled on land close to the Oneida village of Kanowalohale as well as in the Susquehanna valley, the Tuscarora maintained their own identity and were added as a separate nation to the original five. Their hereditary chiefs could convene and make decisions at council meetings within their own nation, but as those chiefs were not included in the roll call of the founding chiefs of the League, they could only participate in Grand Council debates, not be included when decisions were made.[11]

In similar fashion the Nanticoke nation, an Algonquian people who were fleeing armed aggression and loss of land in Delaware and Maryland in 1743, sought safe haven within the Confederacy, traveling up the Susquehanna River's north branch and overland to attend the Grand Council at Onondaga. The council granted their request to settle on the Susquehanna and placed them under the jurisdiction of the Oneida whose Chief Shickellamy had previously been placed by the Six Nations as overseer of the Susquehanna region. The Nanticoke's subsidiary position with the Oneida was evident in a speech given by one of their chiefs at a conference with the British government's representative William Johnson at the Mohawk village of Canajoharie in April 1759. The Nanticoke said they would respond to Onondaga's request for support against the British only after speaking with the Oneida "under whose direction they were and take [their] advice upon it."[12]

The significance of the Oneida as guardians and benefactors of the "fallen log" was amplified by the advantages bestowed on them by the geographical location of their ancestral lands. While not at the political center of the Iroquois as the Onondaga were, the Oneida's pivotal position within the Confederacy extended beyond their perceived control of the east–west route near Kanowalohale. Just to the west of the "fallen log" and claimed by the Oneida as within their jurisdiction was the Carrying Place, a two-mile stretch of land that connected the headwaters of the Mohawk River with Wood Creek. Traveling east from the Carrying Place, one would follow the Mohawk River through neighboring Mohawk territory until meeting the Hudson River north of Albany, from there going south to the Atlantic Ocean. Heading west from the Carrying Place, Wood Creek allowed the traveler to descend the Oswego River to Lake Ontario. Geographically as well as symbolically, the Oneida were no doubt aware they could easily "descend" when journeying to the territory of other nations, whereas others had to work hard to "come up" to their location. As long as they maintained ownership of the portage of the Carrying Place, the Oneida were in a position to control a major portion of movement by water from the mid-Atlantic colonies to Lake Ontario. In addition, smaller rivers emptying near the Carrying Place, adding further incentive for them to monopolize its use, facilitated access to Lake Ontario from the Susquehanna and Delaware Rivers to the southeast. The Oneida claimed responsibility for the Susquehanna valley as the southern extremity of their homelands, which provided them with the added prestige of what might be considered a southern door to the Iroquois Confederacy, promoting communication with the distant Wyoming and Minisink valleys.

The number of villages the Oneida occupied during the second half of the eighteenth century is impossible to calculate because of the seasonal nomadic nature of the inhabitants and the frequency with which they relocated. However, it is safe to conclude that four relatively stable communities existed between 1750 and their destruction during the revolution. The principal village of Kanowalohale was located near the Carrying Place portage. It was connected with the east–west trail running parallel to the Mohawk River as well as with the overland and water routes providing access to the south. It was in a strategic position both for Indian intertribal communication and for colonial commercial, political, and military relations. This community might have developed as a suburb of Old Oneida, a village considered of great antiquity but further removed from the Carrying Place and trails to the south. A few miles to the east was Oriska, also older than Kanowalohale and of considerable significance during the revolution. Many smaller villages that considered themselves, and were thought of by others, to be predominantly Oneida were clustered along the tributaries of the Susquehanna River, the foremost of these being Oquaga. Situated at the crossroads of numerous southern trade routes, Oquaga was destined to become a diverse community that would provide both beneficial and adverse influences for the Oneida.[13]

Living in a frontier town on the southern extremity of Oneida territory, Oquaga residents became as involved in the expanding economic rhythm of the Susquehanna valley as had the northern Oneida in that of the Mohawk River. As early as 1722 they were dealing with colonial traders, and in 1737 the colonial surveyor general Cadwallader Colden noted that goods could be carried on boats between the interior of Oneida territory and destinations in Pennsylvania, Maryland, and Virginia. Oquaga served as a depot, where shipments were transferred between vessels appropriate for both larger and smaller waterways. Oquaga caught the attention of William Johnson in 1739, a year after his arrival in the colony. Writing to request supplies from his uncle Peter Warren, Johnson stated his intention to use Oquaga as a trade center, as he could "dispose of [items] to the Indians there better than at Oswego [on Lake Ontario] because there are too many Indians there." Johnson's trade at Oquaga contributed greatly to his financial success and enabled him in 1749 to build a large fortified home, Fort Johnson (reminiscent of those in his Irish homeland), on the north bank of the Mohawk River, which not only served as the hub of his trade network (extending from New York to Fort Niagara) but in which his "fireplace" was the setting for numerous economic and political councils with the Iroquois, other Indian deputations, and colonial authorities in his later position as superintendent of Indian Affairs.[14]

Despite the Oneida's perceived strength and leadership within the Confederacy, the arrival of European traders brought changes to Iroquoian socioeconomic conditions that negatively affected Oneida's political leadership. Glimpses of European commodities within Oneida communities can be seen in the seventeenth-century journals of van den Bogaert. When visiting an Oneida village in 1634 in an effort to ascertain the reason behind the decline in furs, Bogaert reported to the Dutch traders in Albany that the paucity of gifts they had brought with them was a source of derision for an Oneida chief, who said the Dutch were "worthless scoundrels" as they brought so little compared with the French. Bogaert noticed this chief had axes, French clothing, and razors among his possessions. A century later William Johnson listed blankets, cottons, strouds, vermilion, guns, cutlasses, knives, axes, red binding for hair, bullets, powder, blades, flints, kettles, mirrors, scissors, and razors as items needed to outfit Indian warriors.[15]

The influx of European products is not surprising, considering Oneida's geographic position, as well as the volume of French, Dutch, and later British trade filtering from the trade routes to the villages. These economic changes would undoubtedly have had an adverse effect on Indian politi-

cal leadership. Traditional hunting for community survival, with its associated spirituality stressing harmony between the hunted and the hunter,
was replaced by killing for profit, with no regard for maintaining animal
populations, for the ecosystem, for the seasonal rituals that formed community, or for the associated religious and social norms established in the
past. Within a relatively short time, male identity within the community
as defined through success in the hunt was replaced by advancement in a
new material culture. The ritual exchange of gifts formerly was essential to
Indian diplomacy, indicative of a chief's support and prestige within the
community, and established the participants as being on an equal footing.
Accumulation of commodities indicated an Indian's new dependence on
European goods rather than on his support from his community. In addition, material possessions could undermine former means of exercising
political power; for, once in the hands of the general community, material
possessions were no longer essential as tools of influence for the leaders.[16]

Missionary efforts, although equally invasive, were not as successful in
achieving conversions, despite their material inducements. William Andrews, sponsored by the Church of England's Society for the Propagation of
the Gospel (SPG), extended his ministry among the Mohawk to the Oneida
in 1714. His efforts there were futile, and within a year he was banished
from their midst. Nevertheless, there can be little doubt that his use of
gifts intended to promote school attendance was not in vain. His distribution of penknives, paper, food, glass beads, scissors, mirrors, rings, buttons,
buckles, combs, ear-bobs, blankets, shirts, and stockings rivaled the largesse
provided by the traders. The Oneida would not escape the influence of
the Reverend Doctor Eleazar Wheelock, a Puritan divine enlivened by the
enthusiastic revivalism of the Great Awakening of the 1730s. Wheelock's
home in Connecticut became a boarding school from which numerous Indian and white graduates, including a number of Oneida themselves, fil-
tered into Oneida territory in the mid-1750s as schoolteachers, interpreters,
and resident clergy.[17]

A chronological investigation of the Oneida between 1750 and 1800 provides evidence indicating that the resilience and adaptability of their leaders
in the face of constantly changing conditions negates the theory that they,
and their Iroquois confederates, were spiraling with their people into political oblivion. Although by 1800 they had failed to secure their homeland for
posterity, they repeatedly accommodated to the circumstances confronting
them and maintained the support of those they represented. In the following study, Chapter 1 focuses on the Oneida at war in the 1750s. Although
they possessed a considerable number of speakers already well trained in
dealing with confederates and colonists at conferences, they did not an-
ticipate the degree to which unanimity advocated within the Confederacy
and their own nation would come under strain. Their allegiance was sought
by the British and the French and extended to distant Iroquoian relatives,

the Mingo in the Ohio valley, and the Caughnawauga near Montreal in Canada. Both these latter groups had roots in Iroquoian culture—before they broke away in the seventeenth century, because of internal conflicts, and formed new communities in their respective areas. With the decline in Mohawk dominance to the east, the Oneida took advantage of new opportunities to enhance their own prestige and to adapt to the changing political climate.

In Chapter 2, the Oneida are at peace. Following the British victory over the French in 1760 and the attempted extension of British control of the Iroquois, Oneida leaders became discouraged as their relationship with the British disintegrated. Alliances forged during the war, despite the Oneida's desire to maintain neutrality as advocated by the Confederacy regarding relations with the Europeans, did not mean that promises were kept during peace. Oneida's alienation from the British was augmented by tensions caused by Confederacy representatives who denounced Oneida's escalating tendency to act independently as negotiators for the Iroquois.

An opportunity for Oneida diplomacy arose at the Fort Stanwix conference of 1768, a pivotal event examined in Chapter 3. An agreement designed by the English authorities and engineered by William Johnson would have severely eroded land at the heart of Oneida's homeland, creating spiritual and cultural ramifications for its inhabitants. Three prominent Oneida speakers at the conference contended successfully with colonial governors hungry for territory, traders seeking land in recompense for wartime losses, missionaries eager to extend their influence, and an Indian superintendent desperate to regain his former prestige. In doing so, these speakers established a reinvigorated diplomatic leadership position for the Oneida.

The Oneida's overt behavior as rebels between 1774 and 1776, in their abandoning the Confederacy and aligning with the Patriots, is the theme of Chapter 4. Acting against the advice of the Cayuga and Onondaga, the Oneida warriors show increased allegiance with the colonists, eventually promising to serve alongside their fighters against Loyalist forces, British troops, and those Iroquois who supported them. In this way the Oneida were not led passively into the revolution. They took the initiative to protect and advance their own interests, a development that takes on added significance considering the influence of a forceful missionary at Kanowalohale, continued friction with the British, uncertainty regarding the allegiance of their Patriot colonial neighbors, added pressure arising from involvement with the settlement of Christian Indians from New England, and increased criticism from within the Confederacy.

Chapter 5 sees the Oneida drawn inexorably into the revolution as spies, guides, guerrilla fighters, army volunteers, and commissioned officers. This publicly indicated their allegiance to the Patriots, yet in private they tried stoically to limit their own attacks on their pro-British Confederates to destruction of crops, livestock, and homes—to the exclusion of killing their kin. Their active involvement in the battles of Barren Hill, Saratoga, and Valley Forge become the stuff of Oneida legend and identity. Yet, simultaneously, they grasped at every straw that might offer a hope of rejuvenated Iroquois unity and neutrality, and to leave the colonists to sort out their differences among themselves. By the end of the war, the debauchery suffered by the Oneida makes their valiant efforts during the revolutionary conflict all the more tragic.

Chapter 6 refutes the argument that the Oneida were a defeated people. Granted, a phenomenal decline in population resulted from the revolutionary war and the subsequent displacement of people, as unscrupulous congressional and state representatives, speculative land companies, and private individuals all grabbed increasing amounts of acreage between 1784 and 1795. External factors beyond Oneida control militated against a successful outcome to their struggle to keep their lands intact. However, the high number of Oneida participants at the conferences, and as signatories to the treaties, and the fluidity with which chiefs and warriors combined and exchanged their traditional roles, all indicate the determination of the Oneida nation to continue their position as a people whose log across the pathway to the future is not to be disregarded.

SOME ARBITRARY DECISIONS had to be made in the writing of this study. Acknowledging the absence of material written by the Oneida themselves, total reliance has been placed on indirect sources: contemporary colonial government documents, missionary papers, military journals and reports, correspondence, and accounts of traders and travelers. In numerous cases cross-referencing these records has resulted in considerable frustration arising from their being either incomplete, incompatible, or just plain inaccurate.

Contemporary translators had obvious handicaps in expressing the grammatical nuances employed by Oneida spokesmen and in many cases conveyed a meaning unintended by the original speaker. In fact it is probable that the scribes at conferences referred to a speaker as sachem, being unaware that the person could have been a leading warrior or a Pine Tree chief. These distinctions become particularly important in any attempt to trace the rise or decline of the status of the speakers.

The spelling of names is fraught with danger. Attempts by various scribes using new combinations of letters in order to approximate and improve on accuracy only served to cause variations of such extreme that the original has been lost in the process. I have used the spelling of an Indian name as it appears most frequently in the records. Other options are shown beside that spelling in the Biographical Information of Oneida Leaders.

In an attempt to honor the names the Oneida would have used for each other in the eighteenth century, I have preferred to use Oneida names throughout the study. For example, the majority of historians writing about the Oneida in this period have referred to a leader by the name Good Peter; I have used his name Agwrongdongwas, with his English name appearing in a note and the Biographical Information. Although "Amerindian," "indigenous," "aboriginal," "native," and "First Nation" have all been accepted terminology used in recent years when referring to the people who first inhabited the Americas, "Indian" was the word the Oneida would have heard in the eighteenth century, and that is the word used in this study. Similarly, "white" is used to designate any person not of Indian ancestry.

My referring to Oneida in the singular when alluding to them as a group is in recognition of their being a distinct nation, a community with a unique heritage. This is in line with the custom of saying that Germany was defeated, rather than the Germans were defeated, in World War II. When referring to the members of that nation, then I use "Oneida" as a plural noun as well.

I acknowledge that records of conferences and treaties mentioned leaders of Indian nations other than the Oneida. To include them was not the purpose of this study, however. That is material for someone's future endeavor.

# CHAPTER ONE

# THE ONEIDA DURING WAR, IN THE 1750s

The Oneida had good reason to be anxious in the summer of 1750. Only two years had passed since the cessation of hostilities between the British and the French, and nerves were strained because of the likelihood that renewed fighting would revive the friction within the Iroquois Confederacy created by the European nations' vying with each other for Indian allegiance. The Oneida promoted their own sense of political centrality, buoyed by their traditions, their geographical location, and their corps of leaders who followed in the footsteps of the late Shickellamy. As Younger Brother loyal to ancient tradition, however, they found themselves bound to their neighboring elders—the Mohawk on the east, allied strongly with the British, and the Onondaga on the west who had swung heavily toward the French. Oneida leaders faced the challenge of maneuvering to become recognized by the Six Nations as spokesmen for the Confederacy, at the same time as currying favor with the British in order to get the best deal for the Iroquois without becoming pawns of the imperial authorities. Toward the end of the decade, the Oneida were not in the position they had anticipated.

A generation had passed since 1701 when the Iroquois Confederacy formally adopted a neutral position in matters dealing with the British and French authorities. The Iroquois then turned their collective backs on the fighting of the past twenty years, in which they had lost their infamous military strength. They were constantly threatened by the aggressive attitude of the French and by the increasing independence of the Indians of the Ohio region—where the Mingo continued to resist the oversight of their Iroquois cousins; the Shawnee shifted loyalties between the British and the French depending on what best suited their interests, and despite Iroquois persuasion; and the Delaware tried to assert domination, having moved there to escape colonial seizure of their lands in Pennsylvania. In particular the Oneida, clinging to their clout by controlling the movement of goods through the Mohawk valley via the Carrying Place, were feeling a negative economic breeze, as the fur trade was conducted increasingly between the Europeans and the western Indians through the Albany–Montreal route along the Hudson River valley, thereby bypassing the Iroquois. The Confederacy aimed to maintain their neutral stance, though admittedly they steered closer to the British camp as a result of the British victory over the French in the warfare of 1744–1749 and the increasing prestige of William Johnson's trade network. They were trying to generate better trade relations with the Indians of the Ohio and Montreal regions, through diplomacy as they had failed to do so by warfare; to extend their influence over the Delaware living in the Susquehanna and Delaware river valleys of Pennsylvania; and to restore their legendary military status by subjugating their traditional enemies the Catawba and Cherokee, living to the south in the Carolinas. These initiatives were working reasonably well, until the disruptions caused by the mid-1740s warfare made it increasingly necessary for the Iroquois to reevaluate their position, and especially that of neutrality.[1]

In August 1750 the Oneida leaders at Kanowalohale became themselves involved in the already well-established tug-of-war between the British and the French for loyalty among the Iroquois. They learned that Conrad Weiser, a German immigrant trader fluent in the Iroquois dialects since his youthful sojourn among the Mohawk and now in the employ of the Pennsylvania Provincial Assembly, was traveling through their territory on his way to Onondaga. His mission was to ascertain the degree to which the Iroquois were being lured into the French orbit, and at the same time to promote trade with the British in an attempt to retain Six Nations' loyalty. The Oneida trusted Weiser, for in the previous decade he had been the protégé of the Oneida ambassador Shickellamy in Pennsylvania. They also shared the British concern about Onondaga infidelity. Drawing on the significance of their log across the trail they detained Weiser at Kanowalohale, primarily to discuss the defection of many Onondaga to the French. The Oneida sachem Disononto had been taken prisoner by the French as a young man and had more recently fought to defend the Mohawk against the French. He lamented the growing tendency among some Oneida to abandon the British and join the pro-French Onondaga. In good health despite being in his seventies, Disononto was chosen to lead an Oneida delegation to accompany Weiser to the Onondaga Grand Council meeting.[2]

A younger Oneida sachem, Conoquhieson, dominated the gathering, however. He embodied a strategic position as spokesman for the Oneida living at Kanowalohale, as his community had bestowed on him the title reserved for the successor of a founding hereditary chief who represented the Oneida nation when the Iroquois League originated. In his opening ad-

dress (a condolence speech for the death of an Onondaga chief who had vehemently opposed his nation's drift into the French orbit), Conoquhieson
stated his determination that the Oneida resist the French. As was his custom, his terminology reflected that of a traditional sachem: he "removed
the tears" from the eyes of those present, "cleaned their throat," cleansed
their seats from any lingering "deadly Distemper" that might lure the Onondaga and their confederates away from their British allies, and completed
the condolence with the exchange of wampum and "covering of the grave"
of the deceased pro-British chief.[3]

His prestige among the British authorities was undoubtedly advanced
by his acceptance and defense of Protestant Christianity. A missionary
visiting Onondaga in 1749 had recorded what he called a "friendly dispute between Ganachquaieson a Protestant Convert and one of the Deputies of Oneida and the good Man of the House where [they] lodged . . . ,
a professed Roman [Catholic] and head of the affairs at Onontago." He
indicated that the debate revolved around Roman Catholic and Protestant doctrines concerning the authority of scripture and life after death.
The Onondaga argued from his priest's teaching that souls can be rescued
from torment by the prayers of the faithful on earth, and Conoquhieson
countered that the false teachings of the priest were exposed by the bibli-
cal truth that no salvation was possible without repentance and faith in
Jesus Christ.[4] His repudiation of teachings alien to those held by British
Protestants would not have gone unnoticed by the imperial authorities
courting his favor.

At discussions ensuing at Onondaga that September, the apprehension
felt—by both the British and the Iroquois loyal to them concerning increased numbers of Iroquois adhering to the French cause—would have been
palpable. Two years earlier Johnson had joined New York governor George
Clinton in efforts to lessen French influence among the Oneida. They denied the Roman Catholics permission to build a church at Lake Oneida and
to appoint a priest to reside among them. French persistence had intensified since then. Johnson now received complaints that the French were a
"very stirring people," visiting among the Oneida and clothing them "from
Head to Foot," while giving them "powder and lead in plenty all for nothing." Pennsylvania governor James Hamilton had informed his Provincial
Council that the French had by their "indefatigable Industry . . . been using
all possible Artifices to corrupt the Six Nations at Onondaga" and had been
sending "a large and valuable Present" to be distributed among the neighboring Indians at Oneida.[5]

Toward the end of the Onondaga conference, Conoquhieson made an
extraordinary announcement. He stated that, in light of Onondaga's pro-
French sympathies, the conference delegates would remove to Kanowalohale, the Oneida's principal village. Once there, he led the delegates in rejecting an invitation offered by Weiser to meet at Philadelphia. He voiced

the Oneida's intention of traveling to the colonial settlement at Albany, where the Oneida would host future meetings of the Confederacy. Under Conoquhieson's leadership as a pro-British traditional sachem sympathetic to Christianity, a major shift was taking place; the Oneida were assuming political primacy within Confederacy proceedings. After all, he could rightly argue, the Onondaga had moved officially to the French camp and, in so doing, had relinquished their traditional right to light the council fire. In addition, the Mohawk were openly angry at British mismanagement of their lands; the Cayuga had sent no representatives to the conference but had deputized the Oneida to speak for them; and the Seneca had decided to boycott the gathering. For these reasons alone Conoquhieson felt justified that the Oneida should displace the Onondaga in hosting the concluding discussions at Albany.[6] His role in transferring the pivotal location of future Indian-colonial conferences from its traditional council fire at Onondaga to one sponsored by the Oneida at Albany accentuated a strategic change taking place in Oneida's relationship within the Confederacy and with the British.

Aquiotta, the Oneida leader associated with the southern Oneida village of Oquaga, was, like Conoquhieson in Kanowalohale, also dealing with the tension between the British and the French. In September 1746 he pleased the British by reporting to Governor Clinton that fourteen of his community declared they would "never lay down their Hatchet until the French and their Indians [were] entirely conquered." As with Conoquhieson, aspects of Christianity tinged his lengthy service as traditional sachem in his community. Only three years earlier, Weiser had written affirming the seventy-year-old Aquiotta as a longtime acquaintance. Accompanied by Shickellamy, Weiser and Aquiotta had participated in a conference at the Onondaga Grand Council fire at which Aquiotta represented the Oneida in welcoming the Nanticoke into their territory. When chosen by his Iroquois peers to represent the Confederacy, Aquiotta incorporated both traditional custom and Christian teaching in the ceremony, thanking the host Onondaga. Holding a belt of wampum and speaking in the "Singing way" of Iroquois oratorical practice, he called out the names of former chiefs who were "now God's and dwell in heaven." At a later conference at Albany in 1751, Aquiotta was again chosen by the Iroquois delegates to represent the Confederacy in expressing their thanks to the Catawba, to the south, for agreeing to restore peace after a century of war with the Six Nations.[7] Under his leadership, the prestige of the southern Oneida within the Confederacy and with the British equaled that of their kinfolk to the north.

In fact, Aquiotta and other Oneida leaders based in Oquaga were influenced by a British Protestant missionary presence that was stronger than among the Oneida to the north. Two community leaders, Agwrongdong-was and Dakayenensese, attributed their Christian conversion in 1748 to the Reverend Elihu Spencer.[8] Johnson, whose trade post had functioned there for over a decade, no doubt encouraged this early missionary presence in Oquaga. In 1751 the Reverend Jonathan Edwards commented on the Oneida as having "made religion their main concern, rather than war, or any worldly affairs." Determined to see a school established, Edwards wrote the Boston commissioners of the Scottish Society for the Propagation of Christian Knowledge (SSPCK), the Presbyterian missionary organization, that the "dependence of the establishment, as to continuance and prosperity, [was] chiefly on the Onohohquaugas, who [were] much the best disposed of any of the Iroquois and most likely to come in considerable numbers." Anticipating that Oquaga could be a potential center for future missionary work in the upper Susquehanna valley, he wrote enthusiastically in 1753 to the Boston commissioners that both the residents and the geographical position of Oquaga presented good prospects for the future of Christian missions.[9]

Despite the anticipation of British clerics, the southern Oneida were ambiguous about accepting the European way of life. Edwards's protégé Gideon Hawley became the missionary at Oquaga in June 1753. He provided valuable glimpses into the people's adherence to traditional customs. One of his Indian guides on the journey to the village threw a stone onto "a heap which for ages had been accumulating by passengers like him." Although the Indian did not want to go into detail about this practice, Hawley recognized it as a general custom among the Indians with whom he traveled, the stones collected being an "acknowledgement of an invisible being, . . . an oblation of the traveller which, if offered with a good mind, may be as acceptable as a consecrated animal." During his ministry at Oquaga from 1753 to 1756, Hawley also reflected on the numerous tensions caused by contact with Europeans at a frontier trading post: the vicious gossip spread about a minister in the Mohawk village of Schoharie, the burning and burial of a Tuscarora chief by his comrades as they were hunting in woods near Oquaga, and the inordinate eagerness of Oquaga residents to combat against the French. Paramount among Oquaga's problems, in Hawley's opinion, were the deleterious effects of Christianity and colonial trade. Hawley considered Dutch traders who came to Oquaga from Albany to be jealous of Johnson, whose perceived enthusiasm for Christianizing the Indians would severely curtail the traders' alcohol sales. Chief Dakayenensese told Hawley how the Dutch would feign friendship with the Indians to relate news that the English were plotting the downfall of the Indians using Christianity as their ploy. Alcohol abuse added tension within the community. The morning after Hawley's arrival, the injury of a local boy by one of the missionary's horses created such a furor among some inebriated Oquaga residents that Hawley had to hide for safety.[10] The Oneida residents of Oquaga faced a dilemma when deciding the degree to which their lives would benefit or suffer from increased involvement with any of the European settlers.

Throughout the 1750s, Oneida speakers from Kanowalohale and Oquaga were cognizant of the continuing rivalry between the British and the French that permeated their communities and of the potentially harmful consequences of alienating the religious traditionalists by aligning too closely with European Christianity. These speakers tried to heighten their prestige both within the Confederacy and in the eyes of the colonial authorities. Such was the case at a meeting at Onondaga in September 1753, when Johnson, as representative of the New York authorities, convinced the Oneida to meet at Onondaga rather than at Albany.

Utilizing the good terms he had with the Mohawk as a result of his lengthy residence among them, Johnson symbolically used a "white wing" to cleanse the council space and reset the "tree of peace" in an upright position to provide shade for those who sat under it. He advised the Seneca to renew their allegiance to the Confederacy and warned the Cayuga against aligning with the "delusive [French] people," suggesting they move closer together within their territory to present a more solid defense against enemies. To the Oneida, however, Johnson afforded special commendation. He sanctioned their recently self-proclaimed appellation as people of the Standing Stone; he symbolically brushed the moss from their stone so they could again provide good leadership; and he welcomed the Tuscarora and Nanticoke as the Oneida's adoptees as "New Strings to the Cradle."[11] This affirmation of the Oneida in fulfilling their traditional role within the Confederacy, proclaimed by a British authority figure at a meeting of the Six Nations' membership, would have fitted well with the Oneida's agenda but not necessarily with that of any confederates who disliked the Oneida's growing sense of self-importance.

A new voice advocating Oneida's crucial role was that of Scarooyady. In autumn 1753, it was becoming increasingly urgent for the British to maintain the support of the Iroquois in their struggle with the French. At a conference called by Governor Hamilton to address this issue at Carlisle that November, Scarooyady was conscious of the faltering allegiance to the British among the southern Oneida. Acting as a traditional sachem, he offered condolence for the deaths of leading members of participating nations before proceeding with the conference, only to be informed that the items needed as condolence gifts had not yet arrived. Acknowledging that Scarooyady was a "Person of Great Weight" in Indian councils, the governor sought his advice. Scara "frankly declared . . . that the Condolences could not be accepted unless the Goods intended to cover the Graves were actually spread on the Ground before them." After the necessary items arrived, the French who were present circulated rumors among the Delaware that the condolences had not been properly performed. Scarooyady reassured those present that the gifts had been properly placed and that he had correctly conducted "the Forms of Condolences which depend entirely on Indian Custom." After leading in the welcoming speeches and acknowledging the commissioners' exhortation that all the nations represented remain loyal to the British, Scarooyady insisted that preventing colonists from Pennsylvania and Virginia from settling on Oneida lands would aid the British cause. Complaining that English goods were sold at too high a price, he urged that reliable persons be selected to conduct trade with the Indians, and that they replace rum with items of value.[12] By the conclusion of this conference, it was obviously becoming more difficult for the British to maintain Iroquoian loyalty because of the imperial authorities' failure to adhere to two promises: to protect Indian land and to provide suitable trade goods at appropriate prices.

With the outbreak of the Seven Years' War (also known as the French-Indian Wars) in summer 1754, the Oneida continued to capitalize on the British feeling of urgency to maintain Iroquois support, particularly in the face of mounting French inducements and possible colonial mismanagement of Indian land and trade agreements. Although the Albany congress has been presented as a predominantly Mohawk affair, the eight chiefs from the Mohawk nation were outnumbered by four Oneida, one Onondaga, four Cayuga, three Seneca, and one Tuscarora. The low attendance of 150 Iroquois participants and observers at this conference indicates a lack of Iroquois trust in British promises, however. Considerable anger against the British resonated among the Mohawk speakers: one picked up a stick and threw it over his back, accompanying the gesture with accusations of British neglect in the face of French seduction. Another ranted about the lack of governmental support for his people in the face of continued loss of land. The Oneida were placed in a difficult position, as they faced criticism by colonial traders who deplored their boarding the boats traveling from Albany westward along the Mohawk River to the trading post at Fort Oswego, stealing rum, using "invective language," threatening death, and charging exorbitant prices for the use of horses as pack animals.[13]

To alleviate the tension, the British commissioners assured the Iroquois that their land and trade grievances would be investigated. The British also acknowledged many things. They had not prevented French incursions into Iroquois lands or stopped the French from "continually drawing off the Indians from the British interest," especially among the Seneca and Onondaga. They acknowledged that the "divided and disunited state" of the colonies had aggravated "the very great neglect of the affairs of the Iroquois," that the Indians had been "supplied with rum by the traders in vast and almost incredible quantities," and that the unregulated purchase of lands from the Indians had "been the cause of great uneasiness and discontents." To rectify matters the British commissioners suggested that an Indian superintendent be appointed, and that "discreet persons" reside in each nation as advisors of the superintendent. They recommended that trade with the Indians be regulated, that forts be "built for the security of each nation," and that complaints about land grants be addressed immediately. These recommendations were particularly appropriate in light of a secret meeting held simultaneously at Montreal in September 1754. A delegation of Oneida approached Ange Duquesne de Menneville, the governor of New France, requesting permission to reside with their relatives in Canada and assuring the French that they would forbid their "young men to touch or look at an English hatchet."[14]

Shickellamy's son, Tachnechdorus, probably having heard of proceedings at Albany in the summer of 1754, took advantage of this information by affirming Oneida's leadership role among the Iroquois at a meeting in Pennsylvania in autumn 1754. He joined Scarooyady in speaking for the Oneida. Lack of support by the British, economic problems connected with trade and alcohol, and aggression on the part of the French were troubling the Oneida of the Susquehanna area as much as those living near the Mohawk River. The Susquehanna Oneida sent word to the Pennsylvania Provincial Council that the Oneida were becoming uneasy at the "Backwardness of the English" and were tending to believe the rumors spread by the Delaware that the British were afraid of the French. Tachnechdorus's position as leader was publicly endorsed in the position of his father, Shickellamy, as "their [Susquehanna Valley] Agent and Representative, giving him Orders to take Care of them . . . , charging him if he should find any White People attempting to settle their Lands, to make Complaint thereof immediately to the Government and to have them removed." In December 1754 Tachnechdorus addressed the Pennsylvania Provincial Council regarding improper land dealings, making sure that council members knew he was an Oneida sachem, duly appointed by and made responsible to the Six Nations Confederacy.[15]

When he addressed a provincial council meeting held at Philadelphia in March 1755, Scarooyady continued to stress his conviction that the Oneida were essential in British negotiations with the Iroquois. He reported the Mohawk's urging to encourage the Confederacy to support the British, but to do so from within Oneida territory, since "nobody cared to do business at Onondaga." It seemed that "all persons who were in the English Interest and had Business to do with the Six Nations of late came round about Onondaga and passed by the Town," preferring to deliver their messages via the Oneida. Scarooyady also disclosed that, when delivering these messages at Oneida, he was approached by a Caughnawauga delegation from Canada, with an invitation to visit the French governor at Quebec. As both the Oneida and the Caughnawauga were pressured by the colonial authorities to part with their lands, a united front against the aggressors might have greater success at preserving their territory. Scarooyady went on to warn the British representatives that French success in gaining Indian allies was based on their generosity in giving more than adequate clothing and gifts, thereby encouraging friendships among the Iroquois.[16]

The Oneida's insistence on promoting Iroquois loyalty to Britain began to meet with opposition from other Iroquois nations, especially the Mohawk, as they began to react negatively to this relatively new direction being taken by their Younger Brother. With the approval of the Iroquois, the council fire was relocated from Albany and rekindled by Johnson at his home at Fort Johnson, from which he was conducting his expanding trade network as well as increasing numbers of meetings with the Iroquois. This arrangement would have annoyed the Oneida, who had earlier moved the council fire from Onondaga to Albany. It also fed the rivalry between the Oneida and the Mohawk as to who represented the main political force within the Confederacy. The tension increased in April 1755, when the New York governor, James DeLancey, eager to implement the advice of the commissioners at the Albany conference, placed Johnson in charge of the forces being raised to attack the French. At a council called in June, Johnson's commission to lead a campaign at Lake George provided him with an opportunity to apply his new responsibilities as superintendent and to improve his rapport with the Six Nations. He was pleased with the Indians' response, exultant that "there are more Men than ever before known to come to any meeting." The attendance of 408 Mohawk and 200 Oneida, out of a total 1,071 participants, indicated an understandable support by the Mohawk, Johnson's friends, as well as a source of tension for the Oneida.[17]

The superintendent delivered an impassioned speech reminding the council of the British friendship that could now be repaid by Iroquois warriors' support for campaigns against the French at Forts Duquesne, Oswego, and Crown Point. To reinforce his plea, Johnson read a letter sent by the Oneida's southern chief, Scarooyady, indicating the willingness of their brothers to the south to fight against the French. The Oneida, however, were consistently problematic at the conference in their efforts to maintain their perceived position of leadership within the Confederacy despite the Mohawk predominance. They complained about the presence of rum at the discussions, a fact Johnson hastened to remedy. Testing the superintendent's interest in their political system, the Oneida requested that he install a young man as sachem to replace one of the Oquaga sachems who had recently died. Johnson's promise to comply led to the Oneida's presenting two additional youths to be installed as sachems. Conoquhieson knew of Johnson's familiarity in installing new Mohawk sachems within their nation; he was not as certain of the superintendent's interest in the Oneida and apologized for appearing to stand too much on form and ceremony. Later in the conference, word arrived from Scarooyady that six young Mohawk had been killed while serving the British, and the Onondaga offered to conduct the condolence to the "elder" Mohawk brothers on Scarooyady's behalf. Aquiotta, the venerable Oneida sachem, insisted that the responsibility lay with his nation in their capacity as the Mohawks' "younger" brother to officiate in that ceremony.[18] However, that he had to accentuate this fact indicates that additional challenges to Oneida's leadership were hovering on the horizon.

Conoquhieson was anxious to show Oneida's independence from the British to the confederates. Eager to assert his responsibility as head sachem, he reintroduced the sensitive topic of land ownership. However, the Onondaga sachem still harbored pro-French sentiments and reacted negatively to Johnson's request that the scattered members of the Six Nations and their allies live in closer proximity in order to protect themselves from the French. How could they do this, he asked, when their land base was shrinking because of Europeans' buying or stealing large portions of Iroquois territory? At this point Conoquhieson commandeered the meeting and angrily accused Johnson of illegally allowing settlers in New York and Pennsylvania to obtain land from the Iroquois. When Johnson summoned Conoquhieson and the other Oneida sachems the following day to discuss in private the fortifications intended to protect their territory, Conoquhieson rebuffed Johnson, voicing his concern about the German Palatines living on land at their eastern border without paying for it. Johnson promised he would try to see justice done; having witnessed the potentially disruptive efforts of the Oneida to dominate the proceedings, he exhorted the Six Nations to reside together as amicably as possible at a time when enemies were trying to divide and destroy the Iroquois Confederacy.[19]

As open hostility intensified between the French and the British, the Oneida continued to be vocal at conferences, but increasingly as a nation flexing its independence from the British. While feeling it their responsibility to gain the greatest advantages for the Confederacy through loyalty to Britain, they did not want to appear to be British lackeys. By late autumn 1755 the British defeat at Fort Duquesne, failure at Fort Niagara, and slim victory at Lake George, diminished by the loss of numerous Mohawk leaders, had all contributed to lessen enthusiasm among the Six Nations for the British campaign against the French. Anxious to prevent the troublesome Delaware from further conversations with the French or attacks on the Pennsylvania border, Johnson called a council in December 1755 to urge the Six Nations to assert their authority. The response was not encouraging. The Seneca preferred to send a delegation to Canada to meet the new French governor Pierre François Vaudreuil, the Onondaga ignored the conference altogether, and the Oneida and Tuscarora were represented by an irate Conoquhieson. He assured Johnson that his people were on their guard against the French and had never been guilty of the charge of failing to care for the southern Shawnee allies. He had no intention that his people attack the French fort at Oswegatchie on the Saint Lawrence River to the northwest. Why should they, he asked, as the fort long promised by the British to protect the Oneida in their own territory had never materialized?[20]

Meanwhile Scarooyady to the south voiced similar sentiments. He complained that the British, despite promises of adequate supplies, were humiliating the Indians by not giving them sufficient funding with which to purchase clothing suitable for attending meetings in Pennsylvania. In a letter to Johnson, the secretary of the Pennsylvania Provincial Council described the Oneida chieftain as a brave warrior, with an aversion to the French, and eager at any opportunity to strike them, but using meetings with the Six Nations to subversively entice the Indians to side with the French. Scarooyady's intentions were suspect, the secretary insisted, when he chose a large black wampum belt when invited to a meeting with the Six Nations, fearing they would justifiably interpret it as a message of war despite the Oneida sachem's assurance that a black belt without a hatchet was of no significance. Although the secretary acknowledged that Scarooyady was "a mighty good man and worthy of all kind of Notice from the Six Nations," the Oneida leader's outspoken denunciation of a British general following his death, condemning his pride and ignorant attitude toward the Iroquois, was not conducive to cordial British-Iroquois relations.[21]

The Confederacy's approbation of the Oneida serving as their mediator with the colonial authorities seemed strengthened at the February 1756 conference at Fort Johnson, where Johnson again struggled to maintain the support of the Iroquois. When representatives of all Six Nations were present, Johnson directed much of the subsequent business toward the Seneca, requesting greater assistance from them against the French and stronger support for the British. His aim was to form alliances with as many Indian nations as possible. They should "not be any longer wheedled, blindfolded and imposed on by the artful speeches of the French," they should relocate their villages so as to better defend themselves, and they should act against any who threaten the British or any member of the Confederacy. In their reply the Seneca requested that the Oneida be responsible for considering these suggestions. Acknowledging that the Mohawk had been the head of the Confederacy and that management of the Delaware and Shawnee affair could be left to them, the Seneca made a point of reminding the delegates that it was the Oneida who had previously arranged an interview between the two groups when two messages sent by the Seneca had failed to obtain a response. The Seneca speaker insisted on Oneida assistance on this occasion, anticipating a meeting in the Susquehanna River area that would be organized by the Oneida as the recognized representative of the Confederacy.[22]

However, this amicable relationship was tenuous at best. Conoquhieson's attitude at the February 1756 conference at Fort Johnson with a delegation from Kanowalohale betrayed the Oneida's increasingly strained relationship both with their confederates and with the British. By this time Conoquhieson's adherence to ancient custom was well-known within the Confederacy and beyond, and his late arrival at this conference speaks volumes. His explanation for the delay reinforced his concern that tradition be honored; he pointed out that other members of the Confederacy had neglected to perform the customary condolences before proceeding to the conference, a fact that the Oneida rectified. Complaints against the imperial powers voiced by Conoquhieson on behalf of the Oneida and their associated nations had been made before; Britain's consistent defaulting on commitments to the Oneida was jeopardizing any expectation that the entire Confederacy would support them in their campaigns against the French. Before the conference ended, Johnson had no option but to attend a private meeting with the Oneida at the request of Conoquhieson, who reminded him that the promised construction of a fort was long overdue: this should be not only completed quickly but also by carefully chosen men so that no liquor was brought to the community.[23]

The southern Oneida were voicing similar disenchantment with the British because of their laggardly response to requests for support. In March 1756 Scarooyady reported directly to the Pennsylvanian authorities in Philadelphia that he found their Delaware neighbors to be against the British to the point that he and his companions were in mortal danger. When he had tried to initiate discussions with them, they pushed aside a peace belt with a stick in a contemptuous fashion, declaring their intention of killing all the British. To make matters worse, Scarooyady found Tachnechdorus had joined a Delaware war party. After Scarooyady upbraided him for his disloyalty both to the British and to his late father, the unfortunate man retorted that he had done so only under threat of death. Later, in the spring of 1756, Scarooyady attended a conference at Onondaga at which Delaware delegates were to explain their reasons for siding with the French. They claimed the British had treated them "like dogs," taking no pity on them whether starving or drunk but turning them out of their homes and beating them. The Delaware concluded that if they had not joined the French they would have ended up slaves of the British. Scarooyady, regretting that the Delaware would not listen, encouraged the British to declare war on them.[24]

The Oneida, concerned about the French destruction of Fort Oswego on Lake Ontario where they traded with the British, requested that Johnson immediately attend a meeting, in the eastern extremity of their territory, at German Flats on the north bank of the Mohawk River. They were well aware of the economic and military ramifications of the destruction of this trade post. Conoquhieson reminded Johnson that, although he had often told the general to maintain his guard at Fort Oswego, the French had been too cunning. He ridiculed Johnson's advice to attack the French at the Oneida Carrying Place, sarcastically suggesting the Oneida could only "pluck off a hair from the enemy" without adequate fortifications. Johnson reiterated that others of the Six Nations agreed with him that defense of the Carrying Place was essential for the welfare of the whole valley, chiding Conoquhieson that the Oneida were too unsteady and "unaccountable." In fact Johnson insinuated that the Oneida had played "a treacherous and deceitful part" in the fall of Fort Oswego. Conoquhieson angrily objected to these charges, but to no avail. Two days later a more conciliatory tone was offered by two Oneida elders who lacked Conoquhieson's aggressive approach. Tesanonde felt the only recourse was to follow the advice of their ancestors and to "drive away the Spirit of Anger and discord from [their] hearts and bury it under a large Pine Tree according to their custom in order that [they] might deliberate maturely." Akonyoda, listed as the most senior Oneida sachem in attendance, said that the loss of Fort Oswego affected his people as much as it did Johnson, but that the general should plan for the future and not lose heart.[25]

The Oneida's relationship with the British continued to deteriorate, despite their lagging hope that the British would supply their needs in return for their loyalty. At a meeting with Johnson in August 1756, Conoquhieson presented his usual list of requirements: clothing, arms and ammunition, a fort with a good officer and a company of soldiers supplied with powder and lead. Johnson approved, but when the Oneida requested payment for military service, he balked. He knew the Iroquois were paid when serving as recruits for the abortive Fort Niagara campaign in 1755. He needed Iroquois warriors now but offered no payment, insisting that the innovation was an expensive disruption of tradition. He informed the Oneida that this unfortunate custom had set a bad precedent, which should not have been accepted considering the amount of goods and ammunition given them daily. Using Conoquhieson's respect for tradition to his own advantage, Johnson added that their ancestors had never expected payment when they fought against the French. Conoquhieson, however, argued vehemently that the British were responsible for this development and should not try to renege, especially as they had forbidden the Oneida to go to Canada where all their wants would be supplied.[26] By this point any respect remaining between the Oneida and the British was wearing very thin.

Scarooyady was also disenchanted with the British that year. Referring to his unsuccessful visit among the Susquehanna Delaware in the winter of 1755, he informed the governor of Pennsylvania that it was gratifying to be so warmly welcomed by the Oneida and Oquaga where he was seen as a man "of Gravity and Experience" worthy of their obedience. He knew that the Oneida had asked Johnson to support their request that Scarooyady should live among them as "a Captain among the Warriors and a Counsellor in their Councils." This would mean leaving his home near Logstown, Ohio, where he had been aiming to lead a multi-tribal coalition against the French, in defiance of the pro-French Onondaga. As this venture was proving unsuccessful, largely because of the pro-French faction among the Iroquois, Scarooyady accepted the Oneida's invitation and moved to the Mohawk valley. It was here that he died from smallpox in 1757.[27]

The Oneida found the restriction placed on their visits to Canada by the British authorities to be particularly irksome. Members of their nation continued to maintain economic and familial connections with the community of Caughnawauga on the north bank of the Saint Lawrence River, which they had helped establish in 1667. While it was understandable that the British suspected these Oneida of spying for the French, for Conoquhieson and his people such suspicion further weakened the Oneida-British alliance.

At a meeting with the Six Nations in November 1756, Johnson chided their representatives for sending delegates to Canada without his knowledge or consent; it was clearly contrary to his request that the Iroquois not conduct secret negotiations with the enemy. In Johnson's defense, he had reason for concern. The previous July, a delegation of Oneida and Onondaga had gone to Montreal in response to Governor Vaudreuil's invitation. Having listened to the governor's litany of British offenses and French promises, the Indian delegation accepted his installation of a new Onondaga sachem, his presentation of canoes and gifts, and his promise to improve trade with the Six Nations by driving the British out of Fort Oswego. In response to Johnson, Conoquhieson retorted that British stinginess drew the Oneida to the French. Johnson thundered in reply that the Oneida were bringing shame to the loyalty of their forefathers who would never stoop to such "base foolish conduct."[28]

There was more to the story. One Oneida chief, Gawehe, was consistently associated with the French. In the summer of 1756 the British honored him as a chief warrior of the Oneida nation, and Johnson persuaded him to accept a war belt on behalf of the British rather than Governor Vaudreuil's invitation to side with the French. However, by the autumn he was back in Montreal. Conoquhieson reported that belts sent by Johnson to the Onondaga, Cayuga, and Seneca never reached their destination; once Gawehe reached Cayuga he concealed the belts from all but one Cayuga chief with whom he privately arranged to travel to Canada. According to Conoquhieson, no news had arrived from Canada because Gawehe and other Oneida who traveled with him were intoxicated the entire time they were in that country. At Christmas 1756, Gawehe was again in Montreal. He declared his personal loyalty to the French, submitting two medals previously awarded by the British as an indication of his sincerity.[29]

The matter did not end there, either. In December 1756 one hundred Indians led by the Oneida and including Cayuga, Onondaga, Nanticoke, Tuscarora, and Seneca traveled to Montreal to declare their commitment to the French. Governor Vaudreuil thanked "his children the Oneida [for their] proofs of loyalty," complimenting them for their foresight, as the British were plotting to build the forts as requested by the Confederacy but with the intention of then taking control of Iroquois territory. The following May, Vaudreuil had further meetings with an Oneida delegation. He doubted their fidelity as they had not burned the British forts as they had promised him on a previous occasion. After secret meetings with the Oneida leaders, he reported they had renewed their pledge of support, sung and danced a war dance, and accepted "the French hatchet with ardour."[30]

Conoquhieson had no option but to acknowledge that French enticements continued to be a major obstacle to unity among the Oneida. In the spring of 1757, the Oneida were described as a nation in which spying for the French was encouraged; some were reluctant to attend meetings at the appointed time, while others would do nothing without the presence of the

French faction. An Oneida supporter of the British named Tianoga visited Johnson in the company of Aquiotta, the elderly Oneida sachem, and related the news gained from an Oneida spy suspected of supporting the French, that they were proceeding with plans to attack the Iroquois living along the Mohawk River between Fort Oswego and Albany. Tianoga had also visited Oquaga, soliciting their support, fearing the influence of the pro-French Delawares living near that settlement. However, they had already declared their loyalty to the British in response to a message received from Conoquhieson. As for attending a meeting at Onondaga, the Oquaga sachem Adarockquaghs declined, for fear of internal factions dominating the conference. Johnson was aware of the potential problems caused by Tuscarora and Oneida indecision, especially as he felt many of the Oneida were in favor of supporting the French. Conoquhieson knew about the divided loyalties among his people and admitted to Johnson that although many Oneida were in the French interest because of the commodities made available to them, the majority were "determined to keep fast hold of the Ancient Covenant Chain with [their] Brethren the English and [would] not quit it."[31]

However, Oquaga seemed committed to adhering to the British cause. In the spring of 1757 Johnson was informed that Agwrongdongwas was providing an English education for the Oquaga community. Although several residents could read and write, he needed more material if he was to continue his role as schoolmaster. Adarockquaghs, now recognized as a leading sachem at Oquaga, attended a meeting of the Oquaga, Tuscarora, and Nanticoke at Fort Johnson. He informed Johnson that his people were not lazy. Their absence from meetings at Onondaga was because of illness in the village. The leaders also needed to stay home because they had no adequate fortifications against the French. Reaffirming their allegiance to the British, Adarockquaghs declined to encourage his people to attend a future conference as the potential was high for further factions to develop.[32]

Conoquhieson, still acting as the leading Oneida sachem at meetings, was determined to promote his nation's importance within the Confederacy despite Johnson's sentiments to the contrary. In September 1757 Johnson was planning a conference at Onondaga to encourage Iroquois loyalty to the British in the face of increasing warfare with the French. Conoquhieson, expressing frustration that two Oneida chiefs sent to Canada to request a cessation of hostilities on the Mohawk River area were disregarded by the French governor, was composing a message to the Cherokee nation, distant relatives of the Iroquois, urging their support against the French. Conoquhieson included in the message an invitation for their Cherokee relatives to attend a conference in Onondaga, because of its proximity to the "Oneidas, . . . the heads of the Confederacy," thereby assuming the traditional responsibility of the host nation to issue the invitations. In a similar vein the following April, Conoquhieson went to Fort Johnson to invite Johnson personally to a congress at Onondaga; Johnson was also asked to rendezvous with the Mohawks and Súsquehanna Indians who were meeting at Oneida before proceeding to Onondaga. Johnson accepted the invitation, assuming that their intentions would be in accord with the interests of Britain and planning to travel with the Mohawk living near Fort Johnson.[33]

While Conoquhieson continued to advocate for the Iroquois from his home at Kanowalohale, a new Oneida voice arose to fill the void in the Susquehanna and Ohio valleys created by the death of Scarooyady. Usually representing the Oneida warriors and based at Oquaga, Thomas King had appeared at Fort Johnson in the spring of 1756, leading in a condolence for the death of Johnson's sister and brother-in-law at the battle at Lake George the previous autumn and requesting a fort and ammunitions for Oquaga. He accompanied Scarooyady in representing the Oneida at the meetings prior to and during the Lancaster conference in the spring of 1757, and following Scarooyady's death he shared with the Mohawk delegate the responsibilities of speaker for the Iroquois. The following spring, he served as a messenger for the British, delivering a notice to the Cherokee from both Johnson and the Confederacy expressing appreciation for their willingness to join the British against the French, and conveying a speech from the British governor of Boston for Johnson that was first to be read to the Iroquois gathered at Fort Johnson and then to be carried by King to the Six Nations. Traveling to Kanowalohale on Johnson's behalf, King investigated reports of threats against the superintendent's life coming from that community, carrying a testimonial in one hand and a flag in the other as marks of Johnson's trust.[34]

King's uniquely aggressive oratorical style was evident when he challenged the British authorities at the Easton conference in October 1758, where the New Jersey and Pennsylvania governors tried to negotiate peace with the Delaware and Shawnee. King, speaking on behalf of the Younger Brothers and their associated nations, broached the topic of the Delaware's hostility, addressing in what was to become his usual grandiose manner the "Governors and their Councils, and Indian Chiefs and their Councils, as to Warriors of all Nations, White People and Indians, desiring all present to attend carefully to what was going to be related as matters of great Consequence." In answering why the Shawnee became enemies, he charged that it was the British who imprisoned and killed them when they were traveling through South Carolina to fight their enemies in the south. When the British did nothing to correct the problems caused by this unnecessary intervention, said King, the Shawnee brought the pro-French Delaware into hostile action against the British. Similarly, the Seneca turned against the British when a number of Seneca were ambushed and killed by British soldiers in Virginia. The Indians in the Ohio region were treated in the same way, King continued. Their requests of the governors of Virginia and Pennsylvania to protect their lands from the French were ignored, and as the French became their neighbors it was natural that trade would develop into friendly relations between the two groups. Addressing the colonial governors individually, King pointed out that the Indians of Pennsylvania and New Jersey had been swindled, either because lands were not paid for or because territory was taken that should have remained in Indian possession.[35]

The Oneida's difficulty in maintaining a position of leadership within the Confederacy (dealing simultaneously, as they were, with increased frustration over a tenuous relationship with the British) came to a head at a conference at Fort Johnson in December 1758. Shaking with anger, Conoquhieson—observed by the forty Oneida sachems, young men, women, and children who attended the conference with him—inappropriately interrupted Johnson's welcome and refused to accept his suggestion that the proceedings be delayed until the neighboring Mohawk arrive at the meeting. The following day his mood was no better. He dismissed Johnson's concern about not being directly informed of the murder of an Oneida at the hands of pro-French Indians. Reminding Johnson of Oneida's central role in the Confederacy, Conoquhieson leveled attacks against the British concerning the lack of affordable goods and the continuous availability of alcohol in Iroquois territory in general and Oneida lands in particular. Johnson's response abandoned all niceties. He reminded Conoquhieson of the supremacy of the Mohawk as head of the Confederacy and of the apparent inability of the Oneida speaker to remember traditional customs. This was particularly abrasive for Conoquhieson, who could not countenance such public questioning of his promotion of the Oneida nation and his personal adherence to traditional custom.[36]

After a decade of posturing and negotiating from both the members of the Confederacy and the British authorities, much had changed for the Oneida and in ways they had not expected. Arguments with the British over prices of trade goods and the ubiquity of alcohol were constant. Conoquhieson, Scarooyady, and King were consistently vociferous in their displeasure with the British, but they did not advocate the breakdown in their relationship that now seemed inevitable. The Oneida's continuous travels to their colleagues in French territory in Canada did little to advance good relations with the British. The charismatic Shickellamy had been dead for a decade, and his son had disgraced himself by his brief dalliance with the Susquehanna Delaware —whose intention of maintaining a pro-French stance was made evident by their refusal to attend the 1756 Grand Council meeting at Onondaga. British reputation reached a low in the eyes of the Iroquois in August 1757 when the French captured Fort William Henry and the following summer defeated the British at Fort Ticonderoga. Two strong voices, those of Scarooyady and Aquiotta, were silenced when they died in 1757. Conoquhieson and King emerged as pivotal figures for the Oneida during this period, but by the end of the decade they did not carry the clout they had anticipated. If their effectiveness as leaders depended on their ability to get their demands met by the British, they could be considered failures. If it was based on their mastery of presenting the Oneida nation as a conduit for discontent against the

British, they were successful. A cluster of future leaders were being primed at Oquaga, a community painfully aware of the pressures brought to bear by the clash of cultures. Given what we know about the Oneida leaders and the impact of the hostilities between Britain and France on the Six Nations, the 1750s was a decade in which the Oneida nation encouraged leadership that demonstrated significant determination and adaptability, but which begged the question as to whether these men and the nation they represented would be able to survive in the face of changing circumstances over which they had little control.[37]

# CHAPTER TWO

# THE ONEIDA AT PEACE, 1760–1765

The arrival of peace, inaugurated as the British and their Iroquois allies defeated the French in the early 1760s, brought new challenges to the Confederacy. The Six Nations, having unanimously agreed in 1759 to support William Johnson at a conference at Canajoharie, expected a more positive response to the demands they repeatedly made of the British. It was one thing for the Iroquois to negotiate alliances during the uncertainties of war; however, it was quite another to gain concessions promised by the victors once the need for armed service had diminished. Striving to regain Oneida's dominance in the eyes of the British after the embarrassment resulting from the 1758 debacle when he lost his temper in public, Conoquhieson as chief sachem speaking for the Oneida in their northern area and Thomas King as head warrior representing them in the south persevered in maintaining a strong Oneida presence at conferences initiated by the British. They would face new issues in 1763—arising from the newly expanded British jurisdiction, the uprising attributed to Pontiac, and the disruptive behavior of a branch of their western Elder Brothers, the Chenussio Seneca. Despite their determination, the Oneida found themselves in an even worse position by 1765 than when the decade began.

Conoquhieson continued to press for Oneida leadership, both within the Confederacy and in the eyes of the imperial authorities, as the British victory over the French at Louisburg in late July 1758 and the Saint Lawrence valley in 1760 presented the Oneida with new opportunities to be on good terms with the British. This relationship continued to be illusive, however. The association between the Iroquois, Johnson, and the British military leadership became increasingly strained after General Jeffrey

Amherst arrived as representative of the British government in colonial America. Amherst's capture of the French fort at Louisburg made him an obvious choice, in the opinion of the British government, to command British forces; his lack of social graces was considered of minor consequence in light of his military capabilities.[1]

This situation was only one of many facing Conoquhieson that were beyond the Oneida's control, continuing conditions from prior to the British victory. In April 1759 a conference summoned by Johnson at Canajoharie, in Mohawk territory to the west of Albany, started on an inauspicious note. As superintendent, Johnson berated the Iroquois for their continued visits into Canada and stressed the benefits of maintaining their allegiance to Britain. Conoquhieson was understandably tired of hearing these sentiments. On this occasion he taunted Johnson by repeating gossip—supposedly originating from Vaudreuil, the governor of New France, and delivered to an Oneida delegation recently returned from Montreal—that in due time the English would "throw off the mask" and use the forts constructed in Oneida territory to destroy the entire Confederacy. Tiring of Johnson's suspicions of Iroquois loyalty, warranted though they were, Conoquhieson concluded, "this was the Governor of Canada's speech with the hatchet belt he gave. We have faithfully repeated it to you and now give it to you, a clear Demonstration of our confidence in our Brethren the English and that we will act with unreserved sincerity towards you we here deliver you the hatchet belt. . . . We will have nothing to do with it—take it and make what use you please of it—you may cut Your wood with it if you will."[2]

In an effort to create a more harmonious atmosphere at this conference and to deliver unanimous Confederacy support for the British offensive against the French, Johnson led the condolence of those who had died in the service of Britain. Conoquhieson was not about to be eclipsed by Johnson's actions, however. He reminded Johnson that, as a Cayuga warrior had committed the recent murder of a colonial trader, the warriors at the conference would eventually decide on the "sort of medicine or plaster" to be applied. As the French were suspected to be behind the Cayuga's actions, the warriors would be responsible should the Confederacy "determine to exert themselves unanimously" in the British cause against the French. Since British prisoners had been earlier delivered by the Iroquois and all participants were in attendance, Conoquhieson took the initiative to declare that the Six Nations were united in their "determination to stand or fall" with Johnson. After wampum belts were exchanged, Conoquhieson assured Johnson that the Oneida would take the added responsibility of publishing the resolutions of the meeting to others within the Confederacy. By the meeting's adjournment, it was obvious that Conoquhieson had very much been in control of the proceedings.[3]

It is possible that the Oneida contributed to the mellowing of General Amherst's long-standing caustic approach to the Iroquois, which created problems as much for them as for their advocate and stalwart British citizen, William Johnson. As plans for an attack on the fort at Quebec were forming, in the winter of 1759, Johnson's constant requests for money to furnish Indian supplies strained Amherst's patience, especially as the reticence of the home government to send funds augmented his already parsimonious nature. Warning Johnson against divulging military plans to the Indians, Amherst stated he placed little value in their loyalty, as he found them to be a "most idle worthless set" that feigned sickness to avoid action. For him, execution was "the best way of treating Indians" when disloyal. Amherst's attitude softened slightly when he accepted Johnson's invitation in the summer of 1760 to evaluate the Iroquois in person. Johnson took him to Kanowalohale, which he subsequently described as "a pretty location." There Johnson introduced Amherst to some Oneida involved in Christian prayer and in the curing of copious supplies of fish. Then wishing "to please the Indians," Amherst launched a ship from Fort Oswego under the name *Onondaga*. Glasses of punch and closing speeches interpreted by Johnson ended the festivities; the Indians "were greatly delighted with the whole [and] promised to be fast friends."[4]

The jovial air dissipated, however, once the attack commenced on the French camped near Montreal in August 1760. As the British routed the French among the Saint Lawrence River islands, neither Johnson nor Amherst could control the Indians, who destroyed everything they found of value in any enemy Indian village. Nevertheless, the Indians who remained loyal to the campaign received material benefits from the British. In September Johnson received gifts for the Indians from the newly appointed British governor of Montreal, Thomas Gage: "sixty four necklaces for women, four lace hats for Indian chiefs, two hundred forty-two pounds of silver trinkets, one hundred nineteen pounds of wampum in belts, six thousand cord of bark for canoes and forty-four [containers] of brandy." At a ceremony held later, at a meeting in Montreal in April 1761, General Amherst awarded 182 Iroquois silver medals for military service; Gawehe and Thomas King were among the 16 recipients from Oquaga and Kanowalohale.[5]

At the request of General Amherst, Johnson planned a conference at Fort Detroit with the Iroquois and western Indians to formalize their loyalty to the British once the French had been defeated. However, on Johnson's arrival at German Flats in July 1761, he encountered thirty Oneida and Tuscarora chiefs who were about to leave for Fort Johnson to discuss the recent murder of a German settler by Oneida youth.[6] Violent incidents between Indians and colonists often resulted in fatalities, which damaged the fragile relationship between the two groups. The Oneida demanded an immediate meeting with Johnson, which provided an opportunity for them to discuss a number of issues related to the murder. Conoquhieson, speaking on behalf of the Oneida and Tuscarora, began with the usual protocol of wiping away the tears of the participants, removing the axe from the heads of the English, and covering the grave of the deceased by burying the "late accident" under the roots of the "Great Tree" so that the event might "never more be remembered." Acknowledging the extreme concern felt by the Oneida, Conoquhieson reminded the gathering that an Englishman had killed two Oneida recently, an event for which the Oneida "never received any redress." He went on to voice optimism that his ceremonies might keep the "Covenant Chain bright and lasting," but he warned that, if the English continued to "look so cooly" on them and made no effort to preserve the chain of friendship, "it might prove of fatal Consequence and end up in the destruction of one of us." Conoquhieson admitted that the Oneida were not totally innocent in this affair: their youth had become intoxicated and refused to listen to the warnings of their sachems against "committing any Violence" to persons or property. "Unfortunately for us, we are not (more than you) exempt from bad people, who will not hearken to advice."[7]

Introducing a different topic, Conoquhieson spoke about the relentless advance of Europeans onto Indian land, admitting his own desire to "kick the German inhabitants" and "drive them into the sea." In his reply Johnson explained that General Amherst, being unfamiliar with native tradition, would expect the Oneida to deliver the murderer so he could be brought to justice, especially as this would indicate the Oneida nation's dislike for crime and eagerness for justice. Johnson discounted the previous murder of two Indians as they were found in the act of plundering the house and destroying the property of the man who killed them, and since Indians had committed many similar killings, Johnson felt Conoquhieson was "frivolously palliating the crime." He encouraged the Oneida to continue in their desire to "preserve the Covenant Chain bright and lasting," reminding them that drunkenness did not negate the Oneida's responsibility to comply "with Amherst's demand of delivering up the offender to justice." Acknowledging that the suspected perpetrator had escaped to a distant area, and realizing the strain this situation was placing on British-Oneida relations, Conoquhieson assured Johnson that, when caught, the man would be handed over to the appropriate authorities.[8]

To admit that Oneida youth were opposing traditional authority would have been a difficult thing for Conoquhieson to do. However, hoping to maintain Oneida loyalty, Johnson portrayed the Oneida favorably in a letter he wrote to Amherst on the same day as this meeting. He indicated that it was their chiefs who had initiated a settlement, that they always cautioned their young men not to insult the settlers in any way, that the leaders had no prior knowledge that the murder was being committed, that they would deliver the offender once found, and that the whole incident was "contrary to their Inclinations or Intentions." Amherst replied, with a stern practicality for which he had become well-known, that the disappearance of the offender was merely an excuse and delay tactic, that he would see justice done, and that the lack of redress for the earlier murder of two Oneida was merely a matter of neglect that did not negate the need for justice to be upheld in this situation. There was little that Johnson or Conoquhieson could say in rebuttal.[9]

Conoquhieson was probably unaware that Johnson's attempts to convince Amherst of the benefits of extending financial and moral support to the Iroquois put the superintendent in an awkward position. Johnson had been knighted in 1756, as a sign of Britain's faith in his abilities, and his situation had thus changed. Humiliated by his losses in the Lake George campaign, which had cost him considerable credibility with the Mohawk nation, Johnson was now encountering opposition from Amherst, the high-ranking British official who, operating on the local scene, was capable of damaging the rapport Johnson had cautiously been nurturing with the Oneida. Johnson's communication with Amherst following the murder of the German settler indicated the benefit of crediting the Oneida for taking the initiative in calling a meeting to settle the issue. However, when Johnson reiterated the pressure felt by the Indians over the apparent loss of their lands, Amherst repeated his commitment not to "interfere with their Lands" providing their conduct supported this privilege, saying he would "Reward them as far as it is in [his] power if they merit it, and punish them if they Deserve it." A subsequent letter from Johnson stressing Oneida remorse received a biting reply: Amherst would use his authority to "punish the delinquents with Entire Destruction, which [he was] firmly resolved on, whenever any of them give [him] Cause." Amherst's inflexibility, lessened somewhat after his earlier visit to Kanowalohale, was becoming again a major obstacle.[10]

Conoquhieson's adamant position regarding the retention of Oneida land undoubtedly troubled Johnson, especially in light of Johnson's efforts to advocate for them to Amherst. The chief was confident that he spoke for the entire Confederacy: "this land which was given us by the Divine Being, we love as our lives, and therefore hope you will secure the possession of it to us, which has been ours from the beginning, by preventing any more of your people from settling higher in the Country agreeable to the desire of all these Nations." How was Johnson to address this matter with integrity, knowing his tenuous position under Amherst? Conoquhieson would not be satisfied by Johnson's reminder of an earlier order made by the English king that no further lands could be granted or sold without the permission of the Oneida, and that they could only blame themselves if any further grants were made "contrary to [their] inclinations."[11]

The push by settlers from Connecticut for land in Pennsylvania still angered the Oneida, who continued to claim rights of ownership in their southern territory. In February 1761 Governor Hamilton of Pennsylvania had written to Johnson expressing apprehension of a "renewal of the Indian war from a most Wicked revival of the Connecticut claims," admitting the Indians would have just cause since the land belonged to them and not to the colonists of either Connecticut or Pennsylvania. Hamilton was particularly anxious that Johnson convey to the Six Nations that he recognized the "proprietary rights" of the Iroquois in the face of the "mischievous set of Intruders." Another letter, from the Pennsylvania Provincial Council, echoed this concern, recognizing that the issue harked back to the dealings of colonists against which Conoquhieson had spoken in the mid-1750s. Johnson voiced his apprehension, noting the critical significance of the problem, at a time when the Iroquois were particularly sensitive regarding the French influence, only recently replaced by British authority; he felt that Amherst's intervention was the only means of concluding this issue, but of this he indicated little hope.[12]

Amherst's unwillingness to restrain what the Oneida perceived as the illegal sale of their land was matched by his reluctance to spend money on them in ways he considered extravagant. Conoquhieson's speech at a meeting with Johnson in June 1761 indicated his frustration over less powder being made available to the Oneida hunters. When Johnson supported Conoquhieson's view and broached the topic with Amherst, the latter expressed his aversion to buying the allegiance of the Indians rather than encouraging them to be independent supporters of British interests. Johnson disagreed. When Amherst had questioned the large sum involved when Johnson applied for reimbursement for costs incurred in purchasing gifts for the Iroquois at the meetings en route to Fort Detroit, Johnson rebutted by indicating the Indians were already noticing the lack of presents and ammunition available since the British took charge of the treaty process. He still thought it inadvisable to alienate Conoquhieson and the Oneida by cutting off these commodities at a time when the English had just assumed the jurisdiction of Indians who had recently received considerable largesse from the French.[13] This debate between the two British officials remained unresolved at Amherst's departure in November 1763 and did nothing to relieve tensions between the Iroquois and the imperial authorities.

The quandary created by alcohol abuse among young Indian men, mentioned by Conoquhieson when meeting with Johnson at German Flats, would plague the Oneida as long as they depended on British forts for protection and British traders for supplies. The distress of an Oneida woman from Kanowalohale was evident when she approached the personnel at Fort Stanwix for assistance against the French and their allied Indians, explaining that all the men at the village were either absent or drunk. The dilemma faced by the British authorities stationed at the forts was not alleviated when the Indians requested alcohol at conferences. The Indians indicated that it contributed to a more jovial atmosphere; it seemed to them that its manufacture, when revealed to the British, was sanctioned by God. Yet the British authorities feared the Indians would, when drunk, accuse the British of offering peace with one hand and the suffering caused by alcohol with the other. Conoquhieson tried to excuse the Oneida who murdered the German settler by reminding Johnson that his drunken state was due to the alcohol supplied by the British; at the same time Conoquhieson pointed out that the same commanding officers at the forts were prevented from selling the powder necessary for the young men to hunt for food.[14]

The demoralizing effect of alcohol as indicated by Conoquhieson was frequently at the root of the tension between the older Oneida sachems and the younger warriors when competing for authority in their communities. When young Oneida fighters, angered by the conservative and conciliatory mood of the elders, vented their frustrations in drunken and destructive behavior, they weakened the relationship being sought by the Oneida with the British. Conoquhieson realized that his lament—that the murder of the German settler was precipitated by the anger of drunken warriors—did not absolve them from responsibility for their behavior, especially in the eyes of the elders who warned the youth against alcohol abuse. The warriors felt differently: "We the Warriors . . . are in fact the People of Consequence for Managing Affairs, our Sachems being generally a parcell of Old People who say Much, but who Mean and Act very little, so that we have both the power and Ability to Settle Matters."[15] The Oneida had enough problems of their own, without external factors creating even more internal divisions.

In January 1762 the Confederacy chose the Oneida to challenge Johnson's command. The previous year, in August 1761 at Fort Johnson, the Mohawk had joined the Oneida in chastising the Seneca for disobeying Johnson and continuing their attachment to the French during the British-French war. The Seneca's "imprudent steps" had placed the whole Confederacy in a state of uneasiness, and their good behavior was necessary to ensure future cooperation from the English. But at a subsequent conference called by Governor Hamilton at Easton, Pennsylvania, also in August 1761, the mood had changed. Five hundred Indians including the Seneca, Onondaga, Cayuga, and Oneida took the opportunity to criticize Johnson's administration of Indian affairs, especially his failure to prevent fraudulent land sales and the high prices of his trade goods. Then, over the winter, the Mohawk continued to grumble over their loss of land and the fact that the Seneca were dealing more with western tribes than with the Confederacy. In January 1762 the Iroquois chiefs turned to Conoquhieson to speak for the entire Confederacy in presenting their case: "We have for sometime past heard that our Brethren the English were wanting to get more Lands from us, and several came amongst us for that purpose last year. Whereupon, the whole Six Nations assembled, to consider thereon, and have required us, the Oneidas in their Names to desire you will prevent your People from Coming amongst us for that purpose."[16]

Johnson's reply echoed those of previous occasions. He reassured them that the king had ordered all the colonial governors not to make grants or to arrange sales without the Indians' permission. He added that he would advise the authorities that no further land transactions were wanted by the Six Nations. Johnson's assurances rang hollow, however. Conoquhieson and other Iroquois leaders attended further meetings at Fort Johnson later that month and sympathized with the Mohawk sachems' frustration over George Klock, a trader who continued to avoid the counsel of the elders and to entice the young men to his house, ply them with alcohol, and then gain their support for the proposed land deals by falsely telling them he had obtained the consent of the elders.[17]

Struggling to reestablish his authority and to reunite the Six Nations, Johnson summoned the Confederacy to a conference at his home in April 1762. The event did not begin auspiciously. Johnson was angry with the Seneca for plotting with the Indians near Fort Detroit to attack the British at the same time he was celebrating the French defeat at Montreal. When Conoquhieson felt that matters were amicably settled between Johnson and the Elder Brothers, he commandeered the floor and introduced concerns that, while specific to his nation, were relevant to the whole Confederacy: "I am . . . to Speak to you at the request of the women of the Six Nations, who on your first Summons were desirous to come down . . . but were afterwards Informed you did not Desire their Attendance; however as it has always been our Custom for them to be present on Such Occasions. . . . They now therefore hope you will Consider their fatigue, and . . . afford them Cloathing and Petticoats to cover them, as our Warriors for want of Ammunition cannot take Care of them as formerly." Conoquhieson, and the clan mothers for whom he spoke, had Johnson cornered. For many years the superintendent had relished publicly acknowledging Indians' requirements regarding treaty and conference protocol, and he was now reluctant to lose prestige by diminishing his previous lavish attention on all who attended his meetings because of the restrictions placed on him by Amherst. With the friction existing within the Confederacy, Johnson could not afford to lose further stature by alienating the Oneida. Declaring that he could see no need for women and children to attend "meetings summoned for the Discharge of business," he would nonetheless provide clothing for the women and ammunition for the warriors, providing the latter would "be applied to a proper use."[18]

A brawl at Fort Stanwix in July 1762 was symptomatic of the escalating frustrations affecting the relationship between the British and the Oneida. The captain stationed at the fort wrote to Amherst that a large number of Oneida, without provocation, had insulted his soldiers and attempted to scale the stockades and kill those within. In his letter he included the possibility that the Indians were agitated after some of their youth plundered the home of a trader who refused to sell them rum. Amherst replied that he would advise Johnson to deal with the matter and included a warning that, should any further attacks be conducted by the Oneida or by any tribe, the commander of the garrison in question would be ordered to fire his cannon at the attackers. When corresponding with Johnson, Amherst repeated this warning, telling Johnson "Immediately [to] Call the Oneida Indians to Account for such a Daring attempt at any of the King's Posts" and extending the deterrent to include those who might be "Daring to Plunder the Traders."[19]

The tensions that erupted into the brawl at Fort Stanwix were not felt only by the Oneida. The existence of British forts within Iroquois territory had extensive ramifications for the Indians' economic and political life, and the benefits they sought from trade opportunities under the aegis of the fort commanders were frequently outweighed by the negative influences of these military outposts of the British empire. Yet the Oneida were expected to lead the barrage aimed against the British. Asked by the Confederacy to represent them at the April 1762 conference, Conoquhieson outlined their complaints concerning the British soldiers' attitude: "I am now Directed to Speak to you on behalf of all our Confederacy . . . ; We cannot but express our great Uneasiness, at the ill treatment we Generally meet with at the Several Garrisons, Such as the being debarred the Liberty of fishing, and our People for the Most frivolous Causes abused, threatened to be fired upon and often Run at with Bayonets; this treatment we look upon as not only Unjust, but very Unbrotherlike; besides if we were Starving with Hunger (which is often Our Case) they will not give Us a Morsel of Any thing; a Usage very different from what we had Reason to Expect, or were promised." Johnson had little sympathy, responding that Conoquhieson's frequent mention of the ill treatment of his people could be attributed to their equally frequent drunken state.[20]

Conoquhieson was not alone in verbally attacking the British. Oneida's spokesman in their southern territory, the recalcitrant Thomas King, voiced similar dissatisfaction with the tardiness of the British in fulfilling their promises. He represented the Oneida at a conference called by Governor Hamilton in August 1762 at Lancaster, where the Pennsylvania governor and members of the provincial council met with over 550 Iroquois and Delaware delegates representing the Six Nations. Governor Hamilton was anxious to obtain the release of colonial prisoners, but the Iroquois focused on what they considered an invalid sale to Connecticut settlers of land in the Susquehanna valley. At the conclusion of the customary opening speeches and condolences, King arose and inappropriately interjected that Oneida guns and hatchets were in need of repair. Governor Hamilton tried to proceed by discussing the return of captives. King, however, took control of the agenda and launched into a lengthy speech instructing the delegates about the traditional niceties of clearing the throat, opening the eyes and ears, and taking the thorns out of the feet of all in attendance. Then complaining that the procedure for returning prisoners had not been resolved since the earlier Easton conference, King railed about the change in tradition concerning the release of prisoners. He had always considered prisoners to be the property of his nation when victorious; now, reluctant to return the English captives, he said it would take time to conduct a practice that was not familiar to the Indians. In addition, some of the prisoners that King was escorting had been taken by the garrisons at the English forts, others had run away as opportunity allowed, and others were still the captives of those Indians who were fighting against the Cherokee. He reminded the governors that financial recompense had been promised in return for the safe arrival of the prisoners, and that this reward was now expected. However, King commented, he felt he was dealing with two governors of Pennsylvania since what was said at one time did not always agree with later statements emanating from Philadelphia.[21]

Following a recital of the significance of burying axes signifying hostility under a pine tree and of the interrelation of the members of the Confederacy, King then referred to the domestic political difficulty involving relations between sachems and warriors that had increasingly plagued the Oneida but as yet showed no sign of being resolved: "What we have hitherto said concerning peace, has been concluded upon by our old Counsellors [sachems]. We also desire our Chief Warriors to be strong and assist our old Counsellors, and desire if any thing should be wanting in the old Counsellors, they would assist them in it, in order that our Friendship may be lasting; for the Counsellors can do nothing unless the Warriors should give their Consent to it." Having warned the British about the improper taking of Iroquois land by force, King repeated the opening accusations concerning guns: "You are daily making rifles; I do not know what you do with them. When you gave me any guns, you gave me Yellow stocked ones, that are worth nothing. I have asked you now four times. At Easton you only gave me Gun Locks. What, think you, could I do with them, without Stocks and Barrels? I make no guns."[22] One can imagine the relief that day when King, from fatigue, finally ended his harangue. It would have been the content of his oration rather than the length that caused discomfort for those whose tradition promoted a less caustic approach.

The conference reconvened four days later, and those gathered heard familiar themes in the second installment of the Oneida sachem's diatribe. The original agreement for the construction of the fort at Shamokin, including its dismantling when no longer needed, had not been honored. The time had come, declared King, for both the fort and the soldiers to go. Unruly soldiers did not combine well with young warriors when they encountered each other on the warpath, especially when soldiers blocked warriors on their way to fight the Cherokee. King requested that the trading post remain, but that it be staffed by honest people of his own choosing, as Indians preparing to fight needed the supplies available at the post. Additional trading posts complete with blacksmiths and gunsmiths were necessary, especially since the advent of peace would give the warriors more time to hunt on the lands they were determined to protect. Speaking on behalf of the warriors, King demanded a supply of powder, war paint, and suitable clothing so they could go to war in suitable style. The delivery of British prisoners, King concluded, was not within his power. He admitted that his promise to the governor might have been inappropriate, as he could not speak for those warriors who had taken prisoners and were not present at the council to indicate their own decisions.[23]

Governor Hamilton acknowledged these concerns, but two points remained contentious. He understood that Indians adopted prisoners into their own nations, but the British lacked this custom and expected an exchange of prisoners of war when peace was declared. He denied ever promising payment when prisoners were returned to the British and warned the Indians against accepting any messages or understandings on the part of the British in Pennsylvania other than those issued by the governor himself. Second, while admitting that the British continued to look "with Longing Eyes" at Indian land, the governor denied accusations that he or his government had granted additional land without the Indians' consent. Recalling similar charges from King at the Easton conference, Hamilton asked for a final resolution from the Indians then present as to whether they had consented to colonists from Connecticut purchasing and settling on their land. This increased King's fury. Without consulting any of the chiefs, he replied: "It is very well known that the Land was sold by the Six Nations; some are here now that sold that Land; it was sold for Two Thousand Dollars, but it was not sold by our Consent in publick Council; it was as [if] it were stolen from us."[24] The conference ended. There was no doubt in the participants' minds that cordial relations between the Oneida and the British had little chance of survival after the exchange between King and Hamilton.

British-Iroquois friction was exacerbated and Oneida authority within the Confederacy diminished in November 1762, when two brothers from the Chenussio Seneca murdered two white men. The offenders continued living in their home community of Kanestio and were bragging about their exploit, which caused uneasiness in the community concerning English retribution. Johnson told the Oneida and Tuscarora at a meeting held at Kanowalohale (with his nephew Guy Johnson attending as deputy agent for Indian affairs) that, as the Oneida claimed leadership among the Iroquois, he expected them to use all possible influence at a conference planned for Onondaga to convince the Chenussio to surrender the two murderers to the British. When the Iroquois gathered at Onondaga the following month, Guy Johnson was concerned that the Seneca were not in attendance. Addressing those present, he exhorted them to maintain their friendship with the English by delivering the murderers. Although the Onondaga agreed that the murderers should be apprehended, they wished to see what the Seneca had already done regarding this matter, thereby in effect displacing Johnson's request and bypassing the influence anticipated by the Oneida.[25] The slight would not go unnoticed by the Oneida leaders.

Matters had not been resolved by the following spring. In March 1763 William Johnson held a meeting at his home with representatives of all the Iroquois, with the exception of the Cayuga whose leaders were involved in hostilities with the Cherokee. A messenger sent by the Onondaga to Kanestio brought back word that the two murderers had fled to the Ohio region. Johnson informed Amherst that the delegates present at the meeting were not comfortable with the concept of simply handing over the offenders for punishment; they were "entirely at a loss what Step to take, on the one side, desirous to give [the British] Satisfaction, and on the other apprehensive of a Quarrel amongst themselves." The debate continued, with Johnson paying little heed to the reasons given by the Onondaga for not delivering the guilty parties. It is telling that Conoquhieson was silent during this exchange; though present at the conference, neither he nor any of the Oneida delegates provided the leadership Johnson requested.[26]

On the last day of the conference, the Onondaga speaker was informed that Johnson had not been apprised by the Oneida as to why the Cayuga were not in attendance. Since the young men had left to fight against the Cherokee, their leaders preferred to leave the matter in the hands of the Elder Brothers, since the Seneca were involved. However, if this had no effect, they as Younger Brothers would endeavor to convince the Seneca to deliver the murderers and maintain peace with the British. The Onondaga speaker continued to address Johnson: "We of Onondaga have now only to observe to you that we cannot help thinking that the Oneida, who are the Elder Branch of the Confederacy, act wrong in not advising the Cayugas to Stay at home, and assist in bringing this unhappy Affair to a good End, before they should think of going to War against their Enemies." Johnson responded that he would take charge of the situation. He demanded that the Cayuga attend a future conference at Chenussio so that all the Iroquois would be involved in solving the problem with the Seneca.[27] The Oneida would have noticed the Onondaga reprimand. As the Cayuga regarded the Oneida as their Elder Brother within the junior moiety, it was convenient for the Onondaga to blame the Oneida for not convincing the Cayuga to stay at home and assist the Oneida rather than going south to fight the Cherokee.

By May 1763, the issue of the Chenussio Seneca remained unresolved, and the Oneida continued to be overlooked. The Onondaga had been unsuccessful in persuading the Seneca to surrender the culprits despite numerous meetings. They claimed they could not convince the Seneca to deviate from their tradition, which militated against delivering their members for retribution. It was with Johnson's persuasion that the Onondaga, not the Oneida, sought and obtained the assistance of the Mohawk in arranging for the Seneca to attend a future meeting of the Confederacy at Fort Johnson. Again, the Oneida were snubbed.[28]

In May 1763 Pontiac of the Ottawa nation led a conglomeration of western Indian groups who shared a hatred of the European incursion in an attack on Fort Detroit. The focus of Johnson's conferences with the Iroquois now shifted from the murders committed by the Seneca to the Iroquois nation's involvement in the uprising attributed to the Ottawa warrior. Meeting in Oneida territory, at German Flats in July 1763 with the entire

Confederacy (except the Seneca, who refused to attend), the superintendent impressed upon those present the extreme necessity of declaring their allegiance to the British. The Iroquois representatives understood Johnson's anxiety: successful Indian attacks on numerous British forts to the west of Niagara seemed linked to Pontiac's siege at Fort Detroit, these hostilities were of mutual concern to the Iroquois and the British, and the real sentiments of the Iroquois regarding the situation were difficult to discern. Conoquhieson addressed those assembled, repeating his earlier litany of land and trade grievances, but Johnson was not impressed with Conoquhieson's reasons for Indian hostilities. Johnson responded in a way that angered the Oneida spokesman. The problems concerning trade were trifling and foolish, Johnson claimed. The Indians had lately expressed satisfaction at the amount and price of trade items. In addition, General Amherst's determination to bring the Seneca murderers to trial should by then have been understood and acceptable to the Oneida. Johnson rebutted Conoquhieson's stated displeasure over the continuing presence of British forts and troops. He reminded him that the posts of which the Oneida disapproved had been constructed and occupied by the French, and it was the French who had lost blood and money when the English captured the forts. Since that time, they had been of benefit to both English and Indian as a defensive bulwark against enemies and might well again be of use, as the Indians themselves were concerned the French menace had not totally subsided. Johnson also denied there had been recent attempts to acquire Indian lands against their wishes, despite their claims to the contrary. Conoquhieson should not be concerned regarding improper land deals at the western end of Iroquoia, Johnson stressed; that was now the responsibility of the Seneca.[29] Conoquhieson's leadership had yet again been challenged.

Although the fighting between the French and the British was all but over in the summer of 1763, hostilities continuing under Pontiac's encouragement and conducted by the western Iroquois increased the tensions. The Chenussio Seneca attacked Forts Le Boeuf and Presqu'île in the southwest corner of their territory, and Amherst authorized retribution that resulted in a bloody but indecisive British victory. The strained relations also affected the Oneida. In July Thomas King arrived seeking funds to purchase ammunition for the Oneida at Oquaga. Johnson granted his request but created increased discord within the Oneida by authorizing King to return home by way of Kanowalohale, so he could investigate chatter that some of the Oneida from that community were threatening to do Johnson harm. Even if such comments were nothing more than speculation arising from the tensions of the period, Johnson's now abrasive relationship with the Oneida gave him just cause to be alarmed.[30]

That summer additional rumors resulting from political divisions within the Oneida lessened that nation's prestige. Information reached Johnson that some Oneida were about to attack the British colonists at German

Flats. Three Oneida chiefs, one of whom was the aged Gawehe, were summoned to Johnson Hall. This was an impressive stone edifice complete with separate bastions that had recently been completed some distance west of Johnson's previous (smaller) home, reflecting his increased prestige. Here they declared the Oneida had known nothing of this development before Johnson's messengers informed them of it. Assuring Johnson they were sent as representatives of the entire village of Kanowalohale, they regretted that the warriors had been misled by the sachems. "All the Warriors met at Kanawarohare, and then and there came to a resolution to live for the time to come in greater friendship with their Brethren, and nevermore obey any orders of their Sachems which might be repugnant to their present good Intentions and resolutions, but would follow their advice in anything that tended to the good of their Nation." They assured Johnson that the warriors were ashamed of their complicity with the misguided sachems and begged forgiveness. Gawehe and the other chiefs then acknowledged their faults and reassured Johnson that as soon as possible all the sachems of Kanowalohale would find the best means of removing the uneasiness from Johnson's mind. The superintendent was pleased to hear of this proposal but added that he could not "but express the greatest surprise to hear that those whose duty and business it [was] to preserve peace and good order, should think of Suffering, much less of encouraging the Young Men to commit any Acts of Violence."[31]

As the uprisings fueled by Pontiac and his supporters dragged on into the autumn of 1763, Johnson struggled to maintain Iroquois allegiance to the British, despite the cessation of British-French hostilities. The Seneca were of special concern. Johnson hoped that these Elder Brothers would join the Iroquois and attend a conference at Johnson Hall in September; once the gathering assembled he thanked the Onondaga for persuading at least some Seneca representatives to attend. The Onondaga speaker stressed that the success of his nation's representatives to convince the Seneca was because of the empathy between their sachems and warriors and those of the Seneca. Conoquhieson could not keep his peace about the Seneca's claim and demanded that credit be afforded the Oneida for bringing about the Seneca's presence. He assured Johnson that it was the Oneida who had gone to the Seneca country and persuaded them to cooperate. The Oneida had also sent messengers to the Chenussio who as yet had not returned. In order to maintain good relations with Amherst, Conoquhieson continued, the Oneida had unanimously agreed to keep their warriors at home in case they appeared to be initiating a confrontation. Conoquhieson also asked that Johnson treat the Oneida well should he travel through their territory en route to the western nations. In conclusion he accused the Onondaga of seeking their own self-interest by previously issuing false information.[32] Previous chatter about the residents of Kanowalohale wishing to harm Johnson had not been forgotten.

The Oneida suffered another verbal attack from the Onondaga the following month when the Six Nations met at Johnson Hall. The Onondaga threatened to go to England hoping that a visit to King George III would result in the Iroquois's concerns regarding land and trade being satisfactorily resolved. This maneuver would displease Johnson considerably, for it would add to the British authorities' perception of his increasing inefficiency. The Oneida, together with the Cayuga and Tuscarora, supported Johnson in wanting this trip postponed, for the chiefs who were chosen to travel would be better occupied staying home and settling the Seneca problem. The Onondaga responded by laying the blame for all the problems at the Younger Brother's door, saying that the indiscriminate selling of land by the Oneida was responsible for the antagonism, and that the decision regarding the trip to England should be decided by Johnson and the Mohawk, not by the Oneida.[33] Support within the Confederacy for the Oneida was inexorably crumbling.

To add to their problems, the Oneida were challenged by the Seneca in December 1763 when the latter finally joined the other nations' delegates meeting at Johnson Hall. The Seneca speaker confirmed that it was the messages of the Onondaga that had convinced them to "drop further Hostilities and lay hold of the Chain of Friendship with the rest of the Confederacy." Explaining that much of their trouble was based on a web of intrigue involving the Delaware and the French, the Seneca speaker actually blamed the Oneida for hindering reconciliation, when the people of Kanowalohale intercepted a belt and scalp being sent throughout the Six Nations and decided to bury the scalp. Conoquhieson could no longer hold his tongue. He "stood up on behalf of the Confederacy and with a great deal of Spirit . . . addressed the Chenussios." He accused the Chenussio of trying to exculpate themselves by blaming the Oneida for confusion arising from a message sent to the Chenussio by the Mohawk. He insisted it was a Chenussio who changed the message to indicate Iroquois defection from the British. He shouted that the Chenussio were propagating falsehood, that the Confederacy knew the Oneida had made a "very large Heap of Belts of [their] Wampum" in an effort to restore peace, and that they should repent of what they had done to the British.[34] There was no mistaking Conoquhieson's frustration over the Seneca's attack on the Oneida's integrity, yet no ameliorating comments or gestures were forthcoming.

Conditions were problematic also for the southern Oneida. While Conoquhieson was insisting that the Oneida receive their rightful credit for bringing the Chenussio Seneca to Johnson's conference fire, Thomas King continued to participate vociferously in meetings as an Oneida spokesman representing the Confederacy. Tensions continued to grow between the pro-British Iroquois and the Delaware, who still maintained alliance with the French and would be involved in skirmishes against the British in 1763 and 1764. King was present at councils called in efforts to rally the support of the Iroquois. In the autumn of 1763 he represented the Indians of the south branch of the Susquehanna, stressing that under his leadership the Oneida had encouraged eight Indian communities in the vicinity of Oquaga to follow Johnson's advice to be loyal to Britain in the event of hostile action. Although reports circulated concerning Delaware scalping parties advancing near Oquaga, King demanded credit for guaranteeing that community's support for Johnson should he so request.[35]

As 1763 drew to a close, General Amherst's departure as commander of the British forces offered hope for a brighter future in British-Iroquois relations. Oneida dependence on British military posts as guardians of the trade system, especially with Fort Stanwix being so close to Kanowalohale, had put them in a compromising position during Amherst's tenure. Delegates from all Six Nations had met at Fort Johnson in May 1763 and composed an address to General Amherst that summarized many of their earlier arguments. The British had promised, once the war with the French was concluded, that they would supply reasonably priced goods at the forts. Instead the Iroquois watched as more land was taken over, additional forts were built, and higher prices for goods were charged. The result was that hunting was declining and the people were increasingly impoverished. In contrast they had agreed earlier with the construction of the fort at Oswego as a place for defense and trade, and the prices charged and treatment shown to the Indians had been most favorable. Despite Amherst's lack of support, Johnson had tried to placate the Oneida and issued conversion tables for trade at Fort Stanwix, indicating the number and quality of beaver, mink, martin, deer, muskrat, and raccoon furs that could be used by the Indians to purchase yarn, stroud, clothing, knives, paint, kettles, and gunpowder.[36]

With the arrival of General Thomas Gage as the new commander, Johnson upgraded regulations concerning the activities of traders at forts. By 1765 commanding officers at the forts were charged with the responsibility of monitoring traders' compliance, in efforts to ensure that traders treated Indians fairly. Arrangements such as these would have been pleasing to delegates from Oneida, Tuscarora, and Oquaga who had approached Johnson in January 1764 to reaffirm their loyalty to the British, at the same time requesting protection for their lands and the stationing of fair traders, a smith, and an interpreter at Fort Stanwix.[37]

Problems again surfaced for the Oneida when Johnson—buoyed by his rapport with Gage and anxious to reestablish credibility with his superiors in Britain following his failure to curb Seneca hostility—tried to orchestrate an Iroquois attack on the western Indians who had been unfaithful to the British cause. Unlike Amherst, Gage agreed with Johnson's desire to capitalize on the Iroquois support promised at the 1759 Canajoharie conference and to secure their assistance against the western Iroquois. As Indians knew the woods and hunting grounds, posited Gage, they would give the British troops confidence, especially for a surprise attack on an Indian village.

Caution was needed, however, in treating Indians "on the Principles of Equity Moderation, and Kindness," by giving them small presents and only "rewarding them as they deserved." In February 1764 Johnson focused on the Oneida and obtained the support of two hundred Indians, mostly from Kanowalohale, to attack the Shawnee and Delaware villages and the "nest of Villains at Kanestio." The Oneida were understandably apprehensive, realizing that Kanowalohale could receive the brunt of a revenge attack.[38]

In the planning process Johnson found an unlikely ally in the flamboyant Thomas King. The Oneida leader promised Johnson he would lead a group of Tuscarora, together with some Oquaga, to join the Onondaga and Cayuga living in the Susquehanna area who also agreed to assist Johnson in an attack against the pro-French Delaware. King arrived at Johnson Hall in February 1764, leading a delegation of loyal Iroquois. His oratorical style, as bombastic as usual, reflected that of Conoquhieson when representing the Confederacy. On behalf of the Onondaga sachems present, he declared their loyalty to the British and the obedience of their warriors to their wishes; for the Cayuga sachems he relayed the regrets of their warriors for leaving home to fight the Cherokee when their presence with the elders would have been more beneficial; for the Mohawks he expressed loyalty while apologizing for the lack of eloquent spokesmen; and for the Onondaga and Seneca he assured Johnson of the sincerity of their allegiance.[39]

That summer King, not knowing the humiliation awaiting him and the Oneida, led an expedition of about six hundred Indians mustered by Johnson to accompany over one thousand British troops to advance from Fort Niagara in a show of force designed to impress any enemy Indians as to the power of the British and their allied Iroquois. The British were led by Colonel John Bradstreet who moved west from Albany accompanied by the allied Iroquois with instructions from General Gage to destroy enemy Indians and to leave all peacemaking initiatives to Johnson. However, on the south shore of Lake Erie not far from Fort Sandusky, Bradstreet defied Gage's orders and concluded a peace treaty with a group of Delaware in which forts were surrendered to the British, Indian hostages arranged as guarantees, and plans made for the transfer of British hostages. As Bradstreet approached Fort Detroit, he sent King ahead to carry news of the peace treaty to Pontiac. En route, Pontiac's allies among the western Iroquois taunted King and the Oneida and ridiculed them as fops of the British, allies of a nation whose leaders did not follow instructions, and doomed by promises of an impending French victory led by Pontiac.[40] As word of Pontiac's humiliation of the Oneida was carried back throughout Iroquoia, King's previous bravado and the Oneida's claims of consequence in dealing with the Seneca were hastily undone.

In September 1764, the involvement of King and the Oneida in these events was questioned at a conference at Fort Sandusky. Pontiac was in attendance. He claimed that Seneca messengers had given him the impression the Six Nations had arrived to join him in an attack against the British. He was confused when King carried Colonel Bradstreet's proposal that the Iroquois force accompanying King should assist Pontiac in brokering a peace agreement between the bellicose Indians and the British, an initiative contrary to General Gage's directives. However the Seneca, according to Pontiac, considered the other five nations to be deceitful if they supported the British. Pontiac warned King and the Oneida to return home, as their lives would be in danger if they persevered in their attachment to the English. In his defense, King responded that he acted cautiously after his humiliation at a previous meeting with Pontiac and the Seneca, and that he had been unwilling to take any action as friend or foe until news of Delaware intentions were made known. It seems Johnson overlooked the rapport he had with King at the beginning of the venture; he could not explain the source of King's eventual change of heart and reluctance to carry out the mission. In December 1764, King arrived at Johnson's home extremely hungry and tired, having traveled on limited supplies for two months since his departure from Sandusky. He was now totally distrustful of Bradstreet, who had failed to supply King's supporters with adequate food and transport and had conversed through a French interpreter with some northern Indians while refusing to supply King with any explanation of the proceedings. In fact King was disillusioned with the British in general.[41]

In the spring of 1765, Oneida delegates to a conference at Johnson Hall watched with broken hearts as William Johnson brought to fruition his long-standing vision of a unified pro-British Iroquois Confederacy. The previous summer, seven warriors representing the majority of the Seneca had signed a peace treaty with Johnson at Fort Niagara, bringing the most recalcitrant of the Iroquois under the British aegis. Now in April 1765, all Six Nations were summoned to recognize formally the reinstitution of the Confederacy and the signing of a peace treaty with the Ohio Delaware. Johnson insisted on the presence of the two leading Seneca warriors whose nation had perpetrated the damage east of the Susquehanna during Pontiac's uprising. Eventually, over one hundred Seneca and Delaware arrived with their English prisoners. They stopped in Oneida territory to collect supplies and medicine, a fact that would have been galling to the Oneida. After Johnson greeted the Seneca and Delaware, the Onondaga requested that he install seven young men as sachems so that the Grand Council could properly represent the Confederacy. Twelve Onondaga names were supplied, with seven listed as having elder sachems as sponsors. The Onondaga speaker requested that the seven new sachems declare their agreement with the traditional rules laid down by their ancestors, thereby bringing pleasure to the Onondaga, the Confederacy, and the British. Exhorting them to act in future according to the lofty expectations placed upon the role of sachem, Johnson presented each newly appointed young man with what had become the usual marks of distinction (despite their total lack of traditional Iroquoian culture): a laced coat and hat, a ruffled shirt, and a medal. In this way the Onondaga, witnessed by the Six

Nations including the Oneida and authenticated by Johnson, reasserted their political dominance within the Confederacy. The Iroquois Confederacy having been reaffirmed, Johnson installed a new Mohawk sachem.

No recognition was given of the Oneida's previous leadership. In fact Conoquhieson had no option other than to indicate acceptance of Onondaga's reaffirmed primacy within the Confederacy by offering two new Oneida sachems for Onondaga approval. The Onondaga sachem, mindful of his own nation's similar situation a few days previously, thanked Conoquhieson for involving the Six Nations (including the Chenussio) in the choice of their new sachems and for recognizing with a wampum belt the Mohawk as head of the Confederacy.[42] In these ceremonies, the protracted efforts of the Oneida to maintain leadership within the Confederacy were eclipsed.

The status of the Oneida within the Confederacy, as represented by Conoquhieson and Thomas King at the 1765 conference, was very different from that promoted by Conoquhieson at Canajoharie six years earlier. At that time the assertive sachems dominated the conference, despite its being held in Mohawk territory and under the auspices of the pro-Mohawk superintendent. From that point on, however, Oneida's tendency to prevail declined. Both Conoquhieson as sachem and King as warrior hammered at the British, complaining on behalf of the Confederacy about the failure of the victors to keep the promises they had made in an effort to maintain Iroquois allegiance. The only other voice heard was that of Gawehe, now sounding laconic in comparison with the other two. Circumstances seemed weighted against the Oneida. Johnson wanted their help in solving the Chenussio murders, but the Onondaga did not. During Johnson's negotiations in response to Pontiac's uprising, the superintendent found Conoquhieson's constant litany of complaints irritating; land, ammunition, forts, soldiers, alcohol, and internal conflicts were of little consequence in comparison with the threat posed by Pontiac and his allies. The Onondaga refused to recognize Oneida contribution to the solution regarding the Chenussio. King's chance to bring honor to the Oneida during Bradstreet's campaign resulted instead in humiliation. As the two leading Oneida representatives in the mid-1760s, Conoquhieson and King had no alternative than to watch as the Onondaga leadership position within the Confederacy strengthened. In many ways the Oneida felt this should have been their role, but the Onondaga had convinced their confederates and Johnson they were in the better position to connect with the Seneca. Peace might have come to Iroquoia, but not to the hearts of the Oneida.

CHAPTER THREE

# THE ONEIDA AS DIPLOMATS, 1765-1770

The arrival of over three thousand Iroquois to attend a conference in Oneida territory at Fort Stanwix in 1768 demonstrates the importance of this event to the Six Nations in general, and the potential significance for the Oneida in particular.[1] The Indians came in response to a summons from William Johnson. In his capacity as superintendent of Indian affairs, Johnson organized the event at the request of the British Board of Trade, which, through the 1763 Proclamation, had encouraged that the Allegheny mountain range be the western boundary of the Atlantic colonies. Historical evaluations have tended to focus on those in attendance who represented colonial interests: provincial governors trying to prevent hostilities and solve the simultaneous problems of protecting Indian lands and accommodating future European territorial expansion; speculators eager to acquire land when it was made available by the resulting Treaty of Fort Stanwix; missionary ambassadors intent on furthering their Christian enterprise; and Johnson himself, a royalist figurehead caught in the British government's dilemma of how to impose its authority on increasingly assertive Atlantic colonies. Only passing notice has been given the Iroquois, who are usually presented as a homogeneous group.[2]

The Oneida in particular had struggled to be more than secondary participants at previous colonial attempts in the mid-1760s to create a definite boundary line separating Indian and settler territory. However, records of the Fort Stanwix conference and of subsequent events in Oneida communities during the early 1770s portray the Oneida leaders' increasingly being frustrated in their own strategies by expectations placed on them by the Confederacy, the colonial authorities, and their own people. Coming to terms with pragmatic adjustments to the traditional roles of sachems and warriors, and confronted by the fresh infusion of Protestant missionary enterprise into their northern territory, the Oneida were finally discovering ways to respond to the challenges presented by the new world in which they found themselves.

Shickellamy, Scarooyady, Conoquhieson, and Thomas King represented a generation of Oneida spokesmen who had eloquently reminded the British that peace would prevail in Iroquoia only if the ancestral lands remained in Indian possession. The 1763 Proclamation's statement that Indian lands were to be preserved for Iroquois use and ownership echoed British policy of the 1750s—that colonial governors would not sell or grant Indian lands without the consent of the nations claiming ownership of them. The turmoil of the 1750s had made Johnson and the British government painfully aware of the importance of guaranteeing the Indians possession of their lands, despite demands for colonial expansion and an appreciation of the economic advantages that would accrue. Realizing a boundary line was necessary in order to protect both Indian hunting grounds and colonial settlements, in 1763 Johnson wrote the Board of Trade that the Six Nations would approve a line running along the back of the northern colonies, if they were convinced this would preserve their land and prevent further grievances. The eventual wording of the proclamation was an attempt to come to terms with this reality: the interests and security of the colonies depended on the Indians being neither molested nor disturbed in possession of the lands not ceded or purchased by the British; their hunting grounds must be protected; governors must not issue patents or grants beyond the boundaries of their respective governments; no patents or sales of lands were to occur beyond the heads of rivers flowing into the Atlantic from the west or northwest (in general indicating the Allegheny mountains); any persons living on lands reserved for the Indians were to be removed; and if Indians wanted to sell any of their land, then the transactions were to be conducted with the crown and under the supervision of the local governor, thereby prohibiting private purchases.[3]

Despite these arrangements, however, the Oneida were not immune from continued attempts by colonial figures to cut into their territory. Among the numerous settlers vying for Iroquois land was the eminent missionary and educator the Reverend Eleazar Wheelock. For some time he had looked enviously at land in New York where he might construct a school larger and more comprehensive than the one operating in Connecticut. Growing numbers of Iroquois children, including several from the Oneida nation, were attending his school, which encouraged him in this endeavor despite Johnson's increasing coolness toward the idea. Johnson had worked hard to lessen the influence of the French among the Oneida after the British-French wars, and he had recently fought against maneuvers by the Connecticut-based Susquehanna Company to assume control of large sections of Iroquoia. In 1761 Johnson invited Wheelock to educate Iroquois children and to prepare missionaries to reside in Seneca and Oneida territory, taking advantage of Wheelock's strong anti-Catholic sentiments in order to combat the Jesuits' influence while assuming Johnson could control a possible Presbyterian infiltration by virtue of his authority as superintendent. However, his correspondence with Wheelock became less amicable as Wheelock's plans developed. Within a year, the expanded vision of a settlement of missionaries accompanying the school within Iroquois territory did not please Johnson, who then vigorously opposed what he saw as a scheme of combined Presbyterian proselytizing and Connecticut land grabbing. He warned Wheelock that any such attempts in the Susquehanna area "would prove fatal to those who should attempt to Establish themselves."[4]

Although the southern Oneida had a longer history of interaction with Christian missionaries than those at Kanowalohale, the latter eventually suffered the effects of interdenominational rivalry. Johnson saw the northern community as a bastion of Church of England missionary enterprise, and Wheelock promoted it as an educational center for Puritan Congregationalism. But antagonism increased between the traditional Oneida and Wheelock's Christian Indians from New England when these began arriving in 1761 because of their disdain for their hosts. The first schoolmaster in the village was David Fowler, a Montauk Indian from the Atlantic coast, who began his duties as teacher in the autumn of 1766. He set up home with his new wife, Hannah Garret, a Pequot who had lived among the neighboring Narragansett and who had also been educated by Wheelock. A fifteen-year-old named Joseph Johnson, a Mohegan also from the east coast, arrived in Kanowalohale in 1766 to assist David Fowler at the school. These missionaries, while living as students with Wheelock, would have been affected by his prejudices that white standards of "virtue, decency and humanity" could be attained only through a Christian education.[5]

When Wheelock promoted the relocation of his school to the Iroquois leadership, his condescending tone in addressing the Oneida would not have gone unnoticed: "I hope you will be kind to [David Fowler] as one of your own people, and help him to live among you . . . and instruct you in managing husbandry. . . . God suffers a few lazy savage people to live a hungry miserable life by hunting. . . . You will live much easier and better than you now do or can do by hunting." Fowler wrote to Wheelock that conditions among the Oneida were in stark contrast to the life from which he had come in New England: "I am obliged to eat with Dogs . . . , yea, I have often seen Dogs eating their Victuals when they set their dishes down, they'll only make a little Noise to show their Displeasure to Dogs and take up the Dish, finish of what was left. My cooks are nasty as Hogs; These men are the laziest Crew I ever saw in all my Days . . . lazy and sordid Wretches, but they are to be pitied not frowned [upon]."[6] The attitude of superiority exemplified by Wheelock's graduates would generate hostility toward Christians in general, create difficulties for Christian Oneida leaders in Kanowalohale, and promote tensions between residents who accepted either Church of England or Congregationalist beliefs and practices.

Despite the unease developing among the Oneida because of the Johnson-Wheelock antagonism, Conoquhieson and King represented the Oneida at a conference called at Johnson Hall in April 1765. Johnson had previously received the approval of the Board of Trade in London to create a precise boundary line to delineate land reserved for the Iroquois and the Delaware of both the Susquehanna and Ohio regions. He was now ready to present this proposal to the Oneida. On this occasion the distinction between roles performed traditionally by sachem and warrior appear to be reversed. The warrior leader King conducted the condolence (a ceremony at formal gatherings honoring recently deceased members of participating nations) though this was usually performed by a sachem of the host nation. Johnson then wasted no time in chastising the Delaware and Chenussio Seneca for their lengthy collusion against the British in the recent wars and urged them to agree to a peaceful settlement with the victors.[7] The switch in ceremonial responsibility on the part of sachem and warrior escaped comment on the part of the individual recording the proceedings, and Johnson continued with the business at hand; however, it is evident that a subtle change was taking place in the Oneida's perception of authority and leadership.

When the plan was aired publicly at this conference, the Onondaga (applying the political clout granted them at the conference earlier that month) voiced concern as to the location of this boundary. Blaming the dishonesty of the British in cheating the Iroquois out of their lands, an Onondaga speaker warned that, if their nation was not treated more fairly in the future, the sachems would be unable to curb the anger of the younger warriors. The boundary line as suggested by the Onondaga did not meet with Johnson's approval; he considered their suggestion "ridiculous" as it omitted a section that had long been purchased and settled by the British. Thomas King, again identifying himself as a warrior, spoke in support of the sachems. He offered a compromise and encouraged the Onondaga to adjust their proposal: "Let us follow the example of our Ancestors. . . . They were Wisemen and took care of everything that concerned peace. Let us do the same, and let us make a Line for the benefit of our Children." Conoquhieson (assuming King's earlier aggressive approach) now took the offensive. Concerned more with establishing his nation's status than with conciliation, he admonished the British for their failure to recognize Oneida control over their territory: "You know that we are the Owners of the Land Westward of the German Flats. We hope we are not to be cheated out of it. . . . We think we are strangely dealt with. Our Fathers were asked to sell Farms, and whenever we agreed to it, the White People took Woods and all."[8]

Pleading ignorance and promising to investigate this particular situation, William Johnson was anxious to meet with the Delaware, having in mind his proposals for the articles of peace and for the proposed boundary line. He decided that a grant of land in Delaware territory would restore the losses sustained by traders (who had long complained of hardships encountered during the fighting in Iroquoia and the Ohio) and that "the Delawares [would] engage to abide by whatever Limits shall be agreed upon between the English and the Six Nations." The Delaware would hand over English prisoners in their possession and any members of their nation guilty of crimes against the British would face trial in colonial courts. Allowing no further discussion that might jeopardize his plans, especially with Conoquhieson and King so vociferous in opposition to his proposals, Johnson signed the document on behalf of the Iroquois himself! He then directed the Delaware to add their marks, thereby welcoming them into the Covenant Chain of Friendship and indicating British forgiveness of past sins and expectation of future obedience. Johnson saw to it that the conference was concluded.[9]

The Oneida unwittingly became involved as the tug-of-war between Johnson and Wheelock developed. Wheelock was determined to place his new school within Oneida territory. Johnson, however, returned to a former plan of increasing the Church of England presence in Iroquois villages as a means of countering Wheelock's Congregationalist influence. Pleased at being accepted as a member of the Church of England's Society for the Propagation of the Gospel (SPG) in the autumn of 1766, Johnson contacted the society's leadership in England and New York, enthusiastic to establish a Church of England school on Iroquois land, possibly among the Oneida, as neighboring Iroquois would be willing to attend at that location and thereby avoid "becoming a Gloomy race under the care of the Dissenting Ministers." Such was his conviction as to the necessity of this plan that, should funds for this school be a problem, he would himself provide a clergyman's salary and grounds to accompany the church he had already built, at his own expense, in Johnstown. Certain that his plans would come to fruition, Johnson officially withdrew his financial and moral support of Wheelock in the autumn of 1767.[10]

Meanwhile Thomas King's independent actions as a warrior when conducting land negotiations for his people at Oquaga (a function traditionally performed by a sachem) exacerbated the already troubled relationship between Johnson and the Oneida. In the spring of 1767, two chiefs from Oquaga visited Johnson Hall with the complaint that a land speculator named John Harper had visited their community hoping that they would sell him ten square miles of land between the Susquehanna and Delaware rivers. Johnson advised the chiefs to follow proper procedure by dealing with Harper in the presence of the governor and inviting him to a general meeting of the people of Oquaga. Five days later two other Oquaga chiefs came with the information that Harper had indeed made application to the village council to purchase the land. Johnson now advised them to defer any decision until he could organize a general meeting with the Oneida at Johnson Hall. The following day, Thomas King arrived and informed Johnson that the Oquaga community had already decided, under his leadership, to sell an even larger tract of good quality land. Five months later Thomas King with five others from Oquaga reappeared at Johnson Hall, this time accompanied by John Harper himself, carrying "a licence from the Governor, and Council of New York to purchase a large Tract of land between the Delaware and Susquahana Rivers." King told Johnson that the Oquaga were resolved to sell the land; all that remained was to arrive at a suitable price. Johnson, uncomfortable with this development, questioned the advisability of selling any land without consulting the Oneida nation as a whole, but King assured Johnson that all the Oneida chiefs had approved of the sale. Thankful to be finished with this transaction obviously manipulated by King, Johnson quickly recorded the land sold by the Delaware as requested, but "as to the Price, he left it to their Chiefs to settle with the white People."[11]

In preparation for the major conference to recognize the proposed boundary line officially, Johnson summoned a meeting at his home in March 1768. The Oneida persevered in their efforts to have Johnson hear their land grievances by sending chief Conoquhieson, accompanied by a new spokesman based at Kanowalohale, the head warrior Tagawaron, along with the warrior leader Thomas King from Oquaga. Members of the Cherokee nation, the Six Nations, and the Caughnawauga from Canada also attended; they had previously met together to preserve peace with the Cherokee and to discuss the establishment of the boundary line. Conoquhieson took center stage, having been chosen by the Confederacy chiefs to represent them in offering the condolence ceremony. Before doing so, however, he broke with protocol and took the opportunity to air Oneida grievances with regard to their land: "when our young Men wanted to go a hunting the Wild Beasts in our Country they found it covered with fences, so that they were weary crossing them, neither can they get Venison to Eat, or Bark to make huts for the Beasts are run away and the Trees cut down." When he eventually offered the condolence, he did not perform the ceremonial removal of an axe from the head of the British as was customary. Johnson raised this issue privately with the Confederacy chiefs later that evening, and the following day they apologized to Johnson and performed the ceremony themselves.[12] Conoquhieson was not pleased with this development. It is not known whether Conoquhieson's outbursts were requested or sanctioned by the members of the Oneida nation; or based on his personal agenda, and therefore possibly an embarrassment to their fellow elders; or simply portrayed as such by Johnson, who wished to exonerate himself in having to deal with unruly sachems.

After Johnson welcomed the Cherokee and voiced approval of their desire for peace, their chief presented wampum belts to individual Iroquois nations including the Caughnawauga, to Johnson, and to the Iroquois women and children. Noticeably missing was a belt for the Oneida. When the Iroquois chiefs later gathered in the council room to speak with the Cherokee, they were interrupted by Thomas King who spoke on behalf of the Oneida warriors, requesting that the meeting be held outside to prevent possible secret conversations with the Cherokee. Once assembled Conoquhieson became the main speaker. He congratulated the Cherokee on their desire for peace with the Iroquois, on their trust in Johnson, and on their willingness to attend the Six Nations councils. However, when it came to assurances of safe travel in Oneida and Cherokee lands, Conoquhieson referred to the lack of a wampum belt for his nation: "We are your Elder Brothers and consequently have more understanding than you, We must tell you that you have not done your part thereon as you ought. . . . You have not taken the Axe out of our heads." Although Conoquhieson could conduct the removal of the axe, as he stated, he nevertheless refused the Cherokee request that some Oneida accompany them to "Assist in clearing the road" as he considered it to be unsafe.[13] Yet again the Oneida found themselves in an uncomfortable position.

Johnson brought the focus of the conference back to the matter of Indian lands and the need for agreement on a boundary line. He presented a letter sent by the Board of Trade, which stressed the importance of this decision. An unnamed Iroquois spokesman interrupted, blaming the British for problems in Iroquoia: alcohol abuse, loss of land, violence, racial prejudice, unfair trade practices, high prices of commodities, unnecessary fencing of land, and blockage of trade routes. After accepting responsibility for the deaths of the Iroquois and outlining steps taken by the government in Philadelphia to address the problems and provide compensation, Johnson promised to use the example of the boundary set with the Cherokee as a model for deliberations with the northern Indians.[14]

As the conference concluded, troubling divisions within the Oneida delegation became apparent when Thomas King requested that all present pay attention to their warriors as represented by Tagawaron. Tagawaron then focused on the mistakes made by their sachems when negotiating with the Cherokee. Alluding to ceremonial omissions that indicated unfinished business, he claimed they had left a protruding axe handle that might cause further hostilities and they had not buried all the bones of both nations that lay scattered on the road between their countries. He announced that the Oneida warriors had now corrected both these errors. In addition, the sachems reminded those present that they had not agreed to any Oneida traveling home with the Cherokee for fear of unsafe passage. Tagawaron offered to provide safe travel as suggested by his warriors since the sachems were unable to do so. Johnson—seeing that this difference of opinion between sachems and warriors was counterproductive—tried to restore what he perceived to be the central theme of the conference, thanking the participants for their "unanimity" and "desire for peace" and reminding them that they would be meeting again shortly "to ratify [their] agreement concerning the Boundary Line which his Majesty in his Wisdom [had] agreed to for [their] future Security."[15] The tension between Oneida warriors and sachems was not helping their image at these conferences.

The culmination of Johnson's efforts to resolve the conflict between the Iroquois and the British regarding land depended on the success of the conference being called in September 1768. That autumn the Oneida watched as the impressive gathering representing a divergent array of concerns converged in their territory at the grounds surrounding the derelict Fort Stanwix. A final decision on the boundary line was pending. By 19 September, colonial representatives of Pennsylvania, Virginia, and New Jersey (together with twenty boats laden with presents for the Indians) had congregated at the designated site. Johnson was perplexed; he sent word to Conoquhieson questioning the sachem's tardy arrival with people from Kanowalohale. A return message indicated that the chiefs there were expecting a number of the Cayuga and Seneca nations to arrive for the condolence of a Seneca chief to be conducted by the Oneida leaders. They requested that the conference be held instead at Kanowalohale. Johnson immediately tried to convince the leaders of Kanowalohale of the propriety of holding the condolence at Fort Stanwix: the location was in Oneida territory, all the Iroquois nations were gathering there, their cooperation would facilitate a speedier opening of the conference and reduce the great expense of feeding those who were waiting. The Kanowalohale sachems complied with Johnson's request, and on 24 October thirty-six hundred Iroquois had assembled to begin deliberations in the company of a handful of non-native participants.[16]

Johnson was at a disadvantage, being conscious of his recent loss of stature in the eyes of the British government. By February 1768 his friendship with General Thomas Gage had also diminished. Gage disagreed with Johnson over how to deal with the Indian lands involved in situating the boundary. The general thought that the colonial authorities should negotiate a boundary with the Indians and then pay for land when prospective buyers purchased it. Johnson asserted that the British crown should be willing to reimburse the Indians for their land before the boundary was declared. Johnson had written to the Board of Trade about this problem, urging their support for the authority of the superintendent as the royal representative—only to be informed in return that the Board of Trade had decided the colonial authorities, rather than the superintendent, should have increased control over trade with the Indians and the settlement of the boundary line. In addition to this disadvantage, Johnson was contending with a group of land speculators who had come to this conference determined to acquire land that would provide recompense for losses sustained during previous hostilities with the Iroquois.[17] Whether the Oneida knew of Johnson's predicament is a matter of conjecture, but the role their leaders pursued during conference proceedings suggests they were privy to the situation.

It is also probable that the Oneida were aware of the tactics employed by Wheelock to further his personal agenda among the Iroquois. He was not about to miss such a grand opportunity to further his plans for his school and his objective of increasing a Congregationalist presence in Iroquoia. In early October Wheelock had composed a memorial to Johnson earmarking the Oneida as the nation where "encouraging Prospects" had already developed as a result of their education. Knowing the conference would be attended by all the Iroquois nations as well as by colonial dignitaries, Wheelock sent two representatives to present his case to Johnson and the governors "to solicit [their] favour and assistance" in support of the plan to base missionaries and schoolmasters in Oneida territory. The two delegates —Jacob Johnson and David Avery—had recently begun their ministry with the Oneida at Kanowalohale. In a petition conveyed by these two missionaries, Wheelock requested that the superintendent's previous approbation of the "laudable design of propagating the glorious Gospel among the Indians" be continued, that "the Lands and Inheritances of the Natives not . . . be cut off," but that they be allowed to keep them for their "Temporal . . . and Sacred benefit." Avery met with the Oneida and expressed his suspicion that they were in danger of losing much of their territory, since Johnson's plan of taking the boundary line from Lake Oneida down the western part of Pennsylvania would give the British colonies all the land to the east of the Onondaga territory. In a speech to the Iroquois, Jacob Johnson expressed his fear that the funds set aside for Indian education would be lost or that the Oneida would lose the land on which a new school was being planned; it would mean that the missionaries would "have to ramble all over the world after them" to dispense the benefits of the Gospel and education.[18] These concerns would fuel Oneida determination to achieve their own aims.

At the conference on 24 October, Conoquhieson's opening address as sachem of the host nation was not propitious. He had listened the previous day as William Johnson reminded the delegates that the gathering was initiated by order of the king in June 1768, stated his impatience at having to wait so long for all to arrive, and declared his desire to proceed immediately with the condolences and opening ceremonies. Johnson expected the sachems, counselors, and warriors to consult and cooperate because of their mutual wisdom and good advice. After expressing the same desire for unanimity, Conoquhieson performed the condolence himself, preventing Johnson from assuming that role. He memorialized those who had died among the British and then bestowed an Indian name on William Franklin, the governor of New Jersey, who alone among the governors present had not yet received that honor. Conoquhieson discovered that the Six Nations' delegates were displeased with his arbitrary choice of an Indian name for Governor Franklin without their input and approval. This discontent was exacerbated because Conoquhieson gave his own name, that of a founding chief of the Iroquois League, to the governor; bestowing a ceremonial name required the agreement of the Confederacy chiefs. After publicly acknowledging his error, Conoquhieson assured those present that the Confederacy chiefs had met to discuss this matter and had approved a different name, one that reflected their appreciation of the governor's bringing to justice some murderers of their people.[19]

Reminding the Iroquois that King George III in 1765 had suggested a boundary line should be agreed on in order to prevent colonial incursion onto their lands, Johnson reiterated that the monarch's initiative was in response to Iroquois' complaints about white encroachment. He admitted that many settlers were ignorant of Indian rights and had advanced too far into Indian territory, and that many Indians had been deceived when they agreed to sell land. After two days of consultation, the Oneida speakers as well as others in the Confederacy focused on two concerns: experience had taught them that the white people soon forgot agreements they made when an opportunity to acquire more land arose; and there was not much point to agreeing on a line in the vicinity of Virginia and Pennsylvania to the south if no consideration was given to the northern lands in Iroquois territory itself. Johnson responded by inviting the chiefs of each nation to his tent where they could study his map and consider his suggestions. However, those invited felt that Johnson's proposed boundary line, following the western branch of the Susquehanna and proceeding northward, lay too far to the west and would cut through the heart of Iroquoia, specifically through Oneida territory. Johnson should not expect them to part with land that was "very dear" to them as it contained many of their villages, which were already being threatened by the spread of colonial settlements. They deemed their proposal to be fair, with the line running up the Delaware valley and connecting with Lake George. Johnson countered that this was out of the question: it would protect all but the extreme eastern edge of Mohawk land from white settlement, it would include land that had already been bought from the Iroquois and settled by the colonists, and it would negate his determination to make the southeastern part of Lake Ontario easily accessible to the British. As a result of this impasse, "at night Sir William had a private conference with the Chiefs of the most Influence with whom he made use of every argument to bring matters to an agreeable issue."[20]

To the Oneida, in particular, the issue of land was a "great and weighty matter requiring long deliberation." Johnson found it necessary to convene clandestine meetings at night, for he was impatient at what seemed to him an unreasonable delay. He reported that the Oneida—encouraged by a clergyman sent by Wheelock who "had shewed the Indians the folly of giving up their Lands and cautioned them against it before he left Oneida"—took obstructive measures.[21]

The efforts of the missionaries notwithstanding, on the morning of 30 October, Conoquhieson and Tagawaron, as sachem and warrior, were joined by two other Confederacy chiefs in advocating for the Oneida cause with a compromise proposal that would involve both the Delaware and Susquehanna valleys and still leave most of central and western Iroquoia intact. Johnson was not receptive to this proposal either, explaining that the farther east the boundary was drawn, the less room there would be for colonial expansion and the greater opportunity for friction with the Iroquois. The Oneida continued to offer the greatest opposition to Johnson's plan. Tagawaron, claiming to represent the warriors, informed Johnson that the Oneida were deeply divided on the issue, feeling that they were at a considerable disadvantage since much of their land was involved in the dispute over the northern part of the area under debate. At another nocturnal session, Conoquhieson and Tagawaron brought four additional Oneida chiefs and offered Johnson a further compromise, expressing willingness for the line to run from the Susquehanna north to a location just west of Fort Stanwix and from there in a northeastern direction. Sir William told them that if they would consider extending their proposal further west and include the Carrying Place, they would receive five hundred dollars and a handsome present for each of the chiefs. But Johnson's enticement of money and materials did not work. The Oneida returned with the news that "their people positively refused to agree to any other Line than they had proposed the last night." Although recognizing the benefit of agriculture for revenue and nutrition, they adhered to their need for all their land, as game was becoming scarce. They also saw added advantage in controlling the portage and the transportation of trade goods, thereby earning "somewhat for the support of their families." Johnson retorted that this was an unusual consideration, as the Oneida had "totally neglected carrying goods for so many years." He suggested they would reap greater benefits if they opened up a road to all travelers and traders, including the British, rather than restricting access and encouraging friction.[22]

After further consultation, the Oneida chiefs returned with their final proposal. They would agree to the line being extended to Canada Creek, thereby surrendering the area around the Carrying Place, but with certain provisions: they would have equal use of the Carrying Place with the English; they would be paid six hundred dollars in addition to the customary fees; the boundary line would be "forever binding and conclusive" on both sides, once agreed to by British authorities; no British jurisdiction would ever broach the line; and any future transactions would be conducted directly with the British monarch or his chosen representatives. Later, Conoquhieson indicated that a chief and warrior from each of the Iroquois nations would visit Johnson's quarters and give their consent to this arrangement, with the news being made public to all at the conference the following day. At this time he requested additional conditions: the earlier promise of cheap and plentiful trade goods would be fulfilled; the "inviolable nature" of the boundary line would be maintained; the right of Iroquois warriors to hunt on the ceded lands as necessary for their subsistence would be granted, but with a refusal to allow white people to hunt in their protected lands so as to prevent future contention; and the Mohawk nation, whose land was almost totally ceded to the British, would retain title to any lands within the grant so that they would benefit from its sale. The final treaty, signed on 5 November 1768, bears the mark of one delegate from each of the Six Nations, the Oneida being represented by Conoquhieson.[23]

The conference upon which so many hopes were focused had finally concluded. Why did Johnson fail to credit Conoquhieson and Tagawaron, and the Oneida nation for whom they spoke, with influencing the final delineation of the boundary line? The boundary line prevented the loss of considerably more Indian land than had originally been proposed by the Board of Trade. It improved his standing among the Iroquois with whom he lived. His desire to lash out at Wheelock by means of his ambassadors to the Oneida may have colored his perceptions; their constant references to the wishes of Wheelock indicated their allegiance to him rather than to the Oneida whom they claimed to represent. Similarly the previous inability of the Oneida to negotiate with the Chenussio Seneca, as he had requested, may have lessened his opinion of them. The Oneida had reason to feel some sense of accomplishment following their involvement in the conference, although their relinquishing control of the Carrying Place would have been hard to accept. The loss of the portage did not diminish the importance of Kanowalohale, located as it was on the major land route running parallel to the Mohawk River westward from Mohawk country. However, the Oneida would certainly feel the loss of prestige among the Iroquois and the decline of economic benefits in their community once the portage was in British hands. Nevertheless, the records of the Fort Stanwix conference clearly demonstrate that the two Oneida spokesmen played a central role in the negotiations and were determined to protect the welfare of their nation.[24]

Despite their perceived success at the Stanwix conference, in the years immediately following the signing of the Fort Stanwix treaty the Oneida leaders struggled to advance the interests of their people during the continuing negotiations among the Six Nations, William Johnson, and neighboring Indians. At a conference at German Flats in July 1770, the Oneida delegation formed only 10 percent of the total twenty-three hundred Indians representing twenty Indian nations including the Iroquois, Cherokee, and Canadian Caughnawauga tribes, yet the triumvirate of Conoquhieson, Tagawaron, and Thomas King were very vocal. As host sachem Conoquhieson welcomed Johnson, appreciative that the superintendent had responded to "the particular request" of the Six Nations sachems that he summon the conference so that the Iroquois and the Canadian Indians could hopefully concur with the desire of the Cherokee for support against their enemies. However, divisions within the Oneida again surfaced. When the opening condolences were completed, King chastised Johnson concerning the warriors' frustration that the Oneida sachems had not alerted their warriors about this meeting, which was of utmost importance to all warriors, including "the Cherokee chiefs whose business they [knew was] to us the Warriors." Although Tagawaron usually represented the warriors, on this occasion he acted as a sachem, attempted to effect reconciliation, and "stood up on the part of Sir William Johnson," repeating the words of Conoquhieson in welcoming the Canadian sachems to the conference. With the aim of preventing friction with the Cherokee warriors, Tagawaron also gave them "a very kind and friendly welcome." Then addressing the entire gathering, he hoped that all were ready to discuss the business at hand since the usual forms of greeting should now have been conducted to everyone's "mutual satisfaction."[25]

Johnson, for his part, promised to supply the warriors with all they required providing they behaved "with order and decorum." However, conscious of the harm that might have been triggered by King's outburst, that evening Johnson summoned a sachem and head warrior from each of the nations and conferred with them well into the night. His anxieties were fueled by the warriors' determination to fight the southern Indians and by the sachems' equally strong desire to avoid hostilities. Although the sachems opted for asking the Cherokee delegates to return home and remain at peace, they doubted whether the warriors would support this decision. Tensions were heightened as the traders had disobeyed Johnson's instructions and made alcohol readily available to the Indians. As a result, the settlers in the German Flats area came to fear for their lives and property, because of "the temper shown by many of the warriors." As the congress drew to a close, Conoquhieson informed Johnson that the Oneida had chosen four chiefs to relay news of the decisions to other Indian nations, the head chief being Thomas King, a warrior known for his outspoken views but on this occasion described by Conoquhieson as being one who would "faithfully execute whatever [was] desired of him."[26] The conference had not gone well for the Oneida. Their leaders had not only betrayed their confederates at Fort Stanwix, especially the Mohawk, by surrendering much Mohawk territory while maintaining land for themselves, but they again could not cooperate among themselves when dealing with the Cherokee.

Nevertheless, the political arena provided Tagawaron with opportunity to refine his leadership skills as an Oneida warrior and prepared him for the challenge he would encounter in the person of the Reverend Samuel Kirkland, a Presbyterian missionary trained by Eleazar Wheelock who had moved to Kanowalohale in the summer of 1766. At first Kirkland was reportedly well received by the Oneida, wearing their style of clothing, eating their food, learning their language, and helping settle community disputes. A year later, however, Kirkland's account of an incident in which he was attacked by the angry husband of an intoxicated spouse indicates his impression of Kanowalohale as an unruly community, where the likelihood of persons carrying concealed weapons and the easy availability of alcohol both from white traders and from other Iroquois visitors contributed to a general breakdown of authority within village society. Although Kirkland's Calvinistic theology, gained from his years as Wheelock's student, would have colored his impression of moral standards at Kanowalohale, social conditions in the community were adversely affected by the economic decline resulting from the profit-sharing arrangement for the Carrying Place portage, compounded by the expenses incurred in the village because of its situation on the main east–west route through Iroquoia. Protocol dictated that community residents provide refreshment and supplies as hosts to those in transit. Kirkland lamented the social ramifications involved in the village's location on a public footpath along which five hundred to a thousand Indians would travel and stop for rest and refreshment on their way to a meeting. It was, he wrote in a letter to SSPCK dated 16 September 1771, as if "most of the Five Nations have their eyes fixed upon this place." This resulted in financial hardship for the Oneida inhabitants, especially since the "encroachments of the white people" had disrupted their fishing and hunting.[27]

The Oneida's initial acceptance of Kirkland was probably because at first he lived much as they did, building a "little cottage where to lay [his] head," wearing Indian-style clothing, and sharing in their fare of roasted squash and corn. Writing in 1768, perhaps to the SSPCK, he admitted his first enthusiasm for identifying with his people might have been misguided. His living near starvation had damaged his health, brought shame to the Christian cause, and dishonor to his own ministry. He subsequently informed his flock that his days of manual labor were over, that his primary responsibility was to save their souls, and that in future they would have to look after his needs. He relished reporting that the Oneida begged his forgiveness and complied with his requests, the result being, at least in his estimation, that his "Influence and Character soon rose higher than ever it was brought low—Whatever [he] said was like a Law to them." Yet the Oneida could not have failed to notice and reflect on their preacher's accumulation of material benefits. In 1768 he claimed his household items were limited to little more than a brass kettle, a few "lousy blankets," a horse, and a dilapidated saddle. By 1772, on the other hand, his house and farm had all the accoutrements of a prosperous colonial homestead.[28] Oneida leaders possessing social or political status might well have observed Kirkland's home and surroundings with increasing envy, especially if they found their own authority undermined as their adherents at Kanowalohale transferred their allegiance to the missionary.

In the early 1770s the Oneida at Kanowalohale became involved in another fractious relationship, this time between Kirkland and William Johnson, that was in many ways a continuation of the denominational dispute between Johnson and Wheelock. Johnson was jealous of Kirkland's popularity among the Indians. He felt bitter about the limited financial support he received from the Church of England's society, the SPG, in comparison with the largesse granted the Presbyterian dissenter by the Scottish society, the SSPCK. Both aspects, Kirkland's popularity and Johnson's own limited finances, had a direct impact on the Oneida. In August 1770 Tagawaron made a private visit to Johnson. Confident in his good relationship with Johnson following the German Flats conference that summer, Tagawaron had made efforts to comply with the superintendent's repeated request that the Indians live in closer proximity to each other, by encouraging some Oneida residing around the village of Kanowalohale to relocate within its confines. Conoquhieson, the leading sachem and an erstwhile supporter of Johnson, refused to cooperate with Tagawaron in this, declaring "that he would have nothing more to do with Sir William or the English." Faced with this tension within the village, none of the surrounding Oneida wished to join the English. As a result, Tagawaron informed Johnson that his supporters in Kanowalohale not only would henceforth follow the superintendent's advice but wished him to appoint "the best and Wisest Men" as sachems, thereby effectively overriding the influence of Conoquhieson. Tagawaron also confided to Johnson that "the Minister slackened greatly in the care of the Indians under his Charge," but he had said nothing to Kirkland about his concern as he was not sure of Johnson's reaction.[29]

A second incident that year involved the Oneida's desire for a blacksmith, an issue that had been simmering for six years. In answer to their frequent petitions, Johnson replied that such requests should go to the governor, expecting that the Oneida would contact that office through him. With increased farming resulting from the newly acquired SSPCK support, the added urgency for a blacksmith prompted Tagawaron, encouraged by Kirkland, to arrange for eight Oneida chiefs in December 1770 to apply directly to the governor, bypassing Johnson. Their request was based on their great distance from Johnson's forge, which made it difficult for them to obtain repairs to their hoes, axes, and guns: "we wont mention how many weary and hungry days we are sure to meet with in our journey, and sometimes by a poor old man or an old woman bent in age who can scarcely walk." The governor was advised by an angry Johnson to ignore this request; no blacksmith arrived, and both the Oneida and Kirkland remained dependent upon the facilities at Johnson Hall.[30] It is not known whether Tagawaron was ever apprised of the fact that Johnson sabotaged the mission.

At the same time, the Oneida and their spokesmen were drawn into the clash between Johnson and Kirkland over the construction of a church. Deacon Thomas of Oquaga, well aware of the desire of some in Kanowalohale and Oquaga to have a new place of worship, traveled to Boston with

Kirkland in the fall of 1770 and procured the SSPCK commissioners' promise of financial support for construction. When Johnson's supporters at Kanowalohale informed him of this, Johnson demanded that the sachems accept his suggestion of immediately obtaining an English church through his advocacy with the SPG. Consequently in February 1771 the sachems met in council and informed the village of their decision to comply with Johnson's suggestion. The warriors, however, informed the sachems of their support for Kirkland, a development that surprised but greatly encouraged the missionary. This was not good for the Oneida. Kirkland observed that "the Warriours for the most part are uncontrouled by the Sachems or Lords," while the sachems "were afraid a seperation would ensue between them and the warriors, and were ready to comply with their Terms, be what they would."[31]

Tagawaron's personal support for Kirkland declined, however. Despite his earlier support of the missionary's plan to build a Presbyterian church, in the spring of 1772, as head warrior at Kanowalohale he verbally attacked Kirkland. Claiming to speak on behalf of both the sachems and the warriors of Kanowalohale, Tagawaron stated that Kirkland refused to baptize their children unless the parents possessed strict moral standards and successfully passed a lengthy examination. Tagawaron claimed that Kirkland's stance had brought confusion to the community, since previous Church of England missionaries were satisfied with nominal evidence of Christian conversion on the part of the parents. In his response Kirkland made no effort to acknowledge their perplexity but urged them to believe in his scriptural requirements, calling their notion of baptism "unworthy of any reply, being too ridiculous to mention" and refusing to baptize children of "drunkards, whoremongers, liars, thieves, profane, ignorant and foolish."[32]

Overriding the turmoil in Kanowalohale and the leadership claims of Conoquhieson and Tagawaron, Kirkland proudly announced in the summer of 1773 that the chapel started in the spring was completed. Men and women from neighboring towns gathered to witness the raising of the walls, sachems of Kanowalohale encouraged faithful women to pray that the men be given strength, the total structure was "raised without the help of white people," and "the whole affair was conducted with great decency and indeed solemnity." Not only did Kirkland portray an idyllic scene of communal harmony, with sachems and matrons offering encouragement to the warriors as they labored, he enthused that the entire enterprise brought to the town a renewed sense of distinction that had long been the objective of the Oneida nation. All was not quite as harmonious in the village as Kirkland indicated, however. Neither was he, in fact, the cause of the idyllic scene he portrayed. When, a few months previously, some young warriors broke down his door at night, with unwitting foresight he attributed their negative action to the fact that their "former pagan state had been revived."[33] He was unwilling to acknowledge the possibility that Oneida of lesser fortune might eye his possessions with envy, or that his popularity in the community had decreased to the point that his life was in danger, or that Conoquhieson or Tagawaron might have instigated hostility.

William Johnson wanted to have the last word where this church was concerned. But actually it was the Oneida who had the last word. When Kirkland's congregation argued for a steeple, they were not content unless they placed a bell in the structure, but the only bell available in the vicinity was one owned by Johnson. Some residents of Kanowalohale had arranged with Johnson for this bell to be shipped to their community, but Johnson, not about to miss the opportunity, had his name and the date inscribed on the bell before it was delivered to Kirkland's church. The final decision was with the Oneida people; it was they who held a meeting, made their own plans, and hung the bell themselves.[34]

Tagawaron's political career during this period is of particular interest. He was not a newcomer to the political scene; he had frequently attended conferences at Fort Johnson with Conoquhieson and Gawehe starting in 1757, and by March 1768 he was voicing solid support for Johnson on behalf of the Kanowalohale warriors. His leadership at Fort Stanwix and for half a decade following was cut short by his death in 1772. His story has been used to suggest that Kirkland's ministry brought legitimacy to the warrior faction (of which Tagawaron was an outspoken leader), which previously had lacked the political, social, and spiritual justification for their opposition to the head sachems' traditional authority. William Johnson as promoter of the Church of England has been portrayed as supportive of those who opposed Kirkland's Presbyterian persuasion and as a bulwark for the sachems who grew increasingly wary of the Oneida warriors' power. The alignment was not so simple.[35]

It is significant that when the church was being built in Kanowalohale, members of the conservative establishment—the sachems and leading women —cooperated with the warriors during its construction, and the warriors in Kirkland's congregation were the ones concerned that a steeple be added, so that their structure looked as impressive as the buildings belonging to the Church of England. Yet Tagawaron spoke out against his minister when the community reacted against Kirkland's restrictive policy regarding baptism. Tagawaron's embarrassment at the failure of the blacksmith mission might have contributed to his disenchantment with Kirkland. Both Johnson and Kirkland were offering a church, and Johnson's lengthy connection and influence with the Oneida could easily have swayed community sentiment in favor of a Church of England structure, a fact that Tagawaron could not ignore. Considering the numerous and often conflicting variables operating within Kanowalohale, Tagawaron's pragmatic style was consistent—whether he was acting as an Oneida spokesman at a conference or as a warrior leader at home—and was indicative of a new approach to leadership.

Tagawaron's personal disenchantment with Kirkland may also have allowed him to serve as a conduit for discontent on the part of others reacting against the missionary's endeavors. An unidentified source, reporting to Wheelock from the 1768 Fort Stanwix conference, praised the loyalty of those Oneida who had accepted Kirkland's ministry soon after his arrival, but it neglected to mention the reason for their separation from their colleagues, other than their Christian conversion: "the Oneidas to whom the Gospel has been Successfully preached encamped by themselves and looked behaved and talked like Christians . . . . Their air, and Temper was modest, kind, humble and insomuch that Strangers took notice of it." In 1771 Kirkland contributed a further ingredient that augmented the division within the Oneida: he reported that those who had subscribed to his encouragement of husbandry were taunted and ridiculed as being warriors whose spirits had become as those of "silly women and children."[36] For the warriors who faced derision, however, the implications would be dramatic. Working in the field, growing crops, and tending animals were traditionally within the domain of the women; hunting for food and pelts was the realm of the men. Reversing the gender roles would provide a source of ridicule for any adapting themselves to a new way of life. Farming occupied much less land than hunting, so those favoring land sales also favored the switch to farming. Warriors idle from lack of warfare or frustrated by loss of hunting grounds might be totally adverse to remaking their self-image by accepting Kirkland's transition to agriculture and the form of Christianity he represented. Tagawaron's position as a warrior leader would be compromised if he continued to support Kirkland, when many of those for whom he spoke had legitimate reasons for rejecting Kirkland's mission. Leadership among the Oneida was becoming a position fraught with complications.

By the early 1770s Conoquhieson and King had changed the focus of their leadership. Deflated by the resurgence of Onondaga supremacy as of April 1765, both men seemed confused as to the most appropriate position to take at the conference at Johnson Hall later that month. Their suggestions for solving the problem of Delaware allegiance were overridden by the Onondaga and Johnson, making Oneida mediation unnecessary. Their meetings with the Iroquois and Johnson concerning peace negotiations with the Cherokee were plagued by internal friction between Conoquhieson, Tagawaron, and King. Tagawaron's role at the Fort Stanwix conference provided additional impetus for the Oneida leaders to present a united front, in order to maintain both the traditional and economic benefits of the Carrying Place portage, but their confederates who lost more land than anticipated felt betrayed by the Oneida. What the Oneida gained for themselves in the eventual treaty terms, they lost in their relationship with the other Iroquois. For a time, the Oneida leaders seemed more introspective, turning their attention to the religious and social issues accentuated by Kirkland's ministry. But there was no sense that a change of leadership was necessary. For all their divisions on specific issues, Conoquhieson as hereditary sachem, accompanied by Tagawaron and Thomas King as warrior leaders, maintained their places within their Oneida communities through increasingly troubled times.

# CHAPTER FOUR

# THE ONEIDA AS NEUTRALS, 1770–1776

The Oneida were not directly involved on 19 April 1775, when the opening volley was fired between British and rebel forces at Lexington, Massachusetts. Their main concern in the early 1770s was to provide leadership in maintaining Iroquois neutrality in the growing conflict. By 1776, however, they had gradually, reluctantly, become involved as the majority of their nation supported the Patriots. Other nations chose to place their fortune in the British camp, along with most of the Iroquois Confederacy. The Oneida majority decision to separate from their confederates has frequently been attributed to the influence of their missionary, Samuel Kirkland. Other factors operating simultaneously need to be considered as well, however. These include continuing friction with the British regarding landownership and the scarcity of trade goods; the supportive interaction of colonial and Indian residents of the Mohawk valley, as revolutionary hostilities threatened their homes and livelihood; strained relations within the Six Nations resulting from how the Oneida perceived their role, both within the Confederacy and with neighboring nations such as the Caughnawauga and the Christianized nations from New England; and strategies developed by Oneida political leaders to maintain a strong position for their nation in relation to a growing Patriot military presence. Not only were long-standing and reputable Oneida leaders reacting as active rather than passive respondents to circumstances surrounding them, they were also drawing additional leaders into the deliberations with fellow confederates and neighboring colonists.

The Oneida nation's shift to abandon their affiliation with the Six Nations Confederacy at the beginning of the revolution has been seen as a response to Kirkland's strength of character and singularity of vision.

Considerable evidence supports his allegiance to the Patriot cause whose leaders, realizing an armed clash was inevitable, depended on him to rally the Oneida to the colonists' side. Certainly, at the time, there was nothing similar to Kirkland and his ministry among the Six Nations. His fluency in the Oneida language made him indispensable to both the Indians and the colonial authorities. His name appears frequently as interpreter or witness in the records of conferences and treaties from the period of the revolution until his death in 1808.[1]

Concomitant with Kirkland's influence, however, was the Oneida nation's continuing antagonism toward the British. In the first half of the 1770s, colonial encroachment onto Oneida land increased despite governmental assurances to the contrary. The 1768 Fort Stanwix treaty had resulted in Oneida territory being at the cutting edge of European westward expansion, and as the storm clouds of war were gathering, Oneida representatives negotiated repeatedly with the British, and frequently on behalf of their confederates, in continuing efforts to preserve Iroquois land. Despite his advancing years, Conoquhieson, sometimes of Old Oneida but better known as a resident of Kanowalohale, continued to advocate tirelessly for his people.[2]

In July 1772 William Johnson and New York governor William Tryon met with the Iroquois at Johnson Hall. A Mohawk speaker echoed the familiar Iroquois refrain—that their elders were tired of British delays and had entrusted the "business into the hands of the young Warriors." Johnson expressed his discomfort about dealing with warriors in the time of peace and his preference for negotiating with the sachems. After listening to assurances that both Johnson and Tryon would prevent any further land grievances, Conoquhieson, accompanied by fellow Oneida sachems and warriors, approached the governor. Following the opening salutations, Tryon mentioned that he had heard the Oneida wished to dispose of some of their land. This met with a curt response from Conoquhieson, who clarified that the Oneida would take the initiative if any property was to be made available, and then only on compassionate grounds: "the Great Spirit gave us our lands and we love them so much that we never offered any for sale; but whenever our Brothers the English have appeared in want of Lands, and applied to us, we have always granted their desire." Supported as he was by both warriors and sachems (despite Johnson's stated aversion for dealing with warriors), it is possible that Conoquhieson's magnanimity was instrumental in the Oneida's arranging a potential yet surprising land grant with the Mohawk the following April. Having attended the earlier conference at Johnson Hall, Conoquhieson was aware of the acute nature of their distress, being on the threshold of westward colonial expansion. When the Oneida at Kanowalohale received a Mohawk petition "to give them quarter somewhere in their vicinity," they agreed to grant them space for a settlement within six miles of their town.[3]

Conoquhieson again arrived at Johnson Hall for a major conference called by Sir William Johnson in the summer of 1774, ready to join with fellow Iroquois in complaining relentlessly to their host. The Seneca grumbled about his failure to regulate trade practices in their territory and the disregard of his people for land settlement proceedings as set out in the Fort Stanwix treaty. Cayuga warriors were angry about the availability of rum in their territory as a result of the unethical practices of colonial traders. The Mohawk reiterated how their people continued to lose their land. Johnson, feeling unwell from a lingering illness and fatigued by the barrage of complaints, retired after presenting a round of pipe tobacco and liquor to the chiefs. Two hours later the news of Johnson's sudden death spread rapidly through the Indian gathering. The following morning his nephew and son-in-law, Guy Johnson, assured all at the conference that he would continue his late uncle's work among them. In the afternoon Sir William's body was laid to rest in the family vault in the town he had created. Conoquhieson was chosen by the Iroquois to represent them in leading the condolence ceremony the next morning. With wampum belts he ceremonially cleansed the ground, covered the body and grave of Sir William, and thanked Guy Johnson for ensuring that the fire would be maintained at Johnson Hall. Speaking on behalf of the entire Confederacy, as he had often done before, Conoquhieson requested that King George III of England be informed of Guy Johnson's intentions, because, as he said, "in this alarming time of trouble without [Johnson's] care and attention our affairs will fall into great confusion."[4]

The troublesome time that Conoquhieson anticipated was already evident in Oneida territory, and Kirkland was partly responsible. His familiarity with native traditions enabled him to take advantage of a cultural feature within Kanowalohale, which gained him both supporters and opponents. He had become aware of the Oneida's symbolic "fallen log." He began referring to this representative location as his pulpit, alluding to it when conducting meetings at his home with those traveling through Kanowalohale. The implications of the missionary's intentions would not have been lost on those such as Conoquhieson, whose sensitivity toward cultural tradition would have been affronted—or on the warriors, who would have appreciated the clout given their anti-British sentiments by Kirkland's utilization of an ancient tradition. Kirkland relished the irritation this afforded Johnson. In the spring of 1774 he wrote to an SSPCK commissioner in Boston concerning his appropriation of "the log" as a stopping point for those traveling through Kanowalohale in preference to traveling on to Johnson Hall.[5] For the Oneida, alliance with or opposition to Kirkland was becoming a critical issue when deciding whether to support the British or the colonists.

During the autumn of 1774, the Oneida were drawn into mounting tensions among neighboring Indians within Guy Johnson's jurisdiction. For many years the Shawnee, claiming the Virginia hill country as their ancestral homeland, had shared the Ohio valley with the western Iroquois and had been allies with the French against the British settlers encroaching on their land. They were now fighting the militia summoned by Virginia's governor John Murray, earl of Dunmore, in an attempt to reclaim land he had illegally granted to war veterans, land beyond the boundary line established by the 1768 Fort Stanwix treaty. The Shawnee were fighting despite the Iroquois delegations' requests that they seek a peaceful settlement to their grievances.

Guy Johnson reported that, in September 1774, a group of Shawnee head warriors traveled to Onondaga seeking Seneca warriors' assistance against the British, as some Shawnee young men had died in a skirmish with the Virginians. Johnson claimed credit for a speedy dispatch of reliable messengers throughout the Confederacy, which thwarted Shawnee plans and prevented Iroquois involvement. In his journal Kirkland noted approval of the Oneida's reluctance to be involved in the hostilities. But Shawnee deputies stopped at Oneida on their return from Onondaga. Unable to approach the Confederacy through the agency of an Oneida half-king or overseer resident in the Ohio region (since none had been appointed since the death of Thomas King), the Shawnee urged the Oneida chiefs at Kanowalohale to exert their influence and persuade the Six Nations to assist the Shawnee in their fight. The Oneida, no doubt appreciating the recognition afforded them by the Shawnee, declined the invitation because of their obedience to the Six Nations' decision to "abide by their agreement and Covenant with the English."[6] The fact that the Shawnee approached the Oneida would have increased anxiety among their confederates.

In fact, others in the Confederacy did not feel the importance afforded to the Oneida by the Shawnee. While Guy Johnson was trying to assert his position as new superintendent and to assure the authorities in Britain of Iroquois fidelity, the Six Nations were negotiating their own individual positions within the Confederacy in relation to the British. At a grand council at Onondaga in November 1774, the host nation opened proceedings with a reminder that tradition dictated each nation should speak for itself when declaring its allegiance to the superintendent and to the government he represented. The Onondaga and Seneca speakers resolved to "stand to [their] engagements with the English." So did the Cayuga. The Mohawk sachem, however, spoke for the Oneida and Tuscarora nations as well as for themselves and declared their intention to "hold fast and preserve the peace" as earlier promised to William Johnson.[7] Thus, only the Oneida and their adoptees were given no opportunity to speak for themselves. This was possibly the Elder Brothers' reminder of the Oneida's continuing subordinate position in the Confederacy resulting from the April 1765 conference at Johnson Hall.

By January 1775, while the conflict intensified between the British and the rebel colonies, the Oneida were embroiled in their own domestic problems, arising directly from Kirkland's activities. Two years earlier the residents of Oquaga had witnessed the growing antagonism between Dakayenensese, who had accepted and supported the Church of England's style of Christianity, and Agwrongdongwas, who advocated Kirkland's Congregationalism. Now additional complaints about the missionary's activities at Kanowalohale necessitated Conoquhieson's raising the issue again with Guy Johnson. While still representing those in his village who wished to maintain their loyalty to the king, Conoquhieson's opinions echoed those of the late warrior chief Tagawaron, who opposed the missionary's refusal to baptize their babies: "He goes on in such a manner that our chiefs are desirous to get rid of him; for he has a store in our village and is concerned in trade with his Brother, which is very unbecoming in him, and he minds public affairs more than Religion, for he is always collecting news and telling us strange manners of the white people, whilst he endeavours to represent us as a people of no consequence to them." The Onondaga added their grievances to those of Conoquhieson, expressing concern that a letter they had sent to Johnson had been reputedly stopped by Kirkland who subsequently read it and burned it.[8]

Conoquhieson, however, was not about to abandon his leadership in voicing Kirkland's inappropriate behavior. He not only elaborated on the missionary's religious inadequacies but also recounted Kirkland's efforts to lure those living at Kanowalohale away from their relationship with the English. "These and many other matters are still better known at the Village he lives at, as well, as his carrying stories to and from Boston that gives us great uneasiness, and on these things our Chiefs had several conferences and resolved to come down and lay it before you some time ago." Other Oneida disagreed with Conoquhieson. Gaghsaweda, a Bear clan member and a new voice from among the warriors at Kanowalohale, joined with Deacon Thomas and others in challenging Conoquhieson and in supporting the livelihood of the missionary.[9] Kirkland was not making life easy for those he lived among, and he was becoming a pivotal figure in the tension between Oneida sachems and warriors.

In February 1775 Deacon Thomas, Agwrongdongwas, and Adarockquaghs brought similar grievances from Oquaga to Guy Johnson's attention regarding land and denominational rivalry that had been previously raised with his uncle. Bringing with them a belt incorporating William Johnson's initials, they spoke vehemently of their long-standing loyalty to the British and to the new superintendent. Agwrongdongwas was angry that, despite his people's loyalty to the British, colonists were settling on the lands protected by the Fort Stanwix treaty. Adarockquaghs complained about the actions of their "dissenting minister," whose procedures regarding baptism were similar to those of Kirkland. This minister had sent an accompanying letter, denying he had spoken against the Church of England and indicating that a number of the Oneida and Tuscarora chiefs had requested that he stay at Oquaga.[10]

Guy Johnson, wishing to maintain the loyalty of the Oneida nation, had little recourse other than to confront Kirkland about the charges laid against him earlier by Conoquhieson. Writing to Kirkland the same month as the sachem's visit, and conscious of similar accusations now being made against the minister at Oquaga, Johnson reiterated that the repeated charges of "meddling in matters of a political nature" and the charge of burning a letter from the Onondaga would have "a dangerous tendency with the Indians." In the missionary's eight-page reply, Kirkland laid the responsibility at Conoquhieson's door. He denied charges of political interference and of burning a letter. Kirkland maintained that Conoquhieson had admitted to some Kanowalohale chiefs at a public council meeting that Thayendanega (the Mohawk leader commonly known as Joseph Brant, well-known for his involvement in the French-Indian Wars as a fierce ally of the British and as a friend of William Johnson) had encouraged Conoquhieson to fabricate the stories as it would be pleasing to Johnson. Since a speech that some of the Kanowalohale chiefs (unfortunately not named in the records) had sent to Johnson in support of Kirkland's ministry had apparently not arrived, Kirkland repeated it for the superintendent's edification. "We the Oneida chiefs . . . love our minister—he lives in great peace among us . . . he meddles not in politics. He labours hard in doctrine and teaches us the pure word of God. . . . We don't desire his removal nor are we willing to part with him." A year later, Kirkland admitted that he had addressed political concerns with the Oneida—but only in an attempt to explain the growing dispute between England and the colony as arising from Britain's sending an army to force the colony to raise money to cover the costs of the Seven Years' War.[11] In a small community such as Kanowalohale, however, Conoquhieson and other pro-British Oneida sachems would be aware of their missionary's growing affiliation with the Patriots and of the assumptions made by the pro-British Oneida concerning his possible manipulation of their sentiments.

As the revolution was beginning in the spring of 1775, the Oneida's primary concerns were with conflicting issues within their own communities, Kirkland's influence notwithstanding. Conoquhieson stalwartly provided leadership for those who saw no reason to relinquish their attachment to Johnson or to the British connection he represented. It would have been to this group that another letter was reputedly written in May by Thayendanega and other Mohawk sachems—it was found on a trail after a runner supposedly dropped it. The letter assumed that the Oneida would be eager to assist in protecting Guy Johnson from being taken prisoner by the Bostonians and to encourage the other Iroquois nations to rally in defense of the superintendent. Unfortunately for Johnson, news of a pending attack later in May forced him to flee westward and eventually to seek refuge in Canada. Pausing at Fort Stanwix he sought assistance from the Oneida, but they were either unwilling or unable to share their provisions with him.[12]

Other Oneida caused consternation by maintaining contact with their kinfolk in Canada. They were led by James Dean, a non-native resident of Oquaga who had earned their trust over the years.[13] At the end of June 1775, Dean led the Oneida and a "considerable body of Indians" to Montreal where the Indians were under suspicion of having "accepted the hatchet" from the British governor there.[14]

At the same time, still other Oneida representatives arrived at Albany and requested a conference with the congressional representatives. They were "in a disposition very friendly" to the Patriot cause. These Oneida may well have been accustomed to traveling to Albany for meetings with colonial authorities. They may have heard that the fledgling congress at Philadelphia had decided "that a committee of five be appointed . . . from New York relative to Indian affairs and report what steps [were] necessary to be taken for securing and preserving the friendship of the Indian Nations." It was this latter group who would dictate Oneida's destiny.[15]

Anxious to present themselves to the colonists as a nation of consequence within the Iroquois Confederacy, Oneida representatives frequently took the initiative to develop a rapport with the business leaders of Albany. In May 1775 Thomas Spencer, a youth whose Oneida mother had met his Anglo-American father in the Cherry Valley area and whom the Oquaga of Oneida accepted as one of their speakers, gave a stirring speech on behalf of the residents of Kanowalohale to a gathering of colonists in support of the rebel cause. That summer Oneynyoagat, a Christian convert of the Turtle clan who would be a future leading sachem of the Kanowalohale Oneida, pledged his people's friendship to the settlers represented by the Committee of Correspondence by attending their meetings in Albany.[16]

In June 1775 the committee was informed that the Oneida had declined to accept a bribe offered earlier by Guy Johnson encouraging them to assist the British in the event of hostilities. They had also refused his request "to let him Build a House on their Land and live amongst them," this being a second refusal on the part of the Oneida.[17] Shortly afterward, Tenussa Teaundeanthe, warrior William Thaghthaghgwesere, Kristiaen, and Clenis attended a committee meeting and voiced their pleasure that the council fire had been revived at Albany, "where [their] forefathers first settled their Ancient Friendship" with the colonists. Expressing surprise over Guy Johnson's belligerent attitude, they reiterated their wish to remain neutral—as declared earlier at the meeting at German Flats. To reinforce their importance, they reported that the Onondaga had "thanked them kindly for their Wisdom" displayed at that meeting and "had fixed the Oneida for the place where to apply for intelligence." For their part, the Oneida had refused to succumb to Johnson's threat to block the passage of trade goods through Albany if they did not meet separately with him. They were determined to "keep this Passage open" and to preserve their tradition of attending meetings on behalf of the Confederacy.[18]

Members of the Albany committee resolved "to show their sincerity" toward the Oneida by supporting the continuation of Kirkland's ministry with the Oneida and by attending future council fires at German Flats as a sign of solidarity. The Oneida appreciated this show of support: "We shall take the greatest Care of your Belt which speaks the great Friendship for us the Oneydas. We shall Communicate the same to our Chief Men of the Oneyda Nation." The Albany committee also sent a letter with the Oneidas to be shared at a future Six Nations council at German Flats, expressing pleasure at the leadership shown by the Oneida nation and requesting that the other Iroquois support the Patriots in their struggle against the British. When the meeting actually took place at German Flats, their committee delegates joined with those of Albany in expressing their regret over the actions of Guy Johnson and in complimenting the Oneida and Tuscarora for their willingness to prevent the other Iroquois from being led astray by the British.[19]

In June 1775 the Oneida were aware of the success achieved by Guy Johnson and his Indian agent, Daniel Claus, in securing the support of a large number of Iroquois at a conference at Fort Oswego. Anxious to maintain a noncommittal course between the Patriots and Loyalists who were competing for Iroquois allegiance, the Oneida issued an important document, "the first written declaration of neutrality" in North America.[20] Interpreted and written at Kanowalohale by Aksiaktatye, an Oneida warrior of the Wolf clan whose fluency with English served his people for over two decades, the document declared that "the Chiefs, head men, councillors warriors and young men of the Onoida nation" were "altogether for Peace" and did not want to "meddle with any disputers," whether their English or their New England brothers. "Let all be easy in their minds we are for Peace; ye are brethren that are at varience and this is the reason we desire to be nutrails. We are in sincerity your very dear and true friends Indian of the Onoida nation and we hope that peace may be restored soon between Great Britain and her Colony." Exhibiting their propensity to see themselves as having considerable influence in the Confederacy, they added: "We will exert our utmost Endeavours to keep our Brethren the Six nations and others further Back from disturbing you in the Present difficult times."[21]

The names of those signing this document indicate the cooperation that could exist when necessary between the different factions developing within the Oneida communities. Conoquhieson was the stalwart pro-British Church of England sachem from Old Oneida bearing the title of a founding chief of the Iroquois League. Shononghriyo also carried the title of a founding chief; he would be heavily involved as a traditional leader and as a warrior of the Turtle clan in later land negotiations for his people. Hendrick was from Oriska. Jimmy Tayaheure was a recently appointed Oneida sachem at Kanowalohale. Skenandoah was an adopted Oneida, a Wolf clan warrior, and recent convert to Christianity who befriended Kirkland; he advocated for his people until his death in 1816. Agwrongdongwas was a loyal pro-Kirkland leader from Oquaga who would vehemently support his nation's rights until his death in 1792.

Neutrality was proving an elusive target even for the Oneida, however. The difficulty of the situation was augmented, also, by the arrival of refugees from New England who brought with them a strong anti-British bias. Their eagerness to settle in Oneida territory was understandable, considering that many of their leaders, including Joseph Johnson, had been students at Wheelock's school in the 1760s. They were known to Samuel Kirkland and were familiar with the Oneida, having been employed as their teachers or missionaries. In October 1773, a delegation of five Oneidas visited Guy Johnson at Johnson Hall in response to his late uncle's communication to the Iroquois Confederacy that a nation provide a home for a body of New England Indians who had been dispossessed of their land by European colonists.[22]

Having discussed this proposal at a council of warriors and sachems, the Oneida agreed to respond positively to Sir William's suggestion. They declared their pleasure at welcoming the New England Indians to Oneida territory. Joseph Johnson knew his negative appraisal of the English authorities would "cast a prejudice in [their] Hearts against the English Brethren." He reminded the Oneida that the English had enjoyed taking "advantage of poor, Ignorant and blind Indians," drowning their ancestors in alcohol and stripping them of their possessions. An Oneida speaker informed the Mohegan leader about tensions within the Oneida nation, between those who supported Christianity and those who did not. Although the arrival of Christian Indians would bolster the Christian cause, the speaker stressed that unity within the Oneida nation was of ultimate importance.[23]

In the autumn of 1774, Guy Johnson arranged a land grant of approximately twenty miles square between the Oneida and New England Indians, but the numbers anticipated in the planned migration did not materialize.[24] The attempted migration probably had other results, however. Evidence concerning the rapacious hunger of the English for Indian land that was brought to Oneida by those Indians who did migrate from New England, Joseph Johnson and his Indian colleagues' constant manipulating for additional land in Oneida territory, and the Oneida's own experience of British authorities' unscrupulous land deals, all probably helped weaken the Oneida's resolve to maintain neutrality. Their allegiance to the colonists strengthened in the face of hostilities brewing in the summer of 1775.

Conoquhieson's enthusiasm to preserve Oneida's neutrality was originally matched by that of the merchants at Albany and the congressional commissioners based in Philadelphia. All groups were aware of the ramifications to peace and trade in the Mohawk valley resulting from General Philip Schuyler's planned military offensive into Canada, especially knowing Guy Johnson's success in obtaining the support of many Iroquois warriors. As the

Oneida was the nation closest geographically to the colonial settlements, after the departure of most Mohawk to Canada, neutrality was still the best solution proposed at a conference held in Albany in August and September 1775. By this time, tensions between Indians and the British had grown to the point that the Oneida insisted on holding preliminary meetings with the commissioners in their territory at German Flats before proceeding to Albany. Conoquhieson, still favoring the British cause but fully aware of the rebels' growing antagonism, was accompanied by the Oneida sachem Teyohagweanda in reassuring the merchants and commissioners that all important matters would be relayed by the Oneida to absent confederates. Teyohagweanda expressed the anxiety felt by those such as himself and Conoquhieson who had not openly supported the rebels, that they should be able to travel safely to Albany as they had been invited "to a Council of peace and entire Friendship." Once in Albany, Conoquhieson led the proceedings. With his friend the sachem Senghnagenrat, he informed the commissioners that, as the Oneida had not initially summoned the Indians to the conference, "they thought in good Manners [to] first address themselves to the Committee of Albany." At this meeting Senghnagenrat reminded the citizens of Albany that the Oneida loved the English, whether they lived over the ocean or in the colony; that for this reason they would remain neutral; that they would not listen to rumors about trade at Fort Stanwix being obstructed by the British; and that they wished their minister temporarily removed to safety, so that the Oneida would not be unjustly accused of allowing him to be taken prisoner.[25]

Once all three groups reconvened, Senghnagenrat alerted the committee members and the commissioners that as gossip was rampant among both Indians and whites, the truth about the Iroquois could best be acquired at a council meeting of the Six Nations rather than from any individual nation. The commissioners responded that when they gathered at their council fire in Pennsylvania they represented twelve provinces rather than six and therefore spoke with greater authority than the Iroquois. The Indian delegates were again told of the injustice suffered by the British colonists at the hands of the English king's ministers and of the necessity that the Six Nations remain neutral in a conflict that did not concern them. Not cowed by these veiled threats, Teyohagweanda demanded that improper land deals in the Susquehanna area involving Governor John Penn of Pennsylvania be rectified. The commissioners responded briefly to these grievances: clergy would be allowed to stay in their mission stations; trade would be opened and improved at the two locations as requested; and General Philip Schuyler had already been appointed to protect the council fire at Albany. As for concerns over land, they would have to be presented to the congress in Philadelphia.[26] The mood at the meeting's conclusion was far from congenial, with both the Oneida and the colonists realizing that neutrality was becoming impossible to maintain.

Conoquhieson died in the autumn of 1775 while returning from Albany to Kanowalohale. His participation in Sir William Johnson's funeral rites the previous year had been the pinnacle of his public career. His speeches at German Flats and Albany were brief and limited to ceremonial observances, mild in comparison with his invective against Kirkland earlier that year. Senghnagenrat had been his companion and protégé for many years; they had attended a meeting together at Johnson Hall in March 1763 to represent the Oneida on the issue of the Chenussio murderers being brought to justice, and in December 1766 they had been sent by the Oneida to express displeasure with Seneca land deals. Conoquhieson was also present at the negotiations for the land grant between the Oneida and the New England Indians in 1773. His prominence as an Oneida sachem at the 1775 conference, as well as at subsequent meetings at the outbreak of the revolution, would be welcomed by those of his nation who remained loyal to the pro-British sympathies of Conoquhieson.[27]

The Oneida were not oblivious to developments outside their immediate area. Since Guy Johnson and Daniel Claus had fled to Canada, William Johnson's son John was now the British representative in the Mohawk valley, with John Butler, a wealthy Mohawk valley Loyalist, as his deputy Indian agent. The Oneida were anxious that Guy Johnson might use his familiarity with the Six Nations to encourage Oneida kin at Caughnawauga to side with the British in the growing conflict. To bolster neutrality among their Canadian allies, Henry Cornelius and warriors Aksiaktatye and Honyost Thaosagawat traveled with other Oneida to Caughnawauga in September 1775. Thayendanega and Daniel Claus met them en route and tried to divert them to a meeting with Guy Johnson in Montreal. They declined this offer and, instead, convinced those at Caughnawauga to follow the lead of their Oneida brethren and avoid taking sides in an argument between the British and the Americans.[28]

By 1776 the Oneida's strained relationship with their confederates was almost beyond repair. Their vacillating loyalty to the British continued to gall the Mohawk, who in January angrily questioned Oneida's neutrality stance when they encountered rebel forces sent against John Johnson by General Schuyler. In February 1776, the Oneida, again represented by James Dean, tried to provide necessary leadership by requesting a council in Onondaga to discuss rumors of British hostilities emanating from Fort Niagara, but in deference to Onondaga's unwillingness to call a meeting, the Oneida grudgingly agreed to "gratify them and wait." At the same time the contentious issue of the Oneida's propensity to block messages arose again. An invitation had arrived at Kanowalohale from Governor Penn suggesting the Iroquois Confederacy attend a meeting in Philadelphia. However, the Oneida claimed they "were at a loss to comprehend Penn's design" and decided that the invitation should go no further until General Schuyler advised them.[29] Just where Oneida loyalty lay was increasingly questioned by their confederates.

In March 1776 additional fissures weakened Confederacy cohesion and further alienated the Oneida. Sachems from Cayuga and Onondaga had traveled to Kanowalohale to attend the condolence of an Oneida chief. Following the ceremony, a Cayuga sachem accused their hosts—and not without grounds—of "paying less attention to the ancient council fire at Onondaga than that lately rekindled at Albany." Warning that the Albany people were fickle, he feared bad repercussions if the rebels should ever defeat the British. As Oneida had formed a "well-known attachment" to the colonists, he continued, they ran the risk of not being rightly informed about Confederacy matters by those nations that favored the British. The Oneida admitted sending a delegation to Fort Niagara to learn about British intentions, despite the earlier advice of the Onondaga not to do so, and hoped that their attempt at espionage would ultimately meet with Confederacy approval. However, the Cayuga's main grievance was that a war hatchet presented to the Oneida by Guy Johnson had been given to their friends at Albany; it was one thing not to go to war, but quite another to give away to a committee of rebel colonists a war hatchet presented by the British. The Oneida might well have considered their action to be a gesture of peace toward the Patriots, but the pro-British Iroquois would not have deemed it appropriate. The Cayuga reprimanded the Oneida for not following proper protocol and demanded they go to Albany in the company of some Cayuga warriors to retrieve the hatchet. The Oneida refused and encouraged the Cayuga to return home rather than bring further disgrace to the Confederacy. A fierce debate continued for three days, with the Cayuga finally agreeing to abandon their plan. The Oneida admitted that the conference at Kanowalohale was one of the most heated debates ever held within the Confederacy.[30]

James Dean was a witness to this debate. Of his role in the March 1776 conference, Kirkland wrote that "the Oneidas place great confidence in Mr. Dean and admit him to their cabinet council. Had he not been there to strengthen and encourage the Oneidas, the Cayugas would probably have carried the day." The Oneida's positive relationship with Dean and the fractious nature of the Confederacy were indicated a few days after the closure of the March 1776 meeting at Kanowalohale. A group of "female governesses" from the Oneida, Tuscarora, and Onondaga nations were informed that Dean had received a warning from the Onondaga not to attend their council planned for April 1776, as some "Mohawks who came from Niagara to attend the Congress . . . in one of their drunken frolicks threatened to take [Dean's] life." Despite their urging, he did travel to the conference, but under the protection of warriors from Caughnawauga, Kanowalohale, and Oquaga.[31]

Once the Grand Council proceeded at Onondaga in April, the Oneida were challenged by a Seneca chief concerning a reported plan for some Oneida warriors to travel to Fort Niagara for the purpose of instigating anti-British activity. The Oneida denied this accusation and, despite questions being raised about their loyalty to the British, joined the Six Nations in somewhat unrealistically stating "mutual assurances of their fixed determination to observe a strict neutrality in the present quarrel." Requesting a return of trade opportunities, they demanded that improvements be made at Fort Stanwix. After all, as Senghnagenrat pointed out, it was hard for the Oneida to turn their backs on British generosity toward those of the Six Nations who remained loyal to His Majesty's forces.[32]

When conversation turned to discussions held previously at Albany, the Oneida, Tuscarora, and Caughnawauga "unanimously disapproved" of the position taken by others of the Confederacy—that any decisions made at a council fire other than the one at Onondaga be considered invalid. At the same time, since provisions at Fort Niagara were severely depleted, the Seneca were considering meeting with the commissioners at Albany to request food and clothing. On hearing of this, Senghnagenrat objected to the proposal and requested that the Six Nations "exercise patience" until the Oneida themselves could meet with those in Albany in the coming summer. When later asked by the Cayuga sachems for an explanation as to their position, the Oneida's determination to represent the Iroquois at the Albany council fire "much dissatisfied" the Cayuga, who felt the issue should be brought for consideration before the entire Confederacy.[33]

Council discussion was interrupted by the arrival of a letter from General Schuyler announcing the evacuation of the British troops from Boston. "[E]xpressing his joy and thankfulness" that British trade goods would be available through Quebec now that the Patriots had closed Boston as a supply base, Senghnagenrat stated ironically that the Americans would not be able to close Fort Stanwix as a conduit for trade goods from Canada, that the rebel forces had actually enabled much-needed British supplies to be more readily available to the eastern Iroquois, and that General Schuyler's assistance in securing supplies for those loyal to him was now rendered unnecessary by the very rebels that Schuyler supported. Senghnagenrat then addressed the assembly in a more conciliatory tone and "assured them that the Oneidas and Tuscaroras were unalterably fixed in their determination not to interfere in the present quarrel, or endeavor to obstruct or hinder, by words or otherwise, any of the military operations of the contending parties, while they themselves were uninjured." Conversations continued as participants prepared to leave Onondaga. The Oneida could not understand the Seneca's desire to speak to the commissioners at Albany, unless encouraged to do so for some subversive reason engineered by the British. The Cayuga, possibly motivated by the three Elder Brothers' constant antagonism toward their Younger Brother at this conference, and no doubt remembering their own aggressive hostility toward the Oneida at the meeting the previous month, approached the Oneida in an effort to "settle all difficulties subsisting between them and their brethren, and renewed and strengthened their ancient covenant of brotherhood."[34]

In the midst of this tumultuous meeting, the Oneida became increasingly aware of the hostility their pro-rebel stance inspired in their confederates, and they appreciated the support of the Caughnawauga Indians. Despite similar divided loyalties at home, the majority of the Caughnawauga nation had decided to support the Patriots and demonstrated their allegiance by attending the conferences in February and March 1776. As with the Oneida, there were those among the Caughnawauga who supported the British; they had kept a hatchet presented to them by William Johnson and were "influenced by those Seneca who had been unfriendly to the Colonies." However, Kirkland learned that, during the March conference at Onondaga, the Seneca requested that the Caughnawauga go directly to Onondaga territory and not visit the Oneida as "they were Bostonians." The Caughnawauga refused to comply, preferring to travel to the Oneida first, since they "were of one heart and one mind" with their colleagues and had been originally invited by them.[35]

The year 1776 was proving a pivotal period for the Oneida, as they continued to lose ground in their struggle to provide leadership for Iroquoian neutrality. The British stepped up their recruitment of Iroquois allies at meetings at Fort Niagara. The Patriots struggled to find the resources to offer inducements to the Iroquois that matched the value of the British. Early in May a delegation of Iroquois sachems and warriors met with the congressional commissioners and some citizens of Albany and New York. The commissioners urged the Indians to maintain their neutrality and ignore the invitations to join the Loyalist forces at Fort Niagara. Speakers for the Oneida responded that it was tempting to listen to reports of plentiful food and clothing at that location, especially since trade had diminished and supplies were low among those who supported the rebels.[36]

The same month Henry Cornelius joined representatives from other nations at a meeting with John Butler at Fort Niagara. While others were wooed by British promises of material largesse, Cornelius resisted. In addition, the Oneida were displeased by Schuyler's orders that the Committee of Correspondence at Albany restrict the passage of goods through the Fort Stanwix area. Schuyler's disclosure that traders were breaking their promise to supply only the western Iroquois nations and were diverting goods to British troops in Montreal did not alleviate tensions created by the Albany committee with whom the Oneida were increasingly friendly. The Oneida at Oquaga promised continued neutrality, but only so long as the commissioners supplied powder, lead, and flint. British reinforcements in Canada brought additional concern for the Oneida that other Indians would be enticed to support the British because of their increased control of the Saint Lawrence–Britain trade route. Thirteen Oneidas—led by Henry Cornelius, a young sachem from Kanowalohale named Sewajis, and a Wolf clan member named Kanaghweas (the newly appointed successor to hold the League title of Conoquhieson)—visited Caughnawauga in May 1776. They were discouraged to discover the growth of Iroquois sympathy toward the Loyalists there.[37]

In order to convince the Iroquois of the military strength of the Patriots, Schuyler offered to take members of the Six Nations on a tour of Boston, New York, and Philadelphia, all now in Patriot hands. By the end of May, twenty-one Iroquois were guests of the rebels on the east coast. The nine Oneida including Kanaghweas and Aksiaktatye, four Onondaga, and eight Mohawk (no Seneca or Cayuga traveled) were duly impressed with what they saw of Patriot success over the British, and these increasingly entertained the notion that neutrality was a losing proposition.[38]

The situation in Iroquoia continued to deteriorate. At a council held in June 1776 at Johnstown, the Oneida "utterly disapproved" of the conduct of the staunchly pro-British Mohawk who "were impudent—insulting to a very great degree." They also feared the growing influence of the British with the western Iroquois at Fort Niagara, especially in light of the "apparent delay and want of resolution" on the part of the Continental Congress and of that body's leniency with the Mohawk who had repeatedly broken their promises of neutrality and supported the British. The Oneida, concerned about the derelict state of Fort Stanwix, encouraged Kirkland to press the congress for immediate repairs to the structure, though he was not successful. Schuyler agreed that Fort Stanwix required revamping for the protection of the Oneida and the residents of the Mohawk valley, but first he wanted the congress to call a meeting at German Flats to chastise those Iroquois (especially the Mohawk) who had joined the enemy, and to get a firm estimate of how many Iroquois supported the Patriots.[39]

Realizing their precarious position and considering especially their contentious relationship with the Iroquois supporters of the British, in June 1776 the Oneida sent Senghnagenrat to a meeting at Oneida in yet another attempt to promote Iroquois neutrality, but to no avail. Having exhausted their options, the Oneida joined their declared allies the Tuscarora and Caughnawauga and "entered into a defensive league to support each other against the other nations; being resolved that, if the others [joined] the King's party, they would die with the Americans in the contest." Schuyler considered it likely that the Oneida, Tuscarora, and Caughnawauga nations took this action in light of the improbability of the Mohawk, Seneca, Cayuga, and Onondaga remaining neutral.[40] The defensive league was, after all, a move away from neutrality. The Oneida had previously agreed to stay out of the conflict providing they were not molested in their own territory, but their growing apprehension of a British attack in the Mohawk valley invalidated this agreement in the eyes of those leaning toward affiliation with the rebels. The creation of the league opened the way for those favoring the Patriot movement to drift, albeit hesitantly, into active participation in the revolution.

The close relationship that had evolved between the Oneida and Continental Army personnel was observed by officer Joseph Bloomfield at a conference with the Patriots at German Flats in July and August 1776. The army set up camp in June, in response to repeated requests from the Oneida that military reinforcements be available in case of a Loyalist attack. General Schuyler instructed James Dean to summon the Six Nations to a conference slated for July, and in the interim a troop of soldiers went to inspect "the ruins of the Once strong and beautiful Fort [Stanwix]." Proceeding to Kanowalohale they found the sachems meeting in council "in a Miserable old long Hutt" into which they were invited "with an Assuming air of Dignity." Returning a week later to German Flats, the soldiers were "treated with the greatest kindness and Hospitality" by the Oneida and Tuscarora. By mid-July other Iroquois investigating allegiance to the Patriots had begun to assemble and were welcomed by the Oneida hosts.[41]

Of the seventeen hundred Iroquois men, women, and children who eventually assembled, Bloomfield found the Oneida to be particularly pleasing.[42] They were represented by their chief warriors, Agwrongdongwas and Skenandoah, as well as sachems Jim Tayaheura, Adam Waronwansen, Odaghseghte, and Senghnagenrat. The attendance of Odaghseghte, member of the Wolf clan and bearer of the title of the primary founding sachem of the Iroquois League, accompanied by Senghnagenrat, the protégé of the late Conoquhieson, and the two chief warriors from Kanowalohale and Oquaga indicate the gravity with which the Oneida viewed this event. Noted by Bloomfield as being civil and polite in their dealings, the Oneida hastened to construct for themselves bark shelters approximately twenty feet long, in each of which were housed several families. The women busied themselves making moccasins and other items that they offered for sale to the soldiers. On one occasion a group from Oquaga, accompanied by their minister and an interpreter, visited a gathering of Indians and soldiers. After the social niceties (the partaking of tea, cider, and tobacco), Agwrongdongwas, as the Christian chief warrior, thanked the soldiers for their kind reception at German Flats. The Oneida nation in general consistently received Bloomfield's approbation as he noted their politeness in council, their reverence in worship, and their acceptance of European ways. The solemnity of Sunday service, led by Kirkland preaching and praying in Oneida and in English, and the pleasing harmony of the Oneida singers, contrasted with the behavior of others: "Whilst the religious Oneydoes were at their worship in the morning, the Atheistical Seneka's, Onondagoes and Cauyugas who believe there is no God and make a jest of all religion were beating their Tub singing, Dancing and Carrusing in the most profane Manner." At a game that resembled golf, the Oneida (who usually won at this event) received their defeat by the Tuscarora in good spirits and presented the victors with spoils donated by the Oneida matrons "who generously gave of their wampum, silver, Bead Bracelets, their Earrings, nose-Jewels and Pins . . . , Necklaces, belts etc. and all kinds of Indian-Ornaments."[43]

After more than a month of apparent camaraderie, an impatient Schuyler convened the conference. The congressional commissioners had intended that the Six Nations be cowed by threats of dire consequences should they go to war against the Patriots. Bloomfield's account condensed the discussions into a challenge presented by Schuyler as to whether the Iroquois would be faithful to the Loyalists or the Patriots, with those choosing the former being free to go to their homes and face the consequences. In Bloomfield's evaluation, the Mohawk response to Schuyler's challenge was "full of tri-fying Evasive answers," the Onondaga and Seneca were interested in peace only if it served their own interests, and the Cayuga sachems refused to answer for their warriors. Only the "Honest Oneydoes and Tuscaroras said they were for Peace and always keeping their Friendship with their Broth-ers." Official conference records focus on Schuyler's reaction: he thanked the Oneida and Tuscarora for their loyalty and intentions of neutrality; he warned the Mohawk not to use their drunkenness and John Johnson's ac-tivities as excuses for aggression against the Patriots; he advised the Seneca and Onondaga to prevent their warriors from developing contacts with the British in Canada; and he encouraged the Cayuga to avoid listening to Brit-ish promises of better trade opportunities. Adarockquaghs, who frequently spoke on behalf of the Oneida from Oquaga, warned that neutrality had been jeopardized by continued colonial encroachments on their land and by improper surveys made of their hunting grounds, despite promises made to the contrary at the 1768 Fort Stanwix treaty. The commissioners hurried to assure the Oquaga speaker that the Congressional Congress would "stop the wicked practice."[44] Bonds of friendship between the Oneida and the Patriots that would carry them united into the revolution were solidified at this meeting.

Kirkland's cooperation with the Congressional Congress and affiliation with the Oneida, which biographers have touted as all-important, only par-tially shaped the actions taken by the Oneida during this period. Fluctua-tions in support for or rejection of the missionary were predicated on more than the minister's personality, theology, or political persuasion. Cono-quhieson's accusation in 1771 that Kirkland spent more time tending his shop than his flock was understandable, as was Kirkland's determination to rally support for the Patriots by spreading rumors of expected British blockades of Atlantic shipping and Mohawk River trade routes. Kirkland's plan began to backfire, however, when the Oneida pondered the possibility of acquiring more and cheaper supplies from the British at Fort Niagara and Montreal than they could through his Patriot connections.

During the time leading up to Oneida's involvement in the revolution, their leadership was provided primarily by their sachem Conoquhieson. He remained consistent in his views, representing sachems and warriors simul-taneously with his litany of complaints concerning land, trade, forts, sol-diers, and alcohol. In addition, the warrior Agwrongdongwas kept Oquaga in the picture. Sachems and warriors performed in harmony when taking the initiative to secure their people's interests. Numerous Oneida residents of the Mohawk valley worked to establish good relations with the Albany merchants on the Committee of Correspondence, in an effort to maintain economic stability along the Mohawk River trade corridor in which they held a vested interest. Oneida acceptance of the Christianized Indians of New England resonated with their role as an adoptive nation; no individual Oneida speakers or leaders were highlighted during the process, however. The acceptance of Dean as an individual and of the Caughnawauga as a supportive community helped the drift of the Oneida nation toward the Patriots. An expanded leadership was mustered for the major events such as the signing of the document of neutrality and the major council of July–August 1776 that Schuyler called at German Flats. The neutrality declaration appears to have happened almost in defiance of the ostracism shown the Oneida at the November 1774 conference and of the coolness extended to them by the Confederacy during this period. Enjoying the comfortable relationship between the Oneida and the Continental Army, new speakers began to represent the Oneida at conferences: Agwrongdongwas, Adarockquaghs, Teyohagwegeanda, Odaghseghte, and Senghnagenrat. A sense of national solidarity among those Oneida who supported an alliance with the Patriots may have been the breeding ground necessary for nurturing a cadre of leaders to take the Oneida into the future, but they never could have fully anticipated what lay ahead.

# CHAPTER FIVE

# THE ONEIDA AS REBELS, 1777–1783

 $B$ olstered by the possibilities arising from recent Patriot victories over British forces on the Atlantic coast, the Oneida gradually replaced their predilection for neutrality with a more determined military support of the apparent victors. First by spying, and then by guerrilla raids and active military engagements against the British, Oneida sachems and warriors disregarded their previous animosities, combining their efforts to buttress the colonists' struggle to dethrone the British presence. However, they were hesitant when it came to overt attacks on their fellow Iroquois, with whom they had shared in the Grand Councils of the Six Nations Confederacy until the relatively recent exigencies of contact with the Europeans had stretched that ancient bond to the breaking point. The Oneida were heavily involved in the battles of Oriskany and Saratoga in 1777 and of Barren Hill in 1778. Some of their leaders died in the conflict. Many others, in joining the fight, left behind homes of considerable material security. By the winter of 1780, those of the Oneida nation who remained constant in the decision made three years earlier to fight with the Patriots in the revolution found themselves in an unforeseen situation. With their villages destroyed and huddling scattered, homeless, and demoralized in ramshackle shelters on the outskirts of Schenectady, to the west of Albany, the Oneida were forced to recoup their remaining resources in a landscape very different from any they had ever known.

The rapport evident when the Oneida and the Continental Army met on the fields of German Flats in the autumn of 1776 was augmented by an unexpected development the following winter. The Onondaga's influence among the Six Nations had been symbolized since the formation of the

Iroquois League by the fire that burned at the center of the Grand Council meetings of the Confederacy, a feature problematic for the Oneida who spoke against the Onondaga's increased support of the British. In January 1777 the Oneida sent a message to Colonel Elmore, the commander at Fort Schuyler (the name the Patriots gave Fort Stanwix during the revolution). Ninety Onondaga, including three sachems advocating peace, had succumbed to an unknown disease, and such a loss necessitated extinguishing the council fire, which thereby allowed each nation to act independently. Kirkland advised General Schuyler to initiate a traditional condolence ceremony, using the services of Odaghseghte and Senghnagenrat, thereby encouraging Onondaga's allegiance to the Patriot cause centered at Albany in the same way that Sir William Johnson had accomplished for the British by organizing ceremonies at Johnson Hall.[1]

The Oneida, in Schuyler's estimation, were no longer restricted by former Iroquois League protocol and were now free to replace ideas of neutrality with those of greater loyalty to the rebel fire at Albany. Thayendanega and John Butler continued to summon the Oneida to Fort Niagara in hopes of gaining their allegiance; in January 1777 Agwrongdongwas, Skenandoah, and Deacon Thomas maintained Oneida's tradition of rejecting Thayendanega's invitations. The following month two Oneida sachems agreed to travel there but remained adamant in their loyalty to the rebels: Jimmy Tayaheura was a newly appointed sachem at Kanowalohale, and Kanaghweas from Old Oneida had traveled to the east coast in May 1776 and become duly impressed with the Patriots' military successes. To reassure themselves at the same time about the strength of Washington's rebel forces, the Oneida organized a delegation of warriors and sachems to observe the situation in New England. This sortie was led by two leaders of increasing importance, head warrior William Kayentarongwea and Christian sachem Oneyanha of the Turtle clan. The journey provided ample evidence of Patriot advances.[2]

As the British built up their forces in Canada, accompanied mostly by the Seneca, and as rumors circulated about British attacks eastward from Fort Niagara and south from Montreal, the Oneida's contribution as spies for the rebels intensified. Sewajis, a head sachem from Kanowalohale who by now had become familiar with the route to Montreal, in February 1777 led a group of Oneida carrying a list of questions given them by Schuyler. In May they returned home bearing answers indicating ominous threats of a pending invasion, news largely obtained by virtue of Sewajis's ability to mingle undetected among the Caughnawauga. That same spring the sachem Senghnagenrat assisted some Oneida warrior in reconnoitering the Saint Lawrence River for enemy action. Others traveled to Fort Niagara and subsequently reported their findings to the rebel authorities at Albany. On Sewajis's return from leading yet another delegation to the Caughnawauga in June, he brought with him a dire prognosis. He had overheard the military plans of the British and their reinforcements to attack Fort Schuyler and colonial settlements in the Mohawk River valley in the immediate future.[3] By now the cooperation of sachems and warriors in these ventures was becoming commonplace.

The espionage conducted by Oneida sachems and warriors, indispensable to the rebels, provided the final nudge to bring the Oneida into open conflict with the British. Information that Senghnagenrat brought back from Fort Niagara and the evidence that Sewajis uncovered among the Caughnawauga rattled both the Indians and the settlers living near the Mohawk River. The epicenter of Oneida anger against the British was Oriska. The village was located within the land lost to the Oneida at the Fort Stanwix conference of 1768. The prominent agitator in Oriska was Honyere Tewahongarahkon (usually referred to as Honyere), a leading sachem of the Wolf clan whose wife, Tyonajanegen, and teenage sons, Jacob and Cornelius, shared his enthusiasm for military action.[4] Honyere's moment came when British forces, moving south from Montreal into Iroquoia and accompanied by a number of Seneca warriors, anticipated a rendezvous in the Mohawk valley with troops advancing southeast from Fort Oswego. Fort Schuyler and the nearby Carrying Place, long held by the Oneida and a pivotal area for their economic, cultural, and political identity, were now the focus of British plans to disrupt and weaken the Iroquois Confederacy and penetrate their territory. Early in August 1777, the commander of the Tryon County militia, General Nicholas Herkimer, was moving west from Albany to relieve Fort Schuyler and had stopped at Oriska. Herkimer was joined here by Honyere who served as captain of approximately sixty Indians, most of them from Oriska, including his wife and sons, the two ambassadors Henry Cornelius and Thomas Spencer, his brother Honyost Thaosagwat, and Blatcop.[5]

The ensuing battle in August 1777, named after the neighboring Oriskany Creek, was a defining moment for the Oneida. The valor of Oneida fighters eliminated the colonists' previous anxiety concerning their loyalty after abandoning neutrality and becoming involved in combat against the British and Seneca (both previous Oneida allies). Heroic accounts of battle became interwoven with Oneida identity: the agility of Teaghsweangalolis, the Bear clan youth from Kanowalohale whose skill at running expedited the delivery of many messages between Indian and colonist rebels; the horsemanship of Honyere's wife Tyonajanegen, who alerted those at Fort Schuyler to the pending British attack; the outstanding leadership of Honyere, wielding his sword and gun throughout the conflict despite being wounded in the wrist; the tenacity of his wife, loading his gun as well as firing her own; the bravery in battle of his son Cornelius, which later earned him the position of chief warrior; the fierce attacks of Blatcop as he repeatedly rushed at his opponents with his tomahawk despite his broken leg; the loyalty of Oneida warriors protecting General Herkimer, wounded in the leg from gunshot, as he directed operations from his saddle propped against a tree; the willing-ness of Atayataghronghta, the Caughnawauga warrior, to join the fray in support of the Oneida who had adopted him; and the stamina of Honyere's wife as she procured a horse at the cessation of hostilities to ride and alert her people at Fort Schuyler about the outcome.[6] It was evident that, for the Oneida, their reputation for military aggression and fortitude now eclipsed the former prestige gained through skill at negotiation.

Nevertheless, in truth, the battle was a fiasco for all involved; hundreds of lives were lost and casualties sustained. The Patriot General Herkimer died from loss of blood in a mangled leg amputation. The Oneida suffered the death of Thomas Spencer, one of only a few of their people who had lived successfully on both sides of the cultural divide. Not only was there no de-clared victor between the British and the Americans, but the conflict itself signified the first major shedding of blood between the Seneca and Oneida, what has been called "the beginning of a civil war in the Confederacy." The Seneca were particularly incensed, for they suffered a high number of casualties. Of added significance was the loss of their medicine bundles when rebels raided their camp during the fray. Their desire was so fierce for retaliation against the Oneida that, accompanied by Thayendanega, they destroyed the village of Oriska, the home base of many of the Oneida com-batants. The homes of Henry Cornelius and Honyere burned, other houses and crops were destroyed, and cattle were scattered. The Seneca assisted the British in laying siege to Fort Schuyler immediately following the battle, while Oneida leaders, from various backgrounds and positions but united in loyalty to the Patriot army, helped defend the fort: Honyost, Honyere's brother and chief warrior; Cornelius Kakiktoton, Bear clan negotiator with the Albany Committee of Safety; Oneyanha, Christian Turtle clan mem-ber who would be involved in future land deals; Paul Teaghsweangalolis, Bear clan resident of Kanowalohale; and Anthony Shononghriyo, Turtle clan warrior and bearer of the title of a founding Iroquois League member. While the siege was in progress other Oneida performed admirably. Scouts hastily conveyed messages between Fort Schuyler and German Flats, while others spied on British movements and encouraged the colonists of Tryon County not to lose their resolve after the devastating outcome of Oriskany. In personal redress for Thayendanega's involvement in the destruction of his home in Oriska, Honyere confiscated many possessions from the Cana-joharie home of the Mohawk leader's sister Molly and even lived in her house temporarily with his family as a final affront.[7]

It was many years before claims compensation proceedings for war losses were to begin in 1794. Timothy Pickering undertook the claims compensa-tion for war losses.[8] Calling at Samuel Kirkland's home on 24 November 1794, Pickering initiated proceedings for a general council of the Oneida to be held to discuss the best method for them to receive compensation for what they had lost in the war. Kirkland noted in his journal that the

Indians "urged that should a sum be given in the gross, . . . they were utterly incapable of making a just and equal distribution; both from the inequality of their losses and the jealousies which subsisted among them." It took three days to complete the claims: Pickering and his interpreter, Jasper Parrish, lodging with Skenandoah whom they considered to be the principal Oneida chief, met at Skenandoah's home with the Wolf clan; James Dean interviewed the Turtle clan; Kirkland recorded the claims of the Bear clan. Claims were documented for 101 Oneida, 8 Tuscarora, and 1 Caughnawauga. However, there is no independent evidence indicating whether this represented the entire population of Kanowalohale at the time of Pickering's visit. What is of major significance is the Oneida's desire to use clan membership as a means of deciding communal business in the presence of non-natives. The Oneida generally directed the overall process. They decided the manner in which the claimants would enumerate their losses and be awarded compensation; their being interviewed according to clan allowed for the claims to be open to communal scrutiny. As Kirkland and Dean were fluent in the Oneida language, and as Pickering was accompanied by his interpreter, the residents of Kanowalohale preferred negotiating in their own language. In December 1794, Congress acknowledged Pickering's findings and granted the Oneida $5,000.[9]

Honyere's home in Oriska had been one of considerable wealth: the construction of his twenty-square-foot framed house, larger than average, "made by white people," and paid for with a horse and cow, indicated the cooperation existing between the Indian owner and the colonial community.[10] His wagon, sleigh, and plow might have been communal property and part of the influx of agricultural supplies initiated by Kirkland in 1770, but if owned privately, they demonstrated the financial benefit of adopting agricultural practices, especially in light of the livestock and crops owned. His household objects included numerous tin and copper kettles, pewter plates, blankets, clothing material (linen, stroud, calico), tables, trunks, tea kettles with ten teacups and saucers, pewter table spoons, punch bowls, and linen shirts. The lack of knives and forks to accompany the pewter spoons indicate that the Oneida were selective in their accommodation to European etiquette, according to what was of practical use within their traditional customs. The large amount of brooches and earrings, fine clothing and social accoutrements (tea service, punch bowls) revealed a home in which Honyere's wife was comfortable with European etiquette as well as with traditional Indian fare and enjoyed displaying items to indicate the family's prestige. A two-handed bateau usually associated with river trade, the preponderance of farming supplies, and nearly two hundred horses, cattle, sheep, hogs, and fowl, and the paucity of guns and traps, all reveal a trend whereby prominent Oneida were becoming open to greater reliance upon European commodities. Much of this accumulation could demonstrate a shift away from traditional Indian custom, in which the former lavish giving of presents as an indication of communal status was being replaced by hoarding.

Honyere's social status at Oriska notwithstanding, it was the performance of the Oneida under his leadership at the battle of Oriskany that prompted Schuyler and the congressional commissioners to call a council at Albany in September 1777 to satisfy themselves that the Oneida, now actively participating in hostilities, were indeed committed to the Patriots. All Six Nations were invited, but the majority of those attending were Oneida, accompanied by a few Mohawk, one Onondaga, and no Seneca. Schuyler had received a letter from the Continental Army expressing the hope that several hundred Oneida recruits would come to the army's assistance as a result of the meeting's deliberations. Schuyler took the Oneida aside to discuss this possibility, negotiating with their most influential leaders at the conference: Honyere, Atayataghronghta, and Kanadarok. The Oneida insisted that, although they accepted the regrettable fact that bloodshed among the Iroquois was now inevitable as a result of the fighting at Oriskany, their main purpose in going to war was to capture British soldiers in order to exchange them for captured Iroquois brothers, not to engage in hostilities with their confederates. During these discussions, fighting erupted not far from Saratoga, north of Albany. Hurried plans were made for the Indians to engage again in military action, and approximately 150 Indians, mostly Oneida, joined the Continental Army at the Saratoga battle site in October 1777.[11] Since their efforts to maintain neutrality had been abandoned at the battle of Oriskany, the Confederacy was now fractured as the Oneida marched to fight their brothers at Saratoga.

Oneida scouts again excelled in their accustomed tasks—felling trees to obstruct enemy advances, and engaging in guerrilla raids to hamper the British troops' attempts to obtain food supplies. But rather than kill captured enemy soldiers, instead they frightened and harassed them in order to obtain information concerning troop movements. Oneida warriors were notorious for their ability to paralyze British troops when they appeared suddenly before them and just as quickly disappeared with prisoners. Loyalist troops moving south from Canada into the Lake Champlain region faced numerous problems: the British military leadership was not as experienced at fighting as the Patriots. Their Indian allies seemed more interested in looting and plundering than in preparing for battle. The incident of warriors scalping and mutilating Jane McCrea became fodder for rebel announcements against the enemy.[12] Indians returning to their homes constantly defected, despite British soldiers' desperate efforts to restrain them. For their part, as the fighting drew closer to their territory, the Oneida announced that some were returning to their homes in order to protect their families and to procure provisions for the winter. Nevertheless, with the help of the Oneida, the Saratoga engagement in mid-October 1777 resulted in a decisive Patriot victory. Honyere and his wife Tyonajanwegen received special commendation from General Horatio Gates of the American forces (Tyonajanwegen received sufficient rum to supply her family throughout the winter). Kanadarok received a personal belt from George Washington for his outstanding ability to spy on and ambush the enemy.[13]

The Oneida sachems and warriors themselves were not oblivious to the triumphs of their people. Referring to both engagements, sachems Senghnagenrat and Odaghseghte praised their warriors for the defeat of the enemy, despite the loss of Oriska. Similarly, warriors Hendrick and Agwrongdongwas commended their people's accomplishment. Head warrior William Kayentarongwea traveled to Onondaga, at Kirkland's request, to inform them of the British surrender at Saratoga. There he encountered Thayendanega, mustering support for the Loyalists, but at Kayentarongwea's appearance the Mohawk leader departed, leaving many Onondaga less enthusiastic to follow his directives.[14]

The Oneida nation, which had been increasingly ostracized by its confederates before the fighting began, was now facing the probability of suffering additional acts of revenge from their angry confederates. At a meeting of the Six Nations held at Fort Niagara in December 1777, John Butler hoped to improve relations and gain support among all the Iroquois and cement their appreciation for the British by replacing their items lost during the recent fighting. Representatives of all Six Nations attended, though understandably only two Oneida made the trip. Butler was surprised to see the Oneida and stressed in his speeches that the meeting was intended only for those who were friends of the British. An Onondaga speaker had changed his former conciliatory tone toward the Oneida. He was now vehemently opposed to their support of the rebels, reinforcing that his people would have no further dealings with such traitors. Contrary to what the Oneida expected of the Tuscarora, their speakers present voiced their decision to "stick the Axe into the heads of the Rebels." By the meeting's conclusion, Butler assured the British that he had secured the loyalty of all Six Nations except the Oneida, and that the Oneida faced retribution from their former confederates.[15] Whether he realized that the Onondaga and Tuscarora speakers did not represent their entire nations is a moot point in light of the Oneida's position. They knew they had some support from both nations, but they now faced the publicly declared opposition of the Iroquois and of their renewed alliance with the enemy, the British. The main Oneida loss at present was the obliteration of Oriska. And they knew other communities would be at risk.

It was of prime importance to the Oneida that they receive more tangible support from the colonial authorities. Both the Continental Congress and the New York Committee of Correspondence declared their friendship toward their "trusty friends," stating that an attack against the Oneida would be considered an attack against themselves. The Oneida tried to capitalize on their favored position by reminding Schuyler of badly needed repairs at

Fort Schuyler. In turn Schuyler sent a message in care of James Dean to all the Six Nations, indicating a final chance for them to follow the Oneida's example in renouncing their British connection and obtaining necessary repairs and supplies from the rebels. Schuyler was aware that he had received instructions from the Continental Congress to supply Washington with four hundred warriors willing to enter combat against the British.[16]

In response, over seven hundred Iroquois attended the conference Schuyler called in March 1778 to muster the required troops. Such events were now held at Johnstown. Although established by Sir William prior to his death and named after his son, this location did not have quite the same lengthy connection with the British as did Johnson Hall. The majority of attendees were Oneida and Tuscarora. The Onondaga were well represented, a few Mohawk and Cayuga made an appearance, the Seneca and most Mohawk stayed away. A coup for the Patriots was the visit of the marquis de Lafayette, a young Frenchman of independent wealth who had journeyed earlier to America to volunteer his services. He had served with George Washington the previous winter and would soon be commissioned a general in the northern department for the Continental Army. Earlier in March he had ingratiated himself with the Oneida by promoting their cause (albeit unsuccessfully) to have immediate repairs made to Fort Schuyler and by accepting an Oneida name (Kayewla) when they ceremonially adopted him in recognition of his assistance. Schuyler was counting on the Oneida to keep a promise made earlier by their chiefs, that "a considerable number of their best warriors" would join Washington's forces should their villages' protection be assured. There was also anticipation that the western Iroquois might be lured into the rebel camp in response to Lafayette's presence, because of their former favorable connection with the French.[17]

Sachem Odaghseghte had previously spoken on behalf of the Seneca in an attempt to placate them. Now, knowing this was impossible, his voice predominated as the Oneida spokesman at the conference. Speaking only for his people and the Tuscarora, and promising their loyalty to the rebel cause until either their death or victory, he stressed that this loyalty was predicated on the Patriots' maintaining forts in good repair in Oneida territory, housing small garrisons in each fort, and ensuring sufficient trade goods for economic stability in light of damages incurred in the recent fighting. Schuyler had little recourse but to agree. Odaghseghte addressed the assembly as a principal sachem, expressing his misgivings concerning the war itself as well as the behavior of the warriors willing to fight. Like Senghnagenrat, he said, he regretted the sachems' loss of prestige at a time of war when the warriors became the center of attention: "Formerly the Sachems were instantly obeyed by the Warriors, but now the latter have thrown off all Regard to their Council." He urged the young combatants to be mindful of the elder sachems' wisdom—and of the fact that they would one day be silver-haired themselves: "The Rising Generation will imitate your example and you will then be incapable of enforcing your advice by the measures you now pursue."[18]

A month passed, repairs at Fort Schuyler were at a standstill, and Washington was impatiently awaiting a response from the Oneida to indicate exactly how many would support his military offensive. He had hoped for two hundred fighters, as a more realistic number for the Oneida to muster, but a delegation sent to Fort Schuyler indicated this was not to be. Sachem Senghnagenrat and Deacon Thomas apologized for the absence of Odaghseghte (he was ill) and then explained that two hundred warriors were too many, considering the size of the Oneida community, especially since renovations to the fort had still not materialized. When asked if the Oneida would send fighters once the fort was repaired, they replied in the affirmative.[19]

Fort Schuyler had still not received any improvements when the Oneida gathered there again in April 1778. William Kayentarongwea and Skenandoah optimistically reported the possibility of reconciliation among the Iroquois. They had received word that the Seneca and Cayuga might be willing to attend a Grand Council if the Onondaga rekindled the fire in their community. At this point, however, they gathered primarily to dispatch warriors to Washington's army. The fort's commander hoped that twenty Oneida would volunteer, but forty-seven were enthusiastic to serve. Many among those willing to venture forth had become familiar with fighting with the rebels. These were their captain Honyere, his brother Honyost, Sewajis (the first to respond positively), Aksiaktatye, Henry Cornelius, Deacon Thomas, Skenandoah's son Daniel, and Blatcop. They carried with them an apology to Washington for not being greater in numbers. If the anticipated council fire was revived at Onondaga and proved fruitful, then additional warriors might be forthcoming from other nations.[20] Their motives would have been varied: military service provided adventure and notoriety for young fighters at a time of war; loved ones in vulnerable villages deserved protection against the enemy; and the reciprocity between Oneidas and colonists that grew in the period of peace now needed honoring in time of war.

Prior to their departure, Odaghseghte spoke as a traditional sachem, anxious about the behavior of the warriors. They had a long march ahead of them and would be "exposed to Fatigues and Many Temptations." Their behavior would be watched by many. "Keep in mind that warriors sustain an important Character—they Can do much Good and commit great Enormities. . . . To abuse and plunder (and it may be an innocent) Family is beneath the Character of a Warrior." The character of the entire Oneida nation would be observed, by George Washington in particular, an important consideration if, as hoped, the rebels won the war and Washington became the new American leader. Unity was of the utmost importance: "Be always of one mind—have an Object in view and don't let anyone think himself as Head warrior or that he May use all those Freedoms which are indulged at Home." They must avoid alcohol, "the common Beguiler of Indians," as it would bring disaster. "Your deportment in this Case will resound through the American army, be noticed by General Washington the Chief Warrior— and we Sachems shall then rejoice to hear from you." The warriors listened intently—and replied, voicing obedience to the sachem's admonishment but adding that as warriors they would have to make decisions about how to best protect Oneida lands and they expected the sachems would honor these decisions.[21] How times had changed. Odaghseghte had fulfilled his mandate as a sachem, providing advice to warriors before they sallied into combat, but he could well remember the time, not very far back, when a young warrior would not have dared make such a public rebuttal to a sachem.

Shortly afterward the Oneida warriors set off to join Washington and his troops in Valley Forge in southeast Pennsylvania. The army, driven out of coastal Pennsylvania by the British, had spent the winter there. On arriving in the valley, the Oneida were impressed at the sight of the major encampment of the Continental Army; the soldiers were equally intrigued by the members of the infamous Confederacy. Camaraderie flowed easily. Washington extended hospitality to the Oneida leaders, inviting them to dinner. The Oneida assumed they were also welcome to attend Washington's military councils but were politely led to the door. When another warrior invited himself to attend an officer's meal and help himself to a piece of meat, Washington spoke in his defense, saying that maintaining friendly relations with the Oneida allies was more important than rescuing food. Fortunately the Oneida relationship with the army remained sufficiently solid to withstand these challenges in protocol.[22]

In mid-May Lafayette and his Oneida friends were ordered by Washington to investigate rumors that the British were evacuating Philadelphia. Halfway there, the men stopped and encamped at the village of Barren Hill. Again the Oneida had some spare time in which to entertain Washington's troops. One particular soldier admired an Oneida's marksmanship in archery. Taunted into firing an arrow into a black mass in the corner of a nearby stone church, the Oneida dislodged a horde of bats that were subsequently killed by both Indians and soldiers providing, as that soldier reported, "sport for all hands." Inconsequential as such frolic might have been, it served to reinforce the bond between Oneida and rebel.[23]

Such sport was short-lived. Lafayette was informed that three columns of British troops, determined to strike a major blow against Washington's army, were moving in the direction of Barren Hill. He realized their forces outnumbered his own four to one. Lafayette knew the potential escape routes better than the British had anticipated, however, and once fighting commenced he had little other option than to encourage his troops to retreat. The Oneida were in a different column, and hearing the sound of the approaching British cavalry, prepared for an ambush. The melee of war cries and gunfire and archery sufficiently denerved both combatants that each beat a retreat in the confusion. In what was in effect a stalemate, the British and Continental commanders knew they could not win a conclusive victory; the former retreated to Philadelphia, the latter to Barren Hill and eventually Valley Forge.[24]

Despite the ignominious outcome of the Barren Hill campaign, the bravery of the Oneida warriors did not escape notice. One French officer, A. Louis de Tousard, praised the Oneida for defending him when he was wounded: he "had the occasion to acquaint the British light horses with the hollow [holler] of the Indians and their hability [ability] in firing." Although he could not estimate the numbers killed, he lauded the loyalty of the Oneida as they were the last seen leaving the battle scene. The Oneida made a favorable impression on Washington on this the first and only time they actually fought under his command: their "perseverance and fidelity" was laudable but should not be taken for granted, as removing them so far away from their homes might dampen their enthusiasm for supporting the rebels. It might be advisable, he thought, to utilize their martial ability in defending their homelands rather than in fighting the British in distant campaigns. Washington also realized that their innate ability at scouting and raiding—not so familiar to those trained in European maneuvers—would be better used by augmenting rebel forces in the Mohawk valley, thereby freeing the Continental soldiers to fight against the British troops in the style to which both were accustomed. For moral as well as practical reasons, he asserted, the "Oneidas and Tuscaroras have a particular claim to attention and kindness."[25]

Particularly difficult for the Oneida was the death of Sewajis during the Barren Hill campaign.[26] Not only had this youth, appointed sachem by his peers at Kanowalohale, spied faithfully against the British and been one of the first to volunteer for Washington's army, he had also managed to combine the role of sachem and warrior with great aplomb. He had given distinction to a role that had become critical to the Oneida during the revolutionary period.

Fortunately for the Oneida, Washington executed his plan to send their warriors home. The previous year Thayendanega had established his anti-rebel base of operations at Oquaga, a community formerly with strong Oneida connections. Now he planned retaliatory attacks against the Oneida and allied colonists at German Flats, also in Oneida territory. While the Oneida warriors were at Barren Hill, Thayendanega had already begun raids in that region, devastating small communities in the Mohawk valley and conveying the plunder to Oquaga. In the summer of 1778, he led John Butler and the allied pro-British Seneca on a path of vengeance and destruction through the Wyoming valley in the Susquehanna area, not far from Oquaga. Oneida warriors, having returned from Washington's service, were now available to conduct spy missions in an effort to protect their communities and those of their colonial friends in the Mohawk River region, simultaneously resuming their pleading for better fortifications to be supplied by the rebel authorities. Promises of protection and support emanating from the Continental Congress never came to fruition.[27] That Oneida loyalty remained as strong as it did is remarkable, considering the lack of support during this period from the congress, despite Schuyler's supportive voice.

In September 1778 the Oneida went on the offensive. A war party of Oneida and Tuscarora attacked Unadilla, a community close to Oquaga, when Thayendanega had left that village to bring additional turmoil to German Flats. Although they burned houses and freed cattle, the Oneida pointed out that they exercised restraint in their approach. No harm was done to women and children, and several houses were spared, as were some old men unable to fight. They took prisoners with them on returning to Kanowalohale, delivering most of them to the commander at Fort Schuyler as a gesture of goodwill. Others were given to some visiting Caughnawauga. One prisoner was adopted by Odaghseghte, as apparently the aging sachem had formed a friendship with the young man. On hearing about the Oneida's actions, George Washington was again pleased with his Indian allies who had finally initiated aggression against the seemingly unstoppable Thayendanega. The final destruction of Oquaga was conducted two weeks later, by rebel forces who attacked and destroyed the village by night. The sun rose the following day to find the community in smoldering ruins; there were no human casualties as all had fled.[28]

The devastation of Oquaga disrupted the Oneida's life. Crevecoeur, when his North American ramblings brought him to Oquaga in 1776, wrote favorably about the village of fifty houses, built both "after the ancient Indian manner" and "of good hew'd logs properly dove-tailed at each end," providing "neat and warm habitations." Crevecoeur noted the flourishing appearance of the villagers' agriculture and livestock: "Nothing could be more pleasing than to see the embryo of future hospitality, politeness and wealth disseminated in a prodigious manner of shapes and situations along these banks." The village that Crevecoeur visited in 1776 showed evidence of greater acceptance of European commodities than it had done when Richard Smith passed through seven years earlier. Smith was not impressed by the houses, built with "clumsy hewn Timbers and hewn Boards or Planks" and with sheets of bark for roofing, each containing interior stalls "resembling those of Horse Stables," in each of which lived an entire family, with at least six families making up the household. The house's central fireplace was sparsely encircled by rough furniture, including "Beds with dirty Blankets." By the time the village was totally demolished in April 1779, military records indicated further advancement. The troops were reluctant to "lay waste" to the Oneida communities they encountered, and Oquaga was described as "one of the neatest towns on the Susquehanna . . . with good Log houses with Stone Chimney's and glass windows . . . and a great number of apple trees."[29]

One can only conjecture the impact that the loss of Oquaga had on the Oneida. Although it had become a Loyalist stronghold under Thayendanega, for the Oneida who longed for a return to the way things used to be, it was still the southern "door" of the Confederacy. Most of the Oneida residents had previously fled to Kanowalohale, although the number of refugees (and whether they intended to return to Oquaga when the fighting ended, assuming the rebels were victorious) is not known. The loss of both Oriska and Oquaga and the associated dislocation of people involved must have strained the Oneida leadership's resolve with regard to remaining allied with the rebel cause. Odaghseghte's adoption of an enemy youth at Unadilla might prove strongly symbolic of hope for his people's ultimate vindication.

A mission to Albany in October 1778 led by Agwrongdongwas and two Oneida, together with two Caughnawauga and a Tuscarora, described the plight of the Oneida following the hostilities of the summer and the arrival at Kalowalohale of the refugees from Oquaga. As early as April 1778, Schuyler had approached the Continental Congress seeking help with clothing and supplies for the Oneida—they were suffering severe shortages arising from wartime interruptions to trade—but the results were not satisfactory. Now, in October 1778, the Oneida addressed the Indian commissioners through their leading warrior, himself a refugee from Oquaga. Agwrongdongwas complained that their lack of clothing was critical, that they were "obliged to use Grass for Garters," that things were bound to get worse as the war continued, and that the rebels were duty bound to treat their allies better. He also sought protection for the refugees, as some rebel soldiers considered them enemies rather than friends. In conclusion he urged the commissioners to insist that Kirkland spend more time with the Oneida Christians; the missionary's absence resulting from his new role as chaplain to the Continental forces was damaging the spiritual health of the fledgling congregation at Kanowalohale. In response, Agwrongdongwas was given documents stating that the displaced Oquaga should be afforded safe travel, little could be done about lowering food prices during time of war, and even less could be promised about bringing Kirkland more frequently to Kanowalohale as his military chaplaincy made heavy demands on his time.[30] Agwrongdongwas could not convey much satisfaction to his people at his return from the meeting.

Matters deteriorated for the Oneida in the winter of 1778–1779. In November 1778, British forces, accompanied by their Indian allies, ravaged the Cherry Valley in retaliation for the destruction of Oquaga at the hands of the rebels. Others of the Six Nations blamed the Oneida for the endless rounds of attack and counterattack. If the Oneida had not joined the Patriots, the Iroquois Confederacy would have remained intact and undamaged, they charged. The Cayuga in particular breathed venom toward the Oneida: their persistent spying for the rebels had so "Notoriously Disaffected the

Confederacy that it was neither their interest nor Indeed in their Power to protect them any longer." The Oneida were warned: either "Reunite with their ancient friends . . . in a vigorous opposition against the Common Enemy of the Confederacy" or leave their northern villages and move their people to the Susquehanna River area. This threat was a blow to the morale of the Oneida people, especially as the previous summer, their constant hope for reconciliation within the Confederacy had been buoyed when, as a result of the mediation of Agwrongdongwas and other Oneida sachems, 130 Onondaga had joined the Oneida and requested that a council fire be established at Oneida. At that time the sachem was ecstatic: "We warriors of the Oneidas, Tuscaroras and Onondagas . . . are banded in all our proceedings. . . . But we Indians have not hitherto attacked each other. . . . We wish not to [be] involved ourselves in a war with the rest of the Indians which must inevitably be attended with fatal consequences to us."[31] How things had changed.

The Oneida were now being forced by the Cayuga to decide to abandon either the rebel cause or their homeland. Their response was unconventional. Realizing their dream of reestablishing peace within the Confederacy was dashed yet again, Agwrongdongwas reported that, at a meeting in January 1779, the Oneida departed from customary procedure and allowed each individual member of the nation to decide which course of action to take: "should any chuse to join the enemy, free liberty was given to withdraw from the tribe." However, the majority decided "to stand by each other in Defense of their Lives and Liberty against any Enemy that might be disposed to attack them." If a move to another location was the answer, then so be it. Agwrongdongwas expressed added pleasure that some Onondaga remained loyal to their Oneida hosts, the latter being "in high spirits to find such a number of them so friendly disposed."[32]

The Continental Congress realized that new initiatives must be taken to support the Oneida and to curb the inroads the British and their allied Indians were making into the Mohawk River and Lake Champlain areas. One congressional decision adopted Schuyler's suggestion to strengthen the bond between the Continental Army and the Oneida warriors who had volunteered their services in three conflicts since mid-1777 and whose loyalty could conceivably be eroded. James Dean was to approach the Oneida and Tuscarora for their recommendations as to who should receive military commissions, thereby recognizing their military contribution by title and by payment. The Oneida nominated four as captains: the distinguished warrior Honyere, a Christian sachem of the Turtle clan called John Onondiyo, James Wakarontharane, and Tewaghtahkotte. Cornelius Kakiktoton, Honyost Thaosagawat, Christian Thonigwenghsohare, Totyaneahawi, Cornelius Okonyota, John Sagoharase, Joseph Kanaghsatirhon, and the lone Tuscarora Nicholas Kaghnatsho would be lieutenants. Later suggested as lieutenant colonel was Atayataghronghta, the faithful Caughnawauga ambassador, spy, and warrior.[33]

The second initiative was in response to the Oneida's repeated request that the reconstruction of Fort Schuyler be accompanied by the erection of a fortified village near Kanowalohale. This request was finally heeded in February 1779, and a substantial structure resulted with the assistance of soldiers from the Continental Army. No military corps was assigned to the fortified village, however, and the Oneida were expected to provide their own protection from among the village residents.[34] Nevertheless the Oneida felt more secure, thanks to help from the rebel forces.

A major incursion into Iroquoia, with anticipated support from the Oneida, was intended to punish those Six Nations allied with the British and to discourage further British advances into upper New York. Such was the third and major Patriot initiative of 1779. Continental forces led by Major General John Sullivan, moving northward from Pennsylvania's Wyoming valley, would meet with the forces of Brigadier James Clinton, traveling west from the Mohawk valley, and then move en masse through the heart of western Iroquois lands. The Oneida were expected to help with this offensive, but since an initial major blow was intended to weaken the Onondaga, some of whom were now living with the Oneida, the Patriots were to distract the latter by involving them in a strike against British forces in the Saint Lawrence area. Once the Oneida heard of the rebels' attack on the Onondaga and realized they had been duped, their leaders expressed considerable anger. Agwrongdongwas, Skenandoah, and Dean visited the commander at Fort Schuyler to protest such double-dealing. They were fighting the British, they insisted, not the Indians. Leading sachem Odaghseghte brought some peace to the situation by convincing Colonel Goose Van Schaick, the commander at Fort Schuyler, to allow those Onondaga prisoners who had families at Kanowalohale to live there under Oneida custody.[35]

Sullivan and Clinton's summer campaign did not subdue the pro-British Iroquois as expected; neither was it advantageous for the pro-Patriot Oneida. In June 1779, the British made a surprise attack on the Caughnawauga, suspecting the community was harboring rebel spies, as indeed it was. The faithful and long-serving Deacon Thomas was killed by gunfire after he refused to surrender. The same month James Dean brought a cluster of troops led by Honyere to join James Clinton's men, but the Oneida made it clear that—although the Seneca were deemed enemies—the Oneida could not attack those with whom for centuries they had developed strong bonds. In July 1779 Fort Schuyler was attacked by Canadian Indians lured into the campaign by the British, and the Oneida who escaped were all the more keen to avenge Deacon Thomas's murder. Lieutenant Hanyost, a youthful warrior called Bluebeck, and another Oneida joined the Clinton-Sullivan force in August, but when the Patriots successfully attacked Thayendanega and some British regulars at a native village near Newtown, New York, the Oneida refused to send any of their men to assist Sullivan in scouting for further enemy Indian locations. In September an attack on a principal Seneca village at Chenussio resulted in the death of the highly respected Honyost. His warnings of an ambush by the Loyalist Indians had been ignored. His body was scalped and dismembered. Shortly afterward an attack on the Cayuga was planned, and an Oneida sachem named Teheaniyoghtiwat brought seventy of his warriors to participate. When Teheaniyoghtiwat's plea that the Cayuga be spared was dismissed, many of the Oneida refused to fight and returned to Kanowalohale.[36]

The Oneida of Kanowalohale knew revenge was inevitable, and that they would be in the front line of a pending attack by the pro-British Iroquois. With head sachem Odaghseghte as their spokesman, in February 1780 they asked for and received permission to move to land distant from Kanowalohale so as to have a safer place to plant their corn. At Schuyler's instigation, Odaghseghte and Agwrongdongwas were to travel to Fort Niagara the same month to arrange the release of some prisoners and hopefully to lessen the expected blow against the Oneida by healing some of the wounds between the confederates; the aged Skenandoah made the trip in place of Odaghseghte as the latter felt that, as leading sachem, he should stay in his home community during perilous times. At a community council the emissaries were instructed to bring back the other Iroquois from the British fold. The clan mothers reemphasized their dream that all Iroquois men would reunite so that their offspring would be born in a unified Confederacy. Odaghseghte offered personally to provide safe escort to any Iroquois men who wished to travel to Albany to request a return to neutrality. After the grueling winter trip to Fort Niagara, the Oneida delegation made its case, but still with no success. Instead, the Oneida were accused of being troublemakers. They were placed in the fort's dungeon, where they spent approximately five months. During this time the Oneida fractured further. The families of Agwrongdongwas and Skenandoah moved to Fort Niagara to be near them; Senghnagenrat also moved to Niagara and joined pro-British Oneida; Odaghseghte negotiated with Captain Cornelius Van Dyck at Fort Schuyler for military assistance to move from Kanowalohale to a safer location. In desperation Captain John Onondiyo led the Oneida in abandoning Old Oneida and Kanowalohale and setting up camp in a field near Fort Schuyler.[37]

The summer heat of July 1780 beat down on Agwrongdongwas and Skenandoah as they trudged back to Kanowalohale. They had been released from captivity under the condition that they convince their people to unite with the British at Fort Niagara. The two leaders complied, hoping privately that this ploy would save their people and community from Thayendanega's savagery. Once at the abandoned community, the Mohawks under Thayendanega set fire to the entire village despite pleas from the two elders, exhausted from the trip and from witnessing the destruction of what was once a thriving center of Oneida life.[38]

The extent of the loss incurred by the Oneida in Kanowalohale's flames can be gleaned from the home and possessions of chief warrior and Wolf clan member Skenandoah. By 1780, when he was seventy-four, sufficient contact with the European way of life meant he had accumulated a respectable homestead. His large framed house boasted two chimneys and numerous windows and contained a collection of copper and brass kettles, pewter dishes, teapots, rugs, and a large mirror. A sizable barn held a large grinding stone, nails, shovel and tongs, sleigh, a plow for farming, five steel traps, as well as lead balls and guns for hunting. His livestock included horses, hogs, and cattle. Although his home lacked the social amenities of Honyere's home, it served as a guesthouse for many who traveled to Kanowalohale (including Joseph Bloomfield, who stayed there while awaiting the 1776 conference at German Flats). Although Honyere and Skenandoah were the only men mentioned among the Oneida possessing wampum, Skenandoah's stewardship of specific wampum "given at Philadelphia (as) national property" spoke of his particular esteem as a warrior within the community.[39] His home indicated a blend of European and Oneida cultures; his colonial-style house, a landmark in the community, did not prevent his people from entrusting him with their nation's wampum, yet colonial travelers were comfortable staying in a house supplied with European items.

Odaghseghte was recognized both within and beyond the Oneida community for his knowledge of traditional ways and his desire to maintain neutrality. In contrast he had acquired a high profile prior to 1780, but as a sachem, not a warrior. His house was considered an unpretentious "Indian" log home, with no accumulation of European commodities.[40] His situation in 1780 was meager and could be an indication of the declining prestige of the sachems in comparison with that of the warriors.

Agwrongdongwas had become an influential leader within the community prior to the revolution and continued in that capacity until his death. His frame home was one of a warrior with little time available during this period to devote to maintaining a farm. Yet it was one of the few houses to contain some furnishings worthy of note, such as "sitting chairs" and pewter utensils. His barn was large but contained only a small collection of horses, hogs, a cow, and a sleigh. It is not known at what point he moved from Oquaga to Kanowalohale or whether he, like others, maintained homes in more than one community.[41] His status within his village was not a result of or exclusive to his role in the revolution itself.

Gaghsaweda, a Bear clan member named as one of the warrior leaders who had written to Guy Johnson in defense of Samuel Kirkland in 1775, also owned considerable wealth. His framed house boasted European candlesticks, brass fireplace accoutrements, and a kettle. He had no barn, but he owned numerous horses and cattle, trapping equipment, and a quantity of harvested corn. How he obtained the ornamental commodities is not known; and so is also the significance of his owning a "pleasure sleigh" (the only one mentioned in the community).[42] These items would have provided him with a profile that buttressed his future leadership among the Oneida, and this could support the hypothesis that material possessions contributed to rather than resulted from one's position of leadership.

European influence is clearly evident in the material possessions of the leaders at Kanowalohale in 1780. There was a growing tendency among them to construct buildings reflecting a European style. Of seventy-three structures at Kanowalohale in 1780, forty-four were simple homes built of poles and bark, seven were small log houses, and twenty-two were frame houses of a style common among the colonists, a style that became fashionable when Kirkland's church of similar construction was erected in 1773. However, Oneida interest in Kirkland's agricultural policy seemed to be minimal. The hoe was the most common horticultural implement, but the number of traps and guns, equaling the number of metal hoes, scythes, and spades could indicate that men continued to be engaged in hunting and trapping. When considering the high number of metal tools not necessarily associated with agriculture (axes, saws, augurs, chains, and nails) and presumably used by community males, it is possible that Oneida men were more occupied in building homes than they were in raising crops, although they had adopted the practice common among settlers of raising cows, hogs, sheep, and fowl. The prevalence of horses was striking. More than one-third of the Oneida owned over 120 horses in total and associated paraphernalia: harnesses, saddles, tack, and sleighs. Some horses could have been plow horses in place of oxen, but the saddles and tack indicate a predominant use of horses for personal travel, especially when considered in conjunction with the volume of hunting and trapping gear. Participation in the revolution would have encouraged the warriors to procure mounts.[43] The Oneida—when trying to appear of consequence in the eyes of neighboring colonial society—would also be conscious of the status symbol of owning a horse.

It was heartbreaking for the Oneida to leave the community and its council fire, at which they had decided to support the rebels and for which they had valiantly fought, seemingly in vain. Equally demoralizing was the number of Oneida who, following the example of Senghnagenrat, gave up the fight and sought refuge among the British at Fort Niagara. Among the leaders was the warrior Aksiaktatye who moved there with six family members. Three officers who had previously obtained commissions from the Patriots also joined the Loyalist cause—Christian Thonigwenghsohare, Totyaneahani, and Joseph Kanaghsatirhon.[44]

With Kanowalohale destroyed, the survivors sought refuge first at Fort Schuyler and later that winter in Schenectady.[45] The Oneida originally were lodged in the military barracks in Schenectady, but the lengthy amicable relationship between the Oneida and the soldiers quickly collapsed. Schuyler reported that "Disagreeable Controversys have frequently risen between the soldiery and the Indians. . . . One of the latter having lately been barbarously murdered and others Assaulted and dangerously wounded it became necessary to remove them to the neighboring woods."[46]

The dismal conditions and dire prognosis for the Oneida shivering on the outskirts of Schenectady that winter were movingly portrayed by the marquis de Chastellux, a French officer leading one of his nation's contingents assisting the Continental Army during the revolution. Chastellux reported that their village was an "assemblage of miserable huts" constructed like wartime barracks, each with a central pole and framework covered in bark. The floor was below ground level, with a fire burning in the center and with platforms covered in bark and furs that served as beds. They were supplied with rations of meat and flour to augment the cultivation of corn on the surrounding lands, and when possible they hunted for game whose skins were then frequently exchanged for rum. Chastellux estimated that four hundred Oneida lived in the village, but he considered their future to be bleak: "their cruelty seems . . . to render it impossible for the Americans to consent to have them longer for neighbours; and a necessary consequence of a peace, if favourable to the congress, will be their total destruction, or at least their exclusion from all the country this side of the lakes."[47] Well aware of the Oneida's condition, Schuyler had written Samuel Huntington, the president of the Continental Congress, that their hope of a better life in Schenectady—where hunting might be more plentiful—had evaporated, and that the lack of clothing and the prevalence of smallpox would lead them to "renounce an Alliance which has exposed them to such variety of Calamity, to form one with those who can amply supply every of their wants." Of the numerous Oneida who died as a result of the miserable conditions that winter, one was Lieutenant John Sagoharase of the Wolf clan.[48]

Through 1781 the Oneida continued to eke out an existence near Schenectady, taking part spasmodically in raids against Thayendanega's Indians but simultaneously planning a return to their homeland. Schuyler wrote Huntington that, as enemy Indians were still roaming Tryon County, this venture could potentially result in their being "driven to desperation by the hardships they endure and join the enemy . . . [so that] all beyond [Albany] will be one dreadful scene of Desolation and slaughter." That summer found forty-four Tuscarora and Caughnawauga visiting the congress in Philadelphia. Encouraged by Schuyler and led by Odaghseghte and Atayataghronghta, the delegation's appeal for greater supplies for their people during the coming winter was met with mere promises of "good consequences" once the Patriots won the war—with the Oneida's help, of course.[49]

Word reached the Oneida that October that the British had surrendered to Washington. Thayendanega was reluctant to concede defeat, even though the war was officially over. During the next two years he led numerous skirmishes in the upper New York area. With their villages ruined and the future bleak, however, the Oneida's will to fight had dissolved. In the spring of 1782 James Dean apologized to Schuyler for his inability to organize an Oneida scouting party—those summoned had either gone hunting in the woods or had declined, claiming a lack of suitable snowshoes. The malaise was intensified because of a growing hatred for their Oneida neighbors among the residents of Tryon County. In May 1782 an Oneida was suspected of killing some colonial settlers. Although he was proved to be innocent, Schuyler discovered that the former affection between Oneida and settlers had degenerated to such a degree that colonists were threatening to kill any Oneida on sight. He advised the colonists that any such unjust retaliation against the faithful Oneida could prove distressing, as it would provoke their allies to join the enemy forces and bring "more distress to the frontiers . . . , casting an odious imputation on our national faith."[50]

The rebel military campaign of February 1783, involving the Oneida, was the last campaign of the revolution on the New York frontier. Washington endorsed an attack against the British-held Fort Oswego on the southern shore of Lake Ontario, as a warning to Thayendanega and the British to halt all future incursions. The rebel forces were to be aided in this venture by three Oneida scouts, led by John Otaawighton, one of the four captains commissioned in 1779. Otaawighton repeatedly led the expedition in the wrong direction, however. The campaign resulted in failure. The rebel officer Captain Marinus Willett placed the Oneida captain under arrest, frustrated because of his originally having "as high an opinion of [Otaawighton's] knowledge as a guide as of his fidelity and integrity."[51] The morale of the Oneida in this final revolutionary activity reflects that of their life at Schenectady.

Throughout the revolutionary war, Kanowalohale's leaders and residents were living through both economic and political transition. The possessions of the only traditional league sachem, Odaghseghte, were meager. In contrast, warriors Honyere, Agwrongdongwas, Skenandoah, and Gaghsaweda appeared to enjoy considerable material wealth. The function of the warrior adapted to changing expectations—Honyere appeared strictly a fighter, Agwrongdongwas was also frequently a speaker, Skenandoah fulfilled additional roles of speaker and spy. No distinction in community support resulted from the fact that Agwrongdongwas and Skenandoah were Christians or that Gaghsaweda was a traditionalist. Odaghseghte was a sachem who served as speaker but was noticeably less affluent. Senghnagenrat, previously a sachem and speaker, functioned primarily as a spy during the revolution. The leaders represented all clans: Honyere, Agwrongdongwas, and Skenandoah belonged to the Wolf clan, Ojistalale was Turtle, and Gaghsaweda Bear. In general, Oneida Christian warrior-speaker members of the Wolf clan were more inclined to possess Western commodities. The few possessions held by the captains Honyost, Kakiktoton, and Sagoharase would indicate that recognition by and participation with the Continental Army contributed little to an Oneida's wealth. The sparse evidence of farm implements and produce among the residents and leaders of Kanowalohale indicate that Kirkland's agricultural incentives had taken root within the community but contributed little to economic prosperity. Taking Kanowalohale to be representative, the Oneida were a nation entertaining a growing acceptance of colonial values, led by an increasingly large body of Christian and traditional warrior-speakers whose accumulation of Western possessions surpassed that of the sachems and whose role within the community was at the forefront of a new, almost democratic, approach to Oneida leadership.

# CHAPTER SIX

# THE ONEIDA AS SURVIVORS, 1784–1800

When peace was negotiated between Britain and her newly independent American colonies, at the end of the war in 1783, those Iroquois who had remained loyal to Britain were angry at their betrayal by the British government—which simply ignored its Indian allies in the 1783 Articles of Peace. The Oneida, despite their allegiance to the now victorious Americans, fared no better. During the decade following the declaration of peace, Oneida warriors, sachems, and orators represented their nation—and also their erstwhile confederates, when asked to do so—in opposition to the Americans' insatiable desire for the Indians' land.

State authorities at Albany competed for predominance with congressional delegates from Philadelphia. While the white authorities were vying for the right to negotiate with the Indians, the Indians themselves were simultaneously vying for the right to represent their people in dealing with the whites. Each side was conscious of and willing to exploit the divisions within the other. In the 1790s, French representatives and Quaker missionaries added to what was already a tumultuous, explosive mix. The motives and actions of the Oneida's advocate Samuel Kirkland following his return to Kanowalohale in 1785 were questionable in the eyes of the Oneida. Their leaders had helped their people survive the revolution in ways they thought would stand the greatest chance of benefiting their nation. New leaders, both Christian and traditional, emerged to carry on the struggle, incorporating the new and the old in both leadership patterns and religion. Yet by 1800 most of the territory the Oneida had fought to retain for more than fifty years was no longer in their possession. For the reasons behind this tragedy one must look beyond the explanation that the Oneida were simply outnumbered and outwitted by the Americans. It is important to acknowledge the Oneida's unrelenting efforts to be proactive in their response to this struggle.

The 1783 Treaty of Paris left the status of the Iroquois unsettled, but the voices of the Oneida were muffled by the keen competition between the newly formed Continental Congress at Philadelphia and the state government at Albany vying for the right to negotiate with the defeated Iroquois. Congress saw an opportunity to acquire Iroquois lands, giving in return the right to live peacefully in the newly formed United States. In October 1783, members of congress received a report from the Committee on Indian Affairs stressing the "inseparable connection" between the Iroquois' desire to maintain their lands and the government's expectation of peace. Warning that removal of the Indians from their lands would drive them into the hands of the British, the committee recommended that "lines of property should be ascertained and established between the United States and them, which [would] be convenient to the respective tribes, and commensurate to the public wants." By "separating and dividing the settlements of the citizens from the Indian villages and hunting grounds," it was anticipated (as it had been for half a century) that "all occasion for future animosities, disquiet and contention" on the part of the Indians would be removed. In fact it was expected that those Iroquois who were hostile to America in the revolution would appreciate this opportunity to accept the proposed boundaries as reparation for the losses and damages incurred by them. However, the Oneida nation would be afforded special consideration by Congress in return for their loyalty in the revolution: they and the Tuscarora were to be reassured "of the friendship of the United States and that they may rely that the lands which they claim as their inheritance will be reserved for their sole use and benefit until they may think it for their own advantage to dispose of the same."[1]

In the spring of 1784 the congressional commissioners informed George Clinton, governor of the state of New York, of their intention to hold a conference in Oneida territory at Fort Stanwix (as it was called again after the revolution). Governor Clinton disapproved of Congress's decision. He responded that he had already taken the initiative to invite the Iroquois to a meeting, as they resided within his jurisdiction. Actually, he had already received letters from Thayendanega (Joseph Brant) expressing the Iroquois' desire to hold a conference at Fort Stanwix for their own convenience and their willingness to establish a peaceful relationship with all the American states. Anxious that the conference occur, Governor Clinton nevertheless warned the committee he would not allow Congress to enter any agreement with the Indians "residing within the Jurisdiction of this State prejudicial to its Right."[2] Clinton had the authority of the New York State Constitution to support his position. Article 37 of the constitution adopted in April 1777 stipulated that no land contracts made with the Indians within New

York State after 14 October 1775 would be considered valid "unless made under the authority and with the consent of the legislature of this state." New York State's position was expressed by its delegate to Congress, James Duane, who urged that Indian tribes be viewed as members of the state where they lived; otherwise they could be "considered [by Congress] as independent Nations, detached from the State, and absolutely unconnected with it, [making] the Claim of Congress inconvertible."[3]

The Oneida, during this period considered by the American authorities to be a defeated people, soon had reason to become suspicious of the state's motives. As early as March 1783, the New York Assembly instructed its Indian commissioners "to accomplish an exchange of the district claimed by the Oneidas and Tuscaroras for a district of vacant and unappropriated lands within this State" but without causing "Apprehension that there is the most remote intention to deprive them of the enjoyment of the district belonging to them." Should it become necessary to remove Indian nations from their territory within the state, a relocation of the Oneida and Tuscarora to the subsequently empty Seneca lands would provide a friendly buffer at the western extremity of the state. Shortly before the conference was to commence, however, the commander at Fort Stanwix, Jellis Fonda, wrote Governor Clinton that Samuel Kirkland had "put the Oneida Indians on their guard, not to exchange their lands with you or any other person for any other lands," and that Kirkland had sent word of his actions to Thayendanega.[4]

The Oneida were not present when Governor Clinton convened the conference on 1 September 1784, well in advance of the date the congressional representatives were expected. Clinton preferred to deal with the other Iroquois nations first. He expected the Oneida to be accompanied by Kirkland and was not happy that Kirkland's connection with the Continental Congress might influence the Oneida against him. The Oneida and Tuscarora, reportedly uneasy over the rumors that the state intended to deprive them of their lands, used a time-honored practice and delayed proceedings by their absence. Within a week, representatives of all Six Nations had assembled to hear Governor Clinton's opening address. Anxious to allay their fears over the rumors regarding the state's intention of taking Oneida land, Clinton stressed, "This is not true; you must not believe it. We have no Claim on your Lands."[5]

Instead, the Oneida were urged to delineate the boundaries of their territory in order to prevent further intrusions. The Oneida speakers (unfortunately not named by the conference secretaries) assured Clinton they would not listen to evil reports. They requested help in protecting their land against the plans of Colonel John Harper, who continued to attempt the purchase of Oneida land near Unadilla in the Susquehanna River area. They proceeded as requested to outline the western limit of their lands—roughly a strip from the Unadilla River westward to the Oswego River and extending from the Pennsylvania border northward to Lake Ontario. The conference was interrupted by an unidentified Oneida sachem who produced a letter sent by Samuel Kirkland and James Dean. This letter was from the congressional commissioners, requesting a meeting with the Six Nations, reminding them that a treaty with Governor Clinton had not been authorized by Congress, and instructing the Oneida and Tuscarora to be present at Fort Stanwix on 20 September 1784. Unable to convince the Iroquois not to meet with the U.S. commissioners, Clinton arranged for Major Peter Schuyler and an interpreter to remain at Fort Stanwix, "to observe the conduct of the commissioners, . . . attend the publick speeches and meetings," and if "any thing may Eventually prove Detrimental to the State . . . , to use [his] most undivided influence to Counteract and frustrate."[6]

Three days prior to the arrival of the American congressional commissioners, the trusted French friend and adoptee of the Oneida the marquis de Lafayette arrived at Fort Stanwix with his friend the marquis de Barbe-Marbois. In his journal of the conference, Barbe-Marbois recorded a visit to nearby Kanowalohale and conversations with Nicholas Jordan, an adopted Oneida sporting lead earrings and bone nose rings, his face painted with colored bands, who reflected the continuing French influence among the Oneida by his native eloquence in French. Jordan shared with Barbe-Marbois insights he had gained from living with the Oneida for many years. Barbe-Marbois noted that the Oneida, revealing their poverty in comparison with pre-revolutionary times, now traveled exclusively by foot, on trails created by the horses that had predominated prior to the revolution but which had not been replaced. While visiting with Jordan, Barbe-Marbois commented that "the furnishings of an ordinary cabin consist of a black earthenware pot, a mortar, pestle and two cooking pots."[7] Living conditions were noticeably sparser than those prior to the village's destruction in 1780.

Jordan's conversations with Barbe-Marbois indicated that the Oneida were well aware of developments occurring within the more distant reaches of their territory. They knew that six hundred Stockbridge Indians were in the process of taking up residence on six square miles of land they had given them, as were one hundred Narragansett from Rhode Island and a few of the Mohican and Niantic nations from New England who had also been invited by the Oneida to settle among them. Jordan's explanation reflected the pride of the Oneida in maintaining their own traditions: in contrast, those moving onto their land "all seem disposed to join the Oneidas since they cannot preserve their customs and usages amongst the civilized nations."[8]

In this way the Oneida continued to fulfill the traditional role of adopting outsiders, in this case welcoming a group migration that would not require the obliteration of their earlier identity. The removal of the Mohawk nation to Canada left the Oneida as the "eastern door" of Iroquoia, and the remaining confederates would understandably wish to augment their numbers, hoping to stem the westward flow of colonial settlers. Indians seeking a safe haven might have considered the Oneida the best choice, considering their role in the revolution, and especially if their land was presumed to be protected from American acquisition.

The Oneida's creativity in their encounter with European culture made an impression on Barbe-Marbois. From Jordan's cabin, he reflected that he was writing his journal using ink made "by pounding sassafras charcoal and moistening it with gum," on a tortoise shell made into a writing desk and with thin maple bark as paper. It was a second encounter, however, this time with "the venerable chief" Ojistalale, that enabled Barbe-Marbois to appreciate the Oneida's innovative spirit even further. Having met Barbe-Marbois previously at a meeting in Philadelphia, Ojistalale now cordially invited Barbe-Marbois to the Kanowalohale council house, where he found Ojistalale dressed in a Bavarian hunting costume, worn only on occasions of importance. The welcoming feast did not reflect the stated shortage of provisions in Iroquoia. It included freshly caught salmon, milk, butter, fruit, and honey "in abundance." However, contrary to traditional protocol, the visitors had to cook their own food and provide their own utensils, which they had brought in their luggage. Ojistalale, in response to the visitors' request, summoned the warriors to dance, "some dressed as warriors, others in clothes which they had received from the English, . . . [some] with suits . . . cut into two pieces and half put on their heads." With Ojistalale in his Bavarian outfit and the warriors in their finery accompanied by braided crests of feathers in their hair, paint on their faces, bells on their arms and feet, and colored cloths tied to their bodies, the scene was, according to Barbe-Marbois, "a thoroughly ridiculous variety of colours."[9]

In his role as sachem, Ojistalale invited Barbe-Marbois to witness an Oneida initiative for reconciliation with the Seneca. The estrangement between these two nations had deepened as a result of their divided loyalties during the revolution, and now both were camped near the fort at the request of the congressional commissioners. Neither group had made contact with the other. Ojistalale in his Bavarian garb, accompanied by Oneida chiefs in traditional finery, approached the Seneca cabins but sat at some distance, eventually conversing and smoking the calumet with the Seneca chiefs who came out to meet them. The following day the Seneca chiefs reciprocated. Barbe-Marbois's observations of this ceremony—together with the marriage rituals of the Oneida, their love of dance and song, and their precision in following the cultural details involved in war dances, in the selection of a new chief, or in burial rites—indicate that the residents at Kanowalohale were as determined to maintain their heritage as they were willing to accommodate European ways when necessary.[10]

Lafayette spoke to the assembled Indians, with Kirkland as interpreter, before the American congressional commissioners began official proceedings. He reminded the Oneida of his close relation with them during the revolution, and of the continuing good relationship between the French and the American governments. He urged the Oneida not to sell their lands for a supply of alcohol, or to "make use of the favorable dispositions which the Council of the Great Congress seem to manifest."[11] By meeting with the Oneida before they met with the commissioners, LaFayette had effectively stolen the show. The commissioners would have been relieved when Lafayette and his companions left shortly after his speech, especially after they witnessed the favor shown the French general by Iroquois chiefs in the speeches and presentation of wampum.

Discussions with the U.S. commissioners finally began in mid-October and lasted only a few days. This was providential, considering the acrimonious atmosphere between the U.S. agents and the representatives of the Mohawk, Onondaga, Cayuga, and Seneca nations. The terms of the treaty offered by the commissioners (and with which the Six Nations eventually agreed) were severe in their dealing with the four formerly hostile tribes. Hostages from among the Mohawk, Seneca, Cayuga, and Onondaga were to be detained until all colonial prisoners taken by them in the revolution were returned. A north–south boundary line drawn just east of Fort Niagara would be the western boundary of Iroquois lands, removing them from their territory to the east and opening it for American settlement. Supplies would be granted—as a sign of American "humane and liberal views" toward those who were previously their enemies—providing they exhibited due appreciation by behaving in a peaceful and cooperative manner with the American government.[12]

Speaking for the Iroquois who had sided with the British, Thayendanega's Mohawk friend Aaron Hill declared: "We are free, and independent, and at present under no influence. We have hitherto been bound by the Great King, but he having broken the chain, and left us to ourselves, we are again free and independent." The commissioners replied, "You are mistaken in supposing . . . you are become a free and independent nation, and may make what terms you please. It is not so. You are a subdued people; you have been overcome in a war which you entered into with us, not only without provocation but in violation of most sacred obligations." The attitude of the U.S. commissioners was long remembered by the Iroquois. They told a Quaker observer, James Emlen, at the 1794 treaty of Canandaigua that the commissioners "alledged that the Country was now all theirs and used such haughty and threatening Language, that they were intimidated to such a degree as to sign that which was contrary to their Judgement."[13]

Otyadonenghti and Dayaheari signed the treaty on behalf of the Oneida, the only reference to their nation being that they would be secure on their land.[14] Gone were the opening ceremonies and the mutual condolences that had marked colonial authorities' acceptance of native customs at previous conferences. Conversations between the Oneida leaders and the state commissioners soured the relationship between Albany and Philadelphia. The Oneida knew not to trust the promises made by either set of commissioners concerning the security of their lands, but still, the preferential treatment they received would have widened the separation between the Oneida and the other Iroquois nations, especially the Seneca. The Oneida became passive observers—at a conference in their own territory but at which they were not regarded as the hosts. They listened while the Mohawk, Seneca, Cayuga, and Onondaga nations were verbally chastised and humiliated by visiting governmental authorities who severely diminished these nations' land base.

A major adaptation in Oneida leadership was evident at this same conference. At least five of those present held the titles of founding sachems of the Iroquois League: Odaghseghte, Ataytonneatha, Ataghonghteayon, Shononghriyo, and Dyoghhagweate. A sixth was Alawistonis, listed as a warrior, a traditionalist Wolf clan member who was to become highly influential in the future.[15] It would appear that the Oneida had managed to maintain their core body of Iroquois League sachems through the revolutionary period, despite some historians' assumptions of their political disintegration. Their appearance at the Fort Stanwix conference indicates the importance the Oneida attached to the event—although their admittedly less vocal role shows their weakened and subservient position following the revolution.

Records taken at the Fort Stanwix conference show that the Oneida sachems and warriors not only cooperated when negotiating with the American authorities but also were willing to part with some of their land if it would preserve the remainder. Joining the twelve Oneida warriors present when the New York commissioners convened the meeting in early September were the leading sachems Ojistalale, a frequent speaker at previous conferences, and Odaghseghte. The same predominance of warriors over sachems is evident in Oneida's conversations with the congressional commissioners in October 1784. A letter dated 18 October from the Oneida to the congressional commissioners requesting the rebuilding of their church and the reinstatement of Kirkland as missionary, as well as a speech by Ojistalale on 20 October requesting payment to James Dean for his services as interpreter and then also congressional approval of two square miles given to him by the Oneida nation in appreciation of his friendship toward them, were signed by sachems Ojistalale and Oneyanha and by warriors Agwrongdongwas, Skenandoah, and Gaghsaweda. These same men (with the exception of Skenandoah) assisted in the distribution of gifts brought by the Pennsylvania commissioners.[16] They were joined in November 1784 by sachem Odaghseghte and warriors Thaghtaghgwesere and Aksiaktatye when confirmation of the grant of twenty-four square miles to John Harper, disputed since 1767 among the Oneida, was finally sent to the American commissioners. In the spring of 1785, the Oneida chief Ojistalale complained to the New York commissioners that Harper "by Misrepresentations and other unjust and unlawful Means obtained a Writing for a large Tract of Land in the neighbourhood of Onaquaga and extending on both Sides of the Susquehanna River." The New York commissioners assured the Oneida that Harper's purchase would be refused but warned them to be more cautious in the future and only conduct sales if done through the "good lawful Authority from the State."[17]

The Oneida's relationship with Kirkland became ever more uncertain as they witnessed his allegiance to the American Congress during the conference. He had been absent from their communities during the war, serving as chaplain to the Continental Army (as suggested by George Washington), and as a member of Sullivan's staff in the 1779 expedition. In 1784 he made three brief visits to Kanowalohale as requested by the residents. Listening to his grumbles about living "almost intirely on strawberries, with now and then a little fish" and that his "spirits began to lose some of their ardour for want of sustenance," the Oneida patiently suggested he return when their resources were greater.[18]

Kirkland's financial problems were becoming oppressive. He had lost his home at Kanowalohale when the village was burned. His employment with the SSPCK had terminated prior to the revolution, and his income as military chaplain ended at its conclusion. Hoping to convince the SSPCK board at Boston that his reinstatement as missionary at rebuilt Kanowalohale would be beneficial, he included a letter from some unidentified sachems urging that Kirkland continue as their missionary. The migration of other Indian nations into Oneida territory was seen by Kirkland as providing additional opportunity for evangelism.[19] It is questionable whether the Oneida shared Kirkland's vision of their nation as a beacon for Indians seeking the light of Christianity in the bleakness of postrevolutionary Iroquoia. In fact the Cayuga, Onondaga, and Delaware never did make the planned move to Oneida territory. Perhaps Nicholas Jordan's perception of the Oneida nation as enhancing its position as a haven for those following traditional ways was more valid, especially considering the Oneida's adoptive role within the Confederacy.

As the Oneida witnessed Kirkland observing in silence other attempts of Governor Clinton to wrest away more of their land, the rift widened between those of their nation who approved of relinquishing territory and those who did not. In May 1785 the New York State commissioners assured Governor Clinton that the Oneida were willing to sell land, since they had more than they needed, and that it would be appropriate to involve only the Oneida and Tuscarora since their lands alone were of immediate interest to the state. The Oneida were not so obliging, however. Ojistalale would not agree to the date or place as decided by the commissioners until the Oneida grievance over John Harper's method of obtaining Oneida land was rectified. The Oneida also shared Thayendanega's concerns. Not only should all Six Nations be involved in any land negotiations, but further land acquisition in the proposed area went against the agreement made at the recent Fort Stanwix conference.[20]

Contention between New York State and the Continental Congress resurfaced when Oneida leaders, becoming more vocal once more, met with state commissioners for discussions at Fort Herkimer on 25 June 1785. Governor Clinton mistakenly thought that, although the Oneida were angered by John Harper's attempt to obtain their land, they were willing to sell land if the transaction was conducted to their liking. Clinton posited that an area to the south near the Pennsylvania border should be easily obtained from the Oneida as it was close to white settlements, unsuitable for hunting, and of sufficient value to provide funds with which they could buy cattle and "Utensils of Husbandry."[21]

As the commissioners rose to leave, however, Agwrongdongwas, supported by Ojistalale, called them back. Reminding them of his imprisonment at Fort Niagara during the war and subsequent loss of land and home, and that the United States had promised the Oneida they could keep their remaining lands, he asked that the state help the Oneida to ensure that the American government honor its promises and that it pay for land sales conducted prior to the revolution and for which the Oneida had never received recompense. Explaining that land was important to the Oneida for more reasons than hunting, Agwrongdongwas continued that territorial issues were causing friction with both their Indian and their colonial neighbors. "We look to the Eastward. The Indians who lived there are now settled among us and We have been obliged to give them Lands. This will be our Case should we sell our Lands as they have done. While the Indians had all their Lands, they were important. . . . The German Flatts People, when they were poor, applied to Us for Lands and they were Friends, but now they are rich they do not treat Us kindly." Although they were reluctant to sell, Agwrongdongwas stated the Oneida would be willing to lease lands for farming near the boundary line established in 1768, in the hope of preventing future encroachment, maintaining ownership, and providing a needed source of revenue.[22]

Two days later a disgruntled Agwrongdongwas heard that Governor Clinton believed a rumor that he, as an Oneida leader, maintained affinity with the British. Agwrongdongwas bluntly informed the assembly that his loyalty to New York was well-known and that he would conduct no further business with the state until his reputation had been affirmed by the U.S. commissioners. At this point, the sachem Oneyanha led Oneida's negotiations. Speaking on behalf of the warriors, he offered to sell a section of land near the Unadilla River. Clinton replied that this was less than half of what was expected and not worth all the money available for the transaction. The following day Ojistalale capitulated and informed the commissioners that the Oneida would sell additional land amounting to almost the same as originally requested by the state. He feared that "this News about selling our Lands will make a great Noise in the Six Nations" and hoped that "we shall never be applied to any more for any of our Country." Among the eight signatories were sachems Ojistalale and Oneyanha, accompanied by warriors Agwrongdongwas, Skenandoah, Captain Cornelius Okonyota, and Gaghsaweda, with Kirkland as witness.[23] Not only did Oneida sachems and warriors cooperate in this arrangement but signatories were identified by clan membership, which indicates their determination to be seen as representing their community in ways reflecting their traditional method of conducting business.

Despite internal disagreements over the disposal of their land, the Oneida managed to maintain a position of leadership within the Six Nations, admittedly by favoring the authority of Congress over that of the state. In the autumn of 1785 Thayendanega was organizing a meeting at Fort Niagara in order to maintain good relations among the Iroquois, Shawnee, and Cherokee. He sent a letter to Congress inviting their commissioners to attend and guaranteeing their safety, suggesting their reply be conveyed through the Oneida nation. Oneyanha, Skenandoah, Agwrongdongwas, and Gaghsaweda also wrote to Congress urging its compliance with the wishes of Oneida's "brothers of the Six Nations." James Dean had written to Congress earlier that summer, confirming a decision the Onondaga had made in 1778: the Onondaga had "recognized the Oneida tribe as head of the six late confederated nations, and submitted to their direction. The Oneidas esteem this so auspicious an event that they have desired me to communicate this to Congress."[24]

This recognition made by the Elder Brother Onondaga confirmed Oneida primacy to a greater degree than a similar statement made by the Cayuga (as between Younger Brothers) prior to the revolution. Dean stressed to Congress that Thayendanega and his Iroquois allies "have requested the Oneida to assert their influence to procure the interview proposed." Kirkland provided Congress with a letter from the Cayuga; they also now recognized the Oneida as "the acknowledged friends of Congress and the appointed medium of conveyance from us of the Six Nations to Congress." Included by Kirkland was another letter from Agwrongdongwas, Skenandoah, and Gaghsaweda, asking that Congress honor the request of the Cayuga. Kirkland had also interpreted a letter from Thayendanega written to Skenandoah in August 1785 encouraging that chief to use "his utmost influence" to ensure that Congress listened to the wishes of the Six Nations.[25] Although Congress did not respond enthusiastically to these suggestions, they could not ignore the prestige extended to the Oneida by other Indian nations.

While the Oneida were solidifying their leadership role once again among the tattered remains of the Confederacy, Christianity was reportedly benefiting that nation. Kirkland wrote to the SSPCK board stressing the tremendous outpouring of support he received in the autumn of 1785 as "several hundreds, with many foreign Indians," thronged to his lengthy outdoor services at Kanowalohale where he was assisted by the preaching of Agwrongdongwas. He noted that the attendance at worship noticeably increased when Agwrongdongwas entered the meeting, admitting he "received considerable assistance" when the Oneida leader answered questions posed by "a number of their young men of the first abilities and influence in the nation." Part of his message was recorded by Kirkland and shows a masterful blend of Christian and traditional elements. Agwrongdongwas's exhortation "O Sinners, look on the word of Jesus that is a glass in which you may see that which you are" would have resonated with those hearers familiar with the traditional teachings of the Great Law of the Iroquois League regarding the prophet Deganawidah. In his effort to convert the hunter Hiawatha from his cannibal ways, for example, Deganawidah climbed on the hunter's cabin roof and looked down the smoke hole while Hiawatha was preparing a stew. Hiawatha saw the reflection of the prophet's face in the surface of the cook pot, and thinking that his face had become that of a wise god he was transformed. As Hiawatha resolved to abandon his evil ways and devote his time in promoting peace, Deganawidah later taught him the rituals necessary to establish peaceful interpersonal relations.[26] Kirkland did not indicate this connection with Oneida heritage as a possible source of Agwrongdongwas's effectiveness; it might have dimmed the brightness of his own ability to convert the Oneida.

Although some traditional Oneida were showing an interest in Christian teachings, Kirkland noted an increase in opposition by what he called the pagan party. At a service on New Year's Day 1787, some Oneida at Kanowalohale opposed to Kirkland's ministry disrupted the worship by firing guns in the air, berating those listening to Kirkland, and shouting that the ancient customs were "the true religion of the Indians." They tried to initiate a traditional dance and feast, but when few of Kirkland's followers showed any interest, they resorted to insulting him. Later that evening they broke into Kirkland's house with the intention of seizing him, but he had been forewarned and escaped by hiding in the shed of a Christian Oneida.[27] Later that year, a bad harvest brought hardship to the Oneida and contributed to their seeking an explanation, using what Kirkland considered to be "their ancient superstition respecting the power of witchcraft [that] had revived among them and prevailed to a great degree." An elderly Oneida matron had returned from Seneca country, where she had reputedly caused many deaths by her magic. She had been welcomed by numerous families at Kanowalohale and was seen among them in the form of an owl or a fox. By December 1787 Kirkland regretted that "the profligate and pagan party [had] gained great strength." Even Agwrongdongwas admitted to the dilemma caused by the possibility that his method of promoting Christianity might have resulted in "so many of the Oneidas [having] turned back to their old ways."[28]

Disruptions within Oneida society were matched by external forces over which they had no control. These included the illegal land companies formed by individuals of wealth and prestige, who would negotiate independently with the Indians and increase their profits through speculative sales. The New York Genesee Land Company was one such group. Organized in the autumn of 1787, its membership included lawyers, doctors, former state Indian commissioners, landed gentry, and federalists whose politics prevented them from benefiting from state land policies. Included in the ranks of these swindlers were Oneida friend and interpreter-turned-lawyer James Dean and Major Peter Schuyler, brother of Philip Schuyler who had befriended the Oneida during the revolution. Leasing rather than buying land, so as to convince the Indians that they continued to own it, and promising chiefs annual payments, Peter Schuyler negotiated two leases: one with the Six Nations in November 1787 and the other with the Oneida the following January. The first lease permitted the Genesee Land Company to use all the land owned by the Oneida west of the 1768 boundary line, except the land retained for the chiefs and their heirs; in return the Oneida would receive annual payments of between $1,000 and $2,000 for 999 years. The second lease surrendered another large tract, one not previously involved in the Fort Herkimer treaty, for a graduated annual income for 999 years and with the company sharing any mining profits with the Oneida. Among the nineteen who signed for the Oneida were the warriors Aksiaktatye, Gaghsaweda, Skenandoah, and Agwrongdongwas. James Dean and Samuel Kirkland also signed. Not long afterward, the names of three Oneida representatives appeared with sixty-three other Iroquois in another massive land deal, in which two Massachusetts speculators, Oliver Phelps and Nathaniel Gorham, purchased nearly three million acres of Iroquois land in Seneca territory of western New York.[29]

Why were so many Oneida willing to sign away the rights to their land at a time when it seemed crucial they retain those rights? It seems the Oneida accepted the concept of leasing land as a means of retaining ownership while simultaneously receiving an ongoing income. Leasing must have seemed a viable means of support, as they returned to their territory ravaged by the revolution, and at a time when their own depleted numbers were about to be swamped by crowds of Americans following hot on their heels and with money in their pockets. Philip Schuyler had earned the trust of the Oneida during and after the revolution, especially by advocating on their behalf with Congress during the lean years of the early 1780s. Dealing with the land companies gave the Oneida a sense of independence denied them by the state and congressional authorities, yet it also augmented already existing divided loyalties within their nation. Four Oneida signed a letter to the New York legislature berating the state authorities both for the contempt with which they treated the Oneida's offer to lease rather than sell Oneida lands and for the right they still claimed to dispose of lands they knew belonged to the Oneida nation. "We are your Allies, we are a free People. . . . We wish that our Children and Grandchildren may derive a comfortable Living from the Lands which the Great Spirit has given us and our Forefathers."[30]

The economic hardships faced by the Oneida were aggravated by the harsh winter of 1787–1788, unfavorable summer weather, and a poor harvest. These all placed them in a compromised position when balancing their need for food and supplies with the abundance available from the governor of New York, who wanted another conference with them at Fort Stanwix in the summer of 1788. Governor Clinton was determined to block further actions by the land companies in order to keep any income from land deals within state coffers. Oneida leaders Atayataghronghta, Skenandoah, Agwrongdongwas, Captain David, Alawistonis, and Kayentarongwea agreed to this meeting. Later that spring, however, some Oneida were influenced by the largesse offered by the New York Genesee Land Company and supported company opposition to further state involvement in Oneida land. Commissioner John Tayler countered by sending cash, supplies, and a boatload of corn to the Oneida, in addition to a cash reward to Atayataghronghta if he could encourage the Seneca to attend the conference, which would thwart the company's continuous efforts to prevent as many Iroquois as possible from traveling to Fort Stanwix. Having received word from the Oneida that they were not keen to attend the conference, Tayler advised Governor Clinton to postpone the meeting until September and to reduce the amount of food and supplies made available in the interim, positing that when the supplies were "exhausted [the Indians] will be more anxious to meet the Governor than they appear to be at present."[31]

A few weeks prior to the conference the land company convinced a number of Oneida to meet at Lake Oneida. With the help of Peter Schuyler, a leading member, the company advised the Oneida to disregard any attempts by state delegates to buy or lease their land. The Oneida, however, declared their loyalty to the state, told the company to stay out of Oneida affairs, and refused to accept the gifts offered as a bribe. Their loyalty came at a price. As Tayler predicted, before summer's end, the Oneida were in need of state assistance. Agwrongdongwas, Atayataghronghta, and Skenandoah wrote to Governor Clinton: "We request you to assist us if you can with two Batteaux Loads of Corn, if not, when you come up you will find some of us dead from Hunger, for the young Men cannot hunt because we constantly retain them for the Council, and Indian Corn boiled in Water is poor Stuff."[32]

When the Fort Stanwix conference of 1788 opened, the Oneida delegates already knew, having been informed by Atayataghronghta, that Governor Clinton had obtained a major portion of Onondaga territory and had reiterated to all present the invalidity of company leases. Reminding Clinton that the Oneida were "accustomed to speak decidedly and after due Deliberation," Oneyanha requested that previous private discussions with Ojistalale, Gaghsaweda, and Shononghriyo be repeated so "that all may hear in full Council." Agwrongdongwas chastised Clinton because anything "transacted secretly has a bad Appearance" and put in jeopardy the state's declared position of not taking any more Oneida land. Although the Onondaga had chosen one person to be their main negotiator, Agwrongdongwas asked that the Oneida custom of having two persons be respected. Their resultant choice of Atayataghronghta and Peter Otisquette was not haphazard. Clinton, remembering the connection between the French and American governments, recognized the Oneida's astute maneuver in selecting two speakers familiar with the French—especially Otisquette who as a young adventurer from France had served with the Oneida's friend Lafayette and married an Oneida woman. In one stroke the Oneida aligned themselves with the federal commissioners, who themselves would remember the assistance of the French in the revolution and would provide assistance to the Oneida against the territorial aspirations of New York state, should that become expedient.[33]

The New York governor continued his protestations that he wanted merely to protect Oneida lands against unscrupulous Americans, but this did not alleviate Agwrongdongwas's growing sense of despair: "The whole Blame of being deceived on the present occasion ought not to lay upon us. . . . You may think your Brother the Oneida has no Considerations, but it will take me a long Time to tell you all my Thoughts and Contemplations. . . . Our Powers are nominal; it is utterly vain to say these are the Chiefs. We Chiefs are trodden down and little ones rise above us." Atayataghronghta then vehemently reminded Clinton that he had supported him by fighting in the Continental Army and that he expected the governor's assistance with regard to securing Oneida lands. Pleading his youthfulness to excuse himself, Peter Otisquette's comparison between the social opportunities he witnessed in France and the poor conditions of his people at home implied clearly that, if the state government at Albany would not assist the Oneida, then the American Congress would.[34]

The final outcome of the treaty did not favor the Oneida, despite the assistance given Atayataghronghta and Peter Otisquette by a group of chiefs and warriors including Odaghseghte, Gaghsaweda, and Shononghriyo. State commissioners managed to convince the Oneida that the New York Genesee Land Company had obtained all their land. Without telling them the state had repudiated those arrangements, Clinton convinced them of the state's beneficence in returning their lands to them. Nearly all of Oneida territory was ceded to New York State for a payment of $15,000. A fraction of the original five million acres was reserved for the Oneida and their offspring, and a recommendation was made that an additional two square miles be granted to Kirkland's sons. The elimination of the Oneida as a force worth consideration in the eyes of the Americans was complete. It was exemplified by the fact that all future negotiations between the Oneida and New York were henceforth conducted near Albany. The days were gone when state representatives felt it necessary to travel to Oneida territory bearing gifts. The importance of Oneida interest and involvement in the negotiations, however, was indicated by the numerous warriors, sachems, and leading women who attended the conference and signed the treaty.[35]

The names of numerous Oneida delegates, frequently recorded in correspondence and documentation, continued to appear as their nation was engaged in a series of meetings with the representatives of New York State, Congress, and those Iroquois nations whose lands were eyed with envy by both levels of American governance. For example, when the state commissioners conferred with the Cayuga in the spring of 1789, that nation requested help from the Oneida. The eloquent attempts of Atayataghronghta and Agwrongdongwas to discourage the commissioners had no effect, and with Oneyanha, Skenandoah, and Kakiktoton they signed the final deed and witnessed the Cayuga lose their land, just as the Onondaga and the Oneida had done before them.[36]

Similarly, Oneida signatories who frequently supported their people's claims did so in response to complaints regarding the failure of state authorities to alleviate the shortage of food, to remedy incorrect surveying of Oneida land near Oquaga, and to supply the Oneida warriors with necessary supplies. In the spring of 1790, Skenandoah, Alawistonis, Agwrongdongwas, Oneyanha, and Gaghsaweda wrote to Clinton: "Instead of leasing our Country to you for a respectable Rent, we find we have ceded and granted it forever. . . . We find our Reserve much smaller than we expected, as your Surveyors by beginning at the wrong Place . . . have run the East and West Line almost by our Doors. . . . We are free People; you have ever acknowledged it. We choose to regulate our Affairs and to conduct our Concerns by the Rules and Maxims of our Ancestors, without being governed by the Laws of our Brothers, the white People."[37]

These Oneida who were involved in negotiations were also chosen to administer the annual lease payments from the state; in the summer of 1790, Alawistonis, Gaghsaweda, and Aksiaktatye were among the seven delegates who attended John Tayler's arrival at Kanowalohale. He came bearing $600 for the Oneida nation. At the same time, the Cayuga and Onondaga nations, involved in a dispute with the state over their land arrangements, again requested the help of the Oneida in mediating for them. Peter Otisquette supported their demand that the state commissioners travel to Cayuga territory to discuss the issue, but he eventually convinced the Cayuga to meet himself and other Oneida at Fort Stanwix and to travel to New York in the company of warriors from Onondaga. Agwrongdongwas and Oneyanha were the spokesmen when the party reached New York. Governor Clinton's promise to ensure protection of the reserved portion of Indian land was signed by Oneida representatives Oneyanha, Alawistonis, and Honyere, with Samuel Kirkland and Peter Otisquette among the witnesses.[38]

In July 1790 Congress passed the Indian Trade and Intercourse Act, enforcing the constitutional right of the federal government to control all trade and land negotiations with the Indians, trying to put an end to the conflict, unresolved since the transfer of governance from London to Philadelphia, as to whether the state, Congress, or upstart land companies had authority to deal with the Indians. New York continued to ignore this directive and in the spring of 1793 signed two agreements with numerous Oneida in contravention of the congressional decision. The New York state congress accepted a petition to lease land to Peter Smith, a leading New York businessman and took control of all land, both leased and reserved, belonging to the Oneida, Onondaga, and Cayuga nations, by placing management of the land in the hands of agents selected by the state. Whether the Oneida were aware of the dispute between state and federal authority is not known.[39]

In the early 1790s Congress took action to prevent what its members understood to be the devious and illegal maneuvers of New York State to control Indian land within its territory. To this end George Washington was well served by Timothy Pickering, whom he had appointed an Indian commissioner in September 1790 and who met with the Seneca at Newtown Point in Seneca territory in the summer of 1791. Here Pickering encountered the forthrightness of Agwrongdongwas who, with Oneyanha and over one hundred Oneida, attended the conference. In his lengthy speeches, Agwrongdongwas berated Pickering about the shortage of provisions at the conference and the failure of Congress to keep its promise to protect Indian land. "When we fought, nation against nation, we did not fight for land, we fought for bodies. . . . The [white man] fights for land. . . . [You] who conquer keep the land [you] go over. After we have done fighting, we do not think we have the lands in our grasp." Pickering was able to conclude the conference amicably by inviting the Oneida to choose six representatives to visit General Washington in Philadelphia. But once at Philadelphia in March 1792, Agwrongdongwas lamented: "We Indians are unwise and our want of wisdom is owing to our want of knowledge of the ways of white people. White people say to us 'This measure will be for your good' and we have always been accustomed to obey this voice without inquiry into it as we thought our white brothers meant good to us, and hence we have been deceived in respect to our lands." This was Agwrongdongwas's last appearance as spokesman for his people; he died late in the summer of 1792.[40]

The Christian sachem Onondiyo assumed the role of spokesman for the Oneida at a major conference requested by the federal government at Canandaigua in the autumn of 1794. The Oneida delegation was one of the first to arrive. Despite his people's divided opinions regarding their land, Onondiyo defended their "rules of conduct" with which they maintained their national identity and that were to "be handed down that they might be preserved and practiced by [their] children." He admitted the Oneida had behaved "foolishly": the late Agwrongdongwas and the sachems favored leasing the land to provide the nation with an annual income; the warriors were angry with the sachems since the leases meant that the land was not available to the Oneida; yet both recognized the necessity of living in friendship with their white brothers. Pickering reciprocated by suggesting a formula by which two-thirds of the sachems, two-thirds of the warriors, and two-thirds of other recognized leaders would agree on a land transaction before informing the congressional authorities and receiving a fair price for use of the land. Onondiyo welcomed this effort to unify the Oneida, thereby gaining an advantage over his main rival, the chief warrior Sategaleahtas who headed the traditionalist group at Kanowalohale: "All nations have a head, or officers, to manage their business. The Indians have theirs. Among us, the affairs of peace are conducted by the sachems and councillors. But to speak in plain truth, our head warrior wants to interfer and control them. . . . The restoration of our lands would restore peace to our nation. The want of harmony among ourselves afflicts us more than the loss of our lands." In the wording of the final treaty, Congress abandoned its authoritative position as used at Fort Stanwix in 1784. Pickering now brokered a pragmatic solution to the land issues by confirming the lands reserved to the Oneida, Onondaga, and Cayuga by the treaties with New York State, and by accepting the promise of the Oneida, Cayuga, Onondaga, and Seneca to make no further claims for land within the United States.[41]

Onondiyo's comment concerning the Oneida's "want of harmony" from political rivalries reflected only the tip of the proverbial iceberg on which their nation was floundering. Kirkland's efforts to establish Protestant Christianity on a permanent basis were proving problematic. Even Agwrongdongwas, who served as a Christian leader and political apologist for his people, admitted moments of weakness. In 1791 in a lengthy discussion with Kirkland regarding the propensity of the pagan party to disturb the peace with their "frequent night revels and free use of intoxicating draught," Agwrongdongwas stressed the need that "every friend to religion and lover of order and peace" should support the control of alcohol sales. He knew many of the pagan party would support this view as they were less antagonistic to the Christians, "nor did they appear to be sticklers for the ancient religious rites," when the Catholic priest and traders were in the community. Agwrongdongwas understood this ambivalence as he himself admitted he was attracted to the liturgy of the Catholic priest, though he quickly renounced Catholicism and "redoubled his zeal for the protestant cause." Hanwaleao, one of Kirkland's first converts, fell away from attending worship after the revolution and, without entirely rejecting Christianity, tended to return to the tradition of his ancestors. Another Oneida "appeared to have a partial belief in the Roman Catholic tenets and an equal regard for most of the doctrine of protestantism and presbyterianism and still retained some of the traditions of the fathers." Prior to his death this man admitted to another Oneida that, unlike the ceremonies taught to him in his traditional customs, he had learned nothing in Christianity to prepare him for what to say when he actually met Jesus. Toward the end of his ministry, in 1800, Kirkland was resigned to the inevitability that "some doctrine of revealed religion [would] be intermingled with [the Indians'] ancient superstition."[42]

Kirkland's presence among the Oneida during the 1790s exacerbated the tensions within Kanowalohale. His emphasis on agriculture as a means of economic stability met with limited success because of the antagonism on the part of some and apathy on the part of others, aggravated by the particularly harsh winter and dry summer in 1789. Frequent discussions in 1792 with Agwrongdongwas, Skenandoah, and Oneyanha regarding the high degree of violence in Kanowalohale resulted in a scheme initiated by Kirkland in which the community would be divided: those adverse to Christianity and the sale of land would live at Oriska; Kanowalohale would remain the Oneida's central community where husbandry would be promoted, alcohol forbidden, and land reserved for the Christian Oneida would be organized and rented to outsiders. After lengthy debate the Kanowalohale council rejected this plan, which prompted Skenandoah to consider creating a new community for those wishing to live in peace and sobriety and supporting husbandry and true religion. Skenandoah abandoned this plan also, as he found numerous Oneida objected to a scheme that promoted a lifestyle similar to that of the white people, resulting in a town where there would be "no trait of the genuine Indian."[43]

The Oneida experienced mixed emotions as they watched Kirkland's interest in his mission at Kanowalohale change into enthusiasm for establishing a new educational institution in their territory. In 1793 Kirkland received the support of a dozen leading Oneida sachems and warriors including Skenandoah, Gaghsaweda, and Aksiaktatye, who wrote to the SSPCK requesting its support for the establishment of what would be known as the Hamilton Academy. Yet within a few months, Pickering received a letter from many of the same Oneida sachems and warriors asking that Kirkland be replaced. They complained about his frequent absences during the revolution, his constant grumbles about being short of money and provisions, his appearance at the state and federal treaties at which the Oneida were losing access to their land, and his rushed attitude when among the Oneida. Sachem Onondiyo's role in Kirkland's scheme may have also troubled the Oneida. On the one hand, he was the leading spokesman for their nation at the Canandaigua conference in autumn of 1794, publicly admitting that the Oneida were weakened by the dissensions within their community. Yet two years earlier he had fully supported Kirkland and the Christian Indians by traveling with his mentor to Dartmouth where he greatly impressed the college's board.[44] Onondiyo's leading role as Kirkland's protégé at Canandaigua and Dartmouth would not have sat well with those Oneida who were adverse to Kirkland's influence in the community.

The occasional optimistic accounts of Oneida country recorded by those who visited that area in the 1780s and 1790s were outweighed by the negative factors they encountered. An Italian who visited Oneida in the autumn of 1790, Paolo Andreani, was struck by the negative attitude of the pagans in Kanowalohale. Although comprising only one-ninth of the population, they openly ridiculed those who attended Christian services with "scrupulous attention." The fine quality of singing as well as the leadership of Agwrongdongwas and Peter Otisquette were noted by John Linklaen, when he traveled through Kanowalohale in 1791 as agent for the Holland Land Company. Linklaen also noted, however, that Kirkland's labors of twenty-six years were showing only faint signs of success in civilizing those at Kanowalohale, because of their distaste for farming; the Oneida at Oriska were led by recalcitrant chiefs, possessed no laws, and were unruly to the point that Americans were forbidden to make contracts with them. A visit to Iroquois territory made by a Moravian missionary in the summer of 1793 resulted in the observation that Oneida fared better when allowed to follow a traditional lifestyle.[45]

The most negative appraisal of the Oneida's situation toward the end of the nineteenth century resulted from the 1796 tour of the reverend doctors Jeremy Belknap and Jedidiah Morse, who were sent by the SSPCK Boston board to evaluate the success of Kirkland's mission at Kanowalohale. Their verdict was damning. They found a community torn asunder by conflict instigated by a small but powerful pagan group led by Sategaleahtas, the son of Christian sachem Agwrongdongwas. Only one Oneida, Skenandoah, was consistently sober, but his advanced age precluded any influence he might have. Violence and murders were commonplace, clothing habits were primitive, whites living in their community were of poor moral character, alcohol abuse was rampant, and the chiefs had little authority. Husbandry was disdained by Oneida men and was the source of discord with the nearby New Stockbridge and Brothertown communities as the Oneida looked down on these Indians' success in agricultural pursuits. White education of the Indians had failed: a school graduate was "neither a white man nor an Indian; as he has no character with us, he has none with them." Oneida youth had no wars to fight; their dislike for farming would result in their moving away or living at the expense of the government.[46] In short, in the reverend doctors' evaluation, Kirkland's mission was a failure.

Within months of the reverend doctors' visit to Kanowalohale, the Quakers arrived. Their nonpolitical, proeconomic development and self-sufficiency policies had been considered beneficial influences when Congress approved of their sending a circular letter offering assistance to Indian communities. The Oneida, subscribing to the Quaker premise of "not meddling with the affairs of government but doing all [they] can to preserve and promote peace and good will among all men," were the first to respond. During the three years that the Society of Friends stayed at Kanowalohale, they constructed a model farm in an attempt to familiarize and popularize the concept of farming among the men. They taught the use of the sawmill and hired Indian laborers. Oneida women were encouraged to learn domestic skills such as knitting, sewing, and reading. Opposition to their efforts to divide the land among individual Oneida, while claiming this move would solidify the community, led to their eventual departure from Kanowalohale by 1800, leaving all the implements and produce from the farm to the community as a whole to prove their intention of promoting community solidarity.[47]

Whether by coincidence or design, the two primary divisive factions within Kanowalohale resided in the east end of the village—the Quakers and the traditionalists. It was in this section that those opposed to Christianity performed a ritual, after its absence of over thirty years, known as the White Dog sacrifice. In the autumn of 1798, a Mohawk youth from the Grand River community in Canada had a lengthy vision in which a deity, The Upholder of the Heavens, explained that the problems experienced by the Iroquois were caused by their neglect of traditional ceremonies. Sickness, epidemics, losses in war, failed harvests, and severe weather would no longer plague the Six Nations if they returned to the ways of their ancestors. When the ceremony was enthusiastically received in Canada, Alawistonis and Sategaleahtas, both of Oneida, heard of its success and performed the rite in their home community in the summer of 1799. On this occasion, a former Christian named Thauneyendaugauyoon attended, partly from self-confessed curiosity and partly because he felt he should support those among whom he lived at the east end of the village. At this point it was estimated that one-sixth of Kanowalohale attended the ceremony, comprised of "those who professed no other religion than paganism." When the rite was held there again, in May 1800, the response was far greater. Those attending witnessed a white dog suspended from a pole, strangled, its head painted red and its neck adorned with wampum. After it was cooked, a leader offered prayers to The Upholder of the Heavens asking for a good harvest, freedom from storm, success in hunting, and success for the warriors should war arise. Participants ate a small piece of the cooked animal, pledged loyalty to the deity, and joined in a ten-day feast followed by social dancing. Although the consumption of alcohol was strictly forbidden during the ceremony and associated festivities, it was not until the observance in 1800 that this requirement was achieved.[48]

Traveling through a village on the outskirts of Kanowalohale in the summer of 1796, Belknap and Morse had passed the house of Skenandoah's contemporary Alawistonis, the leader of the traditional group among the Oneida. Near his door stood, as they recorded, "the famous stone which gives the nation the name of Oneida, the 'upright stone.'"[49] Their interest in the symbolic stone at Alawistonis's home was insightful. For a generation the Oneida had placed their destiny in the hands of a growing number of traditional and Christian leaders, who were willing to cooperate with each other and to negotiate with the non-Indian governments in the effort to preserve their ancestral lands. League sachems attended colonial conferences in place of the Onondaga Grand Council fire, which had been extinguished. The community still created leaders to replace those who died. In the tradition of the Pine Tree chiefs, Oneida speakers continued to advocate for their people despite the fact that their negotiations failed to produce the expected results. Accommodation within the leadership continued as warriors served as orators during the period of peace. An increasing number of Oneida members signed their names to documents and treaties, trying to ingratiate themselves with state and congressional authorities by imitating colonial custom. With the exception of the Mohawk (whose numbers in New York were severely depleted), the Iroquois sought the leadership of the Oneida as the pivotal group within the Confederacy.

But by the turn of the century the head warrior Agwrongdongwas and sachems Ojistalale and Oneyanha had died. Skenandoah's advanced age prevented him from performing more than ceremonial functions within his community. The Oneida had placed their hopes for the future in the Christian speakers Agwrongdongwas and Skenandoah who had risen to prominence before the revolution; this trust was maintained despite these leaders' failure to protect the nation's interests in the aftermath. Oneida willingness to compromise by signing leases, petitions, and letters, and to do so with increasing numbers of community members, had not achieved the results they desired. Oneida confidence in white Christian ways had not worked. This failure, however, was not indicative of a collapse in Oneida leadership. Traditionalists would now lead the Oneida. The crises wrought by the revolution and the subsequent loss of Oneida territory provided incentive for Alawistonis and Sategaleahtas to restore traditional practices and prove the validity of their position.

# ONEIDA LEADERSHIP MAINTAINED, 1750–1800

Images of Oneida involvement in the revolution have become part of their heritage. The story of Polly Cooper, an Oneida lady unknown other than for her bravery during the war, has become entrenched within her nation's oral tradition. Employed by George Washington at his encampment at Valley Forge during the revolution, it is said, Cooper with the assistance of the Oneida chief Skenandoah arranged for the delivery of bushels of corn to stave off starvation among the troops. She refused Washington's offer of remuneration in appreciation of her showing the soldiers how to cook the corn properly, affirming that it was her duty to serve her country. Determined to show his gratitude, the general arranged for his wife, Martha, to accompany Cooper to Philadelphia where a shawl, a hat, and a bonnet were purchased and presented to the Oneida matron. Similarly, the fame of a leading Oneida warrior, Honyere, was based on his bravery during the battle at Oriskany in 1777. Those claiming direct descendance from Honyere also honor his wife, Tyonajanegen: she reputedly picked up and returned Washington's sword after he had thrown it down in disgust when surrender seemed inevitable; then she stole a pony and rode forty miles to obtain reinforcements to assist him.[1]

One cannot denigrate the value of such vignettes as they take the place of many political and cultural aspects of Oneida heritage that had changed or been lost since the 1750s. By the end of the century, the earlier respect afforded Oneida rituals when conducting treaty negotiations was a thing of the past. There was no further mention of the Oneida as the People of the Fallen Log, and the Standing Stone erected in front of Alawistonis's house would now be their permanent totem, both factually and symbolically.

Their geographic prominence was of little value now that the American state and federal governments had all but liquidated their title to any land, and the Carrying Place by which the Oneida had previously held sway over much of the economic life stream between the Hudson River and Lake Ontario was no longer in their possession. The towns of Kanowalohale and Oquaga were but shadows of their former selves. With these towns and other communities in shambles and the residents dispersed, the lessons of the Great Law and the Creation Epic were no longer the heartbeat of the communities. With the Mohawk scattered, the Onondaga no longer needed as the custodians of the Grand Council fire, and the Seneca pulled into greater involvement in affairs to the west, the Confederacy was in danger of disintegration. The importance of one's clan membership and identity as sachem, warrior, or speaker had fallen into disuse after a brief resurgence as the Oneida attempted to assert their importance in negotiations with the fledgling American governments. Even the Oneida's pivotal role in the Confederacy as the adoptive female member was eclipsed by the sheer need to survive as a separate Iroquois nation, desperate for recognition as such by the overwhelming demands of the new American nation.[2]

This study of Oneida leaders during the second half of the eighteenth century is intended to provide an additional historical foundation from which to evaluate their nation's place in American and Iroquoian history. Many issues confronted by the Oneida remained constant throughout the period and seemed to militate against their survival as a people. Among these issues was the failure of colonial authorities to honor agreements to protect Iroquois lands, to prevent the excessive flow of alcohol, and to provide adequate defenses against their Indian and white adversaries. There was tension arising from competing loyalties within the Six Nations themselves and frustration resulting from the unpredictable availability and cost of trade goods and supplies throughout Iroquoia. Rather than declining into political dependence and social irrelevance, however, Oneida leaders confronted these issues with remarkable resilience and adaptability.

A survey of the principal leaders representing the Oneida nation during the latter half of the eighteenth century exemplifies the irrepressible nature of the nation itself. Not only did the influence of many extend over a considerable number of years, six had already been representing the Oneida when this study opens in 1750 (see table 1). The most noticeable was Skenandoah, middle-aged by this time, who served as both delegate and speaker at conferences despite his predilection for alcohol. It was not until the closing decade of the century that the Oneida lost their customary cadre of headmen. In the intervening years, the number of individuals who led their people is striking. Many identified themselves as either a warrior or a sachem; others were classified by those who recorded conference proceedings. Such differentiations were frequently disregarded by the leaders themselves, depending on the situation at hand. Sachems would speak on behalf of

**TABLE 1**—*Oneida Leadership, 1750–1800*

| Name | 1750 | 1760 | 1770 | 1780 | 1790 | 1800 |
|---|---|---|---|---|---|---|
| Scarooyady# | (1757) | | | | | |
| Conoquhieson* | | | (1775) | | | |
| Aquiotta# | (1757) | | | | | |
| Gawehe# | | (1766) | | | | |
| Agwrongdongwas# | | | | | (1792) | |
| Skenandoah# | | | | | | (1816) |
| Adararockquaghs | ● | | | | ● | |
| Deacon Thomas# | ● | | | (1779) | | |
| Thomas King# | ● | | (1771) | | | |
| Tagawaron# | ● | | (1772) | | | |
| Dakayenensese | ● | | | ● | | |
| Senghnagenrat* | | ● | | ● | | |
| Ojistalale* | | ● | | (1788) | | |
| Oneyanhe* | | | ● | | (1794) | |
| Aksiaktatye# | | | ● | | | ● |
| Onondiyo* | | | | ● | (1795) | |
| Gaghsaweda# | | | | ● | | (1800) |

Date of death, if known, in parentheses.
Solid line – known dates of leadership.
● – no exact dates known of start or finish of leadership.
(#) indicates the person is usually identified as a sachem; (*) indicates usually identified as a warrior. These categories are provided advisedly. Sachems and warriors could also serve as orators, changing their positions depending on the circumstances.

the warriors if appropriate, and warriors supported the sachems if their combined influence was considered beneficial. Warriors could include any who were not hereditary sachems, including speakers and Pine Tree chiefs.

As hostilities intensified between the French and British in the 1750s, the Oneida were led by men accustomed to negotiating with colonial authorities. Conoquhieson's authority as a Christian Oneida League chief, hereditary sachem, and orator was unique. His influence at conferences at Fort Johnson during this decade, already evident at the 1750 meeting at Onondaga, alerted other participants that his nation was a force to be reckoned with. He was quick to voice a sachem's concerns with regard to traditional protocol, land, trade, and defense. His conversion to Christianity appeared not to have adversely affected his being accepted as a leader of his nation. Associated with the Oneida's principal village of Kanowalohale, Conoquhieson was frequently accompanied and supported by Agwrongdongwas and Skenandoah, leaders who originated from the southern Oneida community of Oquaga and who had also adopted Christianity but without the agenda imposed by Kirkland at Kanowalohale. These men were young and spent their time teaching and preaching in the supportive Christian community within

**TABLE 2**—*Principal Oneida Leaders, 1750s*

| Name | Status* | Spirituality | Community |
|---|---|---|---|
| Scarooyady | Warrior | — | — |
| Conoquhieson | Sachem | Christian | Kanowalohale |
| Aquiotta | Warrior | Christian | Oquaga |
| Gawehe | Warrior | — | Kanowalohale |
| Agwrongdongwas | Warrior | Christian | Oquaga |
| Adarockquaghs | — | — | Oquaga |
| Deacon Thomas | Warrior | Christian | Oquaga |
| Thomas King | Warrior | Traditional | Oquaga |
| Skenandoah | Warrior | Christian | Oquaga |
| Dakayenensese | — | Christian | Oquaga |

*Sachems and warriors could also serve as orators, and they could also change their positions depending on the circumstances.

Oquaga; this education stood them in good stead for their future political responsibilities and possibly contributed to their trust in white men.
Aquiotta and Dakayenensese, also from Oquaga, as converts to Christianity
shared similar backgrounds. Aquiotta, an elderly spokesman in the early
1750s, had already gained considerable influence and prestige among his
people. Dakayenensese spoke infrequently at conferences but was recognized as a dedicated Christian authority in his community.

A survey of predominant leaders representing the Oneida during this period of hostility between the British and the French reveals remarkable features (table 2). The prevalence of warriors emerging as Oneida leaders in a
time of warfare is understandable. Their adherence to Christianity and their
common base at Oquaga, on the other hand, are both noteworthy. This
adherence corresponds with the influence of Christian missionaries, who
arrived earlier in the southern part of Oneida territory than in the northern
part. It also possibly substantiates the theory that acceptance of Christianity provided warriors with new opportunities for leadership in comparison
with the opportunities available to the sachems. The predominance of warriors clearly predates Kirkland's ministry at Kanowalohale and explains the
Oneida sachems' subsequent exasperation concerning the warriors' rising to
power and assuming much of what was formerly the sachems' authority.

Many of the delegates who attended conferences during the 1750s as
delegates or speakers did so infrequently and without major responsibilities.
Their names—recorded as simply attending a conference, such as Albany in
1754 (see table 3)—have remained relatively unknown and have not been
credited with the prestige of the decade's major Oneida leaders. As is the case
with those leaders, however, a greater number of Oneida delegates are on record as coming from Oquaga than from all the other communities combined.
For some others, there is no indication as to their home community. With the
exception of Adarockquaghs, they were present at few gatherings during the
decade, especially prior to the Albany conference of 1754.

In the period of peace during the 1760s, Oneida relations with the Iroquoia Confederacy and with the British became increasingly strained.
Conoquhieson was asked with greater frequency by the Confederacy to
represent them when confronting William Johnson about land grievances,
the excessive availability of alcohol, and the irritation caused by British
garrisons. Johnson complicated matters for the Oneida by attempting to
maneuver them into the role of mediator among their confederates when
it suited his purposes. When he asked the Oneida to resolve the issue of the
settlers' murder by Chenussio warriors, their failure in completing such a
mission illustrates the ease with which the Oneida's leadership role could
be jeopardized, despite the efforts of Conoquhieson to maintain it. The pro-
French faction, led by Gawehe prior to his death in 1766, contributed to the
division within the Oneida nation. Thomas King, frequently representing
the Oneida at meetings in Philadelphia, also attended conferences at Fort

**TABLE 3**— *Additional Oneida Delegates, 1750s*

| Name | From Oquaga | Before 1754 | Albany 1754 | After 1754 |
|---|---|---|---|---|
| Adarockquaghs, Adam | Yes | No | Yes | 1756–1776 |
| Alndaraghniro | Yes | No | Yes | 1758 |
| Aneeghnaxqua | Yes | No | Yes | 1757 |
| Aquiraeaghse | Yes | No | Yes | — |
| Canaghsadiro | Yes | No | No | 1756–1766 |
| Disononto | ? | Yes | No | No |
| Gaweaghnoge | Yes | No | Yes | — |
| Kacneghdakon | ? | No | Yes | — |
| Keandarundie | ? | Yes | Yes | 1757, 1758 |
| Leguchsanyont | ? | No | No | 1758 |
| Nicholaasa | ? | No | No | 1758 |
| Onidyoghgory | ? | No | Yes | 1763 |
| Spencer, Thomas | Yes | Yes | No | 1753, 1763–1777 |
| Taraghorus | ? | No | Yes | — |
| Tesanonda | Yes | No | No | 1756 |
| Tohaghdaaghquyserry | ? | No | Yes | — |

Johnson and elsewhere in Iroquoia. Johnson did not relish King's participation at proceedings at this time, when Johnson's influence as superintendent was being challenged. The last thing Johnson wanted was for this renegade leader to undermine his prestige with the Iroquois any further. The Oneida's status with both the Six Nations and the British could swing either way depending on King's behavior. Unlike the previous decade, during the

1760s only Conoquhieson and Thomas King spoke regularly at conferences, and only two relatively unknown Oneida, Onidyoghgory and Swansee, were recorded as delegates at meetings in 1763 and 1766.

In the late 1760s few Oneida names appear in records and documents, and the headmen focused on issues restricted to their immediate situation in their homelands. At the 1768 Fort Stanwix conference a second warrior chief associated with Kanowalohale—Tagawaron—joined Conoquhieson and Thomas King. This triumvirate tackled daunting issues: the determination of colonial representatives to acquire additional land from the Iroquois; the aspirations of Eleazar Wheelock to expand his educational and evangelistic enterprise into Oneida territory; the maneuvering of Johnson's fellow traders to obtain acreage as recompense for their losses from recent warfare; and Johnson's own agenda of restoring his damaged credibility with the British government. The united approach of Conoquhieson as sachem and King and Tagawaron as warriors refutes later historians' claims that the Oneida, led by Kirkland, were divided permanently into opposing camps of sachems loyal to the British and warriors attracted to the American cause. At the time of the Fort Stanwix conference, Kirkland's ministry was in its infancy at Kanowalohale.

The hypothesis is further weakened by the evidence from the actions of the three Oneida leaders following the missionary's arrival at Kanowalohale. They were prepared to engage the energetic Kirkland who brought a pro-American Presbyterian Christianity to a community already experienced in and supportive of anti-British sentiments. However, Tagawaron disavowed Kirkland's promotion of agricultural pursuits among Oneida men and opposed his attempt to construct a Presbyterian chapel at Kanowalohale before Johnson could complete his Church of England structure. As representatives of the Oneida, these leaders cooperated to resolve national issues ahead of dealing with personal or sectarian ambitions. By the end of the 1760s the focus of Oneida leadership had shifted to Kanowalohale, but this transference was more because of the personality of that community's leaders than to any direction on the part of Kirkland.

Forces impacting on the Oneida made the Loyalist cause increasingly difficult for them to support prior to the outbreak of the revolution. The neophyte sachem from Kanowalohale, Senghnagenrat, accompanied the aging Conoquhieson in expressing Iroquoian support of the British. Although British authorities failed to stem the flow of settlers encroaching on Oneida land, members of the Oneida nation took the initiative to develop good relations with the colonial settlers and merchants in the Mohawk River valley. Representatives of the Oneida attending Committee of Correspondence meetings in Albany assured the committee members of their intentions to maintain neutrality while simultaneously showing an interest in contributing to Patriot forces. At the same time, Conoquhieson and Tagawaron continued to criticize Kirkland's ministry and political activity, despite Tagawaron's original support of the missionary. The two men also defended their nation against charges brought by the Cayuga, Seneca, and Onondaga that they were replacing their allegiance to the Confederacy with one to the Patriots centered at Albany.

Senghnagenrat's assumption of the mantle of leading peace sachem following the death of his mentor Conoquhieson in 1775 coincided with the appearance on the political scene of Agwrongdongwas, the Christian convert from Oquaga. Although no details are discernible as to Agwrongdongwas's rise to prominence as Oneida's primary spokesman, his oratorical skills and status as a warrior-speaker from the Oneida's southern area balanced that of Senghnagenrat as a hereditary sachem from the northern region. His friendly relationship with the Patriot forces at the outbreak of the revolution provided continuity for Christian leadership within the Oneida nation following Conoquhieson's death, notwithstanding the fact that his allegiance was to the Patriot rather than to the Loyalist cause. Agwrongdongwas's rise to prominence at this time was a turning point for his people. Oneida leadership by the early 1770s no longer exhibited the abundance of individuals from Oquaga as had been the case twenty years earlier (see table 4). As new situations arose, representatives from other communities were taking their place beside the venerable delegates from Oquaga. Although records of this period do not provide sufficient information to substantiate a complete picture, those whose home community was indicated reflect the growing influence of Kanowalohale. No indication is given as to the religious affiliation of the additional individuals, and most of them do not appear in future documentation.[3]

The revolution provided the necessary opportunity to bring individual Oneida into greater political leadership. A strong corps of qualified speakers, already existing in the 1750s (see table 2), was available to the Oneida in this period. Skenandoah had been involved in conferences since the 1740s, but during the revolution he became an outspoken ally of Kirkland and a leader among the Oneida subscribing to the Patriot conviction. With Agwrongdongwas he suffered imprisonment at Fort Niagara in 1780 when they were captured during the failed peace mission to the British. Agwrongdongwas had emerged from his classroom and pulpit at Oquaga to become, among the Oneida, a leading advocate for the Patriots. Senghnagenrat abandoned the pro-British sentiments of his mentor Conoquhieson and promoted loyalty to the Patriots among the Oneida's confederates. From 1775 Deacon Thomas aggressively pursued a career as informant between allies in Caughnawauga and the Oneida, which led to his death in 1779. The anti-British Atayataghronghta settled among the Oneida, spied for the Patriots, and participated in the 1779 raids on the Mohawk valley while serving in the Sullivan-Clinton campaign.

Previously unknown members of Oneida became involved in the affairs of their nation during the revolutionary war. Ojistalale appeared as a forceful voice on behalf of the Oneida sachems. The warrior Gaghsaweda, who had declared his loyalty to Kirkland in 1775, was to become a leading representative of the Oneida in the next two decades. Oneyanha and Onondiyo came

**TABLE 4**—*Oneida Delegates in the Early 1770s*

| Name | Community | Date | Significance |
|---|---|---|---|
| Adarockquaghs | Oquaga | 1775–1776 | angry with divisions within Oneida nation |
| Agwrongdongwas | Oquaga | 1770–1776 | concerned about land and religion at Oquaga |
| Clenis | Kanowalohale | 1775 | met with Albany Committee of Correspondence |
| Canadegowus | ? | 1774 | signed deed for land to Brothertown Indians |
| Conoquhieson | Kanowalohale | 1770–1775 | league sachem, speaker |
| Deacon Thomas | Oquaga | 1770–1779 | concerned about land and religion at Oquaga |
| Gaghsaweda | Kanowalohale | 1775 | warrior, defended Kirkland |
| Senghnagenrat | Kanowalohale | 1770–1777 | head speaker after Conoquhieson's death |
| Tagarawon | Kanowalohale | 1770–1772 | opposed to Kirkland |
| Teyohagweanda | ? | 1775 | speaker at conference at German Flats |
| Thaghwaghwesere | ? | 1775 | met with Albany Committee of Correspondence |

to the fore as representatives of the Oneida sachems. Honyere's lengthy association with his people began with his leading sixty Oneida from Oriska into the battle of Oriskany in 1777. Some of those selected by the Oneida to be commissioned officers rose from previous anonymity to prominent positions and continued to serve their nation in succeeding years (see table 5).[4]

By 1780 numerous residents of Kanowalohale, including its leaders, had developed a desire for European commodities, originating perhaps from the prestige they had acquired within Oneida culture, from their close connections with Albany merchants prior to the war, or from spoils they obtained during the fighting. Materials used in house construction and furnishing, the

**TABLE 5**—*Oneida Commissioned Officers, 1779*

| Name | Involvement |
| --- | --- |
| Captain Honyere Tewahongarahkonat | conferences, signed land deeds, 1785–1793 |
| Captain Tewaghtahkotte | ——— |
| Captain Wakarontharane, James | awarded land for military service |
| Captain Otaawighton, John | fighting 1783, awarded land for military service |
| Lieut. Thonigwenghsohare, Christian | signed land deeds in 1780s |
| Lieut. Sagoharase, John | died 1780 due to bad conditions at Schenectady |
| Lieut. Kanaghsatirhon, Joseph (Tuscarora) | Christian, received annuity, requested school (1793) |
| Lieut. Okonyota, Cornelius | signed Herkimer treaty (1785), awarded land for service |
| Lieut. Kakiktoton, Cornelius | signed land treaties, 1790–1794 |
| Lieut. Honyost Thaosagwat | leading warrior, killed 1779 |
| Lieut. Totyaneahawi | joined British at Fort Niagara, 1780 |
| Lieut. Atayataghronghta | signed Ft Stanwix treaty (1784, 1788), land deeds of 1790s |

style of personal clothing and adornments, and the possession of farm animals and accoutrements of husbandry were distributed among the leaders of this period without restrictions imposed according to whether those leaders were traditional or Christian, Church of England or Presbyterian, pro- or anti-American during the revolution. In fact the war loss claims made to Pickering in 1794 could well indicate that the communal spirit of ownership frequently touted as a hallmark of Indian life had been superseded among the Oneida by the appeal of individual possession of European commodities.

A definitive diplomatic corps of Oneida speakers operated throughout the 1780s and 1790s (see table 6). Their nation went on being bombarded by external forces that could undermine any advantages accruing from their support of the Americans in the revolution. Attempts by state or federal

**TABLE 6**—*Leading Oneida Speakers, 1784–1794*

| | Ojistalale | Atayatagh-ronghta | Aksiak-tatye | Gagh-saweda | Agwrong-dongwas | Oneyanhe | Skenandoah |
|---|---|---|---|---|---|---|---|
| Status | S | W | W | W | W | S | W |
| Clan | Turtle | ? | Wolf | Bear | Eel | Turtle | Wolf |
| Fort Stanwix 1784[1] | • | • | • | • | • | | • |
| Fort Herkimer 1785[2] | • | | | | • | • | |
| Fort Stanwix 1788[3] | • | • | | • | • | • | |
| Cayuga land cession, 1789[4] | | • | | | • | | |
| Annuity from NY, 1790[5] | | | | | • | • | |
| Newtown conference, 1791[6] | | | | | • | • | |
| Philadelphia meeting, 1792[7] | • | • | | • | | | |
| Canandaigua conference,1794[8] | | | | | | | • |

*Notes*
[1] Minutes of conference, 4 September 1784, *PCIA*, 1:39–40; compiled from *IIDH*.
[2] Entry of 28 June 1785, *IIDH*, reel 38.
[3] Minutes of conference, 22 September 1788, *PCIA*, 1:178–246.
[4] Minutes of treaty, 25 February 1789, *PCIA*, 2:311.
[5] Delegates to receive New York State annuity, 2 June 1790, *PCIA*, 2:378.
[6] Minutes of conference, 20 June–15 July 1791, TPP, roll 60, 69–109.
[7] Minutes of meetings, 5–11 April 1792, TPP, roll 60, 121–29.
[8] Minutes of meetings from 10 September to mid-October 1794, TPP, roll 60, 195–230.

government and land companies to pry territory away from the Oneida —despite promises by each to the contrary and despite Quaker efforts to provide the Oneida with financial security by means of agricultural pursuits —were all met by a body of Oneida representatives who did their best to present a unified approach in opposition. To this end they continued to place the interests of their nation above their concerns as warriors or sachems. One of the two Christian leaders identified consistently as warriors, Skenandoah, saw his influence as a conference speaker lessening because of his advanced age. Agwrongdongwas spoke at all the events involving the Oneida land issues until his death in 1792. His lengthy participation as speaker, possibly earning him the position of Pine Tree chief, was facilitated by his reputedly natural eloquence and by his people's acknowledgment of his skill from years of negotiating with colonial authorities. Sachems Ojistalale and Oneyanhe continued to address Oneida concerns until their deaths in 1788 and 1794 respectively.

Warriors predominated as speakers at the conferences after 1784 (see table 7).[5] At other events there was an overall balance between warrior and sachem representation from the Oneida. No particular clan had disproportionate representation among these men (see table 6). Of the eight leading speakers, the Turtle and Wolf clans each had two members, Bear and Eel clans one, and the clan affiliation in two cases is unknown. The fact that five Iroquois League sachems attended this conference is significant. Unable to represent the Oneida at the Grand Council meetings at Onondaga since the fire had been extinguished in 1777, these sachems were present but did not necessarily speak at the colonial conferences. Traditionally each of the three clans would have three sachems as representatives; at the Fort Stanwix conference, there were two Wolf, two Turtle, and one Bear. The names of two League sachems, Odaghseghte and Shononghriyo, appear at future events as signers, not as speakers.

During the 1780s and 1790s, far more Oneida leaders than in previous decades were involved in the signing of various documents and letters. Many of the speakers also functioned as signatories (see table 8). It is difficult to ascertain the reasons that certain individuals signed treaties, petitions, leases,

**TABLE 7**—*Principal Oneida Leaders, 1750s*

|  | *Warrior* | *Sachem* |
| --- | --- | --- |
| Fort Stanwix conference, 1784 | 14 | 7 |
| Fort Herkimer conference 1785 | 1 | 2 |
| Fort Stanwix conference, 1788 | 5 | 3 (2 unspecified) |
| Cayuga Land cession, 1789 | 2 | 0 |
| Annuity from New York State, 1790 | 2 | 1 |
| Newtown conference, 1791 | 1 | 1 |
| Philadelphia meeting, 1792 | 2 | 0 |
| Canandaigua conference, 1794 | 1 | 1 |

**TABLE 8**—*Leading Oneida Speakers as Signers, 1784–1794*

| | Ojistalale | Atayatagh-ronghta | Aksiak-tatye | Gagh-saweda | Agwrong-dongwas | Oneyanhe | Skenandoah |
|---|---|---|---|---|---|---|---|
| Status | S | W | W | W | W | S | W |
| Clan | Turtle | ? | Wolf | Bear | Eel | Turtle | Wolf |
| Fort Stanwix treaty, 1784[1] | | | | | | | |
| Harper land grant, 1784[2] | | | • | • | | • | |
| Fort Herkimer treaty, 1785[3] | • | | | • | • | • | • |
| Livingston land grant, 1787/88[4] | | | • | • | • | | • |
| Phelps/Gorham grant, 1788[5] | | | | | | | |
| Fort Stanwix 1788[6] | • | | | • | • | • | |
| Cayuga land cession, 1789[7] | | • | | | • | | |
| Oneida land deed, 1790[8] | | | | • | • | • | • |
| Annuity from NY, 1790[9] | | | • | • | | | |
| Smith land lease, 1793[10] | | | | • | | • | • |
| Use of Oneida land, 1793[11] | | | | • | | | |
| School for Oneida, 1793[12] | | | • | • | | | • |
| Letter vs. Kirkland, 1794[13] | | | | • | | • | • |

*Notes*

[1] Minutes of conference, 4 September 1784, *PCIA*, 1:39–40; compiled from *IIDH*.
[2] Entry of 28 June 1785, *IIDH*, reel 38.
[3] Minutes of conference, 22 September 1788, *PCIA*, 1:178–246.
[4] Minutes of treaty, 25 February 1789, *PCIA*, 2:311.
[5] Delegates to receive New York State annuity, 2 June 1790, *PCIA*, 2:378.
[6] Minutes of conference, 20 June–15 July 1791, TPP, roll 60, 69–109.
[7] Minutes of meetings, 5–11 April 1792, TPP, roll 60, 121–29.
[8] Minutes of meetings from 10 September to mid-October 1794, TPP, roll 60, 195–230.
[9] Delegates to receive New York State annuity, 2 June 1790, *PCIA*, 2:378.
[10] Petition dated 15 January 1793, *IIDH*; TPP, roll 62, 67.
[11] Act signed 19 April 1793, compiled from *IIDH*.
[12] Letter to Rev. Dr. Thacher, Clerk of Trustees, Hamilton Oneida Academy, 27 April 1793, *SKJ*, 255.
[13] Letter of 29 January 1794, TPP, roll 62, 82.

or letters. The act of signing treaties or letters might have been an acknowledgment of westernization that would hopefully guarantee the results, a new means of gaining status within the Oneida community, or an indication that a temporary commitment would be considered satisfactory in the face of a rapidly changing environment. For example, Aksiaktatye signed more documents than he delivered speeches, and Kirkland's previously stalwart friend Skenandoah signed a letter complaining about the missionary's apparent loss of interest in the religious welfare of Kanowalohale. The prominent leaders Ojistalale and Agwrongdongwas were signers and speakers until their deaths. Of particular interest is Gaghsaweda, whose constant contribution as speaker and signer throughout this period could either have resulted from or been the cause of his affluence as indicated in his home at Kanowalohale.

An examination of documentation reveals that an unprecedented number of Oneida who were not influential leaders were involved in signing letters, documents, and treaties from 1784 to 1794. Subtracting the eight who formed the central group (see table 8), eighty-four additional individuals participated in negotiations with the newly formed American government. Of these, five persons are particularly noteworthy (see table 9). Odaghseghte carried the title of a leading Oneida sachem involved at the formation of the Iroquois League and, as such, provided continuity for the nation's political system. Alawistonis was the leader of the traditional faction at Kanowalohale. The other three mentioned serve to illustrate the gaps in information that prevent a more complete analysis. Onondiyo was the only declared Christian of the group listed. He, like Skenandoah, signed the letter protesting against Kirkland's ministry despite being the missionary's protégé. Onondiyo and Shononghriyo both made claims for war losses during Pickering's visit to Kanowalohale; Onondiyo's claim was far below the average, while Shononghriyo's was above. Kakiktoton, the only Oneida officer commissioned from Kanowalohale who represented the Oneida as a signing authority, had a meager claim. As with the core group of signers and speakers, the presence of three warriors and two sachems reflects the balance between the two groups. Regarding the clans, the three Wolf, two Turtle, and one Bear indicate a similar symmetry. As warrior/sachem status and clan membership of the majority of the seventy-nine remaining signers were not recorded, it is impossible to come to any conclusion concerning the significance of these positions. Among this group, fifty-four names signed once, eleven signed twice. Four women also acted in this capacity, and in each case signed the same documents: the 1788 Fort Stanwix treaty and the Peter Smith land lease of 1793. Honyere, famous for his revolutionary war performance, was noticeably restricted to signing the Fort Herkimer treaty, the New York State annuity agreement in 1790, and the land use agreement of 1793.

In an effort to maintain their place in the Iroquois Confederacy and to adapt to the constantly changing political climate of colonial America, the Oneida had moved from having a body of experienced and established leadership in 1750 to one in 1800 of individuals whose distinction—as

**TABLE 9**—*Additional Oneida Signers, 1784–1794*

| | Total Signers | Odaghseghte | Alawistonis | Onondiyo | Shononghriyo | Kakiktoton |
|---|---|---|---|---|---|---|
| Status | | S | W | S | W | W |
| Clan | | Wolf | Wolf | Turtle | Turtle | Bear |
| Fort Stanwix treaty,1784 | 2 | | | | | |
| Harper land grant, 1784 | 4 | • | | | | |
| Fort Herkimer treaty, 1785 | 5 | | | • | | |
| Livingston land grant, 1787/88 | 17 | | • | • | • | |
| Phelps/Gorham grant1788 | 3 | | | | | |
| Fort Stanwix 1788 | 23 | • | • | | • | • |
| Cayuga land cession, 1789 | 2 | | | | | • |
| Oneida land deed, 1790 | 6 | | • | | | |
| Annuity from NY,1790 | 5 | | • | | | |
| Smith land lease, 1793 | 23 | | | | • | • |
| Use of Oneida land, 1793 | 23 | • | • | | • | • |
| School for Oneida, 1793 | 7 | | | | | |
| Letter vs. Kirkland, 1794 | 8 | | | • | | • |

Sources—Same as shown for table 8

Replicas of the original large stone are found in all Oneida communities. This one was erected in 1990 on the occassion of the sesquicentennial of the arrival of Oneida refugees from New York State at what is the Oneida of the Thames settlement in Southwestern Ontario.

Christian or traditional, sachem or warrior, hereditary or Pine Tree chief— diminished to allow for the creation of a mosaic of cooperation. As pressures increased after the revolution, the Oneida enlarged the scope of representation, encouraging the involvement of a wider range of individuals. Many of those experienced in political negotiations had died. Skenandoah, the last surviving Christian leader, was living as a reclusive centenarian. He, like others of the Christian-traditionalist alliance that led the Oneida into the revolution, were not repudiated when their strategy failed to preserve Oneida lands. Although they had chosen the winning side, they were still betrayed in the end. Without any loss of honor, they gradually faded away. Gaghsaweda represented the new era of leadership, which Kirkland classified as "pagan." Gaghsaweda, in the company of Agwrongdongwas's son Sategaleahtas, would have watched with anticipation as Alawistonis revived the White Dog sacrifice at Kanowalohale in 1800, then retired to Alawistonis's homestead where the Standing Stone stood as an embodiment of Oneida inheritance and aspirations for the future.

# APPENDIX 1

Names of Oneida and Tuscarora Participants at Fort Stanwix Conference,
4 September 1784

## SACHEMS

Odaghsaghte[+]—League sachem
Ojistalale, Cornelius[+]
Atayatonneatha, Peter[+]—League sachem
Ataghonghteayon, William[+]—League sachem
Dyoghhagweate, William[+]—League sachem
Ageaghwatha, William[+]
Canatsiagere, John[+]

## WARRIORS

Atayataghronghta[+]
Thonwaghweakaragwea, George (Captain)
Aghnyonken, Cornelius[+]
Anentshontye, Paul[+]
Aksiaktatye[+]
Alawistonis[+]
Shononghriyo, Anthony[+]—League sachem
Feghkatkaghtons, John
Kayentarongwea, William[+]
Gaghsaweda[+]
Agwrongdongwas[+]
Skenandoah[+]

## ALSO

Atoghseronge
Kanaweadon[+]

Those who signed the treaty for the Oneida: Otyadonenghti and Dayaheari

*Note:* The names with a plus sign ([+]) are identifiable as Oneida.

# APPENDIX 2

Oneida Members Involved at the Treaty of Fort Stanwix, 22 September 1788

## DELEGATION CHOSEN BY THE ONEIDA TO MEET WITH THE NEW YORK COMMISSIONERS
Ojistalale#
Gaghsaweda*
Shononghriyo, Anthony*
Odaghseghte#
Thanigeandagayon
Thaghniyongo

## ONEIDA SPEAKERS AT THE CONFERENCE
Agwrongdongwas*
Otisquette, Peter
Aksiaktatye*
Oneyanha#

## SIGNATORIES OF THE TREATY

Odaghseghte#

Kanaghgweaye

Otisquette, Peter

Thaghniyongo

Thonigweaghshale

Ojistalale#

Otsetogon

Teyohagweanda

Thanigeandagayon*

David Keanyako

Sagoyontha

Skenandoah*

Tehoughnihalk Hanwagalet (female)

Kaskonghgwea Kanwagalet (female)

Hononwayele (female)

Oneyanha#

Thaghneghtolis, Hendrick

Shononghriyo, Anthony*

Thaghtaghgwesere

Kanaghsalilgh

Teaghsweangalolis, Paul

Agwrongdongwas*

Shoneghslishea, Daniel

Alawistonis*

Kakiktoton

Hannah Sodolk (female)

*Note:* The sachems are indicated by a number sign (#), the warriors by an asterisk (*).

# APPENDIX 3

Petitioners to the State of New York to Lease Land to Peter Smith, 15 January 1793

## ONEIDA PETITIONERS

John Aenghase

Cornelius Aghnyonken

Denny (David)

Kakiktoton

Kennawagenton

Kanonghsase, William

Kanyeagoton

Otsienhea, Peter

Shononghriyo, Anthony*

Soghraghrowane, Peter

Thaghneghtolis, Hendrick

Skenandoah*

Aghnyeate, Daniel

Anentshontye, Paul*

Gaghsaweda*

Kanadarok

Kanento

Kanonghgwenya

Kayeghtorha

Otsighn'yokare, Thomas

Shotsijowane

Thaghnaghwanekeas

Thaghtaghgwesere*

On 14 May 1793, a group of Oneida leaders wrote to Timothy Pickering requesting that he visit the Oneida, as some of their nation had threatened to kill Peter Smith, Smith's surveyor, and a warrior acting as guide (although all they did was break and hide the surveyor's equipment).

Oneyanha

Kanonghgwenya, Peter

Kayeadanongwea, William

Statsideyowane, John

Thaswenkarorens, Paul

Skenandoah*

Gaghsaweda*

Skenandoah, Thomas

Kentaronhye, Anthony

Witnessed by Aksiaktatye

*Note:* The sachems are indicated by a number sign (#), the warriors by an asterisk (*).

# APPENDIX 4

Oneida Signatories to an Act Relative to the Lands Appropriated by the State of New York to the Use of the Oneida, Onondaga, and Cayuga Indians, 19 April 1793

Alawistonis*
Areaghhoktha, Thomas
Gaghsaweda*
Agwrongdongwas*
Hononwayele (female)
Honyere
Kakiktoton
Kanaghsalilgh
Kanwagalet (female)
David Keanyako
Odaghseghte
Ojistalale(#)
Sagoyontha
Shononghriyo*
Hannah Sodolk (female)
Tekeandyakhon
Thaghswoangalolis
Thagniyongo
Thaghtaghgwesere*
Thanigeandagayon*
Thonigwenghsohare
Toneagshlishea
Teyohagweanda

*Note:* The sachems are indicated by a number sign (#), the warriors by an asterisk (*).

# APPENDIX 5

Oneida Signers of Letter to Timothy Pickering Complaining about Samuel Kirkland, 29 January 1794

Skenandoah, John*
Rotshawatzenhe, Cornelius
Akentyakhen, Laurence*
Deanoyondeah, Augustus
Oneyanha, Peter#
Kanadarok, Peter
Kanyeagoton
Gaghsaweda*
Kakiktoton, Cornelius*
Deyahthadane, John
Onondiyo#

*Note:* Sachems are indicated by a number sign (#), warriors by an asterisk (*).

# APPENDIX 6

Oneida Overseers of East and West Ends of Kanowalohale, 25 February 1799

## FOR THE EAST END OF KANOWALOHALE
Tehonogwesghsoolhaula, Christian
Honyost
Onughseeshooh, Thomas
Shaugoogaudoohaula, Neckis
Tahauweyaudelon, Quedels Peter
Wauts'haudeaghongh, Christian

## FOR THE WEST END OF KANOWALOHALE
Looghshingh, Martinus
Kaunaudauloonh, Quedelh
Kaujathoondautheu, Quedlh
Looghtanddya, Nicholas
Kanneyalode, Christian
Kaghneghtootdau, Saugus

# BIOGRAPHICAL INFORMATION OF ONEIDA LEADERS

*Notes:* Quotation marks indicate commonly used British name or nickname, for example, "Big Bear." Parentheses indicate an alternate spelling, for example, (Aghnyonkea). If the name is capitalized and set in bold, it indicates this leader is mentioned in the text.

**ADAROCKQUAGHS**, Adam
  Sachem
  From Oquaga
  Present at Albany conference, July 1754
  Recognized as chief at Oquaga by 1756
  Speaker representing Oquaga at Fort Johnson conference, 27 February 1756
  Leading sachem in Oquaga by 1757
  Speaker at Fort Johnson conferences, May, September 1757
  Oquaga delegate at Fort Stanwix conference, October 1768
  Complained to Guy Johnson regarding denominationalism and land policies at Oquaga, February 1775
  Was doubtful that Oquaga would remain neutral in revolution, at German Flats conference, July 1776

Adoondaraghirha
  Installed as sachem by William Johnson at Johnson Hall, May 1765

Aenghase, John
  Signed petition to New York State to lease land to Peter Smith, 15 January 1793

Ageaghwatha, William
  Participated at Fort Stanwix conference, September 1784

Agentgahgon, Lawrence. *See* Akentyakhen

Aghnyeate, Daniel
  Signed petition to New York State to lease land to Peter Smith, 15 January 1793

Aghnyonken (Aghnyonkea), Cornelius, "Big Bear"
  Warrior
  Wolf clan
  Participated at Fort Stanwix conference, September 1784
  Signed petition to New York State to lease land to Peter Smith, 15 January 1793
  Included in war-losses claim (1780) at Kanowalohale, November 1794

Aghwistonnisk. *See* ALAWISTONIS

Agweaghwatha, William
  Sachem
  Participated at Fort Stanwix conference, September 1784

Agwenyohta, Cornelius
  Warrior
  Signed congressional land grant to John Harper, 20 November 1784

**AGWRONGDONGWAS** (Agwerontongwas), Peter, "Good Peter"
  From Oquaga
  Warrior
  Eel Clan (wife was Wolf Clan)
  Christian, converted at Oquaga by Rev. Spencer, 1748
  Began preaching and teaching at Oquaga, summer 1753
  Leading preacher and teacher at Oquaga, winter 1756
  Criticized William Johnson regarding land policies, May 1757, August 1762
  Good student at Eleazar Wheelock's school, summer 1765
  Attempted to block John Harper's claim to Oneida land, January 1767
  Oquaga delegate to Fort Stanwix conference, October 1768
  Opposed Church of England baptismal policy at Oquaga, March 1773
  Complained to Guy Johnson regarding denominationalism and land policies at Oquaga, February 1775
  Signed Declaration of Neutrality, June 1775
  Present with Oquaga people at German Flats conference, July 1776
  Rejected Thayendanega's invitation to join the British cause at Fort Niagara, January 1777
  Pleased that Onondaga wanted Oneida to form central fire of Confederacy, July 1778
  Supported role of warriors in revolution at meeting with commissioners at Albany, October 1778
  Justified Oneida's separation from the Confederacy, January 1779
  Spoke at Fort Schuyler meeting against Patriot plans to attack Onondaga, July 1779

Was imprisoned at Fort Niagara by the British, February 1780
Speaker at Fort Stanwix conference, October 1784
·Signed letter requesting grant of land for James Dean, October 1784
Kirkland frequently refers to his preaching and evangelism, 1784–1788
Signed New York State treaty at Fort Herkimer, June 1785
Signed letter to Congress regarding disruptions among Six Nations,
   September 1785
Signed letter to Congress that Cayuga wanted Oneida to speak for the
   Iroquois, October 1785
Increased influence as a Christian preacher using traditional
   symbolism, 1786
Signed Livingstone lease, 8 January 1788
Speaker at Fort Stanwix conference, September 1788
Signed Fort Stanwix treaty, 22 September 1788
Speaker at conference regarding Cayuga land, February 1789
Signed Cayuga land cession with New York State, 25 February 1789
Signed letter to Governor Clinton who wanted control of their land, 27
   January 1790
Kirkland mentions his fierce opposition to the Pagan Party at
   Kanowalohale, July–August 1791
Speaker at Newtown conference with western Iroquois, July 1791
Represented the Oneida at a meeting at Philadelphia, March 1792
Died 1792
His widow included in war-losses claim (1780) at Kanowalohale,
   November 1794

Akentyakhen (Akentyakhon), Powles. Also Lowlence Akeandyakhon,
Lawrence Agentgahgon.
   Warrior
   Signed letter to Governor Clinton complaining about Atayataghronghta's
      pro-French influence over Oneida sachems, 28 October 1789
   Was chosen as delegate to accept New York State annuity, 2 June 1790
   Reported by Kirkland as favoring Oneida's pro-French faction, 8
      January 1792
   Reported by Kirkland as supporting Christianity, 1 January 1794
   Signed letter to Pickering complaining about Kirkland, 29 January 1794
   Reported by Kirkland as being changeable and insincere, 9 February
      1796

**AKONYODA**
   Senior sachem of the Oneida in 1756
   Speaker at German Flats meeting, September 1756

**AKSIAKTATYE**, Jacob, "Jacob Reed"
   Warrior

Wolf clan

Traveled to the Caughnawauga to persuade them to maintain their neutrality, September 1775

Traveled to east coast with Philip Schuyler to witness Patriot power, June 1776

Enlisted to fight for Washington, April 1778

Responded to Lafayette's call for Oneida fighters, May 1778

Moved briefly to Fort Niagara with other Oneida joining the British, autumn 1780

Speaker at Fort Stanwix conference, September 1784

Signed congressional land grant to John Harper, 20 November 1784

Signed Livingstone lease, 8 January 1788

Letter to Congress complaining about land leases, February 1788

Kirkland frequently mentions his service as translator, 1788–1800

Was chosen as a delegate to receive New York State annuity, 2 June 1790

Witness to letter to Pickering for protection for Peter Smith's surveyor, 14 May 1793

Signed letter to SSPCK promoting Kirkland's new school for Oneida, 27 April 1793

Assisted in compilation of, and included in, the war-losses claim (1780) at Kanowalohale, November 1794

**ALAWISTONIS** (Rawistonisk, Aughwistonnisk), Jacob, "Blacksmith," "Silversmith"

Warrior

Traditionalist

Wolf clan

Nephew of Agwrongdongwas

Speaker at Fort Stanwix conference, September 1784

Signed Livingstone lease, 8 January 1788

Signed Fort Stanwix treaty, 22 September 1788

Signed letter to Governor Clinton regarding Atayataghronghta's pro-French influence over the Oneida sachems, 28 October 1789

Signed letter to Governor Clinton demanding control over their own land, 27 January 1790

Was chosen as a delegate to receive New York State annuity, 2 June 1790

Witness to treaties signed with Cayuga and Onondaga at Fort Stanwix, 16, 22 June 1790

Signed act regarding land appropriated by New York for use by the Oneida, Onondaga, and Cayuga, 19 April 1793

Included in war-losses claim (1780) at Kanowalohale, 1794

Keeper of the ceremonial Standing Stone, 1796

Reintroduced White Dog sacrifice at Kanowalohale, winter 1799

Recognized within Oneida as leader of the pagan party, 1800

**ALNDARAGHNIRO** (Anagaraghery)
from Oquaga
Representative at the Albany conference, August 1754
Representative at the Easton conference, October 1758

**ANEEGHNAXQUA** (Anuchuaaqua)
From Oquaga
Representative at the Albany conference, August 1754
Representative at the Easton conference, August 1757

Anentshontye, Paul
Warrior
Wolf clan
Participated in the Fort Stanwix conference, September 1784
Signed petition to New York State to lease land to Peter Smith, 15
    January 1793
Included in war-losses claim (1780) at Kanowalohale, 1794

**AQUIOTTA** (Aguiotta)
From Oquaga
Christian and traditionalist
Warrior
Involved in adopting the Nanticoke nation, 1736
Represented the Oneida (at age seventy) at Pennsylvania conference, 13
    August 1743
Speaker at Albany meeting regarding peace with the Catawba, 8 July 1751
Speaker at conferences at Fort Johnson, April, June 1755
Attended conference at German Flats, 3 September 1756
Visited William Johnson at his home, February–May 1757
Killed, summer 1757
Kirkland mentioned Aquiotta often sought his advice, 17 May 1769

**AQUIRAEAGHSE**
From Oquaga
Attended Albany conference, August 1754

Areaghhoktha (Arakoktea), Thomas
Warrior
Signed letter to Governor Clinton complaining about
    Atayataghronghta's pro-French influence over the Oneida sachems,
    28 October 1789
Signed act regarding land appropriated by New York State for use by the
    Oneida, Onondaga, and Cayuga, 19 April 1793
Signed letter to SSCPK requesting a school for the Oneida, 27 April 1793

Arighwagenhas (Arishwagenha)
Warrior
Signed letter to Governor Clinton complaining about
Atayataghronghta's pro-French influence over the Oneida sachems,
28 October 1789

Asisat, Martinus
Signed letter to SSCPK requesting a school for the Oneida, 27 April 1793

**ATAGHONGHTEAYON** (Adahondeayenha), William
Title of an Oneida chief at the founding of the Iroquois League
Sachem
Participated at Fort Stanwix conference, September 1784

**ATAYATAGHRONGHTA** (Atyatoghhanongwia), "Lewis Cook"
Mohawk-African parentage
Born 1740 at and frequently visited Caughnawauga, Canada, but lived
at Kanowalohale and was considered an Oneida
Adopted by Skenandoah as his "son"
Warrior
Grudgingly supported the British until 1775
Served under Honyere and proved his loyalty to the Oneida as an
adopted member, battle of Oriskany, August 1777
Met with General Schuyler regarding fighting for Patriots, September
1777
Led Oneida fighters at battle of Saratoga, September 1777
Chosen by Oneida to be commissioned lieutenant colonel by Congress,
March 1779
Appealed for supplies from Congress in Philadelphia, summer 1780
Speaker at Fort Stanwix conferences, September 1784, September
1788
Speaker at conference and signed Cayuga land cession with New York
State, 25 February 1789
Considered by Kirkland a disruptive influence, as he married into a pro-
French Oneida family, 18 December 1790
Awarded land due to involvement with Oneida in the revolution,
January 1791
Represented the Oneida regarding land ownership, Philadelphia
meeting, April 1792

**ATAYATONNEATHA** (Adyadonneatha), Peter
Title of an Oneida chief at the founding of the Iroquois League
Sachem
Participated at Fort Stanwix conference, September 1784

Atoghseronge
Warrior
Participated in Fort Stanwix conference, September 1784

**BLATCOP**
From Oriska
Served under Honyere for General Herkimer at battle of Oriskany,
where he became well-known for his bravery, August 1777
Enlisted to fight for Washington, April 1778

**BLUEBECK**
Warrior
Served briefly in Clinton-Sullivan campaign, summer 1779

Bread, Peter. *See* Kanadarok

**CANADEGOWUS**
Bear clan
Signed land deed with Brothertown Indians, 4 October 1774

**CANAGHSADIRO**, Thomas
From Oquaga
Speaker at Fort Johnson conference, 27 February 1756
Scouted for French enemy at Fort Ticonderoga, May 1757
Speaker at Fort Johnson meeting, 24 July 1758
Was awarded silver medal for participating in Amherst's 1760 Montreal
campaign, April 1761
Visited Eleazar Wheelock to evaluate his school, 19 June 1766

Canatsiagere, John
Sachem
Participated in Fort Stanwix conference, September 1784

**CAPTAIN DAVID**
Signed Livingstone lease, 30 November 1787
Present at Fort Stanwix conference, October 1784

**CAPTAIN JOHN**. *See* Onondiyo

**CAPTAIN PETER**. *See* Sategaleahtas

**CLENIS**. *See* Kakiktoton

**CONOQUHIESON** (Canachquayson, Conochquiesa, Kanaghgweaya,
Kanaghgweaye)
Title of an Oneida chief at the founding of the Iroquois League
From Kanowalohale

Sachem
Christian, Church of England supporter
Recorded as rejecting Roman Catholicism, 1749
Represented the Oneida and Cayuga at the Onondaga Council, 1750
Speaker at meetings at Fort Johnson, April, June, December 1755
Speaker at Fort Johnson conference, February 1756, at German Flats,
    September 1756
Personally invited Johnson to Onondaga Grand Council, April 1757
Speaker at Fort Johnson conferences, April, December 1758
Speaker at Canajoharie conference, April 1759
Meeting with Johnson, June 1761
Speaker at meeting with William Johnson at German Flats, July 1761
Speaker for Confederacy at Fort Johnson conferences, April, July 1762
Present, but not speaker, at Johnson Hall conference, March 1763
Speaker at German Flats conference, July 1763
Speaker at Johnson Hall conferences, September, December 1763
Present, but not speaker, when William Johnson reaffirmed Onondaga
    leadership of the Confederacy, May 1765
Speaker at Johnson Hall conference regarding boundary line, April 1765
Visited Johnson Hall, angry concerning loss of lands, December 1766
Speaker at Johnson Hall conference regarding Cherokee, March 1768
Principal negotiator at Fort Stanwix conference, October 1768
Signed Fort Stanwix treaty, November 1768
Speaker at German Flats conference regarding Cherokee, July 1770
Conflict with Tagawaron regarding Kirkland, August–December 1770
Met with William Johnson regarding Oneida land rights, July 1772
Further meetings with Johnson about land, April, August 1774
Led condolence ceremonies at Johnson's funeral, August 1774
Joined Tagawaron against Kirkland's baptismal and political policies,
    January 1775
Signed declaration of neutrality, June 1775
Speaker at meeting of Albany Committee of Correspondence at German
    Flats and Albany, August–September 1775
Died autumn 1775, succeeded by Kanaghweas

**CORNELIUS**, Henry
From Oriska
Traveled to the Caughnawauga to maintain their neutrality, September
    1775
Traveled again to Caughnawauga for this purpose, May 1776
Resisted British overtures at Niagara, May 1776
Served under Honyere for General Herkimer at battle of Oriskany, August
    1777
Home burned after battle of Oriskany
Enlisted to fight for Washington, April 1778

**DAKAYENENSESE**, Isaac, "Old Isaac"
From Oquaga
Was converted to Christianity in 1748 by the Rev. Elihu Spencer
Supported Church of England
Began teaching and preaching at Oquaga, summer 1753
Leading preacher at Oquaga, winter 1756
Teacher at Oquaga by 1757
Occasional speaker at conferences, 1760s
Daughter Peggy married to Thayendanega (Joseph Brant), 1764
Speaker at Johnson Hall conference regarding Oquaga being a Christian
   community, 4 February 1764
Speaker at Johnson Hall about loyalty of Oquaga, 9 February 1767
Was involved in land sale to John Harper, 23 July 1767
Arranged indemnity at Oquaga for robbery of French trader, 21 February
   1774
Served under Honyere for General Herkimer at battle at Oriskany, August
   1777

**DAYAHEARI**
Signed Fort Stanwix treaty, 4 September 1784

Deanoyondeah, Augustus
Signed letter to Pickering complaining about Kirkland, 29 January 1794

Dekanaghtsiasne (Dekanaghtorghhere)
Warrior
Signed letter to Governor Clinton complaining about
   Atayataghronghta's pro-French influence over the Oneida
   sachems, 28 October 1789

Denny, David (Lewis)
Turtle clan
Signed petition to New York State to lease land to Peter Smith, 15 January
   1793
Included in war-losses claim (1780) at Kanowalohale, November 1794

Deyahthadane, John
Signed letter to Pickering complaining about Kirkland, 29 January 1794

**DISONONTO**
Sachem at Kanowalohale in 1750, aged over seventy
Supported the Mohawk in their fight against the French as he had been
   imprisoned by them earlier
Present at Onondaga Grand Council, September 1750

**DYOGHHAGWEATE**, William
Dayohagwendeh is the title of an Oneida chief at the founding of the
Iroquois League
Participated in Fort Stanwix conference, September 1784

Feghkatkaghtons, John
Warrior
Participated in Fort Stanwix conference, September 1784

**GAGHSAWEDA** (Kaghsaweta, Thaghsaweta, Haghjaweta), Ludwig
Warrior
Bear clan
Associated with Kanowalohale
Defended Kirkland against Conoquhieson's charges, October 1775
Speaker at Fort Stanwix conference, October 1784
Signed letter requesting grant of land for James Dean, October 1784
Signed congressional land grant for John Harper, 20 November 1784
Signed New York State treaty at Fort Herkimer, 28 June 1785
Signed letter to Congress concerning disputes among the Six Nations,
15 September 1785
Signed letter to Congress, that Cayuga wanted Oneida to speak for the
Iroquois, October 1785
Signed Livingstone lease, 8 January 1788
Was chosen as delegate to meet with New York State commissioners,
Fort Stanwix conference, September 1788
Signed letter to Governor Clinton demanding control of their own
land, 27 January 1790
Was chosen as a delegate to receive New York State annuity, 2 June 1790
Oneida witness to Cayuga ratification of Fort Stanwix treaty, 27 June
1790
Signed petition to New York State to lease land to Peter Smith, 15 January
1793
Signed letter to Pickering for protection of Peter Smith's surveyor, 14
May 1793
Signed act regarding appropriation of land by New York State for use by
the Oneida, Onondaga, and Cayuga, 19 April 1793
Signed letter to SSPCK promoting Kirkland's new school for the Oneida,
27 April 1793
Signed letter to Pickering complaining about Kirkland, 29 January 1794
Included in war-losses claim (1780) at Kanowalohale, November 1794

**GAWEAGHNOGE**
From Oquaga
Representative at the Albany conference, August 1754

**GAWEHE** (Gawickie)
From Kanowalohale
Warrior
Associated with pro-French faction among the Oneida
Conveyed intelligence to Oneida regarding French attack, March 1756
Speaker at Onondaga Grand Council, 10 September 1756
Frequent visits to Canada, May–September 1756
Carried correspondence to Governor Vaudreuil, March 1757
Alerted William Johnson about possible French attack, 15 September
    1757
Was awarded silver medal for participating in Amherst's Montreal
    campaign, April 1761
Attended meeting at Fort Johnson regarding the Seneca, April 1762
Attended meeting at Fort Johnson regarding French attack on German
    Flats, April 1763
Present at Johnson Hall meeting, 5 August 1763
Visited Johnson Hall, angry about defection of Chenussio Seneca, July 1763
Participated in Bradstreet's campaign, spring 1774
Collected provisions at Johnson Hall, 19 December 1764
Died 1766

Haghjaweta. *See* Gaghsaweda

Haghycande
Signed Cayuga land cession with New York State, 25 February 1789

Hanwagalet (Kanwagalet), Kaskonghgwea
Female
Signed Fort Stanwix treaty, 22 September 1788

Hanwagalet (Kanwagalet), Tehoughnihalk
Female
Signed Fort Stanwix treaty, 22 September 1788

**HANWALEAO**, Cornelius
From Kanowalohale
Died in 1800, having professed both Christian and traditional
    sympathies

Hononwayele
Female
Christian in later years
Wife of warrior Anthony Shononghriyo
Signed Fort Stanwix treaty, 22 September 1788
Signed act regarding appropriation of land by New York State for use by

the Oneida, Onondaga, and Cayuga, 19 April 1793
Involved as "matron" in Kirkland's congregation, 10 February 1800

**HONYERE** (Tehonwaghweanglagakhon, Hanyury, Thawengarakwen, Doxtator), Tewahongarahkon
From Oriska
Sachem
Wolf clan
Husband of Tyonajanegen (Dolly)
Father of Jacob, and of Cornelius whose bravery led to his later becoming a head warrior
Brother of Honyost Thaosagawat
Led Oneida fighters for General Herkimer in battle of Oriskany, August 1777, famous for his bravery at this battle
Home burned in retaliation after battle of Oriskany
Lived in home of Molly Brant, Thayendanega's sister, as retaliation for the burning of his home, autumn 1777
Met with General Schuyler regarding fighting for Patriots, September 1777
Received special commendation for his contribution at the battle of Saratoga, October 1777
Was chosen by Oneida to be commissioned captain by Congress, March 1779
Led Oneida fighters briefly in Sullivan-Clinton campaign but would not kill fellow Iroquois, summer 1779
Requested Congress for payment for war services as a commissioned officer, 5 February 1785
Signed New York State treaty at Fort Herkimer, June 1785
Wrote Congress requesting survey of land and new superintendent, 14 July 1787
Was chosen as delegate to receive New York State annuity, 2 June 1790
Delegate to ratify Onondaga land deal at Fort Stanwix conference, 16 June 1790
Attempted to settle dispute between Oriska and Kanowalohale, 23 July 1790
Awarded land for war service as commissioned officer, January 1791
Signed act regarding appropriation of land by New York State for use by Oneida, Onondaga, and Cayuga, 19 April 1793
Signed letter to Pickering about divisions within Oneida regarding land lease with Peter Smith, May 1793
Died 1793
His widow made claim for war losses (1780) at Kanowalohale, November 1794

Honyost (Hanyost)
Was chosen as an overseer of Kanowalohale, east end, 25 February 1799

Horgale, Jacob
Delegate to meeting at Albany regarding land, 28 January 1800

Ishadekarenghes (Tshadekaronghhis). Also Peter Salckarenghis.
Warrior
Signed letter to Governor Clinton complaining about
Atayataghronghta's pro-French influence over the Oneida sachems,
28 October 1789

Itanyeatakayon
Warrior
Signed letter to Governor Clinton complaining about
Atayataghronghta's pro-French influence over the Oneida sachems,
28 October 1789

Jordan (Jourdain), John
Bear clan
Signed letter to SSPCK requesting a school for the Oneida, 27 April 1773
Involved in war-losses claim (1780) at Kanowalohale, November 1794

**JORDAN**, Nicholas
Former French captive, married daughter of Oneida sachem
Resident of Kanowalohale
Present at Fort Stanwix conference, September 1784

Kaantalongwan, William. *See* Kayentarongwea

**KACNEGHDAKON**
Representative at Albany conference, August 1754

Kagendarongwas, William. *See* Kayentarongwea

Kaghnedoreas (Kaghneghlories)
Signed letter to Governor Clinton demanding control of their land, 27
January 1790

Kaghneghtootdau, Saugus
Was chosen as an overseer of Kanowalohale, west end, 25 February 1799

Kaghnenda. *See* Kanento

Kaghsaweta. *See* Gaghsaweda

**KAKIKTOTON** (Kaichtoton, Kohjauwetan), Cornelius (Clenis)
From Kanowalohale

Bear clan

Met with Albany Committee of Correspondence, 1775

Protected Fort Schuyler in the siege of August 1777

Chosen by Oneida to be commissioned lieutenant by Congress, March 1779

Requested payment from Congress for war service as commissioned officer, 5 February 1785

Signed Fort Stanwix treaty, 22 September 1788

Signed Cayuga land cession with New York State, 25 February 1789

Delegate to ratify Onondaga land deal in Fort Stanwix treaty, 16 June 1790

Was awarded land by Congress for war services, January 1791

Signed petition to New York State to lease land to Peter Smith, 15 January 1793

Signed act regarding appropriation of land by New York State for use by the Oneida, Onondaga, and Cayuga, 19 April 1793

Signed letter to Pickering complaining about Kirkland, 29 January 1794

Included in war-losses claim (1780) at Kanowalohale, November 1794

Signed treaty for land deal concerning Oneida, Tuscarora, and Stockbridge, 2 December 1794

**KANADAROK**, Peter (Peter Bread)

Served under Honyere for General Herkimer at battle of Oriskany, August 1777

Met with General Schuyler regarding fighting for Patriots, September 1777

Special medal given by Washington for services as a spy in the battle of Saratoga, October 1777

Signed petition to New York State to lease land to Peter Smith, 15 January 1793

Signed letter to Pickering complaining about Kirkland, 29 January 1794

Kanaghsalilgh (Shanaghsakigh)

Signed Fort Stanwix treaty, 22 September 1788

Moved briefly to Fort Niagara with other Oneida joining the British, autumn 1780

Was chosen as delegate to receive New York State annuity, 2 June 1790

Signed letter to SSPCK requesting a school for the Oneida, 27 April 1793

Reported by Kirkland to have become Christian, 25 May 1793

**KANAGHSATIRHON** (Kanaghsatyerha), Joseph

Chosen by Oneida to be commissioned lieutenant by Congress, March 1779

**KANAGHWEAS** (Kanaghgweaye, Kanagweaga), "Young Conoquhieson"

Sachem

Wolf clan
Succeeded Conoquhieson after his death, autumn 1775
Traveled to Caughnawauga to encourage them to maintain their
    neutrality, May 1776
Traveled to east coast with Philip Schuyler to witness Patriot power, June
    1776
Traveled to Fort Niagara but rejected Thayendanega's invitation to join
    the British, February 1777
Signed Fort Stanwix treaty, 22 September 1788

Kanagwenton. *See* Kennawagenton

Kanaweadon
Warrior
Participated in Fort Stanwix conference, September 1784

Kanento (Kaghnenda, Kaghnenta, Kaneaton), Peter, "Big Christian"
Signed letter to Governor Clinton demanding control of their land, 27
    January 1790
Signed petition to New York State to lease land to Peter Smith, 15 January
    1793
Included in war-losses claim (1780) at Kanowalohale, November 1794

Kanneyalode, Christian
Was chosen as an overseer of Kanowalohale, west end, 25 February 1799

Kanonghgwenya, Peter
Signed Oneida land deal with Pennsylvania, 23 October 1784
Signed petition to New York State to lease land to Peter Smith, 15 January
    1793
Signed letter to Pickering asking for protection for Peter Smith's
    surveyor, 14 May 1793

Kanonghsase (Kanaghguassea), William
Signed land grant to James Dean, 11 August 1785
Signed petition to New York State to lease land to Peter Smith, 15 January
    1793

Kanyeagoton (Kanyaraton, Kanyarodon), Augustus, "Little Christian"
Signed petition to New York State to lease land to Peter Smith, 15 January
    1793
Signed letter to Pickering complaining about Kirkland, 29 January 1794

Kaskoughguea
Delegate at meeting at Fort Stanwix, September 1788

Kaujathoondautheu, Quedlh
Was chosen as an overseer of Kanowalohale, west end, 25 February
1799

Kaunaudauloonh, Quedelh
Was chosen as an overseer of Kanowalohale, west end, 25 February
1799

Kayeadanongwea. *See* Kayentarongwea

Kayeghtorha, Peter, "Beech Tree"
Son of Oneyanha
Signed petition to New York State to lease land to Peter Smith, 15
January 1793

**KAYENTARONGWEA** (Kayeadanongwea, Kaantalongwan,
Kagendarongwas, Kayendalgweah), William
Warrior
Traveled to east coast to witness the strength of Washington's forces,
1777
Speaker at Fort Schuyler meeting, April 1778
Participated in Fort Stanwix conference, September 1784
Signed letter to Congress regarding discord among the Six Nations,
September 1785
Signed Livingstone lease, 8 January 1788
Signed letter to Pickering requesting protection for Peter Smith's
surveyor, 14 May 1793
Signed letter to SSPCK requesting a school for the Oneida, 27 April 1793

Kayhatsho. *See* Kaghnatstio

**KEANDARUNDIE** (Kindarundie)
Delegate at meeting in Canada, November 1751
Delegate at Albany conference, August 1754
Delegate to meetings at Fort Oswegatchie, September 1756, September
1757
Installed as sachem by William Johnson, March 1758

Keanyako (Keanjako), David
Signed Fort Stanwix treaty, 22 September 1788
Signed act regarding appropriation of land by New York State for use by
the Oneida, Onondaga, and Cayuga, 19 April 1793

**KENNAWAGENTON** (Kanagwenton)
Signed Phelps-Gorham land sale, 8 July 1788

Signed petition to New York State to lease land to Peter Smith, 15 January 1793

Kentaronhye (Kontolonty), Anthony
Signed letter to Pickering requesting protection for Peter Smith's surveyor, 14 May 1793
Included in war-losses claim (1780) at Kanowalohale, November 1794

**KING, Thomas**. Also Saghogsoniont (rarely used)
Associated with Oquaga
Warrior
Successor of Shickellamy and Tachnechdorus as Oneida overseer in the Ohio region, following latter's death in 1748
Present at Fort Johnson meetings, autumn 1755, February 1756
Speaker at Lancaster conference, April, May 1757
Speaker at Easton conference, October 1758
Speaker at meeting at Philadelphia, 1759
Was awarded silver medal for participating in Amherst's Montreal campaign, April 1761
Speaker for Confederacy at Lancaster conference, August 1762
Visited Johnson Hall, performed condolence for William Johnson's father, and sought ammunition for Oquaga, July 1763
Attended meetings at Johnson Hall, October 1763
Supported William Johnson in attacking pro-French Shawnee and Delaware, February 1764
Participated in Bradstreet campaign, spring 1764
Captured Delaware prisoners and took them to Oquaga, spring 1764
Speaker at Fort Niagara conference with Chenussio Seneca, 3 August 1764
Met with Pontiac at Sandusky, September–October 1764
Visited Johnson, annoyed at results of campaign against Shawnee and Delaware, December 1764
Present at conference when Johnson installed Onondaga sachems and reaffirmed Onondaga leadership of Confederacy, April 1765
Speaker at conference at Johnson Hall concerning boundary line, April 1765
Visited Johnson Hall, made independent land deals with John Harper for land at Oquaga, June–December 1767
Speaker at Johnson Hall conference regarding the Cherokee, March 1768
Speaker at German Flats conference regarding Cherokee, July 1770
Attended Fort Pitt conference, January 1771
Died in Charleston, South Carolina, following meetings with the Catawba, September 1771

Kohjauwetan. *See* Kakiktoton

Konnauterlook, Peter
    Turtle clan
    Signed land deal with Oneida, Tuscarora, and Stockbridge, 2 December
       1794
Konnoquenyan
    Wolf clan
    Signed land deal with Oneida, Tuscarora, and Stockbridge, 2 December 1794

Kontolonty. *See* Kentaronhye

**LEGUCHSANYONT**
    Present at meetings at Easton, 24 October 1758

Looghshingh, Martinus
    Was chosen as an overseer of Kanowalohale, west end, 25 February
       1799

Looghtanddya, Nicholas
    Was chosen as an overseer of Kanowalohale, west end, 25 February
       1799

Martinus
    From Kanowalohale
    Christian
    Replaced Captain John as leader following his death, 9 January 1800
    Concerned over Christian-traditionalist split at Kanowalohale
    Attended meetings at Albany concerning hostility by whites, 28
       January–7 February 1800

**NICHOLAASA**
    Invited William Johnson to a meeting with Oneida at Onondaga, 26
       April 1758
    Represented the Oneida at meetings with the Chenussio Seneca, 12
       June 1758

**ODAGHSEGHTE** (Odaghsaghte, Otatshete, Otatsheghte), Peter
    Title of an Oneida sachem at the founding of the Iroquois League
    From Kanowalohale
    Sachem
    Wolf Clan
    Speaker at German Flats conference regarding Cherokee, July 1770
    Kirkland suggested he lead a condolence regarding the extinguishment
       of the Onondaga Grand Council fire, January 1777
    Speaker at Johnstown conference with Lafayette, March 1778

Gave speech to warriors about proper conduct in war, May 1778
Personally adopted a young prisoner, autumn 1778
Arranged for release of Onondaga prisoners, July 1779
Gained permission to establish new village near Fort Schuyler, February
1780
Appealed for supplies from Congress in Philadelphia, summer 1780
Speaker at Fort Stanwix conference, September 1784
Signed congressional land grant to John Harper, 20 November 1784
Signed Fort Stanwix treaty, 22 September 1788
Signed letter to Governor Clinton complaining about
Atayataghrongtha's pro-French influence among the Oneida
sachems, 28 October 1789
Signed act regarding appropriation of land by New York State for use by
the Oneida, Onondaga, and Cayuga, 19 April 1793
Included in war-losses claim (1780) at Kanowalohale, November 1794
Signed land deal with New York State for Oneida, Tuscarora, and
Stockbridge, December 1794

**OGHNAONGOGHTON**
Signed Phelps-Gorham land sale, 8 July 1788

Oghneyanha. *See* Oneyanha

Oghsidago
Was awarded silver medal for participation in Amherst's 1760 Montreal
campaign, April 1761

**OHANODLIGHTON**
Bear clan
Loyalist
Resident of Kanowalohale
Chosen by Oneida as hostage at Fort Stanwix conference, September
1784
Included in war-losses claim (1780) at Kanowalohale, November 1794

**OJISTALALE** (Ojistarare, Hanyarry), Cornelius, "Grasshopper"
Sachem
Turtle clan
Signed letter explaining difficulty in obtaining Oneida fighters, 26 April
1778
Participated in Fort Stanwix conference, September 1784
Signed receipt for $5,000 as payment for Oneida land grant to
Pennsylvania at the Fort Stanwix conference, 23 October 1784
Signed letter requesting grant of land for James Dean, October 1784

Differed with Governor Clinton over Oneida land, May 1785
Speaker at conference and signed New York State treaty at Fort
    Herkimer, June 1785
Was chosen as delegate to meet with New York State commissioners at
    the Fort Stanwix conference, September 1788
Signed Fort Stanwix treaty, 22 September 1788
Died 1788
His widow was included in the war-losses claim (1780) at
    Kanowalohale, November 1794

**OKONYOTA** (Ohonyota), Cornelius
Chosen by Oneida to be commissioned lieutenant by Congress, March 1779
Requested payment for military service as a commissioned officer, 5
    February 1785
Signed New York State Treaty at Fort Herkimer, June 1785

Onderihokde
Was awarded silver medal for participation in Amherst's 1760 Montreal
    campaign, April 1761

**ONEYANHA** (Oneyanhe, Oghneyanha, Oneynya, Oneynyoaget,
Aughneonh), Peter, "Beech Tree"
Sachem
Turtle clan
Christian
Traveled to east coast to witness the strength of Washington's forces, 1777
Defended Fort Schuyler in the siege of August 1777
Signed letter requesting grant of land for James Dean, October 1784
Signed congressional land grant to John Harper, 28 November 1784
Speaker at conference and signed New York State treaty at Fort
    Herkimer, June 1785
Signed deed of land to James Dean, 11 August 1785
Signed letter to Congress regarding discord among the Six Nations,
    September 1785
Speaker at Fort Stanwix conference, September 1785
Signed Fort Stanwix treaty, 22 September 1788
Recorded by Kirkland as successor to Ojistalale as leading sachem
    following the latter's death, 30 November 1788
Signed Cayuga land cession with New York State, 25 February 1789
Signed letter to Governor Clinton demanding control of their land, 27
    January 1790
Speaker at conference and witness to ratification of Onondaga-Cayuga
    land deals, 16, 22 June 1790
Concerned about divisions within Kanowalohale, 4 February 1791

Speaker at Newtown Point (Painted Post) conference, July 1791
Signed land lease with Peter Smith, 15 January 1793
Signed letter to Pickering requesting protection for Peter Smith's
    surveyor, 14 May 1793
Signed letter to Pickering complaining about Kirkland, 29 January 1794
Died summer 1794
Widow included in war-losses claim (1780) at Kanowalohale, November
    1794

## ONEYNYOAGAT
Turtle clan
Christian
From Kanowalohale
Oneida representative at Albany Committee of Correspondence
    meeting, summer 1775

## ONIDYOGHGORY, Nickus
Delegate at the Albany conference, July 1754
Delegate at Onondaga Grand Council, 25 October 1763

## ONONDIYO (Onontego, Ononteyoh), John, "Captain John"
Sachem
Turtle clan
Christian
Was chosen by Oneida to be commissioned captain by Congress, March
    1779
Led Oneida from Kanowalohale to their new village near Fort Schuyler,
    autumn 1780
Delegate at Fort Herkimer conference, 28 June 1785
Signed Livingstone lease, 8 January 1788
Traveled with Kirkland to support creation of school at Dartmouth,
    August 1792–February 1793
Became major negotiator after death of Agwrongdongwas in 1793
Signed letter to Pickering complaining about Kirkland, 29 January 1794
Speaker at Canandaigua conference, October 1794
Assisted in compilation of, and included in, the war-losses claim (1780)
    at Kanowalohale, November 1794
Died September 1795

Ononghsawinghti, James
Signed Livingstone lease, 8 January 1788

Onughseeshoo, Thomas
Was chosen as an overseer of Kanowalohale, east end, 25 February 1799

Onwanotseron
Signed congressional land grant to John Harper, 20 November 1784

Origombe, Peter
Signed Livingstone lease, 8 January 1788

Osauhataugaunlot, Thomas
Bear clan
Signed land deal with Oneida, Tuscarora, and Stockbridge, 2 December 1794

**OTAAWIGHTON**, John
Was chosen by Oneida to be commissioned captain by Congress, March 1779
Imprisoned by Patriots for misguiding troops to Oswego, February 1783
Requested payment for military service as commissioned officer, 5 February 1785
Granted land for military service, January 1791

Otatshete, Peter. *See* Odaghseghte

Oterogon
Delegate to Fort Stanwix conference, September 1788

**OTISQUETTE** (Otswguette, Atisquette), Peter, "French Peter"
Warrior
Served in revolution with Lafayette
Married Oneida woman
Studied in Europe
Speaker at Fort Stanwix conference, September 1788
Signed Fort Stanwix treaty, 22 September 1788
Signed letter to Governor Clinton complaining about Atayataghronghta's pro-French influence among the Oneida sachems, 28 October 1789
Delegate at ratification of Cayuga and Onondaga land deals, 16–22 June 1790
Died as a youth, going west to meet George Washington after a conference at Philadelphia, 1792

Otsetogon (Otsedogan), Paul
Signed Fort Stanwix treaty, 22 September 1788
Signed letter to SSPCK requesting a school for the Oneida, 27 April 1793

Otshogea, Paul
Signed Livingstone lease, 8 January 1788

Otsienhea, Peter,
    Signed petition to New York State to lease land to Peter Smith, 15 January
    1793

Otsighn'yokare, Thomas, "Whitebeans"
    Signed petition to New York State to lease land to Peter Smith, 15
    January 1793

**OTYADONENGHTI**
    Signed Fort Stanwix treaty, 4 September 1784

Owyaghse
    Warrior
    Signed letter to Governor Clinton complaining about
    Atayataghronghta's pro-French influence among the Oneida
    sachems, 28 October 1789

**PAGAN PETER**. *See* Sategaleahtas

Rawistonisk. *See* Alawistonis

Reed, Jacob. *See* Aksiaktatye

Roghnketyea
    Signed letter to Governor Clinton demanding control of their land, 27
    January 1790

Rotshawatgense (Rotshawatzenhe), Cornelius
    Signed letter to Pickering complaining about Kirkland, 29 January 1794

**SAGOHARASE**, John
    Chosen by Oneida to be commissioned lieutenant by Congress, March
    1799
    Died at Schenectady, winter 1780
    Heirs were awarded land grant for his military service as a
    commissioned officer, January 1791

Sagorakorongo, David
    Signed Livingstone lease, 8 January 1788

Sagoyontha (Sagoyantha), Cornelius
    Wolf clan
    Signed Fort Stanwix treaty, 22 September 1788
    Was chosen as delegate to receive New York State annuity, 2 June 1790

Signed act regarding appropriation of land by New York State for use by the Oneida, Onondaga, and Cayuga, 19 April 1793

Included in war-losses claim (1780) at Kanowalohale, November 1794

Sahonwate, Hendrick
Signed Livingstone lease, 8 January 1788
Signed letter to Congress complaining about land leases, February 1788

Salckarenghis, Peter
Signed letter to Congress complaining about land leases, February 1788

**SATEGALEAHTAS** (Sautagaulichles), "Pagan Peter," "Captain Peter"
Influential at Kanowalohale
Son of Agwrongdongwas
Leader of traditional pagan party at Kanowalohale
Opposed land arrangements made at Canandaigua conference, autumn 1794
Wanted to remove Kirkland from Kanowalohale, 24 November 1800

**SCAROOYADY** (Scarouady, Monacatoocha, Monocantha), "Half King"
Warrior
Represented the Oneida in their southern territory
Speaker at Lancaster conference, 1748
Speaker at Carlisle conference, November 1753
Speaker at conference in Philadelphia, September 1754
Addressed Pennsylvania Provincial Council, December 1754
Visited Albany with William Johnson, February 1755
Protested against Susquehanna land purchase, March 1755
Speaker at meetings at Philadelphia, March, May, June 1755
Moved to Mohawk valley and resided with Johnson, winter 1755
Speaker at Iroquois conference at Fort Johnson, March 1756
Speaker at meetings at Philadelphia, January, March, April 1756
Attended Onondaga Grand Council, April 1756
Present at Easton conference, 1756
Attended Lancaster conference, April 1757
Died of smallpox, 1757

Segaoneghseria (Segaoneghserisa), Daniel
Letter to Congress complaining about land leases, February 1788

Seghsenowack
Was awarded silver medal for participation in Amherst's 1760 Montreal campaign, April 1761

Seghskyeghte, "John Baptist"
Was awarded silver medal for participation in Amherst's 1760 Montreal
campaign, April 1761

**SENGHNAGENRAT** (Saghaugarat, Sughnagearah), "Whiteskin"
Sachem
From Kanowalohale
Accompanied Conoquhieson to meeting at Albany, March 1763
At meeting with William Johnson regarding Oneida land, December 1766
Negotiator regarding land for New England Indians, October 1773
Negotiator for Confederacy to promote Patriot cause, August 1775
Speaker at conference with Albany Committee of Correspondence at
German Flats, August–September 1775
Preceded by Conoquhieson and became a leading speaker for the
Oneida following the death of the latter, autumn 1775
Speaker at Kanowalohale conference regarding divisions within the
Confederacy, March 1776
Speaker at Albany conference, May 1776
Kirkland suggested that he lead a condolence regarding the
extinguishment of the Onondaga Grand Council fire, January 1777
Spied for the Patriots in the Saint Lawrence River area, spring 1777
Spied for the Patriots at Fort Niagara, June 1777
Unable to raise sufficient Oneida fighters to meet Washington's request,
April 1778
Moved to Fort Niagara with other Oneida joining the British, autumn 1780

**SEWAJIS** (Sinavis)
Sachem
From Kanowalohale
Led delegation to Caughnawauga to maintain their neutrality, May
1776
Traveled to Caughnawauga to question their neutrality, February 1777
Visited Caughnawauga again, June 1777
Enlisted to fight for Washington, April 1778
Killed during Barren Hill campaign, 1778

Shagoyaghtorghhere
Warrior
Signed letter to Governor Clinton complaining about
Atayataghronghta's pro-French influence among the Oneida
sachems, 28 October 1789

Shanaghsakigh. *See* Kanaghsalilgh

Shaugoogaudoohaula, Neckis
   Was chosen as overseer of Kanowalohale, east end, 25 February 1799

Shejijowane, John
   Turtle clan
   Was included in war-losses claim (1780) at Kanowalohale, November
      1794
**SHICKELLAMY**
   Origin uncertain, adopted as an Oneida
   Married to a Cayuga
   Appointed by Confederacy to represent them in their southern
      territory, June 1728
   Pennsylvania Colonial Council wanted him to discourage sale of rum
      to the Iroquois, 16 August 1731
   Resided at Shamokin, 1737–1748
   Numerous trips to meetings in Philadelphia, 1730s, 1740s
   Speaker at Lancaster conference, 1744
   Received baptism by Moravians, January 1748
   Died December 1748

Shogoyontha, Anthony. *See* Shononghriyo

Shoneghslishea (Segaoneghserisa), Daniel
   Signed letter to Governor Clinton in support of Livingstone lease,
      February 1788
   Signed Fort Stanwix treaty, 22 September 1788

Shononghis, Thomas
   Signed Livingstone lease, 8 January 1788

**SHONONGHRIYO** (Shononleyo, Thononghrigo, Shononghlegs,
Shogoyontha, Shonighleoh, Shonoughleyo), Anthony
   Title of an Oneida chief at the founding of the Iroquois League
   Warrior
   Turtle clan
   Signed Declaration of Neutrality, June 1775
   Defended Fort Schuyler in August 1777
   Participated at Fort Stanwix conference, September 1784
   Signed Livingstone lease, 8 January 1788
   Was chosen as a delegate to meet with New York State commissioners at
      the Fort Stanwix conference, September 1788
   Signed Fort Stanwix treaty, 22 September 1788
   Signed land grant to Stockbridge Indians, 2 December 1790

Signed petition to New York State to lease land to Peter Smith, 15 January 1793

Signed act regarding appropriation of land by New York State for use by the Oneida, Cayuga, and Onondaga, 19 April 1793

Signed letter to Governor Clinton regarding problems at German Flats, 17 January 1800

Shoratowane
Signed Phelps-Gorham land sale, 8 July 1788

Shotsijowane (Statsideyowane), John
Signed petition to New York State to lease land to Peter Smith, 15 January 1793

Skandyoughquathe
Was awarded silver medal for participation in Amherst's 1760 Montreal campaign, April 1761

**SKENANDOAH** (Teounesless), Daniel
Son of John Skenandoah
Warrior
Turtle clan
Enlisted to fight for Washington, April 1778
Signed land deal for Stockbridge Indians, 2 December 1794

**SKENANDOAH**, John
Born in Susquehanna area around 1706, adopted as an Oneida
Warrior
Wolf clan
Christian
Father of Daniel and Thomas
Represented Oneida at conferences in 1740s, frequently under the influence of alcohol
Abandoned use of alcohol after humiliating experience at an Albany meeting, 1754
Acted as spy and informant for British during war with French, 1755–1763
Warned William Johnson of possible French attack, December 1757
Joined Amherst's Montreal campaign of 1760 but parted from troops before they arrived at Montreal
Was converted to Christianity by Kirkland, 1768
Present at Fort Stanwix conference, October 1768
Signed Declaration of Neutrality, June 1775
Provided accommodation for Captain Bloomfield at German Flats conference, June 1776

Rejected Thayendanega's invitation to join the British cause at Fort
 Niagara, January 1777
Speaker at Fort Schuyler meeting, April 1778
Spoke at Fort Schuyler meeting against Patriot plans to attack
 Onondaga, July 1779
Imprisoned at Fort Niagara by the British, February 1780
Speaker at Fort Stanwix conference, October 1784
Signed letter requesting grant of land for James Dean, October 1784
Signed New York State treaty at Fort Herkimer, June 1785
Signed land grant for James Dean, 11 August 1785
Signed letter to Congress regarding discord among the Six Nations,
 September 1785
Signed letter to Congress, that Cayuga wanted Oneida to speak for the
 Iroquois, October 1785
Signed Livingstone lease, 8 June 1788
Signed Fort Stanwix treaty, 22 September 1788
Signed Oneida land cession with New York State, 25 February 1789
Signed letter to Governor Clinton demanding control of their own
 land, 27 January 1790
Signed petition to New York State to lease land to Peter Smith, 15
 January 1793
Signed letter to SSPCK promoting Kirkland's new school for the Oneida,
 27 April 1793
Signed letter to Pickering requesting protection for Peter Smith's
 surveyor, 14 May 1793
Reported by Kirkland as wanting to set up a Christian community
 separate from Kanowalohale, 9 November 1793
Signed letter to Pickering complaining about Kirkland, 29 January 1794
Speaker at Canandaigua conference, October 1794
Hosted Pickering at his home during the war-losses evaluations at
 Kanowalohale, November 1794
Included in war-losses claim (1780) at Kanowalohale, November 1794
Signed land deal for Stockbridge Indians, 2 December 1794
Depressed over continuous religious divisions at Kanowalohale, 1
 January 1800
Died 1816, buried near Kirkland

Skenandoah, Thomas
 Signed letter to Pickering requesting protection for Peter Smith's
 surveyor, 14 May 1793

Sodolk, Hannah
 Signed Fort Stanwix treaty, 22 September 1788

Signed act regarding appropriation of land by New York State for use by the Oneida, Onondaga, and Cayuga, 19 April 1793

Soghraghrowane, Peter
Signed petition to New York State to lease land to Peter Smith, 15 January 1793

Soheghtrane
Installed as sachem by William Johnson at Johnson Hall, May 1765

**SPENCER**, Thomas
From Oquaga and Oriska
Oneida-English parentage
Supported Hawley's mission at Oquaga, 1753
At Johnson Hall meeting, Thomas King requested that Spencer supply trade goods from Schenectady, 17 October 1763
Promoted by William Johnson as gunsmith and "honest trader," July 1767
Present at Fort Stanwix conference, October 1768
Worked as a blacksmith at Kanowalohale, 1770s
Speaker at Albany Committee of Correspondence, May 1775
Fought under Honyere at battle of Oriskany and was killed during the fighting, 1777

Statsideyowane, John. *See* Shotsijowane

Suscuhaloane
One of the hostages following the Fort Stanwix conference, 29 October 1784

**TACHNECHDORUS**, John
Son of Shickellamy
Present with his father at Philadelphia meeting in 1732 and at Onondaga Grand Council, 1743
Assumed for himself the role of the Oneida overseer in the Ohio region after his father's death, 1748
Speaker at Philadelphia conference, and was accepted by authorities as representative of the Oneida, 24 December 1754
Joined a war party of the enemy Delaware, 1756
Dropped out of sight in disgrace after 1756

**TAGAWARON**
From Kanowalohale
Warrior

Attended meeting at Fort Johnson with Gawehe, 15 September 1757
Attended meeting at Fort Johnson with Conoquhieson, 10 April 1762
Speaker at Johnson Hall meeting with Gawehe, 5–6 August 1763
Participated in Bradstreet's campaign, spring 1764
Visited Johnson Hall with Gawehe, 19 December 1764
Speaker at Johnson Hall conference regarding Delaware, 30 January 1765
Speaker at Johnson Hall conference regarding Cherokee, March 1768
Principal negotiator at Fort Stanwix conference, October 1768
Speaker at German Flats conference regarding Cherokee, July 1770
Meeting with Johnson regarding land use, August 1770
Conflict with Conoquhieson regarding Kirkland's ministry, August,
    December 1770
Takes Kirkland's advice to circumvent Johnson regarding a blacksmith
    for Oquaga, December 1770
Expressed loyalty of Oquaga to New York governor, 31 December 1770
Opposed to Kirkland's baptismal practices, March 1772
Died 1772

Tahauweyaudelon, Quedels Peter
Was chosen as an overseer of Kanowalohale, east end, 25 February 1799

Tahtequese, William
Represented Oneida at Albany Committee of Correspondence meetings,
    June 1775

**TARAGHORUS**
Present at Albany conference, July 1754

Tatahonghteayon
Signed deed of land to Pennsylvania at Fort Stanwix conference, 23
    October 1784

**TAYAHEURA**, Jimmy
Sachem
From Kanowalohale
Signed Declaration of Neutrality, June 1775
Present at German Flats conference, July 1776
Traveled to Fort Niagara but rejected Thayendanega's invitation to join
    the British, February 1777

**TEAGHSWEANGALOLIS** (Thaghswoangalolis, Thoghsweanglolis), Paul
From Kanowalohale
Bear clan

Famed for heroic running of messages at battle of Oriskany, August 1777
Defended Fort Schuyler in the siege of August 1777
Signed Fort Stanwix treaty, 22 September 1788
Signed act regarding appropriation of land by New York State for use by
the Oneida, Onondaga, and Cayuga, 19 April 1793
Included in war-losses claim (1780) at Kanowalohale, November 1794

**TEAUNDEANTHE**, Tenussa
Represented the Oneida at an Albany Committee of Correspondence
meeting, summer 1775

**TEHEANIYOGHTIWAT**
Served briefly in Sullivan-Clinton campaign but would not kill Cayuga,
summer 1779

Tehonogwesghsoolhaula, Christian
Was chosen as an overseer of Kanowalohale, east end, 25 February 1799

Tehonwaghweanglagakhon. *See* Honyere

Tekahoweasere, John
Was awarded silver medal for participation in Amherst's 1760 Montreal
campaign, April 1761

Tekanijasece (Tekanajosera), John
Turtle clan
Signed letter to SSPCK requesting a school for the Oneida, 27 April 1793
Included in war-losses claim (1780) at Kanowalohale, November 1794
Tekeandyakhon (Tekcandyakkon)
Was chosen as a delegate to meet with New York State commissioners,
Fort Stanwix conference, September 1788
Signed act regarding appropriation of land by New York State for use by
the Oneida, Onondaga, and Cayuga, 19 April 1793

Teounesless, Daniel. *See* Skenandoah, Daniel

**TESANONDE** (Tesanonda, Tesanunde)
Speaker at German Flats meeting, September 1756
Speaker at Onondaga Grand Council, 10 September 1756

**TEWAGHTAHKOTTE**
Was chosen by Oneida to be commissioned captain by Congress, March
1779

Tewahangataghkon. *See* Honyere

**TEWAHONGARAHKON**, Dolly. *See also* Tyonajanegen
Wife of Honyere

**TEYOHAGWEANDA** (Teyohagwanda, Toyohagweanda, Tiahogwando)
Sachem
Speaker at conference with Albany Committee of Correspondence at
    German Flats, August-September 1775
Signed Fort Stanwix treaty, 22 September 1788
Signed act regarding appropriation of land by New York State for use by
    the Oneida, Onondaga, and Cayuga, 19 April 1793

Teyoneghserise
Was awarded silver medal for participation in Amherst's 1760 Montreal
    campaign, April 1761

Thaghenghororenghte. *See* Thaghneghtolis

Thaghnaghwanekeas, "Big Honyost"
Signed petition to New York State to lease land to Peter Smith, 15 January
    1793

Thaghneghtolis (Thaghenghororenghte, Thagneghtorens), Hendrick
Christian
Signed land grant to James Dean, 11 August 1785
Signed Livingstone land lease, 8 January 1788
Signed Fort Stanwix treaty, 22 September 1788
Signed land lease with New York State to Peter Smith, 1793

Thaghneghtorens. *See* Thaghneghtolis

Thaghsaweta. *See* Gaghsaweda

Thaghswoangalolis. *See* Teaghsweangalolis

**THAGHTAGHGWESERE** (Thagtaghguisea, Thaghtagwisea,
Thotegenwasere, Thahteequesera), William
Warrior
Delegate at meeting of Albany Committee of Correspondence, June 1775
Signed congressional land grant to John Harper, 20 November 1784
Signed Fort Stanwix treaty, 22 September 1788
Delegate chosen to receive New York State annuity, 2 June 1790

Signed petition to New York State to lease land to Peter Smith, 15 January 1793

Signed act regarding appropriation of land by New York State for use by the Oneida, Onondaga, and Cayuga, 19 April 1793

Signed letter to SSPCK requesting a school for the Oneida, 27 April 1793

Thagniyongo (Thaghniyongo), "Big Bear"
Chosen as a delegate to meet with New York State commissioners, Fort Stanwix conference, September 1788

Signed Fort Stanwix treaty, 22 September 1788

Signed act regarding appropriation of land by New York State for use by the Oneida, Onondaga, and Cayuga, 19 April 1793

Thangageandagoyan. *See* Thanigeandagayon

**THANIGEANDAGAYON** (Thangageandagoyon, Thanyeatakayon), Henry
Warrior
Wolf clan
Signed Fort Stanwix treaty, 22 September 1788

Signed letter to Governor Clinton regarding Atayataghronghta's pro-French influence over the Oneida sachems, 28 October 1789

Signed act regarding appropriation of land by New York State for use by the Oneida, Onondaga, and Cayuga, 19 April 1793

Included in war-losses claim (1780) at Kanowalohale, November 1794

**THAOSAGAWAT** (Thaosaquatho), Honyost
Warrior
Brother of Honyere Tewahongarahkon
Was awarded silver medal for participation in Amherst's 1760 Montreal campaign, April 1761

Traveled to Caughnawauga to maintain their neutrality, September 1775

Fought under Honyere at the battle of Oriskany and was wounded during the fighting, 1777

Defended Fort Schuyler in the siege of August 1777

Attempted to gain greater support of Oneida fighters in the revolution, 26 April 1778

Enlisted to fight for Washington, April 1778

Chosen by Oneida to be commissioned lieutenant by Congress, March 1779

Served briefly in Clinton-Sullivan campaign, summer 1779

Killed by the Seneca while serving as a guide for General Sullivan, 1779

Tharontuwagon (Tharondawagon)
Signed Livingstone lands lease, 8 January 1788
Witness to letter to Governor Clinton demanding control of their own
land, 27 January 1790

Thaswenkaroras (Thaswenkarorens), Paul
Signed letter to Governor Clinton regarding Atayataghronghta's pro-
French influence over the Oneida sachems, 28 October 1789
Signed letter to Pickering requesting protection for Peter Smith's
surveyor, 14 May 1793

**THAUNEYENDAUGAUYOON**
Christian resident of Kanowalohale who attended the White Dog
sacrifice out of curiosity, 1799

Thayagonentagetita
Hostage as a result of the Fort Stanwix conference, 29 October 1784

Theenis Teandeantha
Delegate to Albany Committee of Correspondence, summer 1775

Theugereyndack
Delegate to Albany Committee of Correspondence, summer 1775

Thoghsweanglolis. *See* Teaghsweangalolis

**THOMAS**, "Deacon Thomas"
From Oquaga
Warrior
Christian
Supported Hawley's mission at Oquaga, 1753
Traveled with Kirkland to Boston to obtain support for a church at
Oquaga, autumn 1770
Opposed Kirkland's Presbyterian baptismal policy, spring 1772
Supported Kirkland's construction of a church at Kanowalohale, 1774
Complained to Guy Johnson regarding denominationalism and land
policies at Oquaga, February 1775
Attempted unsuccessfully to convince the Seneca to support the
Patriots, April 1775
Rejected Thayendanega's invitation to join the British cause at Fort
Niagara, January 1777
Traveled to Canada as spy for the Patriots, April 1777
Unable to raise sufficient Oneida fighters to meet Washington's request,
April 1778
Enlisted to fight for Washington, April 1778

Traveled to Caughnawauga as a spy against the British and was killed there, July 1779

Thomgatasher, Paul
Signed Livingstone land lease, 8 January 1788

**THONAYUTE**
Bear clan
Loyalist
Hostage as a result of the Fort Stanwix conference, October 1784
Included in war-losses claim (1780) at Kanowalohale, November 1794

Thonigweaghshale. *See* Thonigwenghsohare

**THONIGWENGHSOHARE** (Thonigweaghshale, Thonigweoghsohalte, Thonigraghosghhare), Christian
Wolf clan
Was chosen by Oneida to be commissioned lieutenant by Congress, March 1779
Moved briefly to Fort Niagara with other Oneida joining the British, autumn 1780
Signed Livingstone land lease, 8 January 1788
Signed Fort Stanwix treaty, 22 September 1788
Signed act regarding appropriation of land by New York State for use by the Oneida, Onondaga, and Cayuga, 19 April 1793
Included in war-losses claim (1780) at Kanowalohale, November 1794

Thonigweoghsohalte. *See* Thonigwenghsohare

Thononghrigo, Anthony. *See* Shononghriyo

Thonwaghweakaragwea, George
Warrior
Participated in Fort Stanwix conference, September 1784

Thotegenwasere, William. *See* Thaghtaghgwesere

Tiahaeira
Sachem
Speaker at meeting with Indian Affairs Commissioners at Albany, 7 May 1776

Tiahogwando. *See* Teyohagweanda

**TIANOGA**
Visited Oquaga to gain support against the French, autumn 1756
Delegate to visit William Johnson at Fort Johnson, April 1757

Tiwasgwadeghkon
Signed New York State treaty at Fort Herkimer, June 1785

**TOHAGHDAAGHQUYSERRY**
Present at Albany conference, July 1754

Tohayeuesera, Cornelius
Signed Livingstone land lease, 30 November 1787

Toneaghslishea (Tonaghslishea, Toneghslishea), David
Signed Fort Stanwix treaty, 22 September 1788
Signed act regarding appropriation of land by New York State for use by
the Oneida, Onondaga, and Cayuga, 19 April 1793

**TOTYANEAHAWI** (Totyaneahani)
Chosen by Oneida to be commissioned lieutenant by Congress, March
1779
Moved to Fort Niagara with other Oneida joining the British, autumn
1780

Towaniaghhalese, Daniel
Signed Cayuga land cession with New York State, 25 February 1789

Toyohagweanda. *See* Teyohagweanda

Tshadekaronghhis. *See* Ishadekarenghes

**TYONAJANEGEN**, "Dolly"
Wife of Honyere
Mother of Jacob and Cornelius
Accompanied her husband in battle of Oriskany, and famous for her
valor and her skill on horseback, August 1777
Received special commendation for her contribution at the battle of
Saratoga, October 1777

Tyorhadaghiro
Was awarded silver medal for participation in Amherst's 1760 Montreal
campaign, April 1761

**WAKARONTHARANE**, James
Was chosen by Oneida to be commissioned captain by Congress, March 1779
Requested payment for military service as commissioned officer, 5 February 1785
Granted land as payment for military service, January 1791

**WARONWANSEN**, Adam
Present at German Flats conference, July 1776

Wauts'haudeaghongh, Christian
Was chosen as an overseer of Kanowalohale, east end, 25 February 1799

# NOTES

## ABBREVIATIONS

*AA American Archives.* Edited by Peter Force.

*DHNY Documentary History of the State of New York.* 4 vols. Edited by Edmund B. O'Callaghan.

*DRCHNY Documents Relative to the Colonial History of the State of New York.* 15 vols. Edited by Edmund O'Callaghan.

**EWP** Papers of the Reverend Eleazar Wheelock. Dartmouth College Archives, Hanover, New Hampshire.

*IAP Indian Affairs Papers: American Revolution.* Edited by Maryly Penrose.

*IIDH Iroquois Indians: A Documentary History of the Diplomacy of the Six Nations and Their League; Guide to the Microfilm Collection.* Edited by Francis Jennings, William N. Fenton, Mary A. Druke, and David R. Miller.

*JCC Journals of the Continental Congress, 1774–1789.* Edited from the Original Records in the Library of Congress by Worthington Chauncey Ford.

*JPCPC Journals of the Provincial Congress, Provincial Convention, Committee of Safety and Council of Safety of the State of New York, 1775–1777.*

*JSK The Journals of Samuel Kirkland.* Edited by Walter Pilkington.

*LMCC Letters of Members of the Continental Congress.* Edited by Edmund Burnett.

*MPCP Minutes of the Provincial Council of Pennsylvania.* 10 volumes, plus one-volume index.

*PCC Papers of the Continental Congress, 1774–1789.*

*PCIA Proceedings of the Commissioners of Indian Affairs Appointed by Law for the Extinguishment of Indian Titles in the State of New York.* Edited by Franklin Hough.

*PPGC The Public Papers of George Clinton.* Edited by Hugh Hastings.

**PRSK** Papers of the Reverend Samuel Kirkland. Burke Library, Hamilton College, Clinton, New York.

*PSP* Philip Schuyler Papers. New York State Library.

*PWJ The Papers of Sir William Johnson.* Edited by Frederick Sullivan.

**TPP** Timothy Pickering Papers. Massachusetts Historical Society, Boston.

**194** NOTES TO PAGES 3–9

INTRODUCTION

1. Joseph Brant (whose Indian name was Thayendanega), "Answers to Queries Respecting the Six Nations," vol. 1, Miller Papers, New York Historical Society; L. Hammond, *History of Madison County, State of New York* (Syracuse: Truair, Smith and Company, 1872), 1:85–94; Henry Schoolcraft, *Notes on the Iroquois* (New York: Bartlett and Welford, 1847; reprint, Millwood, NY: Kraus Reprint, 1975), 46–54. Canowaroghere and Ganowarohare are two of the many possible spellings of Kanowalohale—not to be confused with Canajoharie, a major Mohawk community.

2. David Levinson, "An Explanation for the Oneida-Colonist Alliance in the American Revolution," *Ethnohistory* 23 (1976): 265–89; Barbara Graymont, "The Oneidas and the American Revolution," in Jack Campisi and Laurence Hauptman, eds., *The Oneida Indian Experience: Two Perspectives* (Syracuse: Syracuse University Press, 1988), 31–42.

3. Carl Klinck and James Talman, eds., *The Journal of Major John Norton, 1816* (Toronto: Champlain Society, 1970), 103–4; Douglas Boyce, "A Glimpse of Iroquois Culture History through the Eyes of Joseph Brant and John Norton," *Proceedings of the American Philosophical Society* 117 (1973): 286–94.

4. Daniel Richter and James Merrell, eds., *The Ordeal of the Longhouse: The Peoples of the Iroquois League in the Era of European Colonization* (Chapel Hill: University of North Carolina Press, 1992), 37–40; William N. Fenton, *The Great Law and the Longhouse: A Political History of the Iroquois Confederacy* (Norman: University of Oklahoma Press, 1998), 51–65.

5. Barbara Barnes, ed., *Traditional Teachings* (Cornwall, ON: North American Indian Travelling College, 1984), 5; William N. Fenton, "Problems in the Authentication of the League of the Iroquois," in Laurence Hauptman and Jack Campisi, eds., *Neighbours and Intruders: An Ethnohistorical Exploration of the Indians of Hudson's River* (Ottawa: National Museum of Canada, 1978), 263–66; Peter Pratt, "A Perspective on Oneida Archeology," in *Current Perspectives in Northeastern Archeology,* ed. Robert Funk and Charles Hayes (Rochester: New York State Archeological Association, 1977), 51–69.

6. Richard White, *The Middle Ground: Indians, Empires, and Republics in the Great Lakes Region, 1650–1815* (London: Cambridge University Press, 1991), 50–60, 91–93; Laurence Hauptman, "Refugee Havens: The Iroquois Villages of the Eighteenth Century," in *American Indian Environments: Ecological Issues in Native American History,* ed. Christopher Vecsey and Robert Venables (Syracuse: Syracuse University Press, 1980), 128–39; Mary Druke, "Linking Arms: The Structure of Iroquois Intertribal Diplomacy," in Daniel Richter and James Merrell, ed., *Beyond the Covenant Chain: The Iroquois and Their Neighbours in Indian North America* (Syracuse: Syracuse University Press, 1987), 29–39; George Snyderman, "Concepts of Land Ownership among the Iroquois and Their Neighbors," in William N. Fenton, ed., *Symposium on Local Diversity in Iroquois Culture,* Smithsonian Institute, Bureau of American Ethnology, Bulletin 149 (Washington, DC: GPO, 1951), 15–34. See also Nancy Bonvillain, "Iroquoian Women," in Nancy Bonvillain, ed., *Studies in Iroquoian Culture* (Rindge, NY: Occasional Publications in Northeastern Anthropology 6, 1980), 47–58; Mary Druke, "Structure and Meanings of Leadership among the Oneida Indians during the Mid-Eighteenth Century" (Ph.D. diss., University of Chicago, 1982); William N. Fenton, "Locality as a Basic Factor in the Development of Iroquois Social Structure," in Fenton, *Symposium on Local Diversity,* 39–53; William Starna, "Northern Iroquoian Horticulture and Insect Infestation: A Cause for Village Removal," *Ethnohistory* 31:3 (1984): 197–207; Michael Recht, "The Role of Fishing in the Iroquois Economy, 1600–1792," *New York History* 78:4 (October 1997): 429–54.

7. Council minutes, 28 June, 10 October 1728, 16 August 1731, *Minutes of the Provincial Council of Pennsylvania,* 10 vols. and index vol. (Harrisburg, PA: Theo Fenn and Company, 1851–1853; reprint, New York: AMS, 1968; hereafter *MPCP*), 3:330–31,

337, 406, 409; Joseph Powell, Shamokin Pennsylvania diary, 31 January, 12 February, 6, 9 March, 1 May 1748, folder 4, box 121, Records of the Moravian Missions among the Indians of North America, Harvard College Library; James Merrell, "'Shamokin, the Very Seat of the Prince of Darkness': Unsettling the Early American Frontier," in Andrew Cayton and F. Teute, ed., *Contact Points: American Frontiers from the Mohawk Valley to the Mississippi, 1750–1830* (Chapel Hill: University of North Carolina Press, 1998), 16–59; James Merrell, "Shickellamy: A Person of Consequence," in Robert Grumet, ed., *Northeastern Indian Lives, 1632–1816* (Amherst: University of Massachusetts Press, 1996), 227–55; Peter Mancall, *Valley of Opportunity: Economic Culture along the Upper Susquehanna, 1700–1800* (Ithaca: Cornell University Press, 1991). James H. Merrell, *Into the American Woods: Negotiations on the Pennsylvania Frontier* (New York: W. W. Norton, 1999); Barry Kent, *Susquehanna's Indians: Indians of Pennsylvania* (Harrisburg: Pennsylvania Historical and Museum Commission, 1981), 98–107.

8. Barnes, *Traditional Teachings,* 3–13. Dean from Demus Elm and Harvey Antone, *The Oneida Creation Story* (Lincoln: University of Nebraska Press, 2000), 7–27.

9. Karim Tiro, "The People of the Standing Stone: The Oneida Indian Nation from Revolution through Removal, 1765–1840" (Ph.D. diss., University of Pennsylvania, 1999); James Lynch, "The Iroquois Confederacy and the Adoption and Administration of Non-Iroquoian Individuals and Groups prior to 1756," *Man in the Northeast* 30 (Fall 1985): 83–99; Eleanor Leacock, "Ethnohistorical Investigation of Egalitarian Politics in Eastern North America," in Elisabeth Tooker, ed., *The Development of Political Organization in Native North America* (Washington, DC: American Ethnological Society, 1983), 17–31; George Snyderman, "Behind the Tree of Peace: A Sociological Analysis of Iroquois Warfare" (Ph.D. diss., University of Pennsylvania, 1948), 9–29; Nancy Shoemaker, "An Alliance between Men: Gender Metaphors in Eighteenth-Century American Indian Diplomacy East of the Mississippi," *Ethnohistory* 46:2 (Spring 1999): 239–63; Elisabeth Tooker, "Women in Iroquois Society," in Michael Foster, Jack Campisi, and Marianne Mithun, eds., *Extending the Rafters: Interdisciplinary Approaches to Iroquoian Studies* (Albany: State University of New York Press, 1984), 109–21.

10. Speech of William Johnson at conference at Fort Johnson, 26 July 1753, in Edmund O'Callaghan, ed., *Documents Relative to the Colonial History of the State of New York,* 15 vols. (Albany, NY: Weed, Parsons, and Company, 1853–1887; hereafter *DRCH-NY*), 5:343, 371, 6:811 (quote).

11. Letter to Lords of Trade, 25 June 1723, ibid., 5:674; William Johnson to Lords of Trade, 18 November 1763, ibid., 7:573; Douglas Boyce, "'As the Wind Scatters the Smoke': The Tuscaroras in the Eighteenth Century," in *Under an Open Sky: Rethinking America's Western Past,* ed. William Cronon (New York: W. W. Norton, 1992), 151–63; David Landy, "Tuscarora among the Iroquois," in Bruce Trigger, ed., *Handbook of North American Indians,* 15 vols. (Washington, DC: Smithsonian Institute, 1978), 518–27.

12. John Bartram, *Observations on the Inhabitants, Climate, Soil, Rivers, Production and other Matters Worthy of Notice* (London: J. Whiston and B. White, 1751), 61–62; journal of Johnson's proceedings at Canajoharie, 14 April 1759, *DRCHNY* 7:385 (quote); Clinton Weslager, *The Nanticoke Indians: Past and Present* (Newark: University of Delaware Press, 1983). The Nanticoke were known as Skaniadaradihaga by the Mohawk, and as Skaniadaradighronos by William Johnson.

13. Helen Tanner, *Atlas of Great Lakes Indian History* (Norman: University of Oklahoma Press, 1987), 41, 59, 74; Marjory Hinman, *Onaquaga: Hub of the Border Wars of the American Revolution* (Windsor, NY: privately printed, 1975), 3–4; Colin Calloway, *The American Revolution in Indian Country: Crisis and Diversity in Native American Communities* (New York: Cambridge University Press, 1995), 108–28; Hammond, *Madison County,* 1:99–106; Thomas Norton, *The Fur Trade in Colonial New York, 1686–1776* (Madison: University of Wisconsin Press, 1974), 184–97; T. Wood Clarke, *Utica for a Century and a*

*Half* (Utica, NY: Widtman Press, 1952), 3–16; Dolores Elliott, "Otsiningo, an Example of an Eighteenth-Century Settlement Pattern," in Robert Funk and Charles Hayes, ed., *Current Perspectives in Northeastern Archeology* (Rochester: New York State Archeological Association, 1977), 93–105. Oquaga is one of over forty spellings, other common options being Onaquaga, Aughquaga, Ochquaga, Onohoghgwaga, and Onohoghgwage.

14. Francis Halsey, *The Old New York Frontier: Its Wars with Indians and Tories, Its Missionary Schools, Pioneers, and Land Titles, 1614–1800* (New York: Scribner, 1901), 38; William Johnson to Peter Warren, 10 May 1739, in Frederick Sullivan, ed., *The Papers of Sir William Johnson* (Albany: State University of New York Press, 1921–1965; hereafter *PWJ*), 1:7 (quote); James Flexner, *Mohawk Baronet: A Biography of Sir William Johnson* (Boston: Little Brown, 1979); Milton Hamilton, *Sir William Johnson: Colonial American, 1715–1763* (Port Washington, NY: Kennikat Press, 1976); Arthur Pound, *Johnson of the Mohawks: A Biography of Sir William Johnson, Irish Immigrant, Mohawk War Chief, American Soldier, Empire Builder* (New York: Macmillan, 1930); William Stone, *The Life and Times of Sir William Johnson, Baronet* (Albany: J. Munsell, 1865).

15. Charles Gehring and William Starna, trans. and eds., *A Journey into Mohawk and Oneida Country, 1634–1635: The Journal of Harmen Meyndertsz van den Bogaert* (Syracuse: Syracuse University Press, 1988), 13; memorandum of Johnson to Governor Clinton, 1747, *PWJ* 1:110.

16. Jack Campisi, "Fur Trade and Factionalism of the Eighteenth-Century Oneidas," in Bonvillain, *Iroquoian Culture,* 37–46; Wilbur Jacobs, *Wilderness Politics and Indian Gifts: The Northern Colonial Frontier, 1748–1763* (Lincoln: University of Nebraska Press, 1950), 76–89, 160–85.

17. Letters of 17 October 1714, 20 April 1716, 1 September 1717, in Society of the Propagation of the Gospel Letter Books, series A, 10:161, 11:319, 12:327, in James Axtell, *The Invasion Within: The Contest of Cultures in Colonial North America* (New York: Oxford University Press, 1985), 260–61. See also Papers of the Reverend Eleazar Wheelock, Dartmouth College Archives, Hanover, New Hampshire (hereafter EWP); Eleazar Wheelock, *A Plain and faithful Narrative of the Original Design, Rise, Progress, and Present State of the Indian Charity School at Lebanon in Connecticut* (Boston: Richard and Samuel Draper, 1763–1765); James Axtell, "Dr. Wheelock and the Indians," in Foster, Campisi, and Mithun, *Extending the Rafters,* 51–64; Henry Bowden, *American Indians and Christian Missions: Studies in Cultural Conflict* (Chicago: University of Chicago Press, 1981); Nancy Hagedorn, "'A Friend to Go Between Them': The Interpreter as Cultural Broker during Anglo-Iroquois Councils, 1740–1770," *Ethnohistory* 35:1 (Winter 1988): 60–80.

## 1—THE ONEIDA DURING WAR

1. Richard Aquila, *The Iroquois Restoration: Iroquois Diplomacy on the Colonial Frontier, 1701–1754* (Lincoln: University of Nebraska Press, 1983), 85–87, 129–31, 156–58, 205–7; Robert Allen, *His Majesty's Indian Allies: British Indian Policy in the Defence of Canada, 1774–1815* (Toronto: Dundurn Press, 1992), 12–21; Daniel Barr, *Unconquered: The Iroquois League at War in Colonial America* (Westport, CT: Praeger, 2006), iv.

2. Minutes of Onondaga Council, 6, 17 September 1750, in *MPCP* 5:470–72; Paul Wallace, *Conrad Weiser, 1696–1760: Friend of Colonist and Mohawk* (New York: Russell and Russell, 1945), 286–313.

3. Elisabeth Tooker, "The League of the Iroquois: Its History, Politics and Ritual," in Trigger, *North American Indians,* 15:424; Fenton, *Great Law and Longhouse,* 192; Minutes of Onondaga Council, 6, 17 September 1750, *MPCP* 5:473–78 (quotes).

4. The entire debate is quoted in Helga Doblin and William Starna, trans. and eds., *The Journals of Christian Daniel Claus and Conrad Weiser: A Journey to Onondaga, 1750* (Philadelphia: American Philosophical Society, 1994), 16–19 (quotes); Wallace,

*Conrad Weiser,* 315–16. The Onondaga involved in the debate later became head sachem of his people, following the death of pro-British Canasatego and, by his own sentiments, reinforced the pro-French sympathy held by the majority of his nation. It is difficult to discern the source of Conoquhieson's knowledge of Christianity. Clerics sponsored by the Society for the Propagation of the Gospel (SPG) had established themselves at Albany in 1702 and hastily extended their jurisdiction westward to the nearby Mohawk communities at Canajoharie and Fort Hunter in an effort to preserve Mohawk loyalty to Britain. However, they did not venture further west. In contrast, the New England Company (NEC) missions at Oquaga, which began in 1744, had encouraged numerous conversions to Christianity. (The NEC was a group of Puritans of Church of England background who were established in 1649 to promote the conversion of the natives of the East Coast of North America.) It was not until the 1760s that a mission spearheaded jointly by the NEC and the Scottish Society for the Propagation of Christian Knowledge (SSPCK) appeared at Kanowalohale.

5. Speech of George Clinton to Oneida Indians, 1748, 7 September 1749, *PWJ* 1:199, 247; Arent Stevens to Johnson, 11 July 1750, ibid., 288 (complaints); speech of James Hamilton to the Pennsylvania Assembly, 16 October 1750, in George Reed, ed., *Pennsylvania Archives,* 4th ser. (Harrisburg, PA: W. Stanley Ray, 1900), 2:135; Francis Jennings, *Empire of Fortune: Crowns, Colonies, and Tribes in the Seven Years War in America* (New York: Norton, 1988), 139–73.

6. Minutes of Onondaga Council, 6, 17 September 1750 (various speeches over a lengthy meeting), *MPCP* 5:478–80.

7. George Clinton (paraphrasing Aquiotta's words) to William Johnson, 28 August, 16 September 1746, *PWJ* 1:60–61, 64; report of Weiser's journey to Onondaga, 13 August 1743, *MPCP* 4:663 ("Singing way"); Weiser journal, 8 July 1751, Du Simitiere Collection of the Library Collection of Philadelphia, in Wallace, *Conrad Weiser,* 327.

8. Agrongdongwas was commonly referred to as Good Peter; Dakayenensese as Isaac or Old Isaac. In 1744 the Reverend John Sergeant (resident of Stockbridge, Massachusetts, and sponsored by the NEC) was the first of an estimated two dozen Christian missionaries who were to minister in the community over the next thirty years. The Reverend Elihu Spencer (also of the NEC) was the first resident missionary in 1748. John Hankin, "Bringing the Good News: Protestant Missionaries to the Indians of New England and New York, 1700–1775" (Ph.D. diss., University of Connecticut, 1993), 516–64; and Marjorie Hinman, *Onaquaga: Early Missionary Outpost, 1748–1777* (Onaquaga, NY: Old Onaquaga Historical Society, 1968), 1–2.

9. Jonathan Edwards, "A Letter from Rev. Jonathan Edwards to Honourable Thomas Hubbard, Esq. of Boston, Relating to the Indian School at Stockbridge," August 1751, *Collections,* Massachusetts Historical Society, ser. 1, vol. 10 (1809), 145–46 (quote). See also Sereno Dwight, *The Life of President Edwards* (New York: G. C. and H. Carvill, 1830), 472, 492–94, 527–30; Halsey, *Old New York Frontier,* 52–55.

10. Gideon Hawley, "A Letter from Rev. Gideon Hawley of Mashpee, containing an Account of his services among the Indians of Massachusetts and New York, and a Narrative of his Journey to Onohoghgwage (1753)," *Collections,* Massachusetts Historical Society, ser. 1, vol. 4 (1795), 50–67 (59, 60). An abbreviated version is in Edmund O'Callaghan, *Documentary History of the State of New York,* 4 vols. (Albany, NY: Weed, Parsons, and Company, 1849–1851; hereafter *DHNY*), 3:1031–46; Gideon Hawley Manuscripts (Boston: Congressional Library of the American Congregational Association), 1:7, 11, 13, 15, 16, 18, 23, 2:20–24, 1:8–10.

11. Minutes of meeting, Johnson with the Six Nations near Onondaga Castle, 8–10 September 1753, *DRCHNY* 6:810–15 (810, 813, 815). See also Weiser to Richard Peters, 28 January 1754, Correspondence of Weiser, Historical Society of Philadelphia, 1:43.

12. Minutes of the Provincial Council, 14 November 1753 (recording the transactions of the Carlisle conference commencing 22 October 1753), *MPCP* 5:666–70 (666–67).

13. The four Oneida were identified, using the Pennsylvania Colonial Records, as Aneeghonaxqua, Taraghorus, Tohaghdaaghquyserry, and Kachneghdackon. Francis Jennings, William N. Fenton, Mary A. Druke, and David R. Miller, eds., *Iroquois Indians: A Documentary History of the Diplomacy of the Six Nations and Their League; Guide to the Microfilm Edition* (Woodbridge, CT: Research Publications, 1985; hereafter *IIDH*), reel 16, 381. These four did not represent the Oneida at other conferences. John Alden, "The Albany Congress and the Creation of the Indian Superintendencies," *Mississippi Valley Historical Review* 27:2 (Summer 1940): 193–210; Fenton, *Great Law and Longhouse*, 471, 475; Timothy Shannon, *Indians and Colonists at the Crossroads of Empire: The Albany Congress of 1754* (Ithaca: Cornell University Press, 2000), 117–40. *DRCHNY* 6:858 ("invective language").

14. "Proceedings of the Congress held at Albany in 1754," *Collections,* Massachusetts Historical Society, 3rd ser., vol. 5 (Boston, 1836), 22–74 (67–68); "Proceedings of the Congress held at Albany, 19 June–8 July 1754," *DRCHNY* 6:853–88 (882); the conference of Oneida and Cayuga at Montreal, 23 September 1754, *DRCHNY* 10:266. The names of the speakers at this conference are not recorded.

15. Minutes of meeting, 22 August 1754, *MPCP* 6:141 (quote); Governor Morris to Johnson, 15 November 1754, *PWJ* 9:143 (quote); Pennsylvania Provincial Council minutes, 24 December 1754, *MPCP* 6:216. No date is found for Tachnechdorus's birth—he was a young boy when his father moved the family to the Susquehanna area in 1728. Leadership was not unfamiliar to him as he had witnessed his father's advocacy of the Oneida on previous occasions. In 1732 as a young man he attended a conference in Philadelphia, at which Shickellamy voiced the support of the Six Nations for the British, and a conference at Onondaga in 1743, at which the Oneida welcomed the Nanticoke into their territory. Minutes, 23 August 1732, *MPCP* 3:435.

16. Minutes of meeting, 31 March 1755, *MPCP* 6:340 (quotes), 342–44.

17. Commission of Johnson by DeLancey, 16 April 1755, *PWJ* 1:468–70. In attendance were 67 Seneca, 103 Cayuga, 200 Oneida, 64 Tuscarora, 100 Onondaga, 19 Nanticoke, 101 Delaware, 9 Tutelo, and 408 Mohawk. Minutes, 22 June 1755, *PWJ* 9:189; Johnson, letters to Colden, Governor Hopkins, and Colonel Braddock, 24, 26, 27 June 1755, *PWJ* 1:641 (quote).

18. Minutes of conference, 21 June–4 July 1755, *DRCHNY* 6:964–89; Barbara Graymont, "New York and New Jersey Treaties, 1714–1753," in Alden T. Vaughan, ed., *Early American Indian Documents: Treaties and Laws, 1607–1789,* vol. 10, *New York and New Jersey Treaties, 1754–1775,* ed. Barbara Graymont (Bethesda, MD: University Publications of America, 2001), 89, 106, 107, 109.

19. Minutes of conference, 21 June–4 July 1755, *DRCHNY* 6:964–89; Samuel Earl, "The Palatines and Their Settlement in the Valley of the Upper Mohawk," *Transactions of the Oneida Historical Society* (1881), 31–51.

20. Minutes of meeting, 26 December 1755, *DRCHNY* 6:45–47; also *PWJ* 9:332–34. Pierre François Vaudreuil was born in Quebec and appointed by King Louis XV as governor of New France in 1755.

21. Richard Peters to Johnson, 23 January 1755, *PWJ* 9:154–59 (159); speech of Scarooyady at provincial council meeting, 22 August 1755, *MPCP* 6:589.

22. Johnson, speech to the Six Nations, 23 February 1756, *PWJ* 9:371. General proceedings recorded in ibid., 347–49; *IIDH*, reel 18, 424; Graymont, "New York and New Jersey," 10:147, 149; Proceedings of 26 February 1756, *PWJ* 9:382.

23. Proceedings of 26 February 1756 conference, *PWJ* 9:348–50, 393–94; Minutes of meeting with the Oneida, 25 February 1756, *PWJ* 9:378. Construction of a fort for the Oneida was a lengthy and contentious issue. John Luzander, *The Construction and*

*Military History of Fort Stanwix* (Washington, DC: Office of Archeology and Historic Preservation, 1969), 1–14.

24. Hawley to Governor Morris on behalf of Scarooyady, 4 January 1756, *MPCP* 7:12; Minutes of Provincial Council meeting, 27 March 1756, *MPCP* 7:64–65; Provincial Council minutes, 3, 10 April 1756, *MPCP* 7:71 (quote), 79; report of George Croghan to Johnson, March 1757, *PWJ* 9:728.

25. Johnson journal, describing meetings at German Flats, 28 August–3 September 1756, *DRCHNY* 7:189–93 (189–90, 193). Both Tesanonde and Akonyoda were infrequent speakers, according to conference minutes.

26. Meeting recorded in Johnson's journal, 12 August 1756, *DRCHNY* 7:183–85. Information concerning Johnson's frustration over Governor of Massachusetts William Shirley's use of "every kind of Artifice to destroy [Johnson's] influence" among the Iroquois—including "debauching" them by "sparing no money" when paying for military and service—is found in the correspondence between William Shirley and Johnson, 7 May, 29, 30, 31 July 1755, in *PWJ* 1:491, 789–90, 794–96, 803–6.

27. Speeches given at provincial council, 10, 14 April 1756, *MPCP* 7:81, 90. See also Nicholas Wainwright, *George Croghan: Wilderness Diplomat* (Chapel Hill: University of North Carolina Press, 1959), 122.

28. Johnson journal, describing conference at Fort Johnson, 17 November 1756, *DRCHNY* 7:230, 234–35 (235). The Oneida speakers are unnamed. Meeting of Oneida and Onondaga with Governor Vaudreuil, 28 July 1756, *DRCHNY* 10:455. See also Gretchen Green, "A New People in an Age of War: The Kahnawake Iroquois, 1667–1760" (Ph.D. diss., College of William and Mary, 1991), 25–27; Richter and Merrell, *Ordeal of the Longhouse*, 105–32; Robert Surtees, "The Iroquois in Canada," in Francis Jennings, William N. Fenton, Mary A. Druke, and David R. Miller, eds., *The History and Culture of Iroquois Diplomacy: An Interdisciplinary Guide to the Treaties of the Six Nations and Their League* (Syracuse: Syracuse University Press, 1985), 67–83.

29. Thomas Butler to Johnson, 4 May 1756, *PWJ* 9:448; Johnson's meeting with the Oneida at Onondaga, 5 July 1756, *DRCHNY* 7:152; speech of Conoquhieson at Fort Johnson, 19 November 1756, *DRCHNY* 7:232–33; Indian intelligence at Fort Johnson, 4 March 1757, *PWJ* 2:679; meetings of Gawehe with Governor Vaudreuil, 23, 30 December 1756, *DRCHNY* 10:513, 516; Butler to Johnson, 7 April 1757, *PWJ* 2:699–70.

30. Governor Vaudreuil concerning a May meeting with the Oneida at Montreal, 13 July 1757, *DRCHNY* 10:587.

31. Butler to Johnson, 7 April, 24 May 1757, *PWJ* 2:699–700, 773; Indian intelligence, 18 April, minutes of Indian proceedings, 2 May, Johnson to Earl of Loudon, 3 September, meeting of Johnson at Fort Johnson, 16 September 1757, Johnson to Abercromby, 17 May 1758, *PWJ* 9:681–83, 714, 824–26, 836–37 (837). Adarockquaghs was also known as Adam.

32. Proceedings of meeting at Fort Johnson, 2 May 1757, minutes of Indian Congress, 29 April 1757, *PWJ* 9:714–16, 703–6.

33. Minutes of Indian conference at Fort Johnson, 15–20 September 1757, *PWJ* 9:831–53 (841); invitation to the Onondaga Congress issued at Fort Johnson, 26 April 1758, *PWJ* 2:822–24; William N. Fenton, "Iroquoian Culture History: A General Evaluation," in William Fenton and John Gulick, ed., *Symposium on Cherokee and Iroquois Culture*, Smithsonian Institute, Bureau of American Ethnology, Bulletin 180 (Washington, DC: GPO, 1961), 257–75.

34. King as speaker at conference at Fort Johnson, 29 February 1756, also at conferences at Lancaster, 1 April, 6–19 May 1757, Minutes of meeting at Fort Johnson, 24 July 1758, *PWJ* 9:393–94, 727–65, 957. With Thomas King I depart from my usual naming system as his Indian names, Saghogsoniont and Tagaderiaghsera, were scarcely ever used.

35. Minutes of Easton conference, 15, 17 October 1758, *MPCP* 8:190–99 (191); Stephen Auth, *The Ten Years' War: Indian-White Relations in Pennsylvania, 1755–1765* (New York: Garland, 1989), 99–108; Anthony Wallace, *King of the Delawares: Teedyuscung, 1700–1763* (Freeport NY: Books for Libraries Press, 1949), 192–207.

36. Johnson's journal, 9 December 1758, *PWJ* 10:64–73.

37. Meeting at German Flats, 3 September 1756, *PWJ* 9:518; meetings at Fort Johnson, 23 February, 1 March, 19 April 1757, *PWJ* 9:618, 623, 682.

## 2—THE ONEIDA AT PEACE

1. Amherst's "callous attitude to Amerindians" became legendary. Ian Steele, *Warpaths: Invasions of North America* (New York: Oxford University Press, 1994), 228, also 236. White, *Middle Ground,* 256–60; Michael McConnell, *A Country Between: The Upper Ohio Valley and Its Peoples, 1724–1774* (Lincoln: University of Nebraska, 1992).

2. Johnson journal, describing the conference at Canajoharie, 4 April 1759, *DRCHNY* 7:385. Vaudreuil continued to meet with the Iroquois. In June 1760 he reminded a Confederacy delegation visiting him at Montreal that they would meet the "fury of the English" if the British won the war and took control of Iroquois territory. Meeting, 13 July 1760, *DRCHNY* 10:587.

3. Minutes of conference at Canajoharie, 4–18 April 1759, *DRCHNY* 7:378–92 (391, 387, 387). Johnson's adoption by the Mohawk and his considerable familiarity with Iroquois customs gave him the necessary authority (about which he often spoke at great length) to perform ceremonies not usually conducted by non-Iroquois persons.

4. Amherst's journal entries of 24 September 1759, 7 July, 1 August 1760, in John Webster, ed., *The Journal of Jeffrey Amherst* (Toronto: Ryerson Press, 1931), 173, 173, 216, 223, 223. See also Auth, *Ten Years' War,* 132–36.

5. Compiled from British War Office records by John Long, *Lord Jeffrey Amherst: A Soldier of the King* (New York: Macmillan, 1933), 138. List of Oneida medal recipients, April 1761, *PWJ* 10:251–54; also at 9:176–77, with variations in spelling and with Christian names included.

6. In May 1761, two dozen Oneida had traveled from Kanowalohale to German Flats for the purpose of having some of their younger members baptized and married. For reasons not divulged, on the return trip, one of their party shot a hog belonging to a German settler. When the settler's son inquired as to why this happened, a scuffle ensued during which the son was fatally shot and his opponent fled. Minutes of meeting at German Flats, 7 July 1761, *PWJ* 407; also Peter Mancall, *Deadly Medicine: Indians and Alcohol in Early America* (Ithaca: Cornell University Press, 1995), 160–64.

7. Minutes of meeting at German Flats, 7 July 1761, *PWJ* 3:431–33.

8. Ibid., 432–37 (432, 435–37).

9. Johnson to Amherst, 7 July, Amherst's reply, 11 July 1761, *PWJ* 3:504, 506.

10. Amherst to Johnson, 11 July, 9 August 1761, *PWJ* 3:506, 514.

11. Speeches at the meeting at German Flats, 7 July 1761, *PWJ* 3:432, 435.

12. James Hamilton to Johnson, 10 February, Rev. Richard Peters to Johnson, 12 February, Johnson to Peters, 4 March 1761, *PWJ* 10:212, 215, 231. Delegations to Johnson Hall from Oquaga in June 1763, urging assistance against the influx of settlers from Connecticut, attested to the accuracy of Johnson's prognosis. Speech of Oquaga delegation, in Johnson's journal of Indian affairs, 5 June 1763, and Johnson to the Board of Trade, 1 August 1762, *PWJ* 10:722, 3:851.

13. Amherst to Johnson, 11 June, Johnson to Amherst, 12 June, Amherst to Johnson, 9 August, Johnson to Amherst, 6 December 1761, *PWJ* 10:284, 286, 3:515, 582.

14. Butler from Fort Stanwix, 9 April 1759, minutes of meeting at Fort Pitt, 12 April 1760, minutes of meeting at German Flats, 7 July 1761, *PWJ* 3:25, 216, 432–33.

15. Record of Fort Detroit conference, 9 September 1761, minutes of meeting at Fort Johnson, 21, 24 April 1762, *PWJ* 3:482, 698, 703 (698).

16. Meeting at Johnson Hall, 19 August 1761, *PWJ* 3:466 (quote). Minutes of Easton conference, August 1761, in Julian Boyd, ed. *Indian Treaties Printed by Benjamin Franklin, 1736–1762* (Philadelphia: Historical Society of Pennsylvania, 1938), 245–62; Auth, *Ten Years' War,* 160–61; speeches at meeting, 17 January 1762, *PWJ* 10:360.

17. Speeches at meeting of 17 January 1762, *PWJ* 10:362. For royal instructions to colonial governors, see communication between the Lords of Trade and the British king, 2 December 1761, *DRCHNY* 7:478. Further clarification was sent to Johnson from the Lords of Trade, 5 August 1763, *DRCHNY* 7:535.

18. George Croghan to Johnson, 31 March 1762, *PWJ* 3:662; minutes of conference at Fort Johnson, 2 April 1762, *PWJ* 10:419; Minutes of conference, 21–28 April 1762, *PWJ* 3:690–715, with speeches of Conoquhieson and Johnson on 25 April, *PWJ* 3:707–11. It is hard to believe that, after twenty years of interaction with the Iroquois, Johnson lacked insight concerning the role of clan mothers in decision making.

19. Captain Baugh to Amherst, 20 July, Amherst to Baugh, 1 August, Amherst to Johnson, 1 August 1762, *PWJ* 3:831, 835, 836.

20. Speeches at conference at Fort Johnson, 22, 25 April 1762, *PWJ* 3:693, 707, 711 (707).

21. Minutes of Lancaster conference, 14 August 1762, *MPCP* 8:729.

22. Ibid., 14, 19 August 1762, 741–49 (747, 748).

23. Ibid., 23 August 1762, 752–58.

24. Ibid., 24 August 1762, 758–67 (763, 765).

25. John Johnston (a smith living among the Seneca) to William Johnson, 1 December, instructions from William Johnson to Guy Johnson, Deputy Agent for Indian Affairs, 21 November, speech of Guy Johnson at Kanowalohale, 30 November, record of meeting at Onondaga, 6 December 1762, *PWJ* 10:382, 583, 585–86, 590–91.

26. Meeting at Fort Johnson, March 1763, *PWJ* 10:625.

27. Johnson to Amherst, 18 March, minutes of conference at Fort Johnson, 16–19 March 1763, *PWJ* 10:623–36 (635). The reference to the Oneida being the elder branch of the Confederacy might possibly be a misunderstanding on the part of the secretary at the meeting. The Cayuga had previously spoken of the Oneida as their Elder Brother; see meetings at Fort Johnson, 29 July 1755, 11 March 1758, *PWJ* 9:215, 880. Thus the Oneida were elder within the moiety, not the Confederacy.

28. Minutes of Iroquois conference at Johnson Hall, 20–28 May 1763, *PWJ* 10:679–83.

29. Minutes of Iroquois conference at German Flats, 18–20 July 1763, *PWJ* 10:746–52. The actual contents of Conoquhieson's speech are not recorded in Johnson's papers. See also Gregory Dowd, *War under Heaven: Pontiac, the Indian Nations, and the British Empire* (Baltimore: Johns Hopkins University Press, 2002), 94–105; Michael Mullin, "Sir William Johnson's Reliance on the Six Nations at the Conclusion of the Anglo-Indian War of 1763–1765," *American Indian Culture and Research Journal* 17:4 (1993): 69–90; Jon Parmenter, "Pontiac's War: Forging New Links in the Anglo-Iroquois Covenant Chain, 1758–1766," *Ethnohistory* 44:4 (Fall 1997): 617–54; Gregory Dowd, *A Spirited Resistance: The North American Indian Struggle for Unity, 1745–1815* (Baltimore: Johns Hopkins University Press, 1992), 35–40; Randolph Downes, *Council Fires on the Upper Ohio: A Narrative of Indian Affairs in the Upper Ohio Valley until 1795* (Pittsburgh: University of Pittsburgh Press, 1957); Jon Parmenter, "The Iroquois and the Native American Struggle for the Ohio Valley, 1754–1794," in David Skaggs and Larry Nelson, ed., *The Sixty Years' War for the Great Lakes, 1754–1814* (East Lansing: Michigan State University Press, 2001), 105–24.

30. Journal of Indian Affairs, 9, 27 July 1763, *PWJ* 10:768, 772.

31. Johnson's journal, 5 August 1763, ibid., 794–97 (796, 797).

32. Conference with the Iroquois at Johnson Hall, 7, 9 September 1763, ibid., 830–40.

33. Conference of 20 October 1763, ibid., 902.

34. Johnson's journal of the conference with the Iroquois at Johnson Hall, 5–22 December 1763, ibid., 964–70 (964, 969, 970).

35. Johnson's journal, 12 September, 17 October 1763, ibid., 847–49, 896–97.

36. Johnson to Amherst, 24 September 1762, *PWJ* 3:885; speeches at Iroquois conference at Johnson Hall, 26, 28 May 1763, regulations issued February 1762, *PWJ* 10:679, 683, 389–91.

37. Regulations issued in 1765, *PWJ* 11:990–93; orders for Regulation of Trade, 16 January 1765, 11:535; Johnson's journal, meetings at Johnson Hall, 18 January 1764, 11:28; Johnson to Colden, 16 March 1764, 4:365, all *PWJ*.

38. Johnson to Thomas Gage, 12 December 1763, *PWJ* 10:953–54; Johnson to John Penn, 9 February, to General Gage, 19 February 1764, *PWJ* 4:323, 333 (323).

39. Johnson to Henry Montour, 21 February, and Henry Montour, William Hare, and John Johnston, reply to Johnson, 7 April 1764, *PWJ* 4:336, 392; minutes of Indian conference, 16 February 1764, *PWJ* 11:59–63.

40. For terms of this treaty, see "Treaty of Peace," *PWJ* 11:327–33; minutes of meeting, 7–10 September 1764, *PWJ* 4:526–27; John Bradstreet to Johnson, *PWJ* 11:340–41. Rumors of the French returning to the Great Lakes area continued to circulate among the Indians who had been loyal to them.

41. King's testimony includes his version of what Pontiac said. King, testimony at conference at Fort Sandusky, Ohio, 3 October 1764, proceedings of conference at Fort Sandusky, 5 October 1764, Johnson to Gage, 8 November 1764, Johnson's journal, 15, 16 December 1764, *PWJ* 11:369–72, 373–74, 402, 506–8. William Godfrey, *John Bradstreet's Quest: Pursuit of Profit and Preferment in Colonial North America* (Waterloo, ON: Wilfred Laurier University Press, 1982), 135–36 (dealings with the Delaware, 186–208).

42. Peace treaty between Johnson and the Chenussio and "other enemy Senecas," 6 August 1764, *DRCHNY* 7:652–53; minutes of conference at Johnson Hall, 13–28 April 1765, *DRCHNY* 11:705–11; minutes of conference at Johnson Hall, 29 April–22 May 1765, *PWJ* 7:718–38 (focusing here on 718–22).

## 3—The Oneida as Diplomats

1. Using figures adapted from William Johnson's census of 1763, *DRCHNY* 7:582–84, Elizabeth Tooker estimated an Iroquois population of approximately nine thousand (based on the warriors being one-fifth of the population), which in turns indicates that those present at Fort Stanwix numbered about 30 percent of the total. Tooker, "The League of the Iroquois," 420.

2. Ruth Higgins, in *Expansion in New York, with Special Reference to the Eighteenth Century* (Columbus: Ohio State University, 1931), 93, considered this treaty to be simply one in a series of British attempts to open more land for settlement. Peter Marshall, in "Sir William Johnson and the Treaty of Fort Stanwix, 1768," *Journal of American Studies* 1:2 (1967): 149–79, broadened the investigation to include Johnson's role as a royal agent during Britain's declining influence over colonial affairs (he only briefly mentions the Oneida as a separate nation). Dorothy Jones, in *License for Empire: Colonialism by Treaty in Early America* (Chicago: University of Chicago Press, 1982), 89–92, treats the Iroquois as a homogeneous group, stressing their active participation in the conference as stemming from their perceived position of power. Jack Sosin, in *Whitehall and Wilderness: The Middle West in British Colonial Policy, 1760–1775* (Lincoln: University of Nebraska Press, 1961), 174, mistakenly places Fort Stanwix in Mohawk territory. Fenton, in *Great Law and Longhouse*, 535–540, points out that, of the twenty-seven

Iroquois chiefs who participated in the conference, only four carried titles referring to their position as successors of the founding chiefs of the Iroquois Confederacy, with two of these being Oneida. He gives little credit to the Iroquois, who managed to direct the line of settlement south and west.

3. Johnson to W. Denny, 21 July 1758, *PWJ* 2:879; Johnson to Board of Trade, 13 November 1763, *DRCHNY* 7:578; terms of the 1763 Proclamation, 24 December 1763, *PWJ* 10:982–84. See also Jack Stagg, *Anglo-Indian Relations in North America to 1763, and an Analysis of the Royal Proclamation of 7 October 1763* (Ottawa: Government Printers, 1981); Max Farrand, "The Indian Boundary Line, 1763," *American Historical Review* 10 (1905): 782–91. I differ with Francis Paul Prucha, *American Indian Policy in the Formative Years, 1790–1834* (Cambridge: Harvard University Press, 1962), 13. His claim that the idea of a boundary line delineating "Indian country" was a departure from past policies may have merit in that governmental documentation did not previously establish one, but his claim that a distinct Indian country was a novel idea overlooks much of what had long been envisaged by the Iroquois and promoted by Johnson.

4. Wheelock's ideas for the expanded school included a location at the center of Indian country, a curriculum that prepared Indians as missionaries and farmers, and provision of a cluster of white towns surrounding the school to assist the Indians in preparing for life in the white world. Wheelock's "Proposal for Introducing Religion, Learning, Agriculture and Manufacture among the Pagans in America" (1763), cited in James McCallum, *Eleazar Wheelock* (Hanover, NH: Dartmouth College Publications, 1939), 114–16. Johnson to Robert Monkton, 1 August 1762, James Hamilton to Johnson, 18 May 1763, Wheelock to Johnson, June 1761, *PWJ* 3:853, 10:671–72, 344–45; Johnson to Wheelock, 17 November 1761, in *DHNY* 4:305; Wheelock to Johnson, 8 December 1762, *DHNY* 4:314–15. Quote from Johnson to Wheelock, 16 October 1762, *DHNY* 4:320–21.

5. Wheelock, *Plain and Faithful Narrative,* 10–25.

6. Wheelock's "Address to the Six Nations Chiefs," 29 April 1765, *DHNY* 4:354–55; David Fowler to Eleazar Wheelock, 15, 24 June 1765, in James McCallum, *The Letters of Eleazar Wheelock's Indians* (Hanover, NH: Dartmouth College Publications, 1932), 93–96 (94).

7. Johnson to Lords of Trade, 13 November 1763, Lords of Trade to Johnson, 10 July 1764, speeches at Iroquois and Delaware conference at Johnson Hall, 29 April–1 May 1765, *DRCHNY* 7:572–81, 634–36, 718–21. It is not known whether this was the first occurrence of this change, but its significance would not have been lost on the Oneida observers at the conference.

8. Speeches of 2–6 May 1765, *DRCHNY* 7:722–26.

9. Speeches of 2–6 May 1765, minutes of conference and articles 9 and 10 of Delaware treaty, 8 May 1765, *DRCHNY* 7:726–30, 732, 740 (727); Wainwright, *George Croghan,* 111, 206–14, 243–58.

10. Johnson to Daniel Burton, 8 October, Johnson to Dr. Samuel Auchmuty, 10 October, 4, 20 November 1766, *PWJ* 5:388–89, 392–93, 409–11, 426–29 (389). Johnson later anticipated a much larger school to educate students from all Six Nations. Johnson to Samuel Johnson in Library of Congress, Washington, 2 December 1766, ibid., 440. He eventually hoped to send promising Mohawk, Oneida, and Oquaga youth to New York or England to be trained as clergy. Johnson to Auchmuty, 22 September 1767, ibid., 695. His dreams included the establishment of an American bishopric, and to encourage this he was willing to donate additional lands and funds; Johnson to Auchmuty, 2 December 1767, ibid., 842.

11. Johnson's journal, 16, 21, 22 January, 9, 10 June 1767, *PWJ* 12:259–61, 331–32 (331, 332).

12. Conference with the Cherokee at Johnson Hall, 4, 5 March 1768, *DRCHNY* 8:38–41 (41); Johnson's journal, 8–11 May 1767, *PWJ* 12:309–15.

13. Speeches of 6–7 March 1768, *DRCHNY* 8:40–45 (41, 45).

14. Speeches of 8–9 March 1768, ibid., 45–50.

15. Speeches of 9–11 March 1768, ibid., 50–53 (53).

16. Luzander, *Fort Stanwix*, 51; Johnson's journal of the congress at Fort Stanwix, 15 September–24 October 1768, *PWJ* 12:617–28. Johnson recorded names of the leading sachems of each nation, together with the interpreter John Butler (whose name features largely in the revolution). This information regarding the preliminaries to the conference given by Johnson is considerably condensed in the account printed in *DRCHNY* 8:111–34. Mancall, *Valley of Opportunity*, 90–94.

17. Gage to Johnson, 22 February, Johnson to Gage, 5 March 1768, *PWJ* 6:119–20, 12:459–60; Johnson to Lords of Trade, 20 July 1768, *DRCHNY* 8:83–87.

18. Memorial of the Reverend Mr. Wheelock, 16 October 1768, *DHNY* 4:388–89 (389). For Wheelock's words from the petition, see EWP #768560.1. Avery to Wheelock, 10 October 1768, EWP #768560.1; Jacob Johnson, speech to the Iroquois, 31 October 1768, *DHNY* 4:395; Jacob Johnson to Wheelock, 17 October 1768, EWP #768567. Jacob Johnson and David Avery were both graduates of Wheelock's Charity School and were sponsored by the SSPCK. Avery served as missionary at Kanowalohale in 1768–1769, and again in 1771–1772; Jacob Johnson was the minister and schoolmaster there in 1768–1769.

19. Minutes of Fort Stanwix conference, 25, 26 October 1768, *DRCHNY* 8:116–17.

20. Ibid., 26, 28 October 1768, 117–22 (121, 122).

21. Ibid., 29 October 1768, 122. Johnson does not identify the specific clergyman, probably either Avery or Jacob Johnson. The timing of these clandestine meetings is significant. Iroquois speakers insisted that meetings be held in the daylight, as evil thoughts and bad decisions occurred during darkness. References to nightly meetings are common at this conference, possibly as a utilitarian move by Johnson to hasten a decision with the input of as few people as possible—or more probably to prevent discussions from being witnessed or influenced by those of other nations.

22. Ibid., 29–31 October 1768, 122–25 (125).

23. Ibid., 1 November 1768, 125–28 (126, 127); Fort Stanwix treaty, 5 November 1768, ibid., 135–36; Ray Billington, "The Fort Stanwix Treaty of 1768," *New York History* 25:2 (April 1944): 182–94. The total number of proposals is hard to calculate. Meetings were held continuously from Friday morning until Monday evening and involved more than the Oneida. Tagawaron, map in hand, made three proposals, the last being agreed to in an open meeting of all concerned on the Monday evening.

24. A map showing the original line proposed by the Board of Trade is reproduced in *PWJ* 5:286. Verbal instructions for the placement of the boundary had been sent to Johnson earlier that year by the Board of Trade. Wills Hillsborough to Johnson, 12 March 1768, *DRCHNY* 8:35–36. The Oneida might well have appreciated any available assistance in their struggle to preserve their territory, but there is no evidence they solicited the aid of Wheelock's representatives. I do not agree with the inference made by George Guzzardo, in "The Superintendent and the Ministers: The Battle for Oneida Allegiances," *New York History* 57 (1976): 255–83, that the Oneida were mere pawns in the struggle between Johnson and Wheelock.

25. Speeches at German Flats conference, 18–22 July 1770, *DRCHNY* 8:229–32.

26. Ibid., 232–41 (234, 237, 240).

27. Kirkland journal, 26–30 October 1767, in Walter Pilkington, ed., *The Journals of Samuel Kirkland* (Clinton, NY: Hamilton College, 1980; hereafter *JSK*), 53–58; Kirkland to Elliot, 12 November 1770, Kirkland to Wheelock, 20 December 1769, 4 February 1770, in the Samuel Kirkland Papers (Massachusetts Historical Society), 12b, 4c, 11a; letter to SSPCK, 16 September 1771, recorded in *JSK*, 71–72 (quotes); John Lennox, *Samuel Kirkland's Mission to the Iroquois* (Chicago: University of Chicago Press, 1935). Figures indicating the amount of trade at Fort Stanwix following its repairs in 1758, in

addition to tolls and carrying charges imposed by the Oneida at the portage, would be very helpful if obtainable. The fort's dilapidated condition by 1768 and constant Oneida requests for trade to be resumed indicate considerable decline.

28. Document entitled "Extract of a Letter of Mr. Sam Kirtland [*sic*]," Boston, 22 August 1768, Papers of the Reverend Samuel Kirkland, Burke Library, Hamilton College, Clinton, New York (hereafter PRSK), 3b. In this document, there is no indication of the recipient, and in fact, it reads more like a report than a letter. A complete inventory is supplied in Kirkland's "Journal as Missionary to the Oneida Indians, 1770–1771," 3 August 1772, Massachusetts Historical Society, quoted in Christine Patrick, "The Life and Times of Samuel Kirkland, 1741–1808: Missionary to the Oneida Indians, American Patriot, and Founder of Hamilton College" (Ph.D. diss., State University of New York at Buffalo, 1993), 214–15. In 1772, his modest 256-square-foot house, with a room 64 square feet added as a bedroom, contained possessions that gave rise to an impressive inventory: a featherbed shipped from New York City, curtains, mirror, and clothes brush; household items including fireplace utensils, teapots, coffee cups, cream and sugar bowls, pewter tankards and plates, stone plates, copper kettles, table and chairs, tablecloths, chests and trunks, six iron and brass kettles, pails, a churn, toaster, frying pan, iron stove, coffee pot, basins, and some books dealing with religion and health. For his agricultural and farm use, and for the purpose of encouraging the Oneida to learn farming practices, he boasted ownership of a plough, four axes, two hoes, a spade and shovel, saws, chisels, rakes, and a shallow boat. He included a pair of oxen, two pigs, a horse, and twelve bags of meal.

29. Johnson's journal, 10 August 1770, *PWJ* 12:836–37.

30. Oneida petition, January 1764, *PWJ* 11:28–29; Oneida petition to Governor Dunmore, 30 December 1770, PRSK, 13e (quote).

31. Rev. Moseley to Kirkland, 3 September 1770, Kirkland to A. Oliver, 12 November 1770, PRSK, 10a, 12b; Kirkland journal, 4 February 1771, *JSK*, 67–68 (quotes). Unfortunately Kirkland supplied no names of those who conveyed word to Johnson. Johnson's son-in-law and deputy Indian agent, Daniel Claus, later voiced that "Indians in general are fond of carrying secrets to their Superintendent which they would not choose to come through the mouth of an Interpreter." Daniel Claus to William Knox, 1 March 1777, *DRCHNY* 8:701. Nor did Kirkland name those who represented the warriors at the council meeting. Christian leadership at Oquaga during this period is supplied in Richard Smith, *A Tour of Four Great Rivers: The Hudson, Mohawk, Susquehanna and Delaware in 1769*, ed. Francis W. Halsey (1906; Fort Washington, NY: Ira J. Friedman, 1964), liii–lxix, 62–73.

32. Speeches of 2, 9 March 1772, *JSK*, 73–77 (76, 77).

33. Kirkland to John Thornton, 5 June, Kirkland to A. Oliver, 30 August 1773, PRSK, 42b, 44c. See also Kirkland journal, August 1773, Kirkland to Andrew Eliot, 19 November 1773, PRSK, 44b, 45c. The church was no small enterprise: in his journal he described it as a building measuring thirty-six by twenty-eight by eighteen feet, with provision for a gallery. There were two doors, five eight-by-ten-foot windows with twenty-four panes of glass each, and four seven-by-nine-foot windows with fifteen panes each. Kirkland journal, 3 June 1773, *JSK*, 83.

34. Entry of [information missing], August 1773, Kirkland to Oliver, 30 August 1773, PRSK, 44c; Wallace to Johnson, 19 May 1773, *PWJ* 8:801.

35. Meetings at Fort Johnson, 15 September 1757, 9 April 1762, 19 December 1764, 30 January 1765, *PWJ* 9:831–32, 10:428, 11:512, 554. Tagawaron's death, after a month's illness, is mentioned on 29 June 1772, *PWJ* 12:1000; meeting at Fort Johnson, 5 August 1763, *PWJ* 10:794–98. "Social polarization" (the conflict between sachems and warriors) is an idea strongly advocated by Guzzardo, in "Superintendent and Ministers." For Kirkland and Oneida factionalism, see also Campisi, "Oneida," in Trigger, *North American Indians,* 15:482–83.

36. Unidentified source, 18 October 1768, EWP #768568.1; Kirkland to Wheelock, 21 September 1771, PRSK, 21g. Tagawaron's role predates the nineteenth-century situation described by Alex Ricciardelli, in "The Adoption of White Agriculture by the Oneida Indians," *Ethnohistory* 10:4 (Fall 1963): 309–25. His role also provides a specific case for the Oneida, which is missing from articles such as those by Judith Brown, "Economic Organization and the Position of Women among the Iroquois," *Ethnohistory* 17:4 (Fall 1970): 151–67; Dean Snow, "The First Americans and the Differentiation of Hunter-Gather Cultures," in *The Cambridge History of the Native Peoples of the Americas,* part 1, ed. Bruce Trigger and Wilcomb Washburn (Cambridge, England: Cambridge University Press, 1996), 125–200; Thomas Wessel, "Agriculture and Iroquois Hegemony in New York, 1610–1779," *Maryland Historian* 1:1 (Spring 1970): 93–104.

## 4—THE ONEIDA AS NEUTRALS

1. George Stanley, "The Six Nations and the American Revolution," *Ontario History* 56:4 (December 1964): 221, 223; Laurence Hauptman, *Conspiracy of Interests: Iroquois Dispossession and the Rise of New York State* (Syracuse: Syracuse University Press, 1999), 34–35; Francis Jennings, "The Indians' Revolution," in *The American Revolution: Explorations in the History of American Radicalism,* ed. Alfred Young (Dekalb: Northern Illinois University Press, 1976), 341; Levinson, "Oneida-Colonist Alliance," 270–71. The resources at Hamilton College, Massachusetts Historical Society, and the State Library at Albany, New York, support Fenton's claim that Kirkland was "one of the more considerable personalities among the founders of our nation." Fenton, *Great Law and Longhouse,* 548.

2. Although Kirkland indicated in 1775 that Conoquhieson lived in the village of Old Oneida, the sachem was generally associated with Kanowalohale. See Kirkland to Guy Johnson, 21 February 1775, PRSK, 53c.

3. Proceedings of Congress with Mohawks, 28–30 July 1772, *DRCHNY* 8:304–10 (304, 309); Kirkland journal, 21 April 1773, *JSK,* 82. The Mohawks never took the Oneida up on this offer, presumably since those affected decided to join other Mohawk who had already migrated to Canada. No numbers were mentioned in this petition; if it involved the majority of the Mohawk remaining in New York, it would have effectively made the Oneida the eastern door of the Confederacy. Considering the deepening animosity between Oneida and Mohawk, and the eventual destruction of Oneida communities in the 1779 Sullivan campaign, it was providential that the Mohawk did not accept the Oneida offer.

4. Proceedings, 9–14 July 1774, *DRCHNY* 8:474–82. Guy Johnson (1740–1788) came to America from Ireland in the 1750s, served in the Seven Years' War, and in 1762 became deputy Indian agent while serving as personal secretary to his uncle and father-in-law. He became superintendent at Sir William's death in 1774, was commander at Fort Niagara from 1780 to 1782, and eventually moved permanently to England. It is possible Conoquhieson was chosen to represent the Confederacy at this important occasion because of his lengthy adherence to Anglicanism (see chapter 1). By this time he was an elder statesman, well-known among the Iroquois for he had spoken at conferences for many years. He had also previously conducted many condolence ceremonies, no doubt fulfilling the role as required of the Oneida who were the Younger Brothers of the Confederacy. In this case the Oneida, being "next-door" to the Mohawk, would be expected to perform the rite. Wampum belts were used to indicate affirmation of treaties as they occurred and were presumably made in advance by the women of the nation by whom they were presented. In an unexpected situation such as this, it would be interesting to know which nation had made these belts.

5. Kirkland to Eliot, 28 March 1774, PRSK, 54b.

6. Recorded in Guy Johnson to Earl of Dartmouth, 10 September 1774, *DRCHNY* 8:489–91; Kirkland, journal entries 24 August, 16 September 1774, *JSK*, 96–98 (98); Samson Occom, diary entry 14 August 1774, EWP reel 14. The sources make no mention of a successor to the Oneida overseer Thomas King following his death in 1771. Governor (William) Bull to Governor Hamilton, 6 September 1771, *MPCP* 9:775–76.

7. Congress of Six Nations with Guy Johnson at Onondaga, November 1774, *DRCHNY* 8:524–27 (524, 525).

8. Meeting of the Six Nations with Guy Johnson, 20–27 January 1775, ibid., 536.

9. Kirkland journal, 10–14 March 1773, *JSK*, 81–82; meeting of the Six Nations with Guy Johnson, 20–27 January 1775, *DRCHNY* 8:534–42 (542); Kirkland to Guy Johnson, 21 February 1775, *JSK*, 106–7.

10. Meeting of Guy Johnson with the Oneida and Oquaga, 10–16 February 1775, *DRCHNY* 8:549–55 (552).

11. Guy Johnson to Kirkland, 14 February, Kirkland to Johnson, 21 February 1774, PRSK, 53b, 53c. See also Johnson to the Earl of Dartmouth, 16 March 1775, *DRCHNY* 8:548–49; Harvey Chalmers, *Joseph Brant: Mohawk* (East Lansing: Michigan State University Press, 1955); Isabel Kelsay, *Joseph Brant, 1743–1807: Man of Two Worlds* (Syracuse: Syracuse University Press, 1984). In 1765 Thayendanega (commonly known as Joseph Brant) had married Margaret, a daughter of the Oneida leader Dakayenensese at Oquaga. At her death in 1771, Thayendanega married her half sister. His personal pro-British allegiance added to that of Dakayenensese but contributed to the conflict of loyalties among the Oneida at Oquaga.

12. Guy Johnson, journal, May–November 1775, *DRCHNY* 8:658. See also William Campbell, *The Border Warfare of New York During the Revolution, or, the Annals of Tryon County* (New York: Baker and Scribner, 1849), 50–51. When a copy of this letter, translated into English, was discussed by the members of the Palatine District of the Troy County Committee of Safety, they felt it could only have been written with Guy Johnson's encouragement. See committee minutes of 21 May 1775, in Maryly Penrose, *Mohawk Valley in the Revolution: Committee of Safety Papers and Genealogical Compendium* (Franklin Park, NJ: Liberty Bell Associates, 1978), 6. The term "Bostonian" appeared in speeches and correspondence throughout the revolutionary period. It was frequently (but not exclusively) used by Indians loyal to Britain as a detrimental appellation for the Oneida supporters of the rebel Patriots. Guy Johnson was causing concern among the Patriots in the Mohawk valley, as they received reports of his fortifying his residence and gaining Iroquois support in case of military action against them. Minutes of Palatine District of the Troy County Committee of Correspondence to the Albany Committee, 18, 21 May 1775, in Peter Force, ed., *American Archives* (hereafter *AA*), 4th series, 6 vols. (Washington, DC: GPO, 1837–1846), 637, 665.

13. Eleazar Wheelock had encouraged the connection between the Caughnawauga and the Oneida by sending James Dean there in the spring of 1775. See Wheelock to Governor Trumbell, 16 March 1775, in *AA*, 4th ser., 2:152. In the 1750s Dean's parents had arranged for him to spend his childhood among the Oneida at Oquaga, learning the languages and customs of that multi-ethnic community. Adopted by a resident Oneida sachem's wife, he was described in 1761 by the missionary Gideon Hawley as a "perfect Indian boy." Hawley to Wheelock, 19 September 1761, EWP #761519. Shortly afterward Dean served as interpreter during Christian worship in that community. In 1770 Dean was admitted to Wheelock's new Dartmouth College in Hanover, New Hampshire. In the spring of 1775, he visited Caughnawauga under the auspices of the congressional commissioners. As he wrote in his "Short Account," the Caughnawauga Indians "took the opportunity . . . to inquire into the Origins and Reasons . . . of the present Controversy." Dean's interpretation to them was in keeping with the aspirations of the Continental Congress, as he proceeded "to conciliate and confirm

their friendship to the common Cause of America." The commissioners subsequently sent Dean for the purpose, as he understood it, "to reside . . . in the Country of the Six Nations, to counteract [English] Intrigues and communicate intelligence to the Commissioners of all material Occurrences in that Quarter." James Dean, "A Short Account of a Tour Undertaken 9 March 1775 from Dartmouth College to Canada," box 13, Philip Schuyler Papers (New York State Library; hereafter PSP). For more about James Dean, see Sidney N. Deane, "A New England Pioneer among the Oneida Indians: The Life of James Dean of Westmoreland, NY," a paper read to the Northampton Historical Society, 28 January 1926; Karim Tiro, "James Dean in Iroquoia," *New York History* 80:4 (October 1999): 391–422.

14. General Philip Schuyler to the Continental Congress, 28, 29 June 1775, *PCC,* M247, roll 177, item 153, 1:2.

15. Ibid., 1:5; Minutes of Congress, 16 June 1775, in Worthington Ford, ed., *Journals of the Continental Congress, 1774–1789,* 34 vols. (Washington, DC: GPO, 1904–1937; hereafter *JCC*), 2:93. The actual appointment of congressional commissioners for the northern section of the Department of Indian Affairs did not take place until 12 July 1775. The commissioners appointed were Joseph Hawley, Turbot Francis, Oliver Wolcott, Volkert Douw, and Philip Schuyler. *JCC* 2:175.

16. Thomas Spencer became a blacksmith who worked both at Kanowalohale and in the Cherry Valley. Joseph Glatthaar and James Martin, *Forgotten Allies: The Oneida Indians and the American Revolution* (New York: Hill and Wang, 2006), 89–90, 345nn37, 38. The spelling Oneynyoaget is found in the speech recorded in *AA,* 4th ser., 2:1746–47. He was commonly known as Beech Tree. The spelling Oneyanhe became the later and more common version of his name.

17. Minutes, 22 June 1775, in James Sullivan, ed., *Minutes of the Albany Committee of Correspondence, 1775–1778* (Albany: University of New York, 1923), 1:97.

18. Minutes, 24, 26 June 1775, ibid., 1:102–5, 106–10 (102, 104, 104). William Thaghthaghgwesere was a frequent signatory of land deals made with the Americans after the revolution; Clenis later used the more common name Kakiktoton.

19. Address to the Oneidas and Tuscaroras, 28 June 1775, *AA,* 4th ser., 2:1125; Sullivan, *Minutes,* 1:108, 110; also New York Delegates to the Provincial Congress, 10 June 1775, in Edmund Burnett, ed., *Letters of Members of the Continental Congress,* 8 vols. (Washington, DC: Carnegie Institute, 1921–1936; hereafter *LMCC*), 1:121–22.

20. Karim Tiro used the phrase "first written declaration of neutrality" in "People of the Standing Stone," 107. See also Aquila, *Iroquoian Restoration,* 85–128; Anthony Wallace, "Origins of Iroquois Neutrality: The Grand Settlement of 1701," *Pennsylvania History* 24:3 (July 1957): 223–35; Anthony Wallace, "The Iroquois and the Revolution: The Neutrality Policy," in *Major Problems in the Era of the American Revolution, 1760–1791,* ed. Richard Brown (Lexington: Heath, 1992): 274–77.

21. A handwritten copy of the declaration "To Whom it May Concern" is among Kirkland's correspondence, June 1775, PRSK, 57b. The names of the signatories are in *AA,* 4th ser., 2:1116–17; see also Henry Schoolcraft, "Skenandoah," in *Information Respecting the History, Condition and Prospects of the Indian Tribes of the United States,* vol. 5 (Philadelphia: J. B. Lippincott and Company, 1855), 509–18. In literature concerning this period, Aksiaktatye is most frequently referred to by his English name, Jacob Reed.

22. Record of meeting, 15 October 1773, *PWJ* 12:1037–38. Joseph Johnson was a Mohegan who was influential among the New England Indians. He had taught at the school in Kanowalohale in 1766, attended the 1768 Fort Stanwix conference, and returned to Oneida in March 1773 after a four-year absence to begin negotiations for obtaining land for his people, which included residents of Montauk, Mohegan, Farmington, Groton, Stonington, Niantuck, and Narraganset, all in New England. Unfortunately, the enthusiasm of the New England Indians was less than Joseph Johnson

had expected. He wrote sternly to the various communities that they not exhibit such "Coldness, Lukewarmness and indifference" to the advocacy of William Johnson and the generosity of the Oneida. Joseph Johnson to the New England Indians, 24 December 1773, EWP #773624.1. Yet only he and one other colleague arrived at Johnson Hall in January 1774 to discuss their move to Oneida. Meeting of 13 January 1774, *PWJ* 12:1060.

23. Speeches of Joseph Johnson and the Oneida at Kanowalohale, 20, 21 January 1774. It is unfortunate that no names are given of the Oneida speakers on these occasions. For the Oneida nation's reply to Joseph Johnson, 22 January 1774, EWP ##774120, 774121.

24. Proclamation on the Oneida grant, 4 October 1774, *PWJ* 8:683–84. See also Laura Murray, *'To Do Good to my Indian Brethren': The Writings of Joseph Johnson, 1751–1776* (Amherst: University of Massachusetts Press, 1998), 201–21, 242, 255–61; Anthony Wonderley, "Brothertown, New York, 1785–1796," *New York History* 81:4 (October 2000): 465–91.

25. "Journal of the Treaty held at Albany in August 1775, with the Six Nations," *Collections,* Massachusetts Historical Society, 3rd ser., vol. 5 (1835), 75–100 (77, 83). Minutes of council, 15 August–1 September 1775, *DRCHNY* 8:605–27; PCC, M247, roll 144, item 134, 1–43; Conoquhieson, speech of 15 August 1775, *DRCHNY* 8:608. Senghnagenrat was commonly referred to by his English name, Whiteskin.

26. Minutes of conference, 25 August–1 September 1775, *DRCHNY* 8:611–26; S. Harrison, *Memoir of Lieutenant Colonel Tench Tilghman, Secretary and Aide to Washington* (Albany, NY: J. Munsell, 1876), 79–101; Donald Gerlach, *Proud Patriot: Philip Schuyler and the War of Independence, 1775–1783* (Syracuse: Syracuse University Press, 1987), 50–54.

27. Meeting of Six Nations at Johnson Hall, 16–19 March 1763, *Journal of Indian Affairs,* 24 December 1766, Indian Records, 15 October 1773, *PWJ* 10:626, 12:244, 1037. Conoquhieson's death was noted the following summer in a speech by Oneida sachem Tiahaeira at a meeting with the Indian affairs commissioners in Albany, 7 May 1776, box 13, Philip Schuyler Papers (New York State Library).

28. Reported in Glatthaar and Martin, *Forgotten Allies,* 96–97.

29. General Schuyler to Continental Congress, 23 January 1776, James Dean to Schuyler, 24 February 1776, PCC, M247, roll 172, item 153, 1:431–40, 2:25 (2:25).

30. Dean to Schuyler, 10 March 1776, ibid., 2:79–82 (79).

31. Kirkland to Schuyler, 12 March 1776, ibid., 2:97–100 (98); extract of James Dean's journal, 21–28 March 1776, *AA,* 4th ser., 5:1100–101 (1101, 1100).

32. Extract of James Dean's journal, 21–28 March 1776, *AA,* 4th ser., 5:1100–101.

33. Ibid., 29 March–3 April 1776, 1102–3.

34. Ibid., 2 April 1776, 1103–4. Dean's intimacy with the Oneida and his sensitivity to Iroquoian cultural practices enabled him to provide details in this document that were rarely included in accounts of councils rendered by persons with less experience. Nancy Hagedorn, "Brokers of Understanding: Interpreters as Agents of Cultural Exchange in Colonial New York," *New York History* 76:4 (October 1995), 379–408.

35. Dean to Schuyler, 10 March, Kirkland to Schuyler, 12 March 1776, *PCC,* M247, roll 172, item 153, 2:83, 97–100 (83, 97, 98).

36. Meeting of the Indian Commissioners with the Six Nations at Albany, 2–10 May 1776, box 13, PSP.

37. Schuyler to Albany Committee of Correspondence, 27 May 1776, Oquaga chiefs to Albany Committee of Correspondence, 4 June 1776, *AA,* 4th ser., 6:648, 710; Senghnagenrat to Schuyler, 22 May 1776, *DRCHNY* 8:690.

38. Schuyler, speech to the Six Nations, March 1776, Report of Six Nations to Commissioners, mid-May 1776, Proceedings of the Continental Congress, 11 June 1776, *AA,* 4th ser., 5:772, 6:502–3, 1701; letter to Samuel Johnson, 26 May 1776, *LMCC*

1:465. Glatthaar and Martin, in *Forgotten Allies,* refers to Conoquhieson's successor as "young Conoquhieson" (Kanaghweas).

39. Kirkland to Schuyler, Schuyler to Congress, both 8 June 1776, *AA,* 4th ser., 6:764, 762 (764).

40. Schuyler to Congress, 8 June 1776, *AA,* 4th ser., 6:763. See also Glatthaar and Martin, *Forgotten Allies,* 119–20; Gerlach, *Proud Patriot,* 150–56. It is unfortunate that the names of the Oneida sachems who supported the formation of this league were not recorded.

41. Bloomfield journal, 10–16 July 1776, in Mark Lender and J. Martin, eds., *Citizen Soldier: The Revolutionary War Journal of Joseph Bloomfield* (Newark: New Jersey Historical Society, 1982), 62–74 (65, 65, 66, 67); also Schuyler, report to Congress, 1 August 1776, *AA,* 5th ser., 1:714–15, 825.

42. According to Iroquois population estimates (see Introduction), this figure represents about 20 percent of the total.

43. Bloomfield journal, 18–23 July, 28 July–4 August 1776, in Lender and Martin, *Citizen Soldier,* 76–87, 90–96 (91, 92). Their use of wampum, their occupations of war and hunting, their style of dance and dress, and their predilection for alcohol all received comment. Gerlach, *Proud Patriot,* 174–87.

44. Thomas Jefferson to John Page, 5 August 1776, *LMCC* 2:29–39; Bloomfield journal, 7–10 August 1776, in Lender and Martin, *Citizen Soldier,* 97–99 (98, 98); minutes of Schuyler's conference with the Six Nations, 12–13 August 1776, *AA,* 5th ser., 1:1038–45, 1050 (1050).

## 5—The Oneida as Rebels

1. Message of Oneida chiefs to Colonel Elmore, 19 January 1777, Samuel Kirkland to Schuyler, 19 January 1777, *PCC,* M247, roll 173, item 153, 3:59–60, 70–72. There is no evidence this condolence was ever held. Walter Mohr, *Federal Indian Relations, 1774–1788* (Philadelphia: University of Pennsylvania Press, 1933), 37–91; Dean Snow, *The Iroquois* (Oxford: Blackwell, 1994), 141–58.

2. Kirkland to Schuyler, 25 January 1777, *PCC,* M247, roll 173, item 153, 21; Tayaheura to Guy Johnson, 23 February 1775, *JSK,* 111; speech of William Kayentarongwea to the Tryon County Committee, 1 April 1777, in *Journals of the Provincial Congress, Provincial Convention, Committee of Safety and Council of Safety of the State of New York, 1775–1777,* 2 vols. (Albany: State Printers, 1842; hereafter *JPCPC*), 1:858; James Vivian and Jean Vivian, "Congressional Indian Policy during the War for Independence: The Northern Department," *Maryland Historical Magazine* 63:3 (September 1968): 241–74.

3. Dean to Schuyler, 20 April, Colonel Elmore to Schuyler, 22 April 1777, *PCC,* M247, roll 173, item 153, 3:128–30, 124–26; resolution of 29 April 1777, *JCC* 7:308; report of Tryon County Committee of Safety, 17 July 1777, *JPCPC* 1:1007; Robert Venables, "The Indians' Revolutionary War in the Hudson Valley 1775–1783," in Hauptman and Campisi, *Neighbours and Intruders,* 225–41.

4. Honyere was accepted by the Oneida even though he had a Mohawk mother and a German father. Background information about him and his family makes for interesting reading in the notes assembled by Lyman Draper, February 1878, Draper Manuscripts, Series U (Frontier Papers), State Historical Society of Wisconsin (hereafter Draper MSS), vol. 11, folios 191–95, 200, 210, 216, 242–43. He was later known as Honyere Doxtator. Ibid., 200–201.

5. Box 14, PSP; Draper MSS, vol. 11, folios 200–201.

6. Oneida nation Web site www.oneida-nation.net/historical.html; Glatthaar and Martin, *Forgotten Allies,* 154–55; from anecdotes from interviews with descendants, Draper MSS, vol. 11, folios 191–92, 196–97, 200–204, 213, 215–17, 243; Campbell, *Border Warfare,*

68–70, 72–74, 83; William Stone, *Life of Joseph Brant,* 2 vols. (New York: George Dearborn and Company, 1838), 1:367; Samuel Durant, *History of Oneida County, New York* (Philadelphia: Everts and Fariss, 1878), 101–15; John Scott, "Joseph Brant at Fort Stanwix and Oriskany," *New York History* 19:1 (October 1938): 399–406.

7. Barbara Graymont, *The Iroquois in the American Revolution* (Syracuse: Syracuse University Press, 1972), 129–42 (142). Daniel Claus to William Knox, 16 October, 6 November 1777, *DRCHNY* 8:720–21, 725; Draper MSS, vol. 11, folios 196, 202, 215, and vol. 3, folio 6; letter to Council of Safety, 11 August 1777, *JPCPC* 1:1037; Schuyler to Continental Congress, roll 29, box 14, PSP; evidence supplied by colonial residents, 20 April 1778, box 14, PSP. See also Barr, *Unconquered,* 165–67; Karim Tiro, "A 'Civil' War? Rethinking Iroquois Participation in the American Revolution," *Explorations in Early American Culture* 4 (2000): 148–65; Glatthaar and Martin, *Forgotten Allies,* 155–69, 177; Gerlach, *Proud Patriot,* 292–95; William Hagan, *Longhouse Diplomacy and Frontier Warfare: The Iroquois Confederacy in the American Revolution* (Albany: New York State American Revolution Bicentennial Commission, 1976), 22–25; Lois Feister and Bonnie Pulis, "Molly Brant: Her Domestic and Political Roles in Eighteenth-Century New York," in R. S. Grumet, ed., *Northeastern Indian Lives, 1632–1816* (Amherst: University of Massachusetts Press, 1996), 295–320.

8. From 1790 to 1794 Timothy Pickering was the congressional commissioner responsible for maintaining good relations with the Six Nations. The story of his growing sympathy for the Iroquois, culminating when he stopped to perform the assessment of Oneida losses during the revolution, is given in Edward Phillips, "Timothy Pickering at His Best: Indian Commissioner 1790–1794," *Essex Institute Historical Collections* 102:3 (July 1966): 163–202.

9. Kirkland journal, 24, 25, 29 November 1794, *JSK,* 275, 277 (277). Phillips, "Pickering at His Best," 167–70; J. Parrish, "The Story of Captain Jasper Parrish: Captive, Interpreter and United States Sub-Agent to the Six Nations Indians (from his own notes, compiled by his son, Stephen Parrish, and others)," *Publications of the Buffalo Historical Society* 6 (1903): 527–38; "Treaty with the Oneida, etc., 1794," 2 December 1794, in Charles Kappler, ed., *Indian Affairs: Laws and Treaties* (Washington, DC: GPO, 1904), 2:37–39.

10. Pickering Papers (Massachusetts Historical Society, Boston; hereafter TPP) 62:160. The actual inventory is in handwritten form and is preserved on microfilm at ibid., 157–66.

11. Schuyler to Hancock, 27 September 1777, *PCC,* M247, roll 173, item 153, 3:252–53; Draper MSS, vol. 11, folio 264.

12. The story of Jane McCrea has become a familiar story in the annals of the revolution. She was traveling to be reunited with her fiancé, fighting with the Loyalists, when she was captured by two warriors. A dispute ensued as to which warrior was her rightful captor, and one then forced the decision by killing and mutilating her. The culprit was captured and initially sentenced to death by the British, but he was eventually pardoned so as not to irritate his kinfolk and create a mass defection of his people from the Loyalist forces.

13. Glatthaar and Martin, *Forgotten Allies,* 190–93; Graymont, *Iroquois in the Revolution,* 150–55. Graymont calls the battle of Saratoga the turning point in the revolution, stating that the rebel cause might have faltered without the support of the Oneida in this confrontation. Graymont, "Oneidas and the American Revolution," 37. Glatthaar claims that "Saratoga was arguably the most consequential triumph for the revolutionaries in their pursuit of independence." Glatthaar and Martin, *Forgotten Allies,* 183. Bread's award is mentioned in Draper MSS, vol. 11, folio 265.

14. From contemporary accounts cited in Glatthaar and Martin, *Forgotten Allies,* 184.

15. Ibid., 185–86 (186); Graymont, *Iroquois in the Revolution,* 163.

16. Continental Congress to the Oneida, 3 December 1777, *JCC* 14:996. See also Schuyler to Henry Laurens, 8 February 1778, in Maryly Penrose, ed., *Indian Affairs Papers: American Revolution* (Franklyn Park, NJ: Liberty Bell Associates, 1981; hereafter *IAP*), 111–12; instructions of the Continental Congress, 4 March 1778, *JCC* 10:220–21; James Duane to Clinton, 13 March 1778, *LMCC* 3:129–30.

17. Louis Gottschalk, *Lafayette Joins the American Army* (Chicago: University of Chicago Press, 1937), 145. See also Lafayette, journal of 1779, in S. Idzerda, ed., *Lafayette in the Age of the American Revolution: Selected Letters and Papers* (Ithaca: Cornell University Press, 1977), 1:247; Lafayette to Washington, 13 March 1778, in Louis Gottschalk, ed., *Letters of Lafayette to Washington, 1777–1779* (Philadelphia: American Philosophical Society, 1976), 33–34.

18. Odaghseghte, speech at Johnstown conference, 10 March 1778, *IAP*, 116; also Gerlach, *Proud Patriot*, 346–50.

19. Glatthaar and Martin, *Forgotten Allies*, 201–2.

20. Kirkland, report to A. Louis de Tousard, 24 April 1778, *PCC*, M247, roll 95, item 78, 157–60.

21. Odaghseghte, speech to Party of Warriors, and reply of the warriors, quoted in Tousard letter, 23 May 1778, ibid., 158–59.

22. Thomas Fleming, *Washington's Secret War: The Hidden Story of Valley Forge* (New York: Smithsonian/Collins, 2005), 291–94; Robert Douglas, trans. and ed., *The Chevalier de Pontgibaud: A French Volunteer of the War of Independence* (Paris: Charles Carrington, 1898; reprint, Arno Press, 1960), 69; John Trussell, *Birthplace of an Army: A Study of the Valley Forge Encampment* (Harrisburg: Pennsylvania Historical and Museum Commission, 1976); John Reed, "Indians at Valley Forge," *Valley Forge Historical Society Journal* 3:1 (1986): 26–32.

23. Joseph P. Martin, *Private Yankee Doodle, Being a Narrative of Some of the Adventures, Dangers and Sufferings of a Revolutionary Soldier,* ed. George Scheer (Boston: Little, Brown, 1962), 118–19 (119).

24. Glatthaar and Martin, *Forgotten Allies*, 209–14; Laurens, letter, 28 May 1778, in Philip Hamer, ed., *The Papers of Henry Laurens*, 14 vols. (Columbia: University of South Carolina Press, 1968), 13:347. See also Glatthaar and Martin, *Forgotten Allies*, 412–13; the Battle of Barren Hill receives but passing mention in Graymont, *Iroquois in the Revolution*, 165.

25. Tousard, report to Continental Congress, 23 May 1778, *PCC*, M247, roll 95, item 78, 157–60 (157); George Washington to Schuyler, 15 May 1778, in John Fitzpatrick, ed., *The Writings of George Washington*, 39 vols. (Washington, DC: GPO, 1931–1944), 11:390, 391.

26. Glatthaar and Martin, *Forgotten Allies*, 215–18.

27. Dean to Clinton, 15 June 1778, in Hugh Hastings, ed., *The Public Papers of George Clinton*, 10 vols. (Albany, NY: State Printers, 1899–1914; hereafter *PPGC*), 3:458–59; Schuyler to Laurens, 19 July 1778, *IAP*, 148–49; "Report of Board of War," 10 June 1778, *PCC*, M247, roll 157, item 147, 81–85.

28. Report included in Commissioner Douw to Clinton, 2 October 1778, *PPGC* 4:131–32; George Washington to Commander Stark, 8 October 1778, in Fitzpatrick, *George Washington*, 13:50; William Butler, journal, 1–6 October 1778, *PPGC* 4:223–24; William Gray, report of 28 October 1778, in Fred Cook, ed., *Journals of the Military Expedition of Major General John Sullivan against the Six Nations of Indians in 1779* (Auburn, NY: Knapp, Peck and Thomson, 1887), 288–90.

29. Smith, *Four Great Rivers*, 65–66; Lieutenant Beatty, journal, 14 August 1779, in Cook, *Military Expedition*, 23. See also William Butler, report, 9 October 1778, *PPGC* 4:225–27; H. Bourdin and S. T. Williams, eds., "Crevecoeur on the Susquehanna, 1774–1776," *Yale Review* 14 (1925): 581–83.

30. Meeting of Commissioners of Indian Affairs, 15 April 1778, *IAP*, 124; Dean

to Commissioner Douw, 15 October, speech of Agwrongdongwas to Douw, 21 October, Douw's speech to the Oneida, Agwrongdongwas's reply, Douw's response, 22 October 1778, ibid., 157–65 (159).

31. Summary of speech of Agwrongdongwas outlining Cayuga charges, in Colonel Van Dyck to Clinton, 23 December 1778, *PPGC* 4:417–19 (419); meeting of Oneida with the Indian commissioners, 21 July 1778, box 14, PSP.

32. Colonel Van Dyck to Clinton, 18 January 1779, *PPGC* 4:492–94 (492, 492, 494); Dean to Schuyler, 18 January 1779, *IAP,* 181.

33. Schuyler's request to Commissioner Duane, 7 March 1779, *PCC,* M247, roll 158, item 147, 3:175; "List of Indians to have Commissions," n.d., box 14, PSP; Pickering to president of Congress, 5 June 1779, *PCC,* M247, roll 158, item 147, 3:391. The list is also in *IAP,* 99, and with the English meanings of the Indian names in Draper MSS, vol. 11, folios 200–210.

34. George Washington to Captain Copp of Fort Schuyler, 19, 25 January 1779, in Fitzpatrick, *George Washington,* 14:23–24, 43; Captain Copp to Captain [?], 24 February 1779, *PCC,* M247, roll 173, item 153, 3:424; T. W. Egly, *History of the First New York Regiment, 1775–1783* (Hampton, NY: Peter Randall, 1981), 113–41.

35. Joseph Fischer, *A Well-Executed Failure: The Sullivan Campaign against the Iroquois, July–September 1779* (Columbia: University of South Carolina Press, 1997); Arthur Parker, "The Indian Interpretation of the Sullivan-Clinton Campaign," *Rochester Historical Society* 8 (1929): 45–59; Stone, *Joseph Brant,* 2:407–9; Oneida meeting with the commissioners, 21 July 1779, Schuyler to Commissioner Douw, 10 August 1779, *IAP,* 224–29.

36. James Madison to Thomas Jefferson, 2 June 1780, *LMCC* 5:181–82; Glatthaar and Martin, *Forgotten Allies,* 247; James Clinton to Governor Clinton, 10 August 1779, *PPGC* 5:189; Sullivan, speech to the Oneida, 1 September, Sullivan to John Jay, 30 September, Oneida sachem to Sullivan, 8, 18 September 1779, in Otis Hammond, ed., *The Letters and Papers of Major General John Sullivan,* 3 vols. (Concord: New Hampshire Historical Society, 1939), 3:114–15, 129–31, 115–16; David Freemoyer account, September 1779, in John Dann, ed., *The Revolution Remembered: Eyewitness Accounts of the War for Independence* (Chicago: University of Chicago Press, 1980), 289–305. See also Tiro, "People of the Standing Stone," 127–32; Fischer, *Well-Executed Failure,* 85–96; Hagan, *Longhouse Diplomacy,* 34–42; Max Mintz, *Seeds of Empire: The American Revolutionary Conquest of the Iroquois* (New York: New York University Press, 1999); Donald McAdams, "The Sullivan Expedition: Success or Failure?" *New York Historical Society Quarterly* 54 (January 1970): 53–81; Parker, "Indian Interpretation," 45–49.

37. Request of Oneida and answer of Indian Commissioners, 9, 10 February 1780, PSP, roll 7 (quote); Kanowalohale council recorded at same meeting, 9 February 1780, ibid.; Colonel Van Schaick to Cornelius Van Dyck, 3 July 1780, *PPGC* 5:912–14; Schuyler to Samuel Huntingdon, 10 October 1780, *PCC,* M247, roll 173, item 153, 3:541; Morgan Lewis to George Clinton, 24 June 1780, *PPGC* 5:883–84; Kirkland to Douw, 3 July 1780, *IAP,* 260; Colonel Van Schaick, 24 June 1780, *PPGC* 5:883; Gerlach, *Proud Patriot,* 418–20. Senghnagenrat later explained to his people that he had been forced into appearing to switch his allegiance to the British; his presence at later councils led the British to believe his defection from the rebels was genuine. But his loyalty to the Americans was later affirmed, both by them and by the Indians. Schuyler to Knox, 13 January 1786, *PCC,* M247, roll 165, item 151, 141–43.

38. Reports, 14 January 1784, box 14, PSP; Draper MSS, vol. 11, folios 204–9, 237–44; entries in *PPGC* 6:288, 480–83; Van Schaick to Cornelius Van Dyck, 3 July 1780, *PPGC* 5:912–14; Schuyler to Huntingdon, 10 October 1780, *PCC,* M247, roll 173, item 153, 3:541; Governor Haldimand to Lord Germain, 25 October 1780, in K. Davies, ed., *Documents of the American Revolution, 1770–1783,* 21 vols. (Shannon: Irish University Press, 1978), 18:208.

39. Inventory from Skenandoah's home, TPP 161; Anthony Wonderley, "An Oneida Community in 1780: Study on an Inventory of Iroquois Property Losses during

the Revolutionary War," *Man in the Northeast* 56 (Fall 1988): 19–41.

40. Inventory of Odaghseghte's home in TPP 166a.

41. Inventory of Agwrongdongwas, ibid., 161.

42. Inventory of Gaghsaweda, ibid., 160a.

43. Extrapolated from the records as shown in Pickering's inventory, TPP 157–66. No mention is made of items of Indian manufacture (such as clothing made of hide or fur) or wooden utensils, as they would not have had any financial value in the minds of the evaluators. For the influence of Kirkland's church, see Kirkland journal, 3 June 1773, *JSK*, 83. Kirkland reported to Congress that he had purchased two milk cows from the Oneida in the summer of 1780. Petition to Congress, 26 April 1785, *JCC* 28:306. There is a clear connection between material status and clan membership in Kanowalohale: when Pickering calculated the value of the 111 claims made for 1780, Wolf clan leaders had consistently greater financial status than Bear and Turtle clan members. Within each clan, 10 percent of the members formed an elite group with considerably greater financial value than others in their clan.

44. Colonel Weissenfels to George Clinton, 9 December 1780, *PPGC* 6:480–83. The three officers joining the British must have done so only temporarily, like Aksiaktatye, who returned to the rebels after six months. All four names appear on treaties between the Oneida and the American government when negotiations start in the early 1780s. Glatthaar and Martin discuss the possible number of Oneida who transferred their loyalty to the British and those who remained with the rebels. Glatthaar and Martin, *Forgotten Allies,* 379nn25, 26.

45. Colonel Van Schaick to Governor Clinton, 24 June 1780, *PPGC* 5:882–84. Guy Johnson reported that 156 Oneida had been killed or captured as a result of Thayendanega's raids that summer. Guy Johnson to Lord Germain, 26 July 1780, *DRCHNY* 8:796–97.

46. Willis Hanson, *A History of Schenectady during the Revolution* (privately printed, 1916), 112.

47. De Chastellux journal, 27 December 1780, in Howard Rice, trans. and ed., *Travels in North America in the Years 1780, 1781, and 1782 by the Marquis de Chastellux* (Chapel Hill: University of North Carolina Press, 1963), 2:208–9. De Chastellux served with the Continental Army from July 1780 to January 1783 and later maintained correspondence with George Washington and Benjamin Franklin.

48. Schuyler to Huntington, 2 December 1780, *IAP*, 266. New York Delegates to Governor Clinton, 11 March 1781, *LMCC* 6:22–23; "List of Necessary Clothing for 406 Indian men, women and children," *PCC*, M247, roll 173, item 153, 3:545; Draper MSS, vol. 11, folios 200–201; Gerlach, *Proud Patriot,* 440–58; Hanson, *History of Schenectady,* 109–13; M. Wright, trans. and ed., *Memoirs of the Marshall Count de Rochambeau, relative to the War of Independence of the United States* (Paris: French, English and American Library, 1838; reprint, New York: Arno Press, 1971), 22–26.

49. Schuyler to Huntingdon, 18 January 1781, *PCC*, M247, roll 173, item 15, 3:555; speech of Atayataghronghta to Congress, 11 September 1781, ibid., roll 98, item 78, 14:498; reply of Committee of Congress to Oneidas, Tuscaroras, and Kahnawakes, 13 September 1781, *IAP,* 276–77.

50. Dean to Schuyler, 20 February 1782, box 13, PSP; Schuyler to inhabitants of Tryon County, 1 May 1782, ibid., cited in Tiro, "People of the Standing Stone," 141–42. See also Russell Barsh, "Native North American Loyalists and Patriots: Reflections on the American Revolution in Native American History," *Indian Historian* 10 (1977): 13–36; J. Bloomfield, *The Oneidas* (New York: James Stewart, 1909), 102–59; Morris Bishop, "The End of the Iroquois Mystique," *American Heritage* 20:6 (October 1969): 28–33, 77–81; Colin Calloway, "The Continuing Revolution in Indian Country," in Frederick Hoxie, ed., *Native Americans and the Early Republic* (Charlottesville: University of Virginia Press, 1999), 3–33.

51. Willett to Washington, 5 March 1783, in Fitzpatrick, *George Washington,* 26:190; Stone, *Joseph Brant,* 2:233–34; Howard Thomas, *Marinus Willett, Soldier-Patriot, 1740–1830* (Prospect, NY: Prospect Books, 1954), 146–50.

## 6—THE ONEIDA AS SURVIVORS

1. Report of the Committee on Indian Affairs to the Continental Congress, and resolutions arising from the report, 15 October 1783, *JCC* 25:681–87 (681, 682, 684, 687). See also Gerlach, *Proud Patriot,* 504–6; Reginald Horsman, *Expansion and American Indian Policy, 1783–1812* (East Lansing: Michigan State University Press, 1967), 16–21; George Shattuck, *The Oneida Land Claims: A Legal History* (Syracuse: Syracuse University Press, 1991); J. David Lehman, "The End of the Iroquois Mystique: The Oneida Land Cession Treaties of the 1780s," *William and Mary Quarterly* 47 (1990): 521–47.

2. Chiefs and Warriors of the Six Nations to George Clinton, 12 April 1784, in Franklin Hough, ed., *Proceedings of the Commissioners of Indian Affairs Appointed by Law for the Extinguishment of Indian Titles in the State of New York* (Albany, NY: Joel Munsell, 1861; hereafter *PCIA*), 1:13–15; Joseph Brant (Thayendanega) to Governor Clinton, 14 April 1784, ibid., 1:22–24; Brant to Clinton, 6 June 1784, *PPGC* 8:323–25; George Clinton to Congressional Commissioners, *PCIA* 1:21 (quote). See also Barbara Graymont, "New York State Indian Policy after the Revolution," *New York History* 57 (1976): 438–74.

3. For Article 37, *Reports of the Proceedings and Debates of the New York Constitutional Convention, 1821* (reprint, New York: Government Publications, 1970), 19; Duane to Governor Clinton, *PCIA* 1:21–22n1. See also *PPGC* 8:328–32; Jack Campisi, "New York–Oneida Treaty of 1795: A Finding of Fact," *American Indian Law Review* 4:1 (Summer 1976): 71–82.

4. Instructions, 17 March 1783, New York Assembly Papers, 49:5, in Henry Manley, *The Treaty of Fort Stanwix, 1784* (Rome, NY: Rome Sentinel, 1932), 28. See also Jacob Read to George Washington, 13 August 1784, *LMCC* 7:583–85; commissioner Peter Ryckman to commissioner Henry Glen, 23 August, Jellis Fonda to George Clinton, 31 August 1784, *PCIA* 1:32–33, 35 (quote).

5. Proceedings of Fort Stanwix Treaty, 1–14 September 1784, *PCIA* 1:36–42 (41).

6. Ibid., 1:43–65 (48); also *PPGC* 8:337, 349–79; Horsman, *Expansion,* 47–49.

7. Eugene Chase, trans. and ed., *Our Revolutionary Forefathers: The Letters of François, Marquis de Barbe-Marbois, 1779–1785* (New York: Duffield, 1929), 188–215 (201). See also Marquis de Barbe-Marbois, "Journey to the Oneidas," in Dean Snow, William Starna, and Charles Gehring, eds., *In Mohawk Country: Early Narratives about a Native People* (Syracuse: Syracuse University Press, 1996), 300–317; Louis Gottschalk, *Lafayette between the American and the French Revolutions, 1783–1789* (Chicago: University of Chicago Press, 1950), 96–108. Jordan emigrated to Canada in the 1750s, took part in the war between France and England, was taken captive by the Oneida, but was spared from death when he was adopted by the family of an Oneida widow, whom he later married. Jordan considered his wife to be of considerable social standing at that time; her dowry consisted of "six hundred pins, one hundred needles, linen cloths, vermillion, a gun, powder and shot, a club, a knife, twenty bundles of furs, two pots, a house, a cow, and a garden. . . . She also had a dozen scalps, to the Indians these [were] family jewels." Chase, *Marbois,* 191–92.

8. Chase, *Marbois,* 193–204 (194).

9. Ibid., 194–97 (194, 195–96).

10. Ibid., 206–11.

11. The English text of Lafayette's speech is provided in Neville Craig, ed., *The Olden Time: A Monthly Publication devoted to the Preservation of Documents and other Authentic Information in Relation to the early Explorations and the Settlement and Improvement of the Country around the Head of the Ohio* (Pittsburgh: Wright and Charlton, 1848), 2:428–29. See also "Account of Lafayette's Meeting with the Six Nations," 3–4 October 1784, in Idzerda, *Lafayette*, 5:255–56; Madison to Arthur Lee, 11, 17 October 1784, in Julian Boyd, ed., *The Papers of Thomas Jefferson*, 21 vols. (Princeton: Princeton University Press, 1953), 7:439–41, 444–47 (a footnote to Madison's letter of 17 October includes Lafayette's speech and the responses made by chiefs of the Mohawk, Seneca, and Huron nations); Boyd, *Papers of Jefferson*, 447–51.

12. Manley, *Treaty of Fort Stanwix*, ch. 22; *PCIA* 1:64–65 (65); Craig, *Olden Time*, 2:409–27; Leonard Sadosky, "Choosing Conquest: Power, Sovereignty and Negotiation in the Treaty of Fort Stanwix, 1783–1784," paper for colloquium, Omohundro Institute of Early American History and Culture, 30 September 2003. The New York commissioners recorded no figures for attendance. The congressional commissioners' reports indicated an attendance of 613 (including 308 Oneida, 20 Caughnawauga, 5 Onondaga, 7 Cayuga, 33 Tuscarora, 25 Mohawk, and 2 Seneca), 27 October 1784, *IIDH*, reel 39. Of the five hostages chosen, two (Ohanodlighton and Thonayute) can be identified as being Oneida. *PCC*, M247, roll 37, item 241. They were Loyalist Bear clan residents at Kanowalohale and made meager claims for war losses at Pickering's visit in 1794.

13. Hill recorded in Craig, *Olden Time*, 2:424, 426. See also James Monroe to Thomas Jefferson, 1 November 1784, *LMCC* 7:605–6; William N. Fenton, ed., "The Journal of James Emlen kept on a Trip to Canandaigua, New York, Sept. 15 to Oct. 30, 1794," *Ethnohistory* 12 (1965), 307.

14. *PCIA*, 1:65. The name of Dayaheari does not seem to appear elsewhere, despite his important function in this event.

15. Minutes of Fort Stanwix conference, 4 September 1784, *PCIA* 1:39–40; Barnes, *Traditional Teachings*, 35. For the identity of these league sachems, and others attending, see Appendix 1.

16. Oneida nation to the congressional commissioners, 18, 20 October 1784, *PCC*, M247, roll 69, item 56, 137, 309. See also Madison to Arthur Lee, 11, 17 October 1874, in Boyd, *Papers of Jefferson*, 7:439–41, 444–47; documents, 23 October, 20 November 1784, *IIDH*, reel 38.

17. Document dated 20 November 1784, *IIDH*, reel 38; Ojistalale to NY commissioners, NY Commissioner Abraham Cuyler to Governor George Clinton, 13 May 1785, *PCIA* 1:72–74 (73, 74).

18. Kirkland to James Bowdin, SSPCK, 14 January 1785, *JSK*, 125. See also Parker Thompson, *The United States Army Chaplaincy, from Its European Antecedents to 1791* (Washington, DC: Department of the Army, 1978), 176–88; Fitzpatrick, *George Washington*, 10:400, 11:78, 105–6, 12:401; Cook, *Military Expedition*, 249–50.

19. Kirkland to James Bowdin, SSPCK, 18 February, 10 March 1784, PRSK, 84a, 85c.

20. Commissioner Cuyler to Governor Clinton, 14 May, commissioners to the Oneida, 13 May, Thayendanega to the commissioner Peter Schuyler, 23 May 1785, *PCIA* 1:70–71, 73–74, 85.

21. Minutes of the conference at Fort Herkimer, 25 June 1785, *PCIA* 1:89–101 (100).

22. Ibid., 1:89–101 (92).

23. Ibid., 27–28 June 1785, *PCIA* 1:102–7 (106). Clan affiliations were recorded in *IIDH*, reel 38.

24. Thayendanega to Congress, September 1785, *PCC*, M247, roll 37, item 471; Oneida chiefs to Congress, 15 September, James Dean to Congress, 11 July, ibid., items 472, 479.

25. Dean to Congress, 15 September, Kirkland to Congress, 14 September 1785, ibid., items 473, 475; Thayendanega to Skenandoah, August 1785, PRSK, 96b.

26. Kirkland journal, 4, 11 March 1787, *JSK,* 129–30. See also Paul Wallace, *White Roots of Peace* (Philadelphia: University of Pennsylvania Press, 1946), 17–19.

27. Kirkland journal, 1 January 1787, in the Lothrop Family Papers, Massachusetts Historical Society, quoted in Patrick, "Samuel Kirkland," 396–97 (396). See also Kirkland journal, 28 January, 9 March 1787, *JSK,* 128–29.

28. Kirkland diary, 16 August, 4, 9 December 1787, in Tiro, "People of the Standing Stone," 161–63 (161, 163, 163).

29. Shaw Livermore, *Early American Land Companies* (New York: Octagon Books, 1968), 198–203. For the terms of the Livingston leases, see *PCIA,* 1:122–24; Orasmus Turner, *History of the Pioneer Settlement of the Phelps and Gorham Purchases* (Rochester, NY: J. W. Brown, 1851). Names of those who signed the Phelps-Gorham deal—three Oneida (Kennawagenton, Oghnaongoghton, and Shoratowane), three Mohawk, eight Onondaga, twenty-two Cayuga, twenty-three Seneca, seven chief women, together with James Dean, Samuel Kirkland, and Thayendanega—are in the *New American State Papers: Indian Affairs,* 4 vols. (Wilmington: Scholarly Research, 1972), 4:108–10. See also George Lewis, *The Indiana Company, 1763–1798* (Glendale, CA: Arthen Clark, 1941).

30. Oneida to the New York legislature, February 1788, *PCIA* 1:124–25n. The four Oneida were Jacob Reed (Aksiaktatye), Hendrick Sahonwate, Peter Salckarenghis, and Daniel Segaoneghserisa.

31. John Tayler to Governor Clinton, 9 April, 16 May, 8 June 1788, *PCIA* 1:132–33, 135, 140–41, 145–46, 147 (145).

32. Oneida sachems to Governor Clinton, 27 June 1788, ibid., 154. See also Jack Campisi, "From Stanwix to Canandaigua: National Policy, States' Rights, and Indian Land," in Christopher Vecsey and William A. Starna, eds., *Iroquois Land Claims* (Syracuse: Syracuse University Press, 1988), 49–65.

33. Minutes of the Fort Stanwix conference, 29 August 1788, *PCIA* 1:179. Peter Otisquette (also known as French Peter) was an Oneida member of the Wolf clan. He served under Lafayette during the revolution, then traveled with him to France in 1784 where he immersed himself in French culture. He returned to America and married an Oneida woman but became known for drunkenness. He died in 1792 while attending a conference in Philadelphia.

34. Minutes of the Fort Stanwix conference, 30 August–22 September 1788, *PCIA* 1:236–51 (239).

35. Minutes of the Fort Stanwix conference and resulting treaty, 30 August–22 September 1788, *PCIA* 1:236–51. The numerous names of the Oneida speakers and signatories are in Appendix 2.

36. *PCIA* 2:267–311.

37. For the names of the eleven who wrote, see Oneida sachems and warriors to Governor Clinton, 27 January 1790, *PCIA* 2:360–62 (361). Alawistonis, often with the first name Jacob, was also known as Blacksmith and Silversmith.

38. Minutes of meetings, 1–16 June 1790, *PCIA* 2:376–402.

39. For the names of Oneida signatories to the Peter Smith lease, see Appendix 3. For the names of Oneida signatories to the act of 19 April 1793, compiled from *IIDH,* see Appendix 4. See also William Starna, "'The United States will protect you': The Iroquois, New York, and the 1790 Nonintercourse Act," *New York History* 83:1 (Winter 2002): 5–33.

40. Minutes of conference at Painted Post (Newtown), 20 June–15 July 1791, TPP, roll 60, 69–109; Agwrongdongwas, speech to Pickering, March 1792, TPP, roll 62, 10; minutes of meetings of Iroquois with Washington, 5–11 April 1792, TPP, roll 60, 121–29; Agwrongdongwas's death in Kirkland to Pickering, 5 September 1792, TPP, roll 62, 61. For details of the Philadelphia meeting, see Katherine Turner, *Red Men Calling on the Great White Father* (Norman: University of Oklahoma Press, 1951).

41. Minutes of meetings at Canandaigua, 10 September–mid-October 1794, TPP, roll 60, 195–230 (219, 219, 221, 230). The only Oneida members mentioned by name in these documents are sachem Onondiyo, war chief Sategaleahtas, and interpreters Skenandoah and James Dean. For terms of the treaty of Canandaigua, 11 November 1794, see *New American State Papers,* 4:148–49. No names of the fifty-nine Iroquois signatories are given. For terms of the treaty with the Oneida on 2 December 1794, see *New American State Papers,* 4:149. Again, no names of the fifteen signing sachems and war chiefs are given.

42. Kirkland journal, 1 August 1791, 26 February 1800, *JSK,* 215–16, 362–63 (215, 216, 363, 363).

43. Kirkland journal, 8 April, 22 June 1789, *JSK,* 161, 166; discussion of 2 November 1793, ibid., 265–66. In the spring of 1799, Kirkland and Skenandoah succeeded in the scheme of separating Christian from non-Christian residents of Kanowalohale and divided the community into an east and west section. From the names of the overseers chosen (see Appendix 6), it would appear that a majority of the pro-sachem Christian Oneida lived at the eastern end, and the pro-warrior traditionalist adherents at the west. Kirkland journal, 25 February 1799, *JSK,* 309–10; Joseph Ibbotson, "Samuel Kirkland, the Treaty of 1792, and the Indian Barrier State," *New York History* 19:1 (October 1938): 374–91.

44. Names of Oneida signing the letter to the SSPCK, 27 April 1793, are in Kirkland's journal, 20 May 1793, *JSK,* 255; Oneida to Pickering, 29 January 1794, TPP 62:82 (see Appendix 5 for names of signatories); Kirkland journal, 13 August–19 October 1792, *JSK,* 225–30; Horsman, *Expansion,* 61–65.

45. "Travels of a Gentleman from Milan, 1790," in Snow et al., *Mohawk Country,* 318–20 (319); Kirkland journal, 28, 30 September 1790, *JSK,* 202–3; John Lincklaen, *Travels in the Years 1791 and 1792 in Pennsylvania, New York, and Vermont* (New York: G. P. Putnam's Sons, 1897), 68–70; John Heckewelder (the Moravian missionary), journal entries of 18 May, 21, 28 July 1793, in Paul Wallace, ed., *Thirty Thousand Miles with John Heckewelder* (Pittsburgh: University of Pittsburgh Press, 1958), 302, 314–15.

46. Jeremy Belknap and Jedidiah Morse, "The report of a committee of the board of correspondents of the Scots Society for propagating Christian knowledge, who visited the Oneida and Mohekunuh Indians in 1796," in *Collections of the Massachusetts Historical Society, for the year M,DCC,XCVIII* (Belknap, 1796; New York: Johnson Reprint, 1798), 5:12–32 (30). Sategaleahtas was commonly known by the colonists as Pagan Peter, in contrast to his Christian father, Agwrongdongwas, who was known as Good Peter.

47. William Savary, *A Journal of the Life, Times and Religious Labours of William Savary, a Minister of the Gospel of Christ, of the Society of Friends, late of Philadelphia* (Philadelphia: Friends' Book Store, 1861), 90. Pickering reassured Congress that the Quakers did not teach "peculiar doctrines" but focused on "useful practices . . . in husbandry and the plain mechanical arts and manufactures directly connected with it." Pickering, letter, 14 February 1796, TPP 62:235. See also Kirkland journal, 6, 7 January 1800, *JSK,* 330–32; Sydney James, *A People among Peoples: Quaker Benevolence in Eighteenth-Century America* (Cambridge, MA: Harvard University Press, 1963), 303–4; Rayner Kelsey, *Friends and Indians, 1655–1917* (Philadelphia: Associated Executive Committee of Friends of Indian Affairs, 1917); Christopher Densmore, "New York Quakers among the Brothertown, Stockbridge, Oneida and Onondaga, 1795–1834," *Man in the Northeast* 44 (Fall 1992): 83–93; Diane Rothenberg, "The Mothers of the Nation: Seneca Resistance to Quaker Intervention" in *Women and Colonization: Anthropological Perspectives,* ed. Mona Etienne and Eleanor Leacock (New York: Praeger, 1980), 61–87; Daniel Richter, "Believing that Many of the Red People Suffer Much for the Want of Food: Hunting, Agriculture and the Quaker Construction of Indianness in the Early Republic," *Journal of the Early Republic* 19:4 (Winter 1999): 601–28.

48. Kirkland to Abraham Miller, 24 May 1800, PRSK, 211c. Events of 1798 to 1800 in Kirkland journal, 23, 26 January 1800, *JSK*, 360, 364–66. See also Harold Blau, "The Iroquois White Dog Sacrifice: Its Evolution and Symbolism," *Ethnohistory* 11:3 (Summer 1964): 97–119; Elizabeth Tooker, "The Iroquois White Dog Sacrifice in the Latter Part of the Eighteenth Century," *Ethnohistory* 12 (Spring 1965): 129–39; Joel Martin, "Cultural Contact and Crises in the Early Republic," in Hoxie, *Native Americans,* 226–60.

49. Jeremy Belknap and J. Morse, *Journal of a Tour from Boston to Oneida, June 1796* (Cambridge, MA: John Wilson and Son, 1882), 21. See also Charles A. Haguenin, "The Sacred Stone of the Oneidas," *New York Folklore Quarterly* 8 (1957): 16–22.

## CONCLUSION

1. The story of Polly Cooper is recorded as an example of Oneida oral tradition in Campisi and Hauptman, *Oneida Indian Experience,* 145. Lyman Draper's interviews in the 1870s with numerous Oneida then living on their reservation in Wisconsin indicate that most of them were familiar with family histories that included involvement in battles during the revolution, especially the battle at Oriskany. See Draper MSS, vol. 11. The tradition of the Doxtator family, as descendants of Honyere, was recounted by a land-claims researcher for the Oneida First Nation at Wisconsin. Campisi and Hauptman, *Oneida Indian Experience,* 145–46.

2. Michael Pomedli, "Eighteenth-Century Treaties: Amended Iroquois Condolence Rituals," *American Indian Quarterly* 19:3 (Summer 1995): 319–39; Jack Campisi, "The Iroquois and the Euro-American Concept of Tribe," *New York History* 78:4 (October 1997): 455–72; Louis Roper, "Old Wine in New Bottles: New York, the Federal Government, and the Oneida Land Claim Cases," *New York History* 72:2 (April 1991): 133–54; James Merrell, "Declarations of Independence: Indian-White Relations in the New Nation," in *The American Revolution: Its Character and Limits,* ed. Jack Greene (New York: New York University Press, 1987), 197–223; Francis Prucha, *American Indian Treaties: The History of a Political Anomaly* (Berkeley and Los Angeles: University of California Press, 1994), 23–59, 94–96; Philip Lord Jr., "The Mohawk-Oneida Corridor: The Geography of Inland Navigation across New York," in Skaggs and Nelson, *Sixty Years' War,* 275–90; Deborah Doxtator, "What Happened to the Iroquois Clans? A Study of Clans in Three Nineteenth-Century Rotinonhsyonni Communities" (Ph.D. diss., University of Western Ontario, 1996).

3. Agwrongdongwas's role as warrior reflects a previous conclusion that nonhereditary chiefs were considered warriors, Pine Tree chiefs, and speakers.

4. Lack of information about most of these men prevents me from ascertaining why they were chosen. Thaosagwat is the exception; he received a silver medal for his involvement with other Oneida in Amherst's campaign against Montreal in 1760.

5. In the case of the 1784 conference at Fort Stanwix, records indicate the names of many Oneida as "participants," leaving it unclear as to whether they were designated speakers.

# SELECTED BIBLIOGRAPHY

## MANUSCRIPT SOURCES

*Collections.* Massachusetts Historical Society, Boston, 1792–1899. Series 1–7.

Deane, Sidney Norton. "A New England Pioneer among the Oneida Indians: The Life of James Dean of Westmoreland, NY." Paper read to the Northampton Historical Society, 28 January 1926.

Draper Manuscripts, Series U (Frontier Papers), State Historical Society of Wisconsin.

Gideon Hawley Manuscripts. 4 vols. Boston: Congregational Library of the American Congregational Association.

*Journals of the Continental Congress, 1774–1789.* Washington, DC: GPO, 1904–1937.

*Journals of the Provincial Congress, Provincial Committee, Committee of Safety and Council of Safety of the State of New York, 1775–1777.* 2 vols. Albany, NY: State Printers, 1842.

Samuel Kirkland Papers. Burke Library. Hamilton College. Clinton, New York.

Samuel Kirkland Papers. Massachusetts Historical Society. Boston.

Miller Papers. Vol 1. New York Historical Society.

*Papers of the Continental Congress, 1774–1789.* U.S. National Archives, Washington, DC.

Timothy Pickering Papers. Massachusetts Historical Society. Boston.

Joseph Powell. Shamokin Pennsylvania Diary. Folder 4, box 121, Records of the Moravian Missions among the Indians of North America, Harvard College Library.

Sadosky, Leonard. "Choosing Conquest: Power, Sovereignty and Negotiation in the Treaty of Fort Stanwix, 1783–1784." Paper for colloquium, Omohundro Institute of Early American History and Culture, 30 September 2003.

Philip Schuyler Papers. Boxes 13 and 14. New York State Library.

Eleazar Wheelock Papers. Dartmouth College Archives. Hanover, New Hampshire.

## PUBLISHED SOURCES

Alden, John. "The Albany Congress and the Creation of the Indian Superintendencies." *Mississippi Valley Historical Review* 27:2 (Summer 1940): 193–210.

Allen, Robert. *His Majesty's Indian Allies: British Indian Policy in the Defence of Canada, 1774–1815.* Toronto: Dundurn Press, 1992.

Aquila, Richard. *The Iroquois Restoration: Iroquois Diplomacy on the Colonial Frontier, 1701–1754.* Lincoln: University of Nebraska Press, 1983.

Auth, Stephen F. *The Ten Years' War: Indian-White Relations in Pennsylvania, 1755–1765.* New York: Garland, 1989.

Axtell, James. "Dr. Wheelock and the Indians." In Foster, *Extending the Rafters,* 51–64.

———. *The Invasion Within: The Contest of Cultures in Colonial North America.* New York: Oxford University Press, 1985.

Barbe-Marbois, Marquis de. "Journey to the Oneidas." In Snow et al., *In Mohawk Country,* 300–317.

Barnes, Barbara, ed. *Traditional Teachings.* Cornwall, ON: North American Indian Travelling College, 1984.

Barr, Daniel. *Unconquered: The Iroquois League at War in Colonial America*. Westport, CT: Praeger, 2006.

Barsh, Russell L. "Native North American Loyalists and Patriots: Reflections on the American Revolution in Native American History." *Indian Historian* 10 (1977): 13–36.

Bartram, John. *Observations on the Inhabitants, Climate, Soil, Rivers, Production and other Matters Worthy of Notice*. London: J. Whiston and B. White, 1751.

Belknap, Jeremy, and Jedidiah Morse. *Journal of a Tour from Boston to Oneida, June 1796*. Cambridge, MA: John Wilson and Son, 1882.

———. "The report of a committee of the board of correspondents of the Scots Society for propagating Christian knowledge, who visited the Oneida and Mohekunuh Indians in 1796." *Collections of the Massachusetts Historical Society, for the year M,DCC,XCVIII*, vol. 5, 12–32. Belknap, 1796; New York: Johnson Reprint, 1798.

Billington, Ray. "The Fort Stanwix Treaty of 1768." *New York History* 25:2 (April 1944): 182–94.

Bishop, Morris. "The End of the Iroquois Mystique." *American Heritage* 20:6 (October 1969): 28–33, 77–81.

Blau, Harold. "Historical Factors in Onondaga Iroquois Cultural Stability." *Ethnohistory* 12:3 (Summer 1965): 250–57.

———. "The Iroquois White Dog Sacrifice: Its Evolution and Symbolism." *Ethnohistory* 11:3 (Summer 1964): 97–119.

Bloomfield, J. K. *The Oneidas*. New York: James Stewart, 1909.

Bonvillain, Nancy. "Iroquoian Women." In Bonvillain, *Studies on Iroquoian Culture*, 47–58.

Bonvillain, Nancy, ed. *Studies on Iroquoian Culture*. Rindge, NY: Occasional Publications in Northeastern Anthropology 6, 1980.

Bourdin, H. L., and S. T. Williams, eds. "Crevecoeur on the Susquehanna, 1774–1776." *Yale Review* 14 (1925): 552–84.

Bowden, Henry W. *American Indians and Christian Missions: Studies in Cultural Conflict*. Chicago: University of Chicago Press, 1981.

Boyce, Douglas W. "'As the Wind Scatters the Smoke': The Tuscaroras in the Eighteenth Century." In *Under an Open Sky: Rethinking America's Western Past*, ed. William Cronon, 151–63. New York: W. W. Norton, 1992.

———. "A Glimpse of Iroquois Culture History through the Eyes of Joseph Brant and John Norton." *Proceedings of the American Philosophical Society* 117 (1973): 286–94.

Boyd, Julian, ed. *Indian Treaties Printed by Benjamin Franklin, 1736–1762*. Philadelphia: Historical Society of Pennsylvania, 1938.

———. *The Papers of Thomas Jefferson*. 21 vols. Princeton: Princeton University Press, 1953.

———. *The Susquehanna Company Papers*. Wilkes Barre: Wyoming Historical and Geological Society, 1930. Reprint, Ithaca: Cornell University Press, 1962.

Brown, Judith. "Economic Organization and the Position of Women among the Iroquois." *Ethnohistory* 17:4 (Fall 1970): 151–67.

Burnett, Edmund, ed. *Letters of Members of the Continental Congress, 1775–1778*. 8 vols. Washington, DC: Carnegie Institute, 1921–1936.

Calloway, Colin. *The American Revolution in Indian Country: Crisis and Diversity in Native American Communities*. New York: Cambridge University Press, 1995.

———. "The Continuing Revolution in Indian Country." In Hoxie, *Native Americans*, 3–33.

Campbell, William W. *The Border Warfare of New York During the Revolution, or the Annals of Tryon County*. New York: Baker and Scribner, 1849.

Campisi, Jack. "From Stanwix to Canandaigua: National Policy, States' Rights, and Indian Land." In Vecsey and Starna, *Iroquois Land Claims*, 49–65.

————. "Fur Trade and Factionalism of the Eighteenth-Century Oneidas." In Bonvillain, *Iroquoian Culture*, 37–46.

————. "The Iroquois and the Euro-American Concept of Tribe." *New York History* 78:4 (October 1997): 455–72.

————. "New York–Oneida Treaty of 1795: A Finding of Fact." *American Indian Law Review* 4:1 (Summer 1976): 71–82.

————. "Oneida." In Trigger, *North American Indians*, 15:481–90.

————. "The Oneida Treaty Period 1783–1838." In Campisi and Hauptman, *Oneida Indian Experience*, 48–64.

Campisi, Jack, and Laurence Hauptman, eds. *The Oneida Indian Experience: Two Perspectives*. Syracuse: Syracuse University Press, 1988.

Cayton, Andrew, and F. Teute, eds. *Contact Points: American Frontiers from the Mohawk Valley to the Mississippi, 1750–1830*. Chapel Hill: University of North Carolina Press, 1998.

Chalmers, Harvey. *Joseph Brant: Mohawk*. East Lansing: Michigan State University Press, 1955.

Chase, Eugene, ed. and trans. *Our Revolutionary Forefathers: The Letters of François, Marquis de Barbe-Marbois, during His Residence in the United States as Secretary of the French Legation, 1779–1783*. New York: Duffield, 1929.

Clarke, T. Wood. *Utica for a Century and a Half*. Utica, NY: Widtman Press, 1952.

Cook, Fred, ed. *Journals of the Military Expedition of Major General John Sullivan against the Six Nations of Indians in 1779*. Auburn, NY: Knapp, Peck and Thomson, 1887.

Craig, Neville, ed. *The Olden Time: A Monthly Publication devoted to the Preservation of Documents and other Authentic Information in Relation to the early Explorations and the Settlement and Improvement of the Country around the Head of the Ohio*. Vol 2. Pittsburg: Wright and Charlton, 1848.

Dann, John C., ed. *The Revolution Remembered: Eyewitness Accounts of the War for Independence*. Chicago: University of Chicago Press, 1980.

Davies, Kenneth, ed. *Documents of the American Revolution, 1770–1783*. 21 vols. Shannon: Irish University Press, 1972–1981.

Densmore, Christopher. "New York Quakers among the Brothertown, Stockbridge, Oneida, and Onondaga, 1795–1834." *Man in the Northeast* 44 (Fall 1992): 83–93.

Doblin, Helga, and William Starna, trans. and eds. *The Journals of Christian Daniel Claus and Conrad Weiser: A Journey to Onandaga, 1750*. Philadelphia: American Philosophical Society, 1994.

Downes, Randolph. *Council Fires on the Upper Ohio: A Narrative of Indian Affairs in the Upper Ohio Valley until 1795*. Pittsburg: University of Pittsburgh Press, 1957.

Doxtator, Deborah. "What Happened to the Iroquois Clans? A Study of Clans in Three Nineteenth-Century Rotinonhsyonni Communities." Ph.D. diss., University of Western Ontario, 1996.

Druke, Mary A. "Linking Arms: The Structure of Iroquois Intertribal Diplomacy." In Richter and Merrell, *Beyond the Covenant Chain*, 29–39.

————. "Structure and Meanings of Leadership among the Oneida Indians during the Mid-Eighteenth Century." Ph.D. diss., University of Chicago, 1982.

Durant, Samuel W. *History of Oneida County, New York*. Philadelphia: Everts and Fariss, 1878.

Dwight, Sereno. *The Life of President Edwards*. New York: G. C. and H. Carvill, 1830.

Earl, Samuel. "The Palatines and Their Settlement in the Valley of the Upper Mohawk." *Transactions of the Oneida Historical Society* (1881): 31–51.

Edwards, Jonathan. "A Letter from Rev. Jonathan Edwards, to Honourable Thomas Hubbard, Esq. of Boston, Relating to the Indian School at Stockbridge." *Collections, Massachusetts Historical Society*, ser. 1, vol. 10 (1809), 142–58.

Egly, T. W. *History of the First New York Regiment, 1775–1783*. Hampton, NY: Peter Randall, 1981.

Elliott, Dolores. "Otsiningo, an Example of an Eighteenth-Century Settlement Pattern." In Funk and Hayes, *Northeastern Archeology*, 93–105.

Elm, Demus, and Harvey Antone. *The Oneida Creation Story*. Lincoln: University of Nebraska Press, 2000.

Farrand, Max. "The Indian Boundary Line, 1763." *American Historical Review* 10 (1905): 782–91.

Feister, Lois, and Bonnie Pulis. "Molly Brant: Her Domestic and Political Roles in Eighteenth-Century New York." In Grumet, *Northeastern Indian Lives*, 295–320.

Fenton, William N. *The Great Law and the Longhouse: A Political History of the Iroquois Confederacy*. Norman: University of Oklahoma Press, 1998.

———. "Iroquoian Culture History: A General Evaluation." In Fenton and Gulick, *Symposium on Cherokee and Iroquois Culture*, 257–73.

———. "Locality as a Basic Factor in the Development of Iroquois Social Structure." In Fenton, *Symposium on Local Diversity*, 39–53.

———. "Problems in the Authentication of the League of the Iroquois." In Hauptman and Campisi, *Neighbours and Intruders*, 263–66.

Fenton, William N., ed. "Journal of James Emlen Kept on a Trip to Canandaigua, New York, Sept 15 to Oct 15, 1794." *Ethnohistory* 12 (1965): 279–342.

———. *Symposium on Local Diversity in Iroquois Culture*. Smithsonian Institute, Bureau of American Ethnology, Bulletin 149. Washington, DC: GPO, 1951.

Fenton, William N., and John Gulick, eds. *Symposium on Cherokee and Iroquois Culture*, 257–73. Smithsonian Institute, Bureau of American Ethnology, Bulletin 180. Washington, DC: GPO, 1961.

Fischer, Joseph R. *A Well-Executed Failure: The Sullivan Campaign against the Iroquois, July–September 1779*. Columbia: University of South Carolina Press, 1997.

Fitzpatrick, John, ed. *The Writings of George Washington*. 39 vols. Washington, DC: GPO, 1931–1944.

Fleming, Thomas. *Washington's Secret War: The Hidden Story of Valley Forge*. New York: Smithsonian/Collins, 2005.

Flexner, James T. *Mohawk Baronet: A Biography of Sir William Johnson*. Boston: Little Brown, 1979.

Force, Peter, ed. *American archives: Fourth series, containing a documentary history of the English colonies in North America from the King's message to Parliament of March 7, 1774 to the Declaration of Independence of the United States*. Washington, DC: M. St. Clair Clarke and Peter Force, 1837–1846. 6 volumes. Fifth series, 3 vols., 1848–1853.

Ford, Worthington, ed. *Journals of the Continental Congress, 1774–1789*. 34 vols. Washington, DC: GPO, 1904–1937.

Foster, Michael K., Jack Campisi, and Marianne Mithun, eds. *Extending the Rafters: Interdisciplinary Approaches to Iroquoian Studies*. Albany: State University of New York Press, 1984.

Funk, Robert, and Charles Hayes, eds. *Current Perspectives in Northeastern Archeology*. Rochester: New York State Archeological Association, 1977.

Gehring, Charles, and William Starna, trans. and ed. *A Journey into Mohawk and Oneida Country, 1634–1635: The Journal of Harmen Meyndertsz van den Bogaert*. Syracuse: Syracuse University Press, 1988.

Gerlach, Donald R. *Proud Patriot: Philip Schuyler and the War of Independence, 1775–1783*. Syracuse: Syracuse University Press, 1987.

Glatthaar, Joseph, and James Martin. *Forgotten Allies: The Oneida Indians and the American Revolution*. New York: Hill and Wang, 2006.

Godfrey, William. *John Bradstreet's Quest: Pursuit of Profit and Preferment in Colonial North America*. Waterloo, ON: Wilfred Laurier University Press, 1982.

Gottschalk, Louis. *Lafayette between the American and French Revolutions, 1783–1789*. Chicago: University of Chicago Press, 1950.

———. *Lafayette Joins the American Army*. Chicago: University of Chicago Press, 1937.

Gottschalk, Louis, ed. *Letters of Lafayette to Washington, 1777–1779*. Philadelphia: American Philosophical Society, 1976.

Graymont, Barbara. *The Iroquois in the American Revolution*. Syracuse: Syracuse University Press, 1972.

———. "New York and New Jersey Treaties, 1714–1753." In Vaughan, *Early American Indian Documents*, 10:136–57.

———. "New York State Indian Policy after the Revolution." *New York History* 57 (1976): 438–74.

———. "The Oneidas and the American Revolution." In Campisi and Hauptman, *Oneida Indian Experience*, 31–42.

Green, Gretchen. "A New People in an Age of War: The Kahnawake Iroquois, 1667–1760." Ph.D. diss., College of William and Mary, 1991.

Grumet, Robert, ed. *Northeastern Indian Lives, 1632–1816*. Amherst: University of Massachusetts Press, 1996.

Guzzardo, John C. "The Superintendent and the Ministers: The Battle for Oneida Allegiances." *New York History* 57 (1976): 255–83.

Hagan, William T. *Longhouse Diplomacy and Frontier Warfare: The Iroquois Confederacy in the American Revolution*. Albany: New York State American Revolution Bicentennial Commission, 1976.

Hagedorn, Nancy L. "Brokers of Understanding: Interpreters as Agents of Cultural Exchange in Colonial New York." *New York History* 76:4 (October 1995): 379–408.

———. "'A Friend to Go Between Them': The Interpreter as Cultural Broker during Anglo-Iroquois Councils, 1740–1770." *Ethnohistory* 35:1 (Winter 1988): 60–80.

Haguenin, Charles A. "The Sacred Stone of the Oneidas." *New York Folklore Quarterly* 8 (1957): 16–22.

Halsey, Francis W. *The Old New York Frontier: Its Wars with Indians and Tories, Its Missionary Schools, Pioneers, and Land Titles, 1614–1800*. New York: Scribner, 1901.

Hamer, Philip M., ed. *The Papers of Henry Laurens*. 14 vols. Columbia: University of South Carolina Press, 1968.

Hamilton, Milton W. *Sir William Johnson: Colonial American, 1715–1763*. Port Washington, NY: Kennikat Press, 1976.

Hammond, L. M. *History of Madison County, State of New York*. 2 vols. Syracuse: Truair, Smith and Company, 1872.

Hammond, Otis G., ed. *The Letters and Papers of Major General John Sullivan*. 3 vols. Concord: New Hampshire Historical Society, 1939.

Hankin, John F. "Bringing the Good News: Protestant Missionaries to the Indians of New England and New York, 1700–1775." Ph.D. diss., University of Connecticut, 1993.

Hanson, J. Howard, ed. *The Minute Book of the Committee of Safety of Tryon County*. New York: Dodd, Mead and Co., 1905.

Hanson, Willis. *A History of Schenectady during the Revolution*. Privately printed, 1916.

Harrison, Samuel. *Memoir of Lieutenant Colonel Tench Tilghman, Secretary and Aide to Washington*. Albany, NY: J. Munsell, 1876.

Hastings, Hugh, ed. *The Public Papers of George Clinton*. 10 vols. Albany, NY: State Printers, 1899–1914.

Hauptman, Laurence. "Command Performance: Philip Schuyler and the New York State–Oneida Treaty of 1795." In *The Oneida Indian Journey from New York to Wisconsin, 1784–1860*, 38–52. Madison: University of Wisconsin Press, 1999.

———. *Conspiracy of Interests: Iroquois Dispossession and the Rise of New York State*. Syracuse: Syracuse University Press, 1999.

———. *The Oneida Indian Journey, from New York to Wisconsin, 1784–1860*. Madison: University of Wisconsin Press, 1999.

———. "Refugee Havens: The Iroquois Villages of the Eighteenth Century." In Vecsey and Venables, *American Indian Environments*, 128–39.

Hauptman, Laurence, and Jack Campisi, eds. *Neighbours and Intruders: An Ethnohistorical Exploration of the Indians of Hudson's River*. Ottawa: National Museum of Canada, 1978.

Hawley, Gideon. "A Letter from Rev. Gideon Hawley of Mashpee, containing an Account of his services among the Indians of Massachusetts and New York, and a Narrative of his Journey to Onohoghgwage." *Collections*, Massachusetts Historical Society, ser. 1, vol. 4 (1795), 50–67.

———. "Narrative of his Journey to Oghwaga in 1753." In O'Callaghan, *State of New York*, 3:1031–46.

Higgins, Ruth. *Expansion in New York, with Special Reference to the Eighteenth Century*. Columbus: Ohio State University, 1931.

Hinman, Marjory B. *Onaquaga: Early Missionary Outpost, 1748–1777*. Onaquaga, NY: Old Onaquaga Historical Society, 1968.

———. *Onaquaga: Hub of the Border Wars of the American Revolution*. Windsor, NY: privately printed, 1975.

Horsman, Reginald. *Expansion and American Indian Policy, 1783–1812*. East Lansing: Michigan State University Press, 1967.

Hough, Franklin. *Notices of Peter Penet and his Operations among the Oneida Indians, including a Plan Prepared by Him for the Governance of that Tribe*. Lowville, NY: Albany Institute, 1866.

Hough, Franklin, ed. *Proceedings of the Commissioners of Indian Affairs Appointed by Law for the Extinguishment of Indian Titles in the State of New York*. Albany, NY: Joel Munsell, 1861.

Hoxie, Frederick, ed. *Native Americans and the Early Republic*. Charlottesville: University of Virginia Press, 1999.

Ibbotson, Joseph D. "Samuel Kirkland, the Treaty of 1792, and the Indian Barrier State." *New York History* 19:1 (October 1938): 374–91.

Idzerda, Stanley J., ed. *Lafayette in the Age of the American Revolution: Selected Letters and Papers*. 5 vols. Ithaca: Cornell University Press, 1977.

Jacobs, Wilbur. *Wilderness Politics and Indian Gifts: The Northern Colonial Frontier, 1748–1763*. Lincoln: University of Nebraska Press, 1950.

James, Sydney. *A People among Peoples: Quaker Benevolence in Eighteenth-Century America*. Cambridge, MA: Harvard University Press, 1963.

Jennings, Francis. *Empire of Fortune: Crowns, Colonies, and Tribes in the Seven Years War in America*. New York: Norton, 1988.

———. "The Indians' Revolution." In *The American Revolution: Explorations in the History of American Radicalism*, ed. Alfred Young, 321–48. DeKalb: Northern Illinois University Press, 1976.

Jennings, Francis, William N. Fenton, Mary A. Druke, and David R. Miller, eds. *The History and Culture of Iroquois Diplomacy: An Interdisciplinary Guide to the Treaties of the Six Nations and Their League*. Syracuse: Syracuse University Press, 1985.

———. *Iroquois Indians: A Documentary History of the Diplomacy of the Six Nations and Their League; Guide to the Microfilm Collection*. Woodbridge, CT: Research Publications, 1985.

Jones, Dorothy. *License for Empire: Colonization by Treaty in Early America*. Chicago:

University of Chicago Press, 1982.

Jones, Pomroy. *Annals and Recollections of Oneida County*. Rome, NY: published by author, 1851.

"Journal of the Treaty held at Albany in August 1775, with the Six Nations." *Collections,* Massachusetts Historical Society, 3rd ser., vol. 5 (Boston: John Eastburn, 1836), 75–100.

Kappler, Charles, ed. *Indian Affairs: Laws and Treaties*. Vol 2. Washington, DC: GPO, 1904.

Kelsay, Isabel T. *Joseph Brant, 1743–1807: Man of Two Worlds*. Syracuse: Syracuse University Press, 1984.

Kelsey, Rayner. *Friends and Indians, 1655–1917*. Philadelphia: Associated Executive Committee of Friends of Indian Affairs, 1917.

Kent, Barry. *Susquehanna's Indians: Indians of Pennsylvania*. Harrisburg: Pennsylvania Historical and Museum Commission, 1981.

Klinck, Carl, and James Talman, eds. *The Journal of Major John Norton*. Toronto: Champlain Society, 1970.

Landy, David. "Tuscarora among the Iroquois." In Trigger, *North American Indians,* 15:518–27.

Leacock, Eleanor. "Ethnohistorical Investigation of Egalitarian Politics in Eastern North America." In Tooker, *Political Organization,* 17–31.

Lehman, J. David. "The End of the Iroquois Mystique: The Oneida Land Cession Treaties of the 1780s." *William and Mary Quarterly* 47 (1990): 521–47.

Lender, Mark, and J. Martin, eds. *Citizen Soldier: The Revolutionary War Journal of Joseph Bloomfield*. Newark: New Jersey Historical Society, 1982.

Lennox, John. *Samuel Kirkland's Mission to the Iroquois*. Chicago: University of Chicago Press, 1935.

Levinson, David. "An Explanation for the Oneida-Colonist Alliance in the American Revolution." *Ethnohistory* 23 (1976): 265–89.

Lewis, George. *The Indiana Company, 1763–1798*. Glendale, CA: Arthen Clark, 1941.

Lincklaen, John. *Travels in the Years 1791 and 1792 in Pennsylvania, New York, and Vermont*. New York: G. P. Putnam's Sons, 1897.

Lincoln, Benjamin. "Journal." *Collections,* Massachusetts Historical Society, 3rd ser., vol. 5 (1836), 150–54.

Livermore, Shaw. *Early American Land Companies*. New York: Octagon Books, 1968.

Long, John. *Lord Jeffrey Amherst: A Soldier of the King*. New York: Macmillan, 1933.

Lord, Philip, Jr. "The Mohawk-Oneida Corridor: The Geography of Inland Navigation Across New York." In Skaggs and Nelson, *Sixty Years' War,* 275–90.

Luzander, John. *The Construction and Military History of Fort Stanwix*. Washington, DC: Office of Archeology and Historic Preservation, 1969.

Lynch, James. "The Iroquois Confederacy and the Adoption and Administration of Non-Iroquoian Individuals and Groups prior to 1756." *Man in the Northeast* 30 (Fall 1985): 83–99.

Mancall, Peter. *Deadly Medicine: Indians and Alcohol in Early America*. Ithaca: Cornell University Press, 1995.

———. *Valley of Opportunity: Economic Culture along the Upper Susquehanna, 1700–1800*. Ithaca: Cornell University Press, 1991.

Manley, Henry S. *The Treaty of Fort Stanwix, 1784*. Rome, NY: Rome Sentinel, 1932.

Marshall, Peter. "Sir William Johnson and the Treaty of Fort Stanwix, 1768." *Journal of American Studies* 1:2 (1967): 149–79.

Martin, Joel. "Cultural Contact and Crises in the Early Republic." In Hoxie, *Native Americans,* 226–60.

Martin, Joseph P. *Private Yankee Doodle, Being a Narrative of Some of the Adventures, Dangers and Sufferings of a Revolutionary Soldier.* Edited by George Scheer. Boston: Little, Brown, 1962.

McAdams, Donald. "The Sullivan Expedition: Success or Failure?" *New York Historical Society Quarterly* 54 (January 1970): 53–81.

McCallum, James D. *Eleazar Wheelock.* Hanover, NH: Dartmouth College Publications, 1939.

———. *The Letters of Eleazar Wheelock's Indians.* Hanover, NH: Dartmouth College Publications, 1932.

McConnell, Michael. *A Country Between: The Upper Ohio Valley and Its Peoples, 1724–1774.* Lincoln: University of Nebraska Press, 1992.

Merrell, James H. "Declarations of Independence: Indian-White Relations in the New Nation." In *The American Revolution: Its Character and Limits,* ed. Jack Greene, 197–223. New York: New York University Press, 1987.

———. *Into the American Woods: Negotiators on the Pennsylvania Frontier.* New York: W. W. Norton, 1999.

———. "'Shamokin, the Very Seat of the Prince of Darkness': Unsettling the Early American Frontier." In Cayton and Teute, *Contact Points,* 16–59.

———. "Shickellamy: A Person of Consequence." In Grumet, *Northeastern Indian Lives,* 227–55.

Mintz, Max. *Seeds of Empire: The American Revolutionary Conquest of the Iroquois.* New York: New York University Press, 1999.

*Minutes of the Provincial Council of Pennsylvania.* 10 vols. and index vol. Harrisburg, PA: Theo Fenn and Company, 1851–1853. Reprint, New York: AMS, 1968.

Mochon, Marion. "Stockbridge-Munsee Cultural Adaptation: 'Assimilated Indians.'" *Proceedings of the American Philosophical Society* 112 (1968): 182–219.

Mohr, Walter. *Federal Indian Relations, 1774–1788.* Philadelphia: University of Pennsylvania Press, 1933.

Mullin, Michael J. "Sir William Johnson's Reliance on the Six Nations at the Conclusion of the Anglo-Indian War of 1763–1765." *American Indian Culture and Research Journal* 17:4 (1993): 69–90.

Murray, Laura, ed. *'To Do Good to My Indian Brethren': The Writings of Joseph Johnson, 1751–1776.* Amherst: University of Massachusetts Press, 1998.

*New American State Papers: Indian Affairs.* 4 vols. Wilmington: Scholarly Research, 1972.

Norton, A. Tiffany. *History of Sullivan's Campaign against the Iroquois.* Lima, NY: published by the author, 1879.

Norton, Thomas. *The Fur Trade in Colonial New York, 1686–1776.* Madison: University of Wisconsin Press, 1974.

O'Callaghan, Edmund B., ed. *Documentary History of the State of New York.* 4 vols. Albany, NY: Weed, Parsons, and Company, 1849–1851.

———. *Documents Relative to the Colonial History of the State of New York.* 15 vols. Albany, NY: Weed, Parsons, and Company, 1853–1887.

Parker, Arthur. "The Indian Interpretation of the Sullivan-Clinton Campaign." *Rochester Historical Society* 8 (1929): 45–59.

Parmenter, Jon. "The Iroquois and the Native American Struggle for the Ohio Valley, 1754–1794." In Skaggs and Nelson, *Sixty Years' War,* 105–24. East Lansing: Michigan State University Press, 2001.

———. "Pontiac's War: Forging New Links in the Anglo-Iroquois Covenant Chain, 1758–1766." *Ethnohistory* 44:4 (Fall 1997): 617–54.

Parrish, J. "The Story of Captain Jasper Parrish: Captive, Interpreter and United States Sub-Agent to the Six Nations Indians (from his own notes, compiled by his son, Stephen Parrish, and others)." *Publications of the Buffalo Historical Society* 6 (1903): 527–38.

Patrick, Christine S. "The Life and Times of Samuel Kirkland, 1741–1808: Missionary to the Oneida Indians, American Patriot, and Founder of Hamilton College." Ph.D. diss., State University of New York at Buffalo, 1993.

Penrose, Maryly, ed. *Indian Affairs Papers: American Revolution.* Franklyn Park, NJ: Liberty Bell Associates, 1981.

———. *Mohawk Valley in the Revolution: Committee of Safety Papers and Genealogical Compendium.* Franklyn Park, NJ: Liberty Bell Associates, 1978.

Pilkington, Walter, ed. *The Journals of Samuel Kirkland.* Clinton, NY: Hamilton College, 1980.

Phillips, Edward. "Timothy Pickering at His Best: Indian Commissioner, 1790–1794." *Historical Collections, Essex Institute* 102:3 (July 1966): 163–202.

Pomedli, Michael M. "Eighteenth-Century Treaties: Amended Iroquois Condolence Rituals." *American Indian Quarterly* 19:3 (Summer 1995): 319–39.

Pound, Arthur. *Johnson of the Mohawks: A Biography of Sir William Johnson, Irish Immigrant, Mohawk War Chief, American Soldier, Empire Builder.* New York: Macmillan, 1930.

Pratt, Peter. "A Perspective on Oneida Archeology." In Funk and Hayes, *Northeastern Archeology,* 51–69.

"Proceedings of the Congress held at Albany, 1754." *Collections,* Massachusetts Historical Society, 3rd ser., vol. 5 (Boston: John Eastburn, 1836), 22–69.

Prucha, Francis Paul. *American Indian Policy in the Formative Years, 1790–1834.* Cambridge, MA: Harvard University Press, 1962.

———. *American Indian Treaties: The History of a Political Anomaly.* Berkeley and Los Angeles: University of California Press, 1994.

Recht, Michael. "The Role of Fishing in the Iroquois Economy, 1600–1792." *New York History* 78:4 (October 1997): 429–54.

Reed, George, ed. *Pennsylvania Archives.* 4th ser., vol. 2. Harrisburg, PA: W. Stanley Ray, 1900.

Reed, John. "Indians at Valley Forge." *Valley Forge Historical Society Journal* 3:1 (1986): 26–32.

*Reports of the Proceedings and Debates of the New York Constitutional Convention, 1821.* Reprint, New York, Government Publications, 1970.

Ricciardelli, Alex. "The Adoption of White Agriculture by the Oneida Indians." *Ethnohistory* 10:4 (Fall 1963): 309–25.

Rice, Howard, trans. and ed. *Travels in North America in the Years 1780, 1781, and 1782 by the Marquis de Chastellux.* Chapel Hill: University of North Carolina Press, 1963.

Richter, Daniel. "Believing that Many of the Red People Suffer Much for the Want of Food: Hunting, Agriculture, and a Quaker Construction of Indianness in the Early Republic." *Journal of the Early Republic* 19:4 (Winter 1999): 601–28.

Richter, Daniel, and James Merrell, eds. *Beyond the Covenant Chain: The Iroquois and Their Neighbours in Indian North America.* Syracuse: Syracuse University Press, 1987.

———. *The Ordeal of the Longhouse: The Peoples of the Iroquois League in the Era of European Colonization.* Chapel Hill: University of North Carolina Press, 1992.

Roper, Louis. "Old Wine in New Bottles: New York, the Federal Government, and the Oneida Land Claims Cases." *New York History* 72:2 (April 1991): 133–54.

Rothenberg, Diane. "The Mothers of the Nation: Seneca Resistance to Quaker Intervention." In *Women and Colonization: Anthropological Perspectives,* ed. Mona Etienne and Eleanor Leacock, 61–87. New York: Praeger, 1980.

Savary, William. *A Journal of the Life, Times and Religious Labours of William Savary, a Minister of the Gospel of Christ, of the Society of Friends, Late of Philadelphia.* Philadelphia: Friends' Book Store, 1861.

Schoolcraft, Henry. *Notes on the Iroquois*. New York: Bartlett and Welford, 1847. Reprint, Millwood, NY: Kraus Reprint, 1975.

———. "Skenandoah." In *Information Respecting the History, Condition and Prospects of the Indian Tribes of the United States*, 509–18. Philadelphia: J. B. Lippincott and Company, 1855.

Scott, John A. "Joseph Brant at Fort Stanwix and Oriskany." *New York History* 19:1 (October 1938): 399–406.

Shannon, Timothy J. *Indians and Colonists at the Crossroads of Empire: The Albany Congress of 1754*. Ithaca: Cornell University Press, 2000.

Shattuck, George. *The Oneida Land Claims: A Legal History*. Syracuse: Syracuse University Press, 1991.

Shoemaker, Nancy. "An Alliance between Men: Gender Metaphors in Eighteenth-Century American Indian Diplomacy East of the Mississippi." *Ethnohistory* 46:2 (Spring 1999): 239–63.

Skaggs, David, and Larry Nelson, eds. *The Sixty Years' War for the Great Lakes, 1754–1814*. East Lansing: Michigan State University Press, 2001.

Smith, Richard. *A Tour of Four Great Rivers: The Hudson, Mohawk, Susquehanna and Delaware in 1769, being the journal of Richard Smith of Burlington, New Jersey*. Edited by Francis W. Halsey. 1906; Port Washington, NY: Ira J. Friedman, 1964.

Snow, Dean. "The First Americans and the Differentiation of Hunter-Gather Cultures." In Trigger and Washburn, *Cambridge History*, 125–200.

———. *The Iroquois*. Oxford: Blackwell, 1994.

Snow, Dean, William Starna, and Charles Gehring, eds. *In Mohawk Country: Early Narratives about a Native People*. Syracuse: Syracuse University Press, 1996.

Snyderman, George. "Behind the Tree of Peace: A Sociological Analysis of Iroquois Warfare." Ph.D. diss., University of Pennsylvania, 1948.

———. "Concepts of Land Ownership among the Iroquois and Their Neighbors." In Fenton, *Symposium on Local Diversity in Iroquois Culture*, 15–34.

Sosin, Jack. *Whitehall and Wilderness: The Middle West in British Colonial Policy, 1760–1775*. Lincoln: University of Nebraska Press, 1961.

Stagg, Jack. *Anglo-Indian Relations in North America to 1763, and an Analysis of the Royal Proclamation of 7 October 1763*. Ottawa: Government Printers, 1981.

Stanley, George F. "The Six Nations and the American Revolution." *Ontario History* 56:4 (December 1964): 217–32.

Starna, William. "Northern Iroquoian Horticulture and Insect Infestation: A Cause for Village Removal." *Ethnohistory* 31:3 (1984): 197–207.

———. "'The United States will protect you': The Iroquois, New York, and the 1790 Nonintercourse Act." *New York History* 83:1 (Winter 2002): 5–33.

Steele, Ian. *Warpaths: Invasions of North America*. New York: Oxford University Press, 1994.

Stone, William L. *The Life and Times of Sir William Johnson, Baronet*. 2 vols. Albany, NY: J. Munsell, 1865.

———. *Life of Joseph Brant*. 2 vols. New York: George Dearborn and Company, 1838.

Sullivan, Frederick, ed. *The Papers of Sir William Johnson*. 14 vols. Albany: State University of New York Press, 1921–1965.

Sullivan, James, ed. *Minutes of the Albany Committee of Correspondence, 1775–1778*. Vol. 1. Albany, NY: University of New York Press, 1923.

Surtees, Robert. "The Iroquois in Canada." In Jennings, Fenton, Druke, and Miller, *Iroquois Diplomacy*, 67–83.

Tanner, Helen H. *Atlas of Great Lakes Indian History*. Norman: University of Oklahoma Press, 1987.

Thomas, Howard. *Marinus Willett, Soldier-Patriot, 1740–1830.* Prospect, NY: Prospect Books, 1954.

Thompson, Parker C. *The United States Army Chaplaincy, from Its European Antecedents to 1791.* Vol. 1. Washington, DC: Department of the Army, 1978.

Tiro, Karim M. "A 'Civil War'? Rethinking Iroquois Participation in the American Revolution." *Explorations in Early American Culture* 4 (2000): 148–65.

———. "James Dean in Iroquoia." *New York History* 80:4 (October 1999): 391–422.

———. "The People of the Standing Stone: The Oneida Indian Nation from Revolution through Removal, 1765–1840." Ph.D. diss., University of Pennsylvania, 1999.

Tooker, Elisabeth. "The Iroquois White Dog Sacrifice in the Latter Part of the Eighteenth Century." *Ethnohistory* 12 (Spring 1965): 129–39.

———. "The League of the Iroquois: Its History, Politics, and Ritual." In Trigger, *North American Indians,* 15:419–41.

———. "Women in Iroquois Society." In Foster, *Extending the Rafters,* 109–21.

Tooker, Elisabeth, ed. *The Development of Political Organization in Native North America.* Proceedings of the American Ethnological Society, 1979. Washington, DC: American Ethnological Society, 1983.

Trigger, Bruce, ed. *Handbook of North American Indians.* 15 vols. Washington, DC: Smithsonian Institute, 1978.

Trigger, Bruce, and W. Washburn, eds. *The Cambridge History of the Native Peoples of the Americas.* Part 1. Cambridge, England: Cambridge University Press, 1996.

Trussell, John B. *Birthplace of an Army: A Study of the Valley Forge Encampment.* Harrisburg: Pennsylvania Historical and Museum Commission, 1976.

Turner, Katherine C. *Red Men Calling on the Great White Father.* Norman: University of Oklahoma Press, 1951.

Turner, Orasmus. *History of the Pioneer Settlement of the Phelps and Gorham Purchases.* Rochester, NY: J. W. Brown, 1851.

Vaughan, Alden, ed. *Early American Indian Documents: Treaties and Laws, 1607–1789.* Vol. 10, *New York and New Jersey Treaties, 1754–1775,* ed. Barbara Graymont. Bethesda, MD: University Publications of America, 2001.

Vecsey, Christopher, and William A. Starna, eds. *Iroquois Land Claims.* Syracuse: Syracuse University Press, 1988.

Vecsey, Chris, and Robert Venables, eds. *American Indian Environments: Ecological Issues in Native American History.* Syracuse: Syracuse University Press, 1980.

Venables, Robert. "The Indians' Revolutionary War in the Hudson Valley, 1775–1783." In Hauptman and Campisi, *Neighbours and Intruders,* 225–41.

Vivian, James, and Jean Vivian. "Congressional Indian Policy during the War for Independence: The Northern Department." *Maryland Historical Magazine* 63:3 (September 1968): 241–74.

Wainwright, Nicholas. *George Croghan, Wilderness Diplomat.* Chapel Hill: University of North Carolina Press, 1959.

Wallace, Anthony. "The Iroquois and the Revolution: The Neutrality Policy." In *Major Problems in the Era of the American Revolution, 1760–1791,* ed. Richard Brown, 274–77. Lexington: D. C. Heath, 1992.

———. *King of the Delawares: Teedyuscung, 1700–1763.* Freeport, NY: Books for Libraries Press, 1949.

———. "Origins of Iroquois Neutrality: The Grand Settlement of 1701." *Pennsylvania History* 24:3 (July 1957): 223–35.

Wallace, Paul. *Conrad Weiser, 1696–1760: Friend of Colonist and Mohawk.* New York: Russell and Russell, 1945.

———. *White Roots of Peace.* Philadelphia: University of Pennsylvania Press, 1946.

Wallace, Paul, ed. *Thirty Thousand Miles with John Heckewelder*. Pittsburg: University of Pittsburgh Press, 1958.

Webster, John, ed. *The Journal of Jeffrey Amherst*. Toronto: Ryerson Press, 1931.

Weslager, Clinton. *The Nanticoke Indians: Past and Present*. Newark: University of Delaware Press, 1983.

Wessell, Thomas R. "Agriculture and Iroquois Hegemony in New York, 1610–1779." *Maryland Historian* 1:1 (Spring 1970): 93–104.

Wheelock, Eleazar. *A Plain and faithful Narrative of the Original Design, Rise, Progress, and Present State of the Indian Charity School at Lebanon in Connecticut*. Boston: Richard and Samuel Draper, 1763–1765.

White, Richard. *The Middle Ground: Indians, Empires, and Republics in the Great Lakes Region, 1650–1815*. London: Cambridge University Press, 1991.

Wonderley, Anthony. "Brothertown, New York, 1785–1796." *New York History* 81:4 (October 2000): 465–91.

———. "An Oneida Community in 1780: Study on an Inventory of Iroquois Property Losses during the Revolutionary War." *Man in the Northeast* 56 (Fall 1988): 19–41.

Wright, M. E., trans. and ed. *Memoirs of the Marshall Count de Rochambeau, relative to the War of Independence of the United States*. Paris: French, English and American Library, 1838. Reprint, New York: Arno Press, 1971.

# INDEX

Adarockquaghs, 31, 88, 136, 155
Adoondaraghirha, 155
adoption, 4, 10, 114, 133
Aenghase, John, 155
Ageaghwatha, William, 155
Aghnyeate, Daniel, 155
Aghnyonken, Cornelius, 156
agriculture, 107, 129; and Kirkland, 71, 138
Agweaghwatha, William, 156
Agwenyohta, Cornelius, 156
Agwrongdongwas ("Good Peter"), 20, 31,
    80, 87, 91, 96, 139, 156–57; assistance
    after the revolution and, 102–6; land
    deals with governments and, 117–28
Akentyakhen, Lawrence, 157
Akonyoda, 29, 157
Aksiaktatye ("Jacob Reed"), 79, 82, 86,
    107, 117, 122, 145, 157–58, 217n30;
    at battle of Barren Hill, 98; and
    Hamilton Academy, 128
Alawistonis ("Blacksmith"), 117, 131–32,
    147, 159, 175; at 1788 Fort Stanwix
    conference, 123; and White Dog
    sacrifice, 130
Albany, 3, 11–12, 20, 31, 51, 78, 91, 95,
    101, 112, 116, 121; conference of
    September 1775, 81; council fire at, 83
Albany Committee of Correspondence,
    Safety, and Protection, 78, 80, 85, 93,
    138; congress of 1754, 23
Albany congress (1754), 23
alcohol, 28, 40; and Albany congress of
    1754, 23; at Oquaga, 21
Alndaraghniro, 159
Amherst, General Lord Jeffrey, 35–36,
    38, 42, 45, 47, 50
Andreani, Paolo, 128
Andrews, Reverend William, 13
Aneeghnaxqua, 159
Anentshontye, Paul, 159
Aquiotta, 20, 25, 31, 136, 159
Aquiraeaghse, 159
Areaghhoktha, Thomas, 159

Arighwagenhas, 160
Asisat, 160
Ataghonghteayon, William, 117, 160
Atayataghronghta, 103, 108, 125, 139,
    160; at 1788 Fort Stanwix conference,
    123–24; at battle of Oriskany, 93; at
    battle of Saratoga, 95
Atayatonneatha, Peter, 117, 160
Atoghseronge, 161
Aughneonh. See Oneyanha
Avery, David, 62

baptism, 69, 76–77
Barbe-Marbois, Marquis de, 114–15
Barren Hill, battle of, 98–100
Belnap, Reverend Doctor Jeremy, 129–30
Blatcop, 92, 161; at battle of Barren Hill, 98
Bloomfield, Major Joseph, 86–87, 106
Bluebeck, 104, 161
Board of Trade, London, 54–55, 57,
    60–61, 65
van den Bogaert, 12
Boston, 84, 68, 86
Bostonians, 85, 207n12
Bradstreet, Colonel John, 51–52
Brant, Joseph. See Thayendanega
Brant, Molly, 93
Bread, Peter. See Kanadarok
Brothertown Indians, 129
Butler, General John, 82, 85, 91, 96, 100,
    204n16

Canada Creek, 64
Canadegowus, 161
Canaghsadiro, Thomas, 161
Canajoharie, 10, 50; conference of April
    1759, 36–37
Canandaigua, 116; conference of 1794,
    126
Canatsiagere, John, 161
Captain David, 123, 161
Carlisle, conference of 1753, 22
Carolina, 10, 18

Carrying Place, 11, 18, 28, 64–67, 92, 133

Catawba Indians, 18, 20

Caughnawauga Indians, 14, 24, 29, 59, 65–66, 82–86, 91–93, 102–4

Cayuga conferences: at Albany congress, 23; at Canandaigua, 126; at Easton, 41; at Fort Stanwix, 61–69, 116–17; at German Flats, 45, 65–66; at Johnson Hall, 49, 52, 57, 59–60, 74; at Johnstown, 86, 97; at Kanowalohale, 83–85; at Onondaga Grand Council, 20, 22, 75

Cayuga Indians, 4, 30, 36, 102–3, 125

Chastellux, Marquis de, 108

Chenussio Seneca Indians, 45, 47, 57, 65, 105, 136

Cherokee Indians, 18, 31–32, 44–45, 59–60, 65–66, 120

Cherry Valley, 78, 102

Church of England, 56, 58, 69, 76

clans, 6, 142, 143, 144, 145, 146; Bear, 76, 92–94, 106; mothers, 7, 42, 83, 87, 105; Turtle, 78–79, 91, 94, 103; Wolf, 79, 85, 87, 92, 94, 108

Claus, Daniel, 79, 82, 205n31

Clenis. *See* Kakiktoton

Clinton, George, 19, 20, 112, 118–19, 123–24

Clinton, Brigadier James, 104

Colden, Cadwallader, 12

Committee on Indian Affairs, 112

condolence: by Conoquheison, 19, 27, 37, 59, 62, 74; by William Johnson, 36; by Thomas King, 32, 57, 66; by Scarooyady, 22; by others, 83, 91

Congregationalist, 56, 58, 62, 76

congressional commissioners, 80–81, 85–88, 112–16, 124

Connecticut, 39, 43, 65

Conoquhieson, 18–19, 25–33, 36, 42, 46–48, 53, 56, 59–62, 68, 73–82, 135–36, 162

Continental Army, 86, 90, 95–99, 104, 118, 124

Continental Congress, 96, 101–3, 108, 112, 118, 120, 126, 129

Cooper, Polly, 132

Cornelius, Henry, 82, 85, 163; at battle of Barren Hill, 98; at battle of Oriskany, 92–93

covenant chain (of friendship), 31, 38, 49, 58

Crevecour, 101

Dakayenensese, 20–21, 76, 136, 163

Dartmouth College, 128

Dayaheari, 116, 163

Dean, James, 9, 78, 82–83, 86, 94, 97, 103–9, 114, 117, 120, 122, 208n13

Deanoyondeah, Augustus, 163

Deganawida (Peacemaker), 4, 6, 121

Dekanaghtsiasne, 163

DeLancey, James, 25

Delaware Indians, 18, 27–29, 32, 49, 51–52, 57

Delaware River, 11, 59, 63

Denny, David, 163

Deyahthadane, John, 164

Disononto, 18, 164

Duane, James, 113

Dunmore, Earl of (James Murray), 75

Dutch traders, 6, 12, 21

Dyoghhagweate, William, 117, 164

Easton: conference of 1758, 32; conference of 1761, 41

Edwards, Reverend Jonathan, 21

Elder Brothers, 6, 9, 25, 75, 84, 120

Elmore, Colonel, 91

Emlem, James, 116

Feghkatkaghtons, John, 164

Fonda, Commander Jellis, 113

Fort Le Boeuf, 47

Fort Crown Point, 25

Fort Detroit, 37, 40, 46–47, 51

Fort Duquesne, 25–26

Fort Herkimer: conference of 1785, 119; conference of 1788, 123–24

Fort Johnson, 12, 24, 27, 37, 41

Fort Niagara, 12, 26, 29, 51–52, 82–86, 91, 96, 105, 116, 119–20

Fort Oswego, 12, 21, 28, 30–31, 37, 79, 92, 109

Fort Presqu'île, 47

Fort Sandusky, 51

Fort Schuyler, 91, 97–98

Fort Stanwix, 40, 42, 50, 61, 73, 77, 87, 92; in disrepair, 84–86

Fort Stanwix conferences: of 1768, 51, 61–67; of 1784, 149; of 1788, 123–24, 150

Fort Ticonderoga, 33

Fort William Henry, 33

Fowler, David, 56

French-Indian Wars. *See* Seven Years' War

French traders, 4, 6

Gage, Thomas, 37, 50–51
Gaghsaweda, Ludwig, 76, 106, 117,
   119–20, 122–25, 128, 139, 145, 147,
   164–65
Garret, Hannah, 56
Gates, General Horatio, 96
Gaweaghnoge, 165
Gawehe, 30, 37, 48, 136, 165
George III, 49, 63, 74
German Flats, 37, 48, 79, 90, 93, 100
German Flats conferences: of 1756, 28; of
   1761, 37, 46; of 1776, 81, 86
German Palatines, 26
Gorham, Nathaniel, 122
Grand River (Canada), 130
Great Awakening, 13

Haghycande, 165
Hamilton, James, 19, 22, 39, 41, 43
Hamilton Academy, 128
Hanwagalet, Kaskonghgwea, 165
Hanwagalet, Tehoughnihalk, 165
Hanwaleao, Cornelius, 127, 166
Harper, John, 58–59, 113, 117, 119
Hawley, Reverend Gideon, 21
Hendrick, 79, 96
Herkimer, General Nicholas, 92–93
Hiawatha, 4, 6, 121
Hill, Aaron, 116
Holland Land Company, 129
Hononwayele, 166
Honyere Tewahongarahkon (Doxtator),
   92–95, 98, 103–4, 125, 132, 140,
   166–67
Honyost, 167
Horgale, Jacob, 167
Hudson River, 6, 11, 18, 133
hunting, 13
Huntington, Samuel, 108

Indian Trade and Intercourse Act (1790),
   125–26
Iroquoia, 55, 86, 92, 104, 114
Iroquois Confederacy, 91, 121; formation
   of, 3–9; founding League chiefs of, 7,
   79, 93, 117, 143; joined by Tuscarora
   and Nanticoke, 10
Iroquois defensive league, 86
Ishadekarenghes, 167
Itanyeatakayon, 167

Jesuits, 56
John, Captain. See Onondiyo

Johnson, Colonel Guy, 45, 74–82, 106
Johnson, Jacob, 62
Johnson, Sir John, 62, 82
Johnson, Joseph, 56, 80
Johnson, Sir William, 10, 12, 20–33, 36,
   39–40, 45–76, 80, 85, 91
Johnson Hall, 48–49, 52–53, 57–59, 68,
   73–74, 80, 97
Johnstown, 86, 97
Jordan, John, 167
Jordan, Nicholas, 114–15, 118, 167, 215n7

Kacneghdakon, 167
Kaghnedoreas, 168
Kaghneghtootdau, Saugus, 168
Kakiktoton, Cornelius (Clenis), 78, 93,
   103, 125, 168, 208n18
Kanadarok, Peter, 95–96, 168
Kanaghsalilgh, 168–69
Kanaghsatirhon, Joseph, 103, 107, 169
Kanaghweas (Young Conoquhieson),
   85–86, 91, 169
Kanaweadon, 169
Kanento, Peter, 169
Kanestio, 45, 51
Kanneyalode, Christian, 169
Kanonghgwenya, Peter, 169
Kanonghsase, William, 169
Kanowalohale, 3, 10–11, 18, 32, 37, 40,
   45–48, 51, 56–57, 61, 66–70, 74, 79,
   82, 91, 101–7, 114–15, 118, 125–30,
   133; Oneida overseers of (Feb. 1799),
   154
Kanyeagoton, Augustus, 170
Kaskoughguea, 170
Kaujathoondautheu, 170
Kaunaudauloonh, 170
Kayeghtorha, Peter, 170
Kayentarongwea, William, 91, 96, 98,
   123, 170
Kayewla. See Lafayette, Marquis
Keandarundie, 170
Keanyako, David, 171
Kennawagenton, 171, 217n29
Kentaronhye, Anthony, 171
King, Thomas, 32, 37, 43–44, 47–52, 55,
   57–60, 65–66, 136, 171
Kirkland, Reverend Samuel, 66–88, 91,
   93–94, 102, 112–29, 138, 205n28
Klock, George, 42
Konnauterlook, Peter, 172
Konnoquenyan, 172
Kristiaen, 78

Lafayette, Marquis, 97, 99, 114–15, 124; adopted as Kayewla, 97
Lake Champlain, 95, 103
Lake George, 63; campaign, 25–26, 32, 39
Lake Oneida, 62, 123
Lake Ontario, 4, 63, 109, 113, 133
Lancaster conferences: of 1757, 32; of 1762, 43
land disputes, 23, 26, 38, 45, 112, 114, 118, 122
Leguchsanyont, 172
Lexington, 72
Linklaen, John, 129
Logstown, 29
Looghshingh, Martinus, 172
Looghtanddya, Nicholas, 172
Louisburg, 35–36
Loyalists, 79, 85, 95

Martinus, 172
Maryland, 12
McCrea, Jane, 95, 211n12
de Menneville, Ange Dusquesne, 24
Mingo Indians, 14, 17
Minisink valley, 11
Mohawk conferences: at Albany congress, 23; at Fort Johnson, 27, 33, 41, 45; at Fort Stanwix, 61–69; at German Flats, 46, 65–66; at Johnson Hall, 49, 52–53, 57, 59–60, 72, 74; at Johnstown, 86; at Kanowalohale, 83–85; at Lake George, 25; at Onondaga Grand Council, 20, 75
Mohawk Indians, 4, 13, 22, 105, 114
Mohawk River, 11, 12, 18, 28, 31, 65, 80, 86, 92, 100, 103–4, 138
Mohegan Indians, 80
Mohican Indians, 114
Montauk Indians, 56
Montreal, 14, 23, 30, 35–37, 82, 85, 91
Moravian missionaries, 8
Morse, Reverend Jedidiah, 129–30

Nanticoke Indians, 10, 22, 30
Narragansett Indians, 56, 114
neutrality, 80–81, 84–86, 91, 105
New England, 14, 56, 80, 91, 114; Indians of, 208n22
New Jersey, 32–33, 61
New Stockbridge, 129
Newtown, 104, 126
New York City, 86, 125

New York Committee of Correspondence, 96
New York Genessee Land Company, 121–24
New York state commissioners, 113, 117–18
Niantic Indians, 114
Nicholaasa, 172
Norton, John, 4

Odaghseghte, 87, 91, 96–97, 101–2, 104–6, 108, 117, 124, 143, 173
Oghnaongoghton, 173, 217n29
Oghsidago, 173
Ohanodlighton, 173, 216n12
Ohio region, 8
Ojistalale, 115, 117–19, 123, 139, 174
Okonyota, Cornelius, 103, 119, 174
Old Oneida village, 11, 79, 91, 105
Onderihokde, 174
Oneida: commissioned officers of (1779), 141; creation epic, 3, 9, 133; declaration of neutrality, (1775), 79; fallen log (Big Tree), 3, 6, 11, 18, 74; Great Law, 3, 9, 121, 133; leadership, (1750–1800), 134, 135, 137, 140, 143; opposed as leaders of the Confederacy 49, 57, 82–84 (by their confederates), 33, 52–53 (by William Johnson), 45, 49 (by the Onondaga Indians); signers of treaties, 151–53; speakers (1784–1794), 142, 144, 146; supported as leaders of the Confederacy 46 (by the Cayuga Indians), 31 (by the Cherokee Indians), 42 (by the clan mothers), 78, 81 (by the Albany Committee of Correspondence, Safety, and Protection), 20, 36, 39, 41–43, 51, 59, 74 (by their confederates), 22, 25 (by William Johnson), 27 (by the Seneca Indians), 75 (by the Shawnee Indians); at war, 92–93, 95, 98–100
Oneida conferences: at Albany congress, 23; at Canandaigua, 126; at Easton, 41; at Fort Herkimer, 119; at Fort Johnson, 26–27, 33, 41; at Fort Stanwix, 61–69, 112–17; at German Flats, 28, 37, 46, 65–66; at Johnson Hall, 48–49, 52, 57, 59–60, 72, 74; at Johnstown, 86, 97; at Kanowalohale, 18, 45, 83–85; at Lake George, 25; at Onondaga Grand Council, 19, 22, 75

Oneida Indians, 4, 5, 9–10, 51, 86, 91–93, 96, 99, 122

Oneyanha ("Beech Tree"), 91, 93, 117, 119, 120–28, 139, 174–75

Oneynyoagat, 78, 175

Onidyoghgory, Nickus, 175

*Onondaga,* 37

Onondaga conferences: at Albany congress, 23; at Canandaigua, 126; at Easton, 41; at Fort Johnson, 45; at Fort Stanwix, 61–69, 116–17; at German Flats, 46, 65–66; at Johnson Hall, 48–49, 52, 57, 69–60, 74; at Johnstown, 86, 97; at Kanowalohale, 83–85; at Onondaga Grand Council, 19, 22, 75

Onodaga Indians, 4, 30, 103–4, 125

Onondaga Grand Council, 7–8, 18, 22, 75, 82–83, 90–91, 130, 133, 143

Onondiyo, John, 103, 105, 126, 128, 139, 175–76

Ononghsawinghti, James, 176

Onughseeshoo, Thomas, 176

Onwanotseron, 176

Oquaga Indians, 29, 31, 50, 85

Oquaga village, 12, 20, 58, 68–69, 76, 85, 100–101, 117, 125, 133

Origombe, Peter, 176

Oriska village, 11, 79, 92–96, 128

Oriskany, battle of, 92–93, 132, 140

Osauhataugaunlot, Thomas, 176

Oswegatchie, 26

Oswego River, 11, 113

Otaawighton, John, 109, 176

Oterogon, 176

Otisquette, Peter (French Peter), 124–25, 129, 176

Otsetogon, Paul, 177

Otshogea, 177

Otsienhea, Peter, 177

Otsignh'yokare, Thomas, 177

Ottawa (Odawa) Indians, 46

Otyadonenghti, 116, 177

Owyaghse, 177

pagan party, 121

Pagan Peter. *See* Sategaleahtas

Patriots, 4, 14, 73, 78–79, 84–88, 91, 93, 102, 104

Penn, John, 81–82

Pennsylvania, 8, 10, 12, 29, 61, 63, 99, 113

Pennsylvania Provincial Council, 8, 18, 27, 40

Pequot Indians, 56

Phelps, Oliver, 122

Philadelphia, 8, 28, 78, 80, 82, 86, 99, 108, 112, 116, 126, 132

Pickering, Timothy, 93, 126, 211n8

Pine Tree chief, 7, 8, 130

Pontiac, 46–48, 51–52

Presbyterian Church, 55, 66, 138

Proclamation of 1763, 54–55

Quakers, 116, 129–30, 142

Quebec, 37

Rhode Island, 114

Roghnketyea, 177

Roman Catholic Church, 19, 56, 127

Rotshawatgense, Cornelius, 177

sachems, 7, 25, 44, 52, 142–146; against the warriors, 48, 60, 66; cooperating with warriors, 79–80, 85–87, 92–99, 117, 120, 124

Sagoharase, John, 103, 108, 177–78

Sagorakorongo, David, 178

Sagoyontha, Cornelius, 178

Sahonwate, Hendrick, 178, 217n30

Salckarenghis, Peter, 178, 217n30

Saratoga, battle of, 95

Sategaleahtas (Pagan Peter), 127, 129–31, 147, 178

Scarooyady, 22, 24–29, 55, 178

Schenectady, 107

Schoharie, 21

Schuyler, Peter, 114, 122–23

Schuyler, Philip: as friend of the Oneida, 80–87; support after revolution and, 91–97, 102, 105–7, 109, 122

Scottish Society for the Propagation of Christian Knowledge (SSPCK), 21, 67–68, 74, 118, 120, 129

Segaoneghseria, Daniel, 179, 217n30

Seghsenowack, 179

Seghskyeghte, 179

Seneca conferences: at Albany congress, 23; at Canandaigua, 126; at Easton, 41; at Fort Johnson, 27, 41, 45; at Fort Stanwix, 61–69, 116–17; at German Flats, 65–66; at Johnson Hall, 48–49, 52, 57, 69–70, 74; at Johnstown, 86; at Kanowalohale, 83–85; at Onondaga

Grand Council, 20, 22, 75
Seneca Indians, 4, 10, 30, 32, 91–93, 122
Senghnagenrat, 81–87, 91, 96, 98, 105, 107, 138–39, 179
Seven Years' War, 23, 77
Sewajis, 85, 91–92, 98, 100, 179–80
Shagoyaghtorghhere, 180
Shamokin, 8, 44
Shaugoogaudoohaula, 180
Shawnee Indians, 8, 26–27, 32, 51, 74–75, 120
Shejijowane, John, 180
Shickellamy, 8, 10, 18, 20, 55, 180
Shoneghslishea, Daniel, 180
Shononghis, Thomas, 180
Shononghlegs. See Shononghriyo
Shononghriyo, Anthony, 79, 93, 117, 123–24, 143, 180–81
Shoratowane, 181, 217n29
Shotsijowane, John, 181
Skandyoughquathe, 181
Skenandoah, Daniel, 98, 181
Skenandoah, John, 79, 87, 91, 94, 98, 105–6, 117–29, 132, 181–83
Skenandoah, Thomas, 183
Skywoman, 9
Smith, Peter, 126, 145
Smith, Richard, 101
Society for the Propagation of the Gospel (SPG), 13, 58, 68
Sodolk, Hannah, 183
Soghraghrowane, Peter, 183
Soheghtrane, 183
Spencer, Reverend Elihu, 20
Spencer, Thomas, 78, 92–93, 183
Standing Stone, 3, 22, 130, 132, 147
Stockbridge Indians, 114
Sullivan, Major General John, 104–5, 118
Sullivan/Clinton campaign, 104–5, 139
Suscuhaloane, 183
Susquehanna Land Company, 55
Susquehanna River, 8, 10–13, 43, 50, 56, 58, 63, 100
Susquehannock Indians, 8

Tachnechdorus, John, 8, 24, 28, 184
Tagawaron, 59–60, 64–70, 76, 184
Tahauweyaudelon, 184
Tahtequese, William, 184
Taraghorus, 185
Tatahonghteayon, 185
Tayaheura, Jimmy, 87, 91, 185

Tayler, John, 123, 125
Teaghsweangalolis, Paul, 92–93, 185
Teaundeanthe, Tenussa, 78, 185
Tegasweangalolis. See Teaghsweangalolis
Teheaniyoghtiwat, 105, 185
Tehonogwesghsoolhaula, Christian, 185
Tekahoweasere, John, 185
Tekanijasece, John, 186
Tesanonde, 28, 186
Tewaghtahkotte, 103, 186
Tewahongarahkon, Dolly. See Tyonajanegen
Teyohagweanda, 81, 186
Teyoneghserise, 186
Thaghnaghwanekeas, 186
Thaghneghtolis, Hendrick, 186
Thaghtaghgwesere, William, 78, 117, 187
Thagniyongo, 187
Thahteequesera. See Thaghtaghwesere
Thanigeandagayon, Henry, 150, 187
Thaosagawat, Honyost, 82, 92–93, 98, 103–5, 188
Tharontuwagon, 188
Thaswenkaroras, Paul, 188
Thauneyendaugauyoon, 130, 188
Thayagonentagetita, 188
Thayendanega (Joseph Brant), 77, 82, 91, 93, 96, 100–5, 108, 112, 118, 120
Theenis Teandeantha, 188
Theugereyndack, 188
Thomas, Deacon, 68, 76, 91, 98, 104, 189
Thomgatasher, Paul, 189
Thonayute, 189, 216n12
Thonigwenghsohare, Christian, 103, 107, 189
Thonwaghweakaragwea, George, 190
Tiahaeira, 190
Tiahogwando. See Teyohagweanda
Tianoga, 31, 190
Tiwasgwadeghkon, 190
Tohagndaaghquyserry, 190
Tohayeuesera, Cornelius, 190
Toneaghslishea, David, 150, 152, 190
Totyaneahawi, 103, 107, 190
de Tousard, A. Louis, 100
Towanuaghhalese, Daniel, 191
Treaty of Paris (1783), 112
Tryon, William, 73
Turtle Island, 9
Tuscarora conferences: at Albany congress, 23; at Fort Johnson, 26, 45; at Fort Stanwix, 61–69, 116–17; at

German Flats, 46, 65–66; at Johnson Hall, 49, 52, 57, 59–60, 74; at Johnstown, 86, 97; at Kanowalohale, 45, 83–85; at Onondaga, 75
Tuscarora Indians, 10, 30, 86
Tyonajanegen, Dolly, 92–93, 95, 132, 191; Jacob and Cornelius, teenage sons of, 92–93
Tyorhadaghiro, 191

Unadilla River, 113, 119
Unadilla village, 101, 113

Valley Forge, 99–100
Van Dyck, Colonel Cornelius, 105
Van Schaick, Colonel Goose, 104
Vaudreuil, Pierre François, 26, 30, 36
Virginia, 12, 32, 61, 63, 74

Wakarontharane, James, 103, 191
wampum belt, 19–20, 27, 30, 36–37, 49, 60, 74, 79, 87, 106, 130, 206n4, 210n43

war hatchet (axe), 27, 30, 36–37, 44, 59–60, 83, 96
Waronwansen, Adam, 87, 191
Warren, Peter, 12
warriors, 7, 44, 142–146; against the sachems, 41, 48, 60, 66; cooperating with the sachems, 79–86, 92, 95–99, 117, 120, 124
Washington, Major General George, 91, 96–101, 108–9, 118, 126, 132
Washington, Martha, 132
Wauts'haudeaghongh, Christian, 191
Weiser, Conrad, 18, 20
Wheelock, Reverend Eleazar, 13, 55, 58, 62, 65–66, 80, 138
White Dog sacrifice, 130
Willett, Captain Marinus, 109
Wood Creek, 11
Wyoming valley, 11, 100, 104

Younger Brother, 6, 25, 32, 84, 120